Janet Giltrow and Dieter Stein (Eds.)
The Pragmatic Turn in Law

Mouton Series in Pragmatics

Editor
Istvan Kecskes

Editorial Board
Reinhard Blutner (Universiteit van Amsterdam)
N.J. Enfield (Max-Planck-Institute for Psycholinguistics)
Raymond W. Gibbs (University of California, Santa Cruz)
Laurence R. Horn (Yale University)
Boaz Keysar (University of Chicago)
Ferenc Kiefer (Hungarian Academy of Sciences)
Lluís Payrató (University of Barcelona)
François Recanati (Institut Jean-Nicod)
John Searle (University of California, Berkeley)
Deirdre Wilson (University College London)

Volume 18

The Pragmatic Turn in Law

Inference and Interpretation in Legal Discourse

Edited by
Janet Giltrow and Dieter Stein

ISBN 978-1-5015-1894-2
e-ISBN (PDF) 978-1-5015-0472-3
e-ISBN (EPUB) 978-1-5015-0468-6
ISSN 1864-6409

Library of Congress Cataloging-in-Publication Data
A CIP catalog record for this book has been applied for at the Library of Congress.

Bibliographic information published by the Deutsche Nationalbibliothek
The Deutsche Nationalbibliothek lists this publication in the Deutsche Nationalbibliografie;
detailed bibliographic data are available on the Internet at http://dnb.dnb.de.

© 2019 Walter de Gruyter Inc., Boston/Berlin
This volume is text- and page-identical with the hardback published in 2017.
Typesetting: RoyalStandard, Hong Kong
Printing and binding: CPI books GmbH, Leck
♾ Printed on acid-free paper
Printed in Germany

www.degruyter.com

Dedicated to the memory of Peter Tiersma

The editors and contributors together dedicate this volume to the memory of Peter Tiersma (1952–2014). Peter was a luminary in the world of language and law. He is remembered not only for his writings, which continue to have great influence on the field, and for his wonderful talks, presented with grace and humor with his beautiful baritone voice, but also for his generosity to a new generation of scholars entering the field, whom he encouraged, and whose work he nurtured. A past president of the International Association of Forensic Linguists, and a co-founder of the International Language and Law Association, Peter as a steward always encouraged new ideas, whether from his close friends and colleagues, or from those emerging scholars he did not yet know.

Peter was born in the Netherlands, and mostly grew up on a dairy farm in central California, where his family moved when he was a child. He was educated at Stanford, the University of California, San Diego, and Berkeley, where he earned, respectively, his undergraduate, doctoral, and law degrees. He was proud of his Frisian heritage, and his early linguistic work included important contributions on the grammar of the Frisian language. After a few years practicing law, he took a position as a law professor at Loyola Law School in Los Angeles, where he spent his entire academic career.

As for Peter's work, his writings on the nature of legal language, on speech acts and legal doctrines, on the jury, on the relationship between law and technology over history, and on the interpretation of laws and contracts, guide scholars from all over the world. Cancer eventually took his life, but not his lasting contributions to our lives, both personal and intellectual. Even as the field adjusts to the sad reality of continuing without him, our respect, admiration and warmth toward him survive and flourish.

Larry Solan

Preface

In July 2014 scholars gathered at the University of British Columbia in Vancouver, Canada, to discuss inference and interpretation in law. Participants came from far and wide. We are grateful for the many investments in costly travel which enabled this gathering of interest in the linguistic measure of legal reasoning. From this gathering emerged the chapters of this volume.

For the staging of the conference itself, we have many to thank. We warmly recognize both the moral support and material contribution of the German Consulate General in Vancouver. We are grateful for support from UBC-administered funds from the Social Sciences and Humanities Research Council of Canada, and also for resources available through the Dean of Arts Office at the University of British Columbia. We are thankful in addition not only for the resources which supported the work of the secretariat facilitating the conference but also for the spirited dedication of the members of this group: Simon Stein at the English Department, Heinrich-Heine-University Düsseldorf; Dan Adleman and Belle Cheung at the University of British Columbia. We thank most heartily Simon for his editorial assistance in preparing the volume's final version, and Donato Mancini at UBC for his work as production assistant.

November 2016
Janet Giltrow and Dieter Stein

Contents

Dedicated to the memory of Peter Tiersma —— v
Preface —— vii
List of contributors —— xi

    Janet Giltrow
1   Introduction —— 1

I **Linguistic-pragmatic approaches to inference in law**

    Laurence R. Horn
2   **Telling it slant: Toward a taxonomy of deception —— 23**

    Meizhen Liao and Yadi Sun
3   **Cooperation in Chinese courtroom discourse —— 57**

    Nicholas Allott and Benjamin Shaer
4   **Inference and intention in legal interpretation —— 83**

    Brian G. Slocum
5   **Pragmatics and legal texts: How best to account for the gaps between literal meaning and communicative meaning —— 119**

    Lawrence M. Solan
6   **One ambiguity, three legal approaches —— 145**

II **Horizons of inference: Extending the context of interpretation**

    Angela Condello and Alexandra Arapinis
7   **Between similarity and analogy: Rethinking the role of prototypes in law and cognitive linguistics —— 167**

    Klaus P. Schneider and Dirk Zielasko
8   **When is an insult a crime? On diverging conceptualizations and changing legislation —— 187**

Frances Olsen
9 **Pragmatic interpretation by judges: Constrained performatives and the deployment of gender bias —— 205**

Shurli Makmillen and Margery Fee
10 **Disguising the dynamism of the law in Canadian courts: Judges using dictionaries —— 233**

III Across borders: New methods for study of inference

Svetlana V. Vlasenko
11 **Legal translation pragmatics: Legal meaning as text-external convention – the case of 'chattels' —— 249**

Friedemann Vogel
12 **Calculating legal meanings? Drawbacks and opportunities of corpus-assisted legal linguistics to make the law (more) explicit —— 287**

Ralf Poscher
13 **The common error in theories of adjudication: An inferentialist argument for a doctrinal conception —— 307**

Dieter Stein
14 **On inferencing in law —— 335**

Subject index —— 369

List of contributors

Nicholas Allott
Department of Literature, Area Studies and European Languages
University of Oslo
Norway

Alexandra Arapinis
University of Roma Tre, Law Department
Angela Condello
University of Torino, Philosophy Department
Italy

Margery Fee
Department of English
University of British Columbia
Canada

Janet Giltrow
Department of English
University of British Columbia
Canada

Laurence Horn
Professor Emeritus of Linguistics and Philosophy
Yale University
U.S.A.

Shurli Makmillen
Department of English and Foreign Languages
Claflin University
Orangeburg, South Carolina
U.S.A.

Meizhen Liao
School of Foreign Languages
Central China Normal University,
Wuhan, People's Republic of China

Frances Olsen
School of Law
University of California at Los Angeles
U.S.A.

Ralf Poscher
Department of Law
University of Freiburg
Germany

Klaus Peter Schneider
Department of English
University of Bonn
Germany

Benjamin Shaer
School of Linguistics and Language Studies
Department of Law and Legal Studies, and
Institute of Cognitive Science
Carleton University, Ottawa
Canada

Brian G. Slocum
University of the Pacific, McGeorge School of Law
Sacramento, CA
U.S.A.

Lawrence M. Solan
Brooklyn Law School
U.S.A.

Dieter Stein
English Linguistics
University of Düsseldorf
Germany

Svetlana V. Vlasenko
Faculty of Law, Public and Private International Law Department
National Research University Higher School of Economics
Moscow, Russia

Friedemann Vogel
Linguistics Department
University of Freiburg
Germany

Sun Yadi
School of Foreign Languages
Central China Normal University
Wuhan, People's Republic of China

Dirk Zielasko
Department of English
University of Bonn
Germany

Janet Giltrow
1 Introduction

This volume follows the gaze of linguistic disciplines as they look into the degree to which the meaning of the sentence depends on the context of its utterance. From this point of view, meaning is not self-contained in a semantics; it is not independent of time, place, person.

The turn towards context is driven by what Sperber and Wilson call the "central problem for pragmatics," namely, that "the linguistic meaning recovered by decoding vastly underdetermines the speaker's meaning" (2002: 3). The turn was initiated by Wittgenstein and Austin, more than half a century ago, and then steered by Grice towards the end of the twentieth century. The turn opens onto all areas of language study, but offers particularly dramatic prospects for study of law and language, where the ideal would anchor meaning beyond contexts and their changing currents of interests, attention, supposition, prejudice or privilege. Ideally, to put law out of reach of partisan privilege, the text of law would be "autonomous" (Tiersma 2010; Stein, this volume): the same for everybody for all time. If meaning in language is, however, inevitably context-dependent – or "vastly" underdetermined by code or system – as pragmatic principle can claim, then legal uses of language will put great stresses on language and its users. And under such duress, language for law has developed characteristic features so pronounced that some declare legal language fundamentally different, and not the same as ordinary uses of language.

Even as it is driven by shared observations of meaning's context-dependency, the pragmatic turn does not run on a single track. Some but by no means all contributions to this volume run along a main track developing out of pragmatic study of language users' resolving indexical expressions and references:

(1) The table was here yesterday. He told me.

Without consulting context, a hearer could not know what table where and when, or who spoke to whom. Example (1) leans heavily on context – to a degree often referred to as the conditions of "everyday conversation," and distinguished from uses of language said to be more formal. The distinction often points to the extent of shared context in conversation in contrast to that found in written language. In writing, mutual awareness may be scant in comparison to that attending *the table*, the teller, and their time and location. Language works

---
Janet Giltrow, University of British Columbia

DOI 10.1515/9781501504723-001

efficiently with, maybe even tends towards – the degree of context-dependency in (1). Legal uses of language may be distinguished by their efforts to fend off this tendency.

Problems of indexicals (*here, yesterday, me*) and reference (*the table...*) are classic to the line of pragmatics which issues from the mid-century turn. Also roughly agreed-upon are the "implicatures" to which, in light of Austin's Speech Acts, Grice pointed: meanings which are *unstated* but intended by the speaker to be inferred from what *is* stated. Some implicatures are readily derived:

(2) *A*: I'm cold.
  B: The window is open.

B's utterance, in context, does not say but is as much as to say *You are cold because the window is open*. Implicatures may also be derived with less certainty:

(3) A and B are in a room.
  B: The window is open.

While it could be feasible for A to infer that B is intending that A infer that A should close the window, other inferences may compete, depending on the relationship between A and B and its history; the house rules or customs for opening or keeping closed the window; questions of security; the residence in the room of a cat who tries to go out at every opportunity....

Implicatures therefore could be said to range from

(a) *strong implicature* (as in (2)), that is, so readily inferable as to require being explicitly defeated (*I'm cold. / The window is open – I don't mean that's why you are cold*) to prevent its being the basis of carrying the interaction forward;

through

(b) *moderate implicature*, that is, reasonably but not so exclusively inferred,

to

(c) *weak implicature*, or what Sperber and Wilson ([1986] 1995) call "poetic effects," that is, inference falling within a span of plausibility at the outer edge of a speaker's conceivable intention.

As Wilson (2011) observes, as the interpretation of an utterance moves further from the "guaranteed" position of strong implicature, more responsibility is taken on by the hearer.

Taking a first step from indexicals and reference to implicature, we may shift our perspective, and see meaning's dependency from a slightly different angle. From this angle, what shows most prominently is not "context" as constituted by material terms and social roles (*table*, teller) and coordinates of time and space. Rather, it is context as constituted by mutual consciousness: in (1), instead of context being composed of table and teller, it is composed of awareness of table and teller; in (3), beyond resolving the reference for *the window*, intelligence of the interaction is in estimating the speaker's intentions in this uttering – and also estimating the speaker's estimate of the hearer's awareness (of cold, of security, of noise, of hearer's proximity to window and thus eligibility for closing it, of dust or odor, of fugitive cat, or of house rules...). We could go so far as to say that "[e]very utterance is an experiment in estimating the consciousness of another" (Giltrow 2015: 208). Following Grice's speaker meaning, and pushing beyond, Sperber and Wilson's ([1986] 1995) Relevance Theory configures context as a domain of mutual assumptions on which communicative acts have "contextual effects": that is, changing what hearers have in mind. The change may be significant, or the effect of the act may be nearly negligible. In the latter case, the utterance's effect on the hearer would be at the outer bounds of relevance.

Even as they may share a point of departure, not all pragmaticists follow Relevance Theory's line of inquiry, a line which can lead to reaches of inference where implicatures are not easily demonstrated. And, in any case, the pragmatic dependence of language on its context of interpretation can also be investigated by means other than linguistic-philosophical ones. As language-users estimate one another's consciousness, these estimates are indicated in the linguistic record. The pragmatic turn can open onto collections of data which harvest such indications, over time for both an historical pragmatics and also a contemporary pragmatics which looks beyond cases, instances or classic puzzles to aggregations, trends, and types. In fact, generalizable patterns have been in view if not pursued from relatively early in the pragmatic project. Levinson (1979) saw Activity Types "[constraining]" language users' contributions, these types being culturally recurring events such as interviewing for a job, teaching a class, playing cricket (1979: 368). While such regularities were at the time being noticed elsewhere in the language disciplines (e.g., Hymes' "speech events"), Levinson's proposal is distinctly pragmatic. The constraints on speakers, he says, are functional: that is, they are known by their *use* in advancing the social activity. These function-bound constraints – sponsored by language users' involvement in Activity Types – have their "mirror image" in "inferential schemata" (1979: 371). In other words, hearers estimate speakers' meaning from the assumptions composing their shared knowledge of the typified activity. One of Levinson's extended examples of an Activity Type is courtroom questioning. Questioning is constrained by function: it has a job to do. At the same time, if one is not aware of its function and role in the activity, the questioning can seem strangely awkward and even uninterpretable.

The pragmatic turn is not a sharp swerve away from established views. Its curve can be seen as continuous with accounts of the historical sedimentations, over centuries, which outsiders to legal professions now experience as impenetrable "legalese"; and also continuous with or ready to come into dialogue with conceptualisations of language from which principles of legal drafting emerge. Pragmatics could also be ready to study the "Plain Language" movements and mandates which have aimed to clear a path for non-specialist readers through the thickets of legalese; such movements are found in the US, the UK, Canada, Australia, the EU, and elsewhere. Most obviously, pragmatic analysis already plays a role in the study of the other "Plain Language," the one advanced by textualism and its fundamental declaration for the autonomy and context-independence of the legal text. Each of these themes in study of law and language could be visited with linguistic-pragmatic methods. And law has been all along in view from pragmatics' foundations. Levinson's turn to the courtroom to exemplify the conditioning of inference by Activity Type is not the first appearance of law in the pragmatic tradition: in Austin's (1962) proposals, some of the first appearances of performative speech acts issue from legal situations.

Further, pragmatic methodologies – developed and extended – could illuminate the rationality of judicial reasoning. As Sullivan (1999) has shown, this rationality is often obscured or deflected by folk notions of language as a code. Further study could show the role of ideologies of literal and "plain" meaning as alibis for other inferential processes.

At the frontier of possibility, could a linguistic-pragmatic approach offer additional techniques for understanding the version of "speaker meaning" encountered in statutes? For several reasons, the idea of "speaker meaning" can itself be found problematic for statutory expression (e.g., Bix 2012, cited in Stein, this volume). In addition, many take the position that there is no role for implicature in statutes. There are grounds for such a position: presumably, legal drafters would avoid the context-dependency that enables implicature (for example, Allott and Shaer, this volume). Moreover, the extensions of implicature in Relevance Theory can be found to be insufficiently systematic for application to questions of law and language. This is also a reasonable position: dubbed "poetic effects" by Sperber and Wilson, weak implicature especially must seem just what legal reasoning cannot entertain. With the reader taking greater responsibility, and the writer reducing the guarantee of meaning, weak implicature could seem to amount to judicial activism and worse: a disturbance to legislative authority, the kind of reading in and acting out which textualism condemns.

Yet, nevertheless, there may be a role for the concept of weak implicature in understanding statutory interpretation. After all, weak implicature is *still ostensive*: a weak implicature is still an effect of the communicative act (the statute). It is at the outer limit of intention – but still within the horizon of intention. So where a statute does not provide examples, or enough examples, for strong implicature or clear application, or when a statute was enacted before certain circumstances came into view or could be contemplated, analysis might show judicial reasoning reaching to weak implicature at what could be argued to be the limit of intention. Or it could show judicial reasoning refusing weak implicature, finding that intention cannot be said to go so far. As Wilson (2011) says, as the strength of implicature shifts to "weak," "responsibility" falls increasingly to the Hearer. Such responsibility may well define the role of judicial interpreters of statutes, and instances of other legal genres, at the outer limit of intention. At the risk of spoiling this possibility by reverting to effects termed "poetic" and shunned by legal language, I suggest that this kind of responsibility is somewhat like that which literary studies assumes when a specialist reader proposes an implicature at the outer limit of a text's ostensive range: that is, a meaning still arguable as to some faint degree intended (or ostensively enabled), but by no means obvious. So a specialist reader might take responsibility for 'saying' to Mark Twain about *Adventures of Huckleberry Finn* that the ornamentations of the Grangerfords' country dwelling project an ante-bellum domestic culture both genteel and primitive, with implications for the family's destiny in a slave society. And Mark Twain might 'say', 'I hadn't thought of it in those terms, they are not the terms we used in those days, but it's not wrong, that could be said,' and his 'saying' this would be audible owing to the specialist reader's argument for the consistency of the weak implicature with other elements of the text and context.

* * *

Contributions to this volume were convened by a conference call to gather in 2014 at the University of British Columbia, in Vancouver, Canada. Participants were welcomed to the "unceded territory of the Musqueam Nation," a portion of which the University of British Columbia occupies. The term *unceded territory* – an historical and political definition of relations amongst peoples and spaces – is itself inferentially active and legally endorsed. It occupies public consciousness, if not public consensus, owing to decades of decisions by Canadian courts on Aboriginal claims to rights and lands. Courts scrutinized historical wordings, and also drew inferences from accessible assumptions in the context of interpretation, and established new assumptions for future inference.

In some cases, these inferences derived from a close focus on wordings in historical legal documents. For example, Canadian courts read the 1760 Treaty of Peace and Friendship between the Mi'kmaq and the British Crown, the Supreme Court of Canada (*R. v. Marshall* No. 1 3 SCR 456) reading the statement about "Truck houses" below differently from the lower courts, which had also differed between themselves in their reading (it is the Mi'kmaq agent who engages, below):

> I do further engage that we will not traffick, barter or Exchange any Commodities in any manner but with such persons or the managers of such Truck houses as shall be appointed or Established by His Majesty's Governor at Lunenbourg or Elsewhere in Nova Scotia or Accadia.

Differing from lower courts, the Supreme Court inferred from this passage that the Mi'kmaq right to hunt and fish was (in pragmatic terms) presupposed by this clause (see Giltrow 2015 for a pragmatic perspective on this case).

More recently, and only six weeks before contributors to this volume gathered in Vancouver, the Supreme Court of Canada handed down a landmark decision on Aboriginal land title in Canada. While a Supreme Court decision nearly twenty years earlier (*Delgamuukw v. British Columbia,* [1997] 3 S.C.R. 1010) had found that Aboriginal title to land existed in principle, it wasn't until *R. v. Tsilhqot'in* [2014] that this principle was applied, and the Xeni Gwet'in were found to have title to 1750 square kilometers of British Columbia. While the Marshall decision (above) can be read as pragmatically anchored in legal wording, and exerting pragmatic (rather than semantic) efforts to interpret the wording, the Tsilhqot'in decision proceeds on a different pragmatic scale. It derives an inference from assumptions in the context of interpretation: namely, the inference that the Xeni Gwet'in own the land in question. The Court looked for evidence of "regular use" (para 27) and

> para 38 [...] evidence of a strong presence on or over the land claimed, manifesting itself in acts of occupation *that could reasonably be interpreted as demonstrating* that the land in question belonged to, was controlled by, or was under the exclusive stewardship of the claimant group. (emphasis added)

The Court found such proof, from which inferences could be made, in record of the Xeni Gwet'in keeping others off the land or permitting others access:

> para 48 The fact that permission was requested and granted or refused, or that treaties were made with other groups, may show intention and capacity to control the land. Even the lack of challenges to occupancy may support an inference of an established group's intention and capacity to control.

A pragmatic illustration of the kind of evidence the Court was seeking, and finding, might go something like this:

   A approaches a location where B stands.
   B: You may pass through here.

A would reasonably infer that *B* controls the territory towards which *A* is heading, and could also reasonably take that control as an intended implicature of *B*'s utterance. So would an overhearer to the utterance reasonably infer that *B* controls that territory.

Delgamuukw, the Supreme Court of Canada decision which enabled *Tsilhqot'in* to find Xeni Gwet'in land title, has been "widely lauded" for "overcoming an unjust evidentiary barrier to the appropriate hearing of Aboriginal claims" (Newman 2005: 433) and finding oral-historical evidence admissible. With this barrier overcome, *Tsilhqot'in* was possible. Yet written evidence had been available all along – since the early 19th century from the region which is now British Columbia, and since the early 18th century, if not late 17th century from regions east of the central plains. Traders acting for both English and French investors sent back to Europe journals recording observations of the customs, practices, and attitudes of the Aboriginal peoples they did business with. Some of the most emphatically stated of these observations were those which recorded the behaviors by which control of territory could be inferred: traders went carefully amongst allies and enemies, and reported intelligence of these territorial circumstances. Why could control – and title – not be inferred for the Tsilhqot'in until 2014? Why was the "court system," for 125 years, experienced by Aboriginal peoples as "unsympathetic"?[1]

Pragmatically-informed study could explore the rationality of the unsympathetic system, just as Olsen (this volume) explores the rationality of 150 years of US decisions perversely oblivious to evidence from which inferences supporting women's rights could readily have been drawn. Without close study on pragmatic principles, we cannot know the pattern of this intransigent rationality regarding Aboriginal title. But it is worth noting for a start that the context for inference changed over the 250 years Aboriginal peoples had been petitioning the Crown, addressing the Privy Council in London, or going before the Supreme Court of Canada. In the first phase of reasoning, when relations between Europeans and Aboriginal peoples were based in trade, the inference of Aboriginal control of territory was readily drawn from context. When the era of settlement arrived, however, and then the era of resource extraction, such inference was not readily drawn.

---

[1] http://www.fonv.ca/nemaiahvalley/thecourtcase/

This short and selective history of recent judicial inference regarding Aboriginal rights and territories illustrates a span of pragmatic focus. It goes from resolving local implications to be derived from certain wordings to inferring from assumptions more broadly introduced into the context. So too might the Tsilhqot'in decision illustrate an outer limit of pragmatic study of legal reasoning. Chief Justice McLachlin's reasons include explanation of the "restriction" on Aboriginal land title:

> para 74 [...] it is collective title held not only for the present generation but for all succeeding generations [...] [the land cannot be] developed or misused in a way that would substantially deprive future generations of the benefit of the land. Some changes – even permanent changes – to the land may be possible. Whether a particular use is irreconcilable with the ability of succeeding generations to benefit from the land will be a matter to be determined when the issue arises.

Offering no examples of permitted use, and anticipating future reasoning, the Chief Justice could be said to be opening the door to weak implicature: inference not guaranteed by the speaker, or even readily accessible from what is said, but still within the broadest conceivable intention of this ostensive action of communicating a decision. For these implicatures the Hearer, or reader, takes greater responsibility.

* * *

Contributions to this volume range not only across the pragmatic span briefly illustrated above by Canadian examples; they also come from a range of disciplinary orientations. Some are closer to traditionally core areas of language study, but even then they are diverse in their methods, from more philosophical to more historical and corpus-based. Contributions come as well from a range of national scholarly cultures, and, especially, national legal cultures. As far as possible, we have kept the door wide open to submissions from these many sites. We hope readers will find the diversity not only provocative or challenging but also inspiring to further inquiry.

In the volume's first chapter, "'Telling it slant': Toward a taxonomy of deception," Horn drives straight (or slant) to a speech practice that is at once adjudicable and also classically pragmatic: the speech action of falsely implicating. (For example, B has had a Swiss bank account. A asks B, *Did you have a Swiss bank account?* B falsely implicates by saying something true: *The firm had a Swiss bank account*.) In a learned survey from antiquity to the modern era, Horn finds reasoning which rates the speaker who falsely implicates as being just as responsible for deception as the speaker who lies – a view which probably aligns with most folk intuition. At the same time, however, folk intuition could also accord with the view which Horn endorses, that is, that the false implicator did not *literally say* what was untrue, so is off the hook. Horn cites Solan and Tiersma's (2005) discussion of lawyers' responsibility in their questioning for closing off escape routes which are paved with literal truths but destined for deception: if the lawyer fails in this responsibility, the false implicator may get off. And, should the lawyer fail in the responsibility, and the false implicator is tracked down by perjury charges, courts can also set the false implicator free – or not, depending on the jurisdiction. The view of false implicature is different in different communicative contexts: in some (but not all) forensic contexts, the Hearer may have to share responsibility for their part in their own deception.

Horn's analysis of false implicature draws crucially and productively on Gricean maxims of Quality and Quantity. Gricean frameworks are also consulted effectively by other contributors, but not all. Liao in "Cooperation in Chinese courtroom discourse" is not alone in challenging Grice's Cooperative Principle ("CP"). Others (e.g., Sarangi and Slembrouck 1992; Poggi 2011, cited by Slocum, this volume) have, like Liao, taken "cooperative" in the folk sense of getting along, working together in agreement towards shared goals while others, e.g., Davies 2007 and Lumsden 2008, have countered by confirming a technical rather than folk sense of "cooperative". CP skeptics find in many social scenes, if not outright oppositions, at least different positions taken by speech participants. Where goals are not aligned, CP skeptics do not see principles of interaction best described as "cooperative." Such readings of Grice may tend to assume by default a conversational model for cooperation – suited to the fragments and inventions traditional to argumentation in pragmatics – and to contrast the cooperation illustrated in such exchanges with what Liao and others call "institutional" discourse. With data collected from Chinese courtrooms, Liao presents lively evidence of interactants being uncooperative: that is, not complying with the Conversational Maxims, which are in this reading of Grice taken to be rules to be obeyed (or defied) rather than as analyzes of structures and rationalities of interaction. In the Chinese courtroom, defendants can be so pronounced in their interactional style that they get scolded by the judge and urged to be "cooperative" in the folk sense, and in a particular sense belonging to Chinese legal culture: the courtroom genres aim for public performance of cooperation, most highly prized when it takes the form of confession. Applying a scale of cooperativeness, from negative to positive, Liao's analyzes show how this application of Maxims can reveal in sharp outline the different roles taken by participants in the genre of Chinese courtroom questioning – and the different interests, values, and orientations attending these roles.

Allott and Shaer ("Inference and intention in legal interpretation") are amongst those who stress the continuity between legal texts and others. In other communicative situations, language-users grasp meaning by figuring out the best explanation for *this Speaker saying this, now, and in this way, to this Hearer*. In other communicative situations, language-users do this without precise attention to the process of figuring-out; and, in other communicative situations, language users understand the sense of a common word from its context rather than from a dictionary. Equally in legal communicative situations, readers can behave in these ways. Allott and Shaer's chapter makes the case for the "inferential-intentional" character of legal communication by first focussing through the lens of Endicott's (1994, 2012) distinction between "investigative" and "creative" interpretation, the former being the extent of utterance interpretation (*what is the statute saying?*), the latter being the extent of legal deliberation (*what is the law?*). In showing how pragmatics applies to utterance interpretation, Allott and Shaer summon many legal examples of meaning being resolved by determining what the writers of the statute intended. These examples confront and challenge two important contemporary positions in reasoning about legal language: Marmor's (2008) claim that the content constructed by the legislature *is* the content rendered in the syntax and semantics of the statute – such is legal language; Perry's (2011) "meaning-textualism." Like Stein (this volume) Allott and Shaer recognize practical bases for retaining a notion of 'the meaning' of a word or words, yet also like Stein (but in somewhat different terms) question using the notion of literal, ordinary, or plain meaning to show the steps in legal interpretation.

While Allott and Shaer join others in describing a continuity between reading legal texts and reading other kinds of texts, they are also not alone in describing statutory genres at least as being different from other uses of language in allowing fewer opportunities for implicature, partly because of the work of drafters but also partly because legal texts, unlike conversations, do not have a "rich" context.

Also recognising the shared conditions of legal and other uses of language, Slocum in "Pragmatics and legal texts" points to what he calls the 'gap' between literal and communicative meaning: communicative meaning is what a reasonable hearer would take a speaker to intend, legal meaning being not identical with but constrained by this communicative meaning. Further, in ordinary interpretation, the reasonable hearer (unselfconscious and "untutored") can do without – be unaware of – "context-independent," literal definitions (no need for a dictionary). Retrieved by judges from dictionaries, such literal meanings can force their way disruptively into communicative meaning. Slocum makes a strong case for these "primary" pragmatic processes (following Recanati 2004) to be established, by pragmatic methodology, as the circumstances for 'ordinary' meaning, thus pre-empting judges' reach for the dictionary, or other interventions in the primary processes. Even as Slocum instates legal reading processes in the territory of "normal" and pragmatically attested reading, however, he also recognizes a discontinuity between legal and other uses of language. Grice's Cooperative Principle, he says, is about "lengthy conversations" – the everyday, the daily – where context is rich; the context of legal texts is, in contrast, 'sparse' (25). Accordingly, Slocum rejects Relevance Theory as too focussed on context-rich occasions to be demonstrably formulated and thereby useful in legal domains.

In "One ambiguity, three legal approaches," Solan shows the law ordinarily or customarily managing some classic pragmatic uncertainties – opaque *vs.* specific reference – as he says, "pragmatically": that is, differently in response to different legal contexts. The law of wills has turned reference towards the opaque: testators do not have to specify – or even know – the grandchildren who are to inherit; whoever belongs to that category at the time of the testator's death will inherit. An interested party might contest with an opportunistic reading of the legal language, but the argument would have small chance of success. Solan says that this rule for interpretation develops from lawyers' familiarity with families' typical intentions. When the same ambiguity of meaning shows up in contract law, however, parties to the contract are taken to agree to the specific terms of the contract, *whether they have read those specific terms or not*, or whether it is feasible to expect the terms to have been read. Once again, context, and in this case a context configured by technological change in "commercial life," influences the interpretive practice. With wills and contracts each sorting according to prevailing understandings of the organisation of interests, the reading of reference in statutes, Solan shows, is broadly variable – statutes unlike wills having no unitary purpose – and can approach "unnatural" readings. While adjudicators might claim "plain language" or literal readings, the meaning, as Solan's analyzes show, is far from plain. These analyzes also show that canons of interpretation – universal measures for resolving uncertainty – are unlikely to be able to handle the pragmatic diversity of interpretation in legal genres.

The perceiving of similarities, the fitting of instances to categories, and the proposing of analogies are common to many if not all domains of language use. Condello and Arapinis, however, in "Between similarity and analogy: Rethinking the role of prototypes in law and cognitive linguistics," make an emphatic case for their custom contribution to legal discourses. Issuing from many speakers, the corpus of texts which constitutes 'the law' is potentially fragmentary and disarticulated. Without the drive for similarities across instances, that corpus would be dis-integrative. But once declared and argued, similarities then bind the pieces of law into a coherence affording both predictability and moral force: things which are successfully argued to be similar must then be treated the same way. One piece of law must have, as it were, other pieces of law *in mind*.

How are the pieces of law kept in mind? Condello and Arapinis find that prototype theory, even in its extended forms, is inadequate to explain the perception of similarity, and take instead a Wittgensteinian approach via family resemblances. This approach finds categories produced by the activity of categorisation (rather than pre-established and waiting for instances to be captured), these activities in turn being "goal-oriented": that is, similarities are discovered, proposed, and successfully argued as a basis for inference to a range of outcomes feasible to the situation. In other words, the ways in which oil and gas rights are found to be like or unlike water rights; cruise ships are found to be like or unlike hotels; spam is found to be like or unlike trespass – the grounds for similarity are grounds for feasible inference towards the goal of adjudication.

In "When is an insult a crime? On diverging conceptualization and changing legislation," Schneider and Zielasko report how revision of Britain's Public Order Act 1986 caught public attention as people considered the kinds of behaviors which might be termed *abusive* or *insulting*, and thus sanctioned by the Act. Seething with conflicting and also consensual notions of what counts as *insulting*, this public attention sustained such a wide range of applications for the term that Schneider and Zielasko find intentionalist approaches to reading the statute unworkable. They cite intentionalism's risk of obscuring a statute's meaning from ordinary readers (who may not have means or inclination to determine the intention); in addition, their own report of the history of the Public Order Act leaves some doubt that intention could be confidently determined anyway, in light of the widely varying situations exciting the Act and its application – from riots and strikes to a teenager's advertising by placard her opinion of Scientology. Schneider and Zielasko then try textualism and dismiss it for judges' over-reach in their notion of their own capacity to know the meaning of a word. And their own inquiry through multiple-dictionary consultation (*abusive* and *insulting* often defined in terms of one another) and corpus analysis confirms that no judge could authoritatively declare the one meaning of *insulting*. Schneider and Zielasko do find grounds, however, for advising the best course for revisions of the statute, and while this advice derives from their study of meaning, it also enforces their stand against "the textualist paradigm: it is nearly impossible to transfer heterogeneous concepts into a rigid code that is either applicable or not applicable in a given situation."

Olsen's "Pragmatic interpretation by judges: Constrained performatives and the development of gender bias" analyzes three historical US adjudications as expressions of legal pragmatism. In each case, the issue is not the classic problem of legal-linguistic pragmatics, namely, the underdeterminacy of the sentence: in each case, the letter of the law was clear and applicable – and in two of the cases in fact repeatedly applied by courts, until overturned. In each case, the problem is instead a finding which answered, according to Olsen's analysis, judges' sense of what was plausible. In each case, as Olsen shows, what was plausible to these adjudicators was what lined up with a gender-biased worldview. In each case, judges consulted assumptions about women which deafened them to manifest claims and directed them to gender-biased decisions. In 1861 New York Superior Court judges described a woman's leaving her husband without posting an "excuse" to be "immoral and illegal," despite lower courts' decisions and the state legislature's statutory position; in *Roe v. Wade* (1973) the court denied standing to a married woman and her husband while granting standing to a pregnant unmarried woman, the court presumably silently consulting an unstated but active assumption that a woman with an unwanted pregnancy would be a single woman and that such a situation embodied all women's abortion concerns. In the third case, reasons for a US Supreme Court decision, overturning earlier decisions, overlooked the fact of sexual violence against women and turned instead, in Justice Scalia's concurring reasons, to the notion of reputation: the assumption that the harm in sexual violence is to a woman's reputation. For Olsen, the decisions are instances of legal pragmatism: jurists defy statutory or precedent principle to shape feasible outcomes. Olsen's response is to propose modification of two linguistic-pragmatic fundamentals. First, she proposes a version of Austin's performative that is "constrained": that is, the speaker is not automatically ratified – via felicity conditions – for the performative but, instead, ratified only in the event of responsibly fulfilling the institution's principles. Second, such responsible fulfilment would include compliance with a "Principle of Communicative Impartiality," which Olsen derives from Grice's Cooperative Principle. Under these revised conditions, judges would be responsible for taking account of claims made in their courts – that is, in their hearing – and demonstrating that responsibility in their reasons.

In answer to questions we might have as to what judges are doing when they stop the reading process, take their dictionaries, and look up a word in common use by speakers of the language, Makmillen and Fee ("Disguising the dynamism of the law in Canadian courts: Judges using dictionaries") suggest that, at some level of intention, judges thereby arrange for observers to infer first that there is a stable "neutral, natural, and self-evident linguistic code" backing up the legal code and to infer second that, since judges consult this authority on the code, they are themselves neutral in their decision-making, even or especially in situations where strong interests collide. At the same time, as Makmillen and Fee also show, the dictionary action which may enable this inference about courts' neutrality can also enable a judge's laying down a platform which extends into a field for future inference. As an instance of such construction, Makmillen and Fee present a Canadian judge's consulting a dictionary on *treaty* and despite finding no definition of a deed as a treaty nevertheless finding that some mid-nineteenth-century colonial-era deeds on Vancouver Island belonged to the category *treaty* – a finding which has extended the reach of judicial inferences into a crucially consequential field in post-colonial socio-political contexts. On another occasion, when courts were asked to determine whether Aboriginal cultural practices – namely, the harvest and sale of fish – were *distinct*, judges again went to the dictionary, and again stipulated their own definition, again with a view to future inference. This time the prospect of future inference was not restricted to Aboriginal rights: in this case – and at that time – judges could hear in the context claims about Québec as a *distinct society*. Dictionaries may be used in some cases to halt a working term, extract it from context, and force it into a literal pose. But the cases Makmillen and Fee report do not arrive at literal meanings. In these cases, what Makmillen and Fee call the dictionary "interlude" seems to permit judges silently to entertain assumptions in context, and provide bases for future inferences: what rights – if any – should flow uniquely to indigenous populations? How separable is Québec from the rest of Canada?

Recognising that, whatever the larger, more holistic or text-contextual principles of interpretation, focus still can narrow to a word – especially in legal translation – Vlasenko ("Legal translation pragmatics: Legal meaning as text-external convention") describes a procedure for sketching the "referential portrait" of a term. Consulting multiple dictionaries and recursively back-translating, this procedure in effect dilates that potentially narrow focus, not only finding the word's complex associations but also installing these into the consciousness and experience of the translator. Vlasenko points to the urgency of developing such a practice in light of projects such as harmonisation in the EU.

Yet the practice offers more than only this first-order utility. With translation protocols being, as Vlasenko says, themselves a research methodology, the procedure offers a glimpse of words' general sense – experienced generally by users of the language – being overtaken in professional settings, such as law, by specialized uses inaccessible from experience of the word's general meaning. In being thus overtaken, the term is converted to historical service to a legal culture. Vlasenko tracks the term *damages* to demonstrate the first point: in the 'general' language one would try to avoid *damage* but in a specialized legal realm one would seek *damages*, the term with its suffix now recording a sense of someone's responsibility for the damage and, in addition, a recourse. Vlasenko's profiling of *chattels* then demonstrates the historical capacity of a legal term, in this case capturing the term's having "put up with" 800 years of the story of possession and dispossession, and now presenting questions as to the destiny of such meanings when legal systems are harmonized across cultures and languages.

In "Calculating legal meanings? Drawbacks and opportunities of corpus-assisted legal linguistics to make the law (more) explicit," Vogel takes the route from the sentence's surface through to meaning and inference via Gumperz and Goffman, and thereby arrives at a view of interpretation which looks back on the process to observe people's coming to understandings of terms through their experience in interaction – their frequenting a word's use and scenes of use. Showing that introspection is not a fully reliable lens for inspecting this accretion of experience, Vogel recommends corpus study as a means of inquiry into terms' sociality. Tracking use of *"Arbeitnehmer"* (employee) in legal genres, Vogel reveals not only a conceptual or doctrinal frame for the term in German legal culture but, in addition, the dynamics of the interests contending around the term's use in arguments about the extent and limits of workers' rights.

Traditional pragmatic methodologies as well as more recent Relevance-Theoretic methods tend to go to small numbers of examples, often repeated from one episode of inquiry to another, for pragmatic methods are soon swamped by quantity. Vogel's chapter suggests a means of proceeding safely and productively to areas of inquiry where traditional methods would be soon inundated. By these means, abundant data become a resource rather than a risk, and possibly a means of detecting the preferred inferential currents which the chapters by Condello, Olsen, and Makmillen and Fee point to.

As we have seen, many contributors to this volume attend to a difference between legal language and other language – a discontinuity or a continuity marked by more or less sharp gradients on the road from generally 'other' uses of language to legal uses. Drawing on the work of historians of legal culture in "The common error in theories of adjudication," Poscher's claim for difference points to cultural development of the "specificity" of legal argumentation over time: argumentation in Ancient Greek legal culture was largely undistinguished from other rhetorical practice; in Roman times, however, forensic argumentation began to show features specific to legal culture. In Poscher's analysis, this specificity – full-fledged in our time – plays a defining role in the adjudication of what he and others, notably Dworkin (1977), call "hard cases," those cases which appear to be "indeterminate" and confounding, compared to those (the majority) which call simply for the application of the general rule of the law to the instance. Poscher's analysis finds a range of responses to the indeterminacy of such hard cases, from formalist and "denial" responses (the law, properly applied, will find the one and only answer) to those responses which send hard cases away from the legal field altogether, to other disciplines (economics, philosophy, politics, for example) for resolution. The extreme expression of this response is the claim that all adjudication is political anyway, a claim emphatically rejected in this chapter, and replaced by an elegant argument on the separation of politics and law.

Stein's "On inferencing in law" picks up threads from most chapters in this volume and weaves them into a broad tapestry of the field as it extends across several national and disciplinary research traditions. As a survey, the chapter might have served as the entrée to the whole volume, and some readers may wish to start with it. However, we position it last for its offering not only a survey but also a summative account which develops a strong position for meaning being a product of interpretation – rather than interpretation being a retrieval of a pre-existing meaning. Stein suggests that this view will be less compatible with some legal cultures than others, for, in rejecting a "folklore," "container" account of meaning, it also challenges more textualist- and literalist-oriented accounts of judicial interpretation. Stein proposes, in addition, that this challenge is an indication of a parallel between legal and linguistic conceptual systems, the pragmatic turn driving new reasoning in both areas. The practice of legal interpretation runs parallel to pragmatics' cline from the lowest-level inferences as to what is 'in the text' to the highest-order inference at implicature. At the highest order, however, as at the lowest, interpretation will be constrained or prompted, Stein proposes, by genre-specific orders of inference, a suggestion supported by other chapters in this volume (Solan; Condello; Poscher). These rules will constrain language users in the kinds and scope of inference and in the "types of knowledge" which can be accessed for inference. Presumably, these constraints or rules would describe lawyers' professional formation, how they arrive at legal uses of language, not only as writers, speakers, readers and hearers, but also as exponents of a theory of language itself. As Stein's chapter emphasizes throughout, the fusion of *the text* with *the law* is more than only an idea of adherents to textualism. It is deeply fundamental to thinking about law in itself and about language in itself, the two trains of thought joining in *the letter of the law*. The merger is, as Stein observes, in important respects a practicality of functioning systems of adjudication and social norms: as such it will not be easily – or possibly even properly – overturned by the pragmatic turn. But the fusion of text and law is, nevertheless, a conceit.

* * *

Many avenues of research extend from the chapters in this volume. One broad avenue leads from several chapters (Allott and Shaer, Slocum, Schneider and Zielasko, Stein) to research into the viability of the notion of literal meaning, or 'plain' meaning, in the staging of legal interpretation: first step – get the literal meaning. More than 15 years ago, Sullivan (1999) used essentially pragmatic means to expose the fallacy of literal meaning in judges' reasoning, and today there is more basis than ever for joining her in questioning the notion. But can judges be stopped from reaching for the dictionary, or otherwise declaring the real meaning of a word – or otherwise interrupting, disrupting, or distracting natural reading processes? Or will stories of arriving at meaning step-by-step from a literal stepping-off point – will these prevail, continuing to offer folk comfort? Useful to legal cultures (as suggested in chapters by Stein and by Makmillen and Fee in this volume), the legend of a stable code, aloof to local interest, is entertained not only in legal cultures but very broadly in educational and national cultures too. And, through ideologies of the standard, the legend of the code can also be a powerful manifestation or rendering of the social order. Is legal culture's tie to code ideologies just like those we find in other domains? Or is it different, and special, in this regard as in others?

Proposing that the literal fallacy be unmasked and rendered unfit as an alibi for inference, Sullivan (1999) also recommends that judges be explicit about the assumptions they consult in making inferences towards findings. She suggests that, if judges' inferences were exposed to view, rather than concealed behind dictionaries or canons of interpretation or laborious searches for 'plain' meaning, their findings would be more credible to the public. In terms Olsen offers in this volume, we could say that judges would thereby earn their status as performative speakers.

But is judicial rationality such that it can be exposed in this way? Several chapters in this volume point to legal inference as trending silently in certain directions, with an unspoken obligation to viable outcomes – not only Olsen's chapter but also Makmillen and Fee's, Condello's, and even Vogel's for its demonstration of timely collocations of issues.

Certainly Poscher's declarations for the distinguishing features of legal argument bring us face-to-face with the constraints which legal genres impose on their users' options for inference – for reasoning from available assumptions. Horn shows us these constraints too, as do Liao and Solan in each of their chapters: constraints which may not be visible to the naked eye, and which call for these kinds of analysis, but which are, nevertheless, second-nature to legal practitioners, and common sense to legal spheres of activity, as Stein argues.

More than once in this volume, legal language is described as crucially different from (although not necessarily discontinuous with) other uses of language. It is said to lack the 'rich' context of other uses of language; its context is 'sparse.' What are these other contexts, other uses? With the exception of Allott and Shaer's mention of Wilson's (2011) consideration of literary genres, the default comparator for not-rich and sparse context is something like 'everyday conversation,' where context is said to be rich and supportive of implicature.

It's true that most illustrations of pragmatic inference can be heard as snippets of something we might call conversation, maybe for lack of a better term, or lack of better means of imagining what would make people say these things. And the language of law is not like the language of these fragments and figments. The default comparison to conversation is no doubt encouraged by the expression of Grice's foundational proposals, but is conversation the only decent guide for exploring the distinctiveness of the language of law? M. M. Bakhtin (1986), arguably the most important theorist of genre in the 20th century, proposed two levels of genre: 'primary genres' were the conversational ones – everyday, daily conversation – whereas 'secondary genres', constituted over time from primary genres, were latched to 'spheres of activity' and issued from the interactions amongst participants in the activity. The legal genres were amongst Bakhtin's handiest examples of secondary genres: ways of speaking tinted with the 'local color' of the values, interests, professional roles and intentions of participants. But the legal genres were not his only examples. He pointed also to the ways of speaking characteristic of science, journalism, political oratory, administrative management, education, publicity, and other fields which we might take today to include sports, celebrity, food, fitness. All these spheres of activity, just as much as law, enable and are enabled by the genres embedded in and expressive of their practice. So, when an impoverished context is claimed for legal genres, one might ask, in comparison to what?

References

Austin, John L. 1962. *How to do things with words*. Oxford: Clarendon Press.
Bakhtin, Michail M. 1986. Speech genres. In Caryl Emerson and Michael Holquist (eds.), *Speech genres and other late essays*, 60–102. University of Texas Press.
Carston, Robyn. 2002. *Thoughts and utterances: The pragmatics of explicit communication*. Malden MA: Blackwell.
Davies, Bethan L. 2007. Grice's Cooperative Principle: Meaning and rationality. *Journal of Pragmatics* 40(11). 12305–12331.
Delgamuukw v. British Columbia, [1997] 3 S.C.R. 1010.
Dworkin, Ronald. 1977. Hard cases. *Taking rights seriously*, 81–130. Cambridge, Mass.: Harvard University Press.
Giltrow, Janet. 2015. Form alone: The Supreme Court of Canada reading historical treaties. In Natasha Artemeva and Aviva Freedman (eds.), *Genre studies around the globe*, 207–224. Trafford Publications: North America and International.
Grice, H. Paul. 1989. *Studies in the way of words*. Cambridge, MA: Harvard University Press.
Endicott, Timothy. 1994. Putting interpretation in its place. *Law and Philosophy* 13(4). 451–479.
Endicott, Timothy. 2012. Legal interpretation. In Andrei Marmor (ed.), *Routledge companion to philosophy of law*, 109–122. Oxford & New York: Routledge.
Marmor, Andrei. 2008. The pragmatics of legal language. *Ratio Juris* 21(4). 423–452.
Levinson, Stephen C. 1979. Activity types and language. *Linguistics* 17. 365–399.
Lumsden, David. 2008. Kinds of conversational cooperation. *Journal of Pragmatics* 40(11). 1865–1895.

Newman, Dwight G. 2005. *Tsilhqot'in Nation v. British Columbia* and civil justice: Analysing the procedural interaction of evidentiary principles and Aboriginal oral history. *Alberta Law Review* 43, 433–449.

Perry, John. 2011. Textualism and the discovery of rights. In Andrei Marmor & Scott Soames (eds.), *Philosophical foundations of language in the law*, 105–129. Oxford: Oxford University Press.

Poggi, F. 2011. Law and conversational implicatures. *International Journal for the Semiotics of Law* 24. 21–40.

R. v. Marshall #1. 3 Canada Supreme Court Reports 456. 1999. Print.

Recanati, François. 2004. *Literal meaning*. Cambridge, England: Cambridge University Press.

Sarangi, Srikant K. & Stefan Slembrouck. 1992. Non-cooperation in communication: A reassessment of Gricean pragmatics. *Journal of Pragmatics* 17. 117–154.

Solan, Lawrence & Peter Tiersma. 2005. *Speaking of crime: The language of criminal justice*. Chicago: University of Chicago Press.

Sperber, Dan & Deirdre Wilson. [1986] 1995. *Relevance: Communication and cognition*, 2nd ed. Oxford UK and Cambridge USA: Blackwell.

Sperber, Dan & Deirdre Wilson. 2002. Pragmatics, modularity and mind-reading. *Mind & Language* 17(1). 3–23.

Sullivan, Ruth. 1999. Statutory interpretation in the Supreme Court of Canada. *Ottawa Law Review* 30(2). 175–227. Print.

Tiersma, Peter. 2010. *Parchment, paper, pixels: Law and the technologies of communication*. Chicago; London: University of Chicago Press.

Tslihqot'in v. British Columbia, [2014] SCC 44.

Wilson, Deirdre. 2011. Relevance and the interpretation of literary works. *UCL Working Papers in Linguistics* 23. 69–80.

Wittgenstein, Ludwig. [1953] 1999. *Philosophical investigations*, trans. G. E. M. Abscombe. Upper Saddle River, New Jersey: Prentice Hall.

I Linguistic-pragmatic approaches to inference in law

Laurence R. Horn
2 Telling it slant: Toward a taxonomy of deception

> Tell all the Truth but tell it Slant –
> Success in Circuit lies
> Too bright for our infirm delight
> The truth's superb surprise
>
> As Lightning to the Children eased
> With explanation kind,
> The Truth must dazzle gradually
> Or every man be blind –
> – Emily Dickinson
>
> Oh, what a tangled web we weave
> When first we practise to deceive!
> – Walter Scott, Marmion, Canto VI

1 "Tell all the truth" or just "Don't tell a lie"?

Are we under an injunction to tell the whole truth? Or an injunction against telling an actual falsehood? There is a rich tradition in philosophy, theology, and jurisprudence of endorsing the latter view, perhaps a weaker goal but an easier one to fulfill:

> The first and most necessary area of philosophy is the one that deals with the application of principles such as "We ought not to lie."
> – Epictetus, *Enchiridon* §52
>
> Thou shalt not bear false witness against thy neighbor.
> – 9th Commandment, *Exodus* 20:16
>
> Do not say what you believe to be false.
> – first maxim of Quality, Grice ([1967] 1989: 27)

For Kant, lying is always abhorrent, but (as recognized since Augustine), some lies are more abhorrent than others. As we shall see, lying may even be considered permissible, depending on the context (Grotius 1625; Mill) or forbidden per se while intentionally misleading is allowed (whence the practice of early modern Jesuits, or what we might call the Clinton Doctrine, expounded below).

Laurence Horn, Yale University

Some, however, see lying as an art form, a ubiquitous defining trait of our species *Homo mendax*. Among those expressing this view is the cynical humanist *par excellence*, Mark Twain (1880):

> None of us could live with an habitual truth-teller. But thank goodness, none of us has to [...]. Everybody lies – every day; every hour; awake; asleep; in his dreams; in his joy; in his mourning; if he keeps his tongue still, his hands, his feet, his eyes, his attitude, will convey deception [...]. Lying is universal – we *all* do it. Therefore, the wise thing is for us diligently to train ourselves to lie thoughtfully, judiciously; to lie with a good object, and not an evil one; to lie for others' advantage, and not our own; to lie healingly, charitably, humanely, not cruelly, hurtfully, maliciously; to lie gracefully and graciously, not awkwardly and clumsily; to lie firmly, frankly, squarely, with head erect, not haltingly, tortuously, with pusillanimous mien, as being ashamed of our high calling. Then shall we be rid of the rank and pestilent truth that is rotting the land; then shall we be great and good and beautiful, and worthy dwellers in a world where even benign Nature habitually lies, except when she promises execrable weather.

To be sure, there are lies and there are lies: *Cui bono?* Twain's dichotomy between altruistic and self-serving lies reflects an ancient intuition. For Aquinas, there is "the LIE JOCOSE," involving irony or game-playing (one might wonder whether this is a lie at all, a point to which we return below), the LIE OFFICIOUS (in defense of oneself or for another, to a child or patient; cf. the WHITE LIE), and finally the LIE MALICIOUS (or INJURIOUS). If the jocose lie is an ironic or sarcastic comment that may not strike us as a lie at all, the altruistic or officious lie is presumably a generous speech act performed for (what we perceive to be) the needs of others. That leaves the true lie, which may be told out of a justified fear of the alternative: "A lie would have no sense unless the truth were felt as dangerous" (Adler 1931: 43). Note too the contrast between telling **the** truth and telling **a** lie: truth is unique, lies are legion.

Nor should it be overlooked that a lie is a something one **tells**; there are falsehoods that one might suggest (intentionally or inadvertently), perhaps by withholding the truth or indeed by telling it slant. This must be built into our definition of lying, a task to which we now turn.

2 To be (a lie) or not to be? Criteria for "*p* is a lie"

How are we to differentiate instances in which I intentionally mislead or deceive you from those in which I can be said to truly commit what Touchstone (*As You Like It* V.iv) calls "the lie direct"? Four criteria have been invoked for what it takes for speaker S to lie to hearer H, criteria distinguished here by different underlining styles:

(1) Criteria for lying
 (C1) S says/asserts that p
 (C2) S believes that p is false
 (C3) p is false
 (C4) S intends to deceive H

To be sure, to **say** something you **correctly believe to be false** with **the intent to deceive** is unquestionably to lie. But must all four of these criteria be satisfied? The Oxford English Dictionary (s.v. LIE, n., 2b), invokes **C3, C1**, and **C4**: a lie is "a **false** statement made with intent to deceive." A slightly different view is endorsed by Augustine in the *Enchiridion:* "Every liar says the opposite of what he thinks in his heart, with purpose to deceive"; thus we have **C1, C2, and C4**. Indeed, the requirement endorsed by Augustine that the liar in stating p must believe not-p (**C2**) is intuitively more plausible than the requirement endorsed by the OED that p be actually false (**C3**). This intuition is explicitly supported by St. Thomas Aquinas (*Summa Theologica* II.II, q. 110; emphasis mine):

> [I]f one says what is false, thinking it to be true, it is false materially, but not formally, because the falseness is beside the intention of the speaker so that it is not a perfect lie, since what is beside the speaker's intention is accidental [...]. If, on the other hand, one utters falsehood formally, through having the will to deceive, *even if what one says be true*, yet inasmuch as this is a voluntary and moral act, *it contains falseness essentially and truth accidentally, and attains the specific nature of a lie* [...]. We judge of a thing according to what is in it formally and essentially rather than according to what is in it materially and accidentally. Hence *it is more in opposition to truth*, considered as a moral virtue, *to tell the truth with the intention of telling a falsehood than to tell a falsehood with the intention of telling the truth.*

Only S's intentions matter, not the actual (accidental) truth of p; as George Costanza famously puts it, "It's not a lie if you believe it" (cf. Fallis 2010 on the Costanza Doctrine).

Perhaps an example will help; here is one based on a scenario described in Updike 1976. Richard tells Ruth that her husband Jerry is having an affair (although he doesn't believe this), with the intention of getting Ruth to sleep with him. Unbeknownst to Richard, Jerry **is** having an affair – with Richard's own wife Sally. On Aquinas's diagnosis, Richard, while telling the (accidental) truth, has lied to Ruth.

Some empirical support for the Aquinas line comes from Coleman & Kay (1981). In their study, they provide subjects with a multiplicity of scenarios variously manipulating the satisfaction of the three conditions I have labeled **(C2)–(C4)**. Their finding is that the greatest unanimity of responses was by those reacting to "prototype" lies in which all three of these conditions were satisfied, but in cases of partial satisfaction "*falsity of belief* is the most important element of the prototype of *lie*, *intended deception* is the next most important element, and *factual falsity* is the least important" (Coleman & Kay 1981: 43; cf. Meibauer 2014a: §2.3 for additional discussion).

3 Lying: toward an Aquinian analysis

Following Frege (1892: 160), Chisholm & Feehan (1977: 152) offer the following definition:

(2) **L lies to D** =$_{df}$ There is a proposition p such that
   (i) L believes that p is false (or at least that p is not true); and
   (ii) L asserts p to D.

Crucial here are L's assertion of p (our **C1**) and L's belief in the falsity of p (our **C2**). Not crucial are the falsity of p (our **C3**) or any attempt on L's part to get D to believe p (our **C4**). How are we to interpret (i)? What if L neither believes that p is true nor believes that p isn't true – or if L doesn't even care about the truth of p? What we have in that case is not a lie but an exemplar of, to use the technical term, *bullshit*:[1]

> It is impossible for someone to lie unless he thinks he knows the truth. A person who lies is thereby responding to the truth, and he is to that extent respectful of it [...] The bullshitter [...] does not reject the authority of the truth, as the liar does, and oppose himself to it. He pays no attention to it at all. By virtue of this, bullshit is a greater enemy of the truth than lies are. (Frankfurt 2005: 61)

4 On (C4): must the liar intend to deceive?

For Frankfurt, the goal of the bullshitter is neither to enlighten the hearer as a truth-teller would do nor to deceive her about the facts as a canonical liar would do, but to inflate his own standing in the bullshittee's assessment. But does a

---

[1] Compare Stephen Colbert's construct of TRUTHINESS or the fallout from Sen. Jon Kyl's (R-AZ) baseless 2011 assertion that "well over 90%" of Planned Parenthood's activity is devoted to performing abortions. When the true figure was subsequently shown to be more like 3%, a staffer helpfully explained that the senator's earlier remark "was not intended to be a factual statement" (cf. http://knowyourmeme.com/memes/events/not-intended-to-be-a-factual-statement).

liar always intend to deceive? What is the status of (**C4**)? This is a matter of debate, and debate it has sparked between deceptionists, who invoke (**C4**), and non-deceptionists, who don't. While the heritage of the deceptionist group harks back to Augustine's "purpose to deceive" and Aquinas's "will to deceive," it is not clear whether this is a necessary condition on all lies or just a marker of prototypic lies.

Knowingly false statements can be intended to deceive a third party without constituting lies to the primary or ratified addressee, so intention to deceive is not sufficient for lying if e.g. (**C1**) is not satisfied. At the same time, it is arguably not a necessary condition on lying either, since a knowingly false assertion can constitute a lie even if the liar assumes that the addressee won't be deceived. Cassandra can lie as well as truthfully assert even if she knows she won't be believed (cf. Pagin 2007 on asserting into the wind).

Recently, the nondeceptionists have focused on the case of the *bald-faced lie* (Carson 2006, 2010; Sorensen 2007; Fallis 2010; Lackey 2013, Stokke 2013a,b; see also Meibauer 2014a: 104–9 for a different view). Now-standard examples include the implausible denial under oath by a frightened witness in a mob trial and the formal but non-credible denial of a plagiarizing student who must simply put on record in the dean's presence his attestation that any misuse of his sources was unintentional. Another case of bald-faced deceit is the transparently unbelievable alibi of an unfaithful spouse:

> That he worked late she did not doubt, but *she knew he did not sleep at his club, and he knew that she knew this* [...]. The regularity of his evening calls, however much she disbelieved them, was a comfort to them both [...]. Even being lied to constantly, though hardly like love, was sustained attention; he must care about her to fabricate so elaborately.
> – Ian McEwan (2001), *Atonement*, p. 139

In each case, S seeks to *go on record as committing to p*, as with "pointless" assertions that are made in good faith: "You're not gonna believe this, but..."

5 A pause for perjury

While courts have long recognized the essential status of (**C1**) in defining perjury (we return below to the distinction between false statements and false implicatures) and the non-essential status of (**C4**), questions about the other two conditions have been dealt with more subtly. Consider the 1911 U.K. Perjury statute and the 1975 revision concerning testimony not given under oath (emphasis added):

http://www.legislation.gov.uk/ukpga/Geo5/1-2/6/section/1/enacted [1911, §1]
If any person lawfully sworn as a witness or as an interpreter in a judicial proceeding wilfully *makes a statement* material in that proceeding, *which he knows to be false or does not believe to be true*, he shall be guilty of perjury [...]

http://www.legislation.gov.uk/ukpga/Geo5/1-2/6/section/1A [1975, §1A]
If any person, in giving any testimony (either orally or in writing) otherwise than on oath, where required to do so by an order under section 2 of the Evidence (Proceedings in Other Jurisdictions) Act 1975, *makes a statement* –
(a) *which he knows to be false* in a material particular, or
(b) *which is false* in a material particular *and which he does not believe to be true*, he shall be guilty of an offence [...]

When we leave the philosophical and theological realms of Augustine and Aquinas for the forensic arena, actual falsity matters, at least in a non-oath context, as seen in the conjunction the highlighted passages in condition (b); Aquinas's "accidental truth" gets one off the hook here, however undeservedly.[2] But under U.S. perjury law, as under the 1911 British statute, perjury can result from any testimony the defendant "does not believe to be true": cf. U.S. Code §1621, http://www.law.cornell.edu/uscode/text/18/1621 (thanks to Larry Solan for the pointer). Thus, "accidental truth" is not exculpatory. One wonders, however, if a witness is ever prosecuted in the U.S. for either (i) stating as true something she neither believes to be true nor believes not to be true (as in the case of dispensing bullshit) or (ii) making a statement she believes to be false that turns out to be "accidentally" true à la Aquinas.

6 Lies and what isn't said: the "silent lie"

In the definitional frameworks for lying and perjury we have touched on, one unchallenged criterion is (**C1**): if it isn't said, it's not a lie. But what is meant by "said"? One case in point is when the speaker gets the hearer to arrive at a false belief by saying nothing at all. In his lament for the lost art of lying, Twain (1880) highlights "the silent lie – the deception which one conveys by simply keeping still and concealing the truth. Many obstinate truth-mongers indulge in this dissipation, imagining that if they speak no lie, they lie not at all." But note Twain's conflation of lie and deception: is this a mere distinction without a difference?

---

2 One puzzle in the interpretation of Section A1 is whether (a) can ever hold when (b) doesn't; it would seem that one cannot *know* p to be false without it being the case both that one *believes* p to be false and that p *is* in fact false.

Those who see lies as crimes against humanity and sins against God (e.g. Augustine or Kant) tend to pardon intentional silent deception when no statement is made. For Kant (1799), the "ground of all duties based on contract" is "*truthfulness in statements which cannot be avoided*, however great may the disadvantage accruing to himself or to another [...]. To be truthful (honest) *in all declarations* is a sacred and absolutely commanding decree of reason, limited by no expediency." Thus if a murderer asks me whether you're hiding in my basement I cannot lie on your behalf – but I can refuse (or at least try to refuse) to make any declaration, or I can change the subject and hope you don't notice. In another of Kant's much cited thought experiments, if I pack my bags to get you to think I'm leaving town (when in fact I have no such intention), I have not lied to you. For Kant, Twain's "silent lie" would be no lie at all.

The suitcase packer makes especially clear the role of Grice's MEANING$_{NN}$ in delineating the realm of the lie, and in particular Grice's distinction between S deliberately and openly getting H to think that p as opposed to S actually telling H that p" (Grice [1957] "Meaning," Essay 7 in Grice 1989). If I don't *communicate* (let alone *assert*) to you that I'm going on a trip, I can't be lying in getting you to reach this incorrect conclusion. This is a point not lost on the Old Testament God or His followers. In his critique of (overt) lies, St. Augustine ("Against Lying," §23) reminds us of the account in Genesis 20:12 of Abraham's silent deception of King Abimelech:

> [T]hey who assert that it is sometimes permitted to lie, conveniently do not mention that Abraham did this concerning Sarah, whom he said to be his sister. For he did not say, She is not my wife, but he said, She is my sister; because she was in truth so near akin, that she might without a lie be called a sister. Which also afterwards he confirmed, after she had been given back by him who had taken her, answering him and saying, And indeed she is my sister, by father, not by mother [...]. Somewhat therefore of truth he left untold, not told anything of falsehood, when he left wife untold, and told of sister [...]. It is not then a lie, when by silence a true thing is kept back, but when by speech a false thing is put forward.

They didn't call him half-honest Abe for nothing.

The fact that one cannot lie without the use of words (or other conventional signals) is a point of convergence between the fathers of the church and the framers of the perjury statutes. To be sure, in common parlance the standards may be relaxed to allow for pragmatic slack (Lasersohn 1999), widening the domain of the lie, whence the "silent lie" excoriated by Twain or the "good lovers' lies" exonerated by Martin (2015):

> Valentine's Day is not a celebration of truth telling. God forbid! Relationships last only if we don't always say exactly what we're thinking. We have to disguise our feelings, to feint, to smile sometimes when we want to shout. In short, we have to lie.

But to "not say exactly what we're thinking" is not to lie – for that, we must say what we're not thinking. Unlike white lies, which are indeed lies (however venial or altruistic), silent "lies" of omission have the same status with respect to actual lies that peanut butter has to butter or phone sex to sex.

7 Lies and what is (and isn't) said: where the truth "lies"

Speech act theory distinguishes what is literally said or spoken in Austin's locutionary sense from what is asserted or otherwise put forth with illocutionary force (e.g. Searle 1969). The latter is the notion relevant for criterion (**C1**). As Chisholm & Feehan (1977) point out, we need to invoke a quasi-Gricean reflexive-intentional notion of asserting that rules out play-acting. The illocutionary definition of *say* or *assert* relevant for characterizing lies must be narrowly defined enough to eliminate non-literal locutions in which no assertion is directly made: irony, sarcasm, banter, pretense, tall tales, (non-conventionalized) metaphor, and so on. At the same time, *say* can't be too strictly defined:

> We must not take the word 'say' so narrowly that a man's speaking or writing is essential to lying. *L* can lie to *D* by nodding his assent, [...] or by using sign language, or by making smoke signals. (Chisholm & Feehan 1977: 149)

But it is the issue of narrowing down what counts and what doesn't count as saying that has proved the more elusive and controversial task.

As Chisholm & Feehan point out (1977: 155), a speaker can convey a false proposition by implicature without lying, e.g. if I utter "My leg isn't bothering me *too* much today" when it's not bothering me at all I may succeed in misleading or deceiving you but – absent the assertion that my leg is bothering me – I do not lie. In the spirit of Chisholm & Feehan, we can characterize lying as an *illocutionary act* in the speech-theoretic sense[3], defined by the speaker's intentional representation of herself as committed to the truth of a proposition she believes to be false (see J. Adler 1997; Meibauer 2005, 2011, 2014a; Horn 2009; Saul 2012; and Stokke 2013a,b for defenses and critiques of this position). As such, it constitutes non-natural meaning (meaning$_{NN}$) in Grice's sense and requires human (or quasi-human) agents. The adage "The moon always lies" is

---

[3] Note that this does not mean that it has a corresponding performative use: *I hereby lie (to you) that...* would be as self-defeating as comparable uses of *flatter* or *boast* (cf. Austin 1962).

prompted by the fact that a waning or decrescent half-moon ☾ appears to self-identify with a letter "C" for 'crescent' and a waxing half-moon ☽ with a letter "D" for 'decrescent'.[4] But heavenly bodies don't really lie (or tell the truth).

While lying is by definition intentional, misleading or deceiving can be accomplished either intentionally (agentively) or unintentionally (non-agentively) – and is typically a *perlocutionary act*, defined by its effect on the addressee or victim. And while lying may or may not be successful in its intended goal, *mislead* and *deceive* are "success" verbs (cf. Mahon 2007, Saul 2012: 71). Thus we have contrasts like those in (3):

(3) Sorry if I {misled you/deceived you/#lied to you}, I didn't mean to.

Don't let the blue sky {mislead you/deceive you/#lie to you} – it's bitterly cold out.

She {lied to me/#misled me/#deceived me}, but I didn't believe her for a minute.

I tried to {mislead/deceive/#lie to} her, but she was too clever to believe me.

Animal and plant kingdoms are replete with deception (or mimicry) that has evolved under natural selection (cf. e.g. Bond & Robinson 1988) but not with lying as such. It is only *homo mendax* who has the ability to lie as well as the ability to (intentionally) deceive, and we are expert at both.

In particular, Kant's suitcase-packer has numerous counterparts on the playing field. We can begin with incidents of "diving" by soccer players – an attempt, according to FIFA regulations, "to deceive the referee by feigning injury or pretending to have been fouled." Diving or "embellishment" is also endemic to hockey, as are "flopping" in basketball and related types of pretense in U.S. football. Intentional misrepresentation in baseball extends from fielders holding up trapped balls as caught to batters who feign being hit by a pitch. Deception in poker is not just incidental but an integral component of the game in the case of the *bluff* – by aggressively betting on weak hand one pretends to have a stronger hand than one really does.[5] More peripheral are the practices of *sandbagging* (checking and then raising a hand, in pretense of having a weaker hand than one does), and *coffee-housing* (dispensing chatter in an attempt to mislead

---

4 The moon only "lies" to those viewing it north of the equator; when seen from the Southern Hemisphere, the moon really is *crescens* when it appears as a C and *decrescens* when it forms a D.

5 The practice of bluffing might be traced back to the Philosopher himself: "Aristotle […] beeyng asked what vauntage a man might get by lying, he answered: 'to be unbelieved when he telleth truth.'" (Baldwin 1571).

one's competitors about the strength of one's hand or more generally to distract them). In none of these cases does the player, absent direct verbal misrepresentation, actually lie. A player who fails to correct a referee's or umpire's misjudgment, allowing a false conclusion to be drawn is rarely considered unethical, especially when the deception benefits the team (cf. Mahon 2008 for overview).

As we shall see in more detail below, there are two distinct questions arising in the assessment of lying and misleading:

(4) (i) is lying (asserting what you don't believe) importantly distinct from intentionally misleading or deceiving (whether by remaining silent or by implicating what you don't believe)?

(ii) if so, is lying in principle worse (morally, ethically, legally) than misleading?

As pointed out by Saul (2012), it is reasonable to accept (4i) while rejecting (4ii); see also Fallis 2010 on deceptive lying, non-deceptive lying, and non-lying deception. Meibauer, who is more inclined to subsume false implicatures under the general rubric of lies, borrows a couplet from Blake as the title of his recent paper on the topic (Meibauer 2014b):

> A truth that's told with bad intent
> Beats all the lies you can invent.
> – William Blake, *Auguries of Innocence* (1803)

But for those who reject Meibauer's conceptual broadening, the moral is that truths you tell with bad intent are still truths and lies you invent are still lies, which doesn't necessarily render the former automatically superior on ethical or moral grounds to the latter. It does mean that the two categories are conceptually distinct, and part of what the account defended here predicts is that this distinction correlates with important and independently arrived at distinctions in the theory of meaning.

8 Liars' advocates

Before delving more fully into the practice of misleading by falsely implicating, we should acknowledge that lying itself has its defenders in philosophical discourse and real life. These include cases in which – to adopt Gricean language – a speaker overrides or opts out of the first Quality maxim, "Do not say what you believe to be false." One frequent overriding factor is politeness or "respecting negative face" (cf. Brown & Levinson 1987, citing Erving Goffman). This yields the "officious" lies of Aquinas or the "prosocial" lies of Meibauer (2014a: §4.9), more popularly known as white lies.

Lies are also excused or endorsed when motivated by the need to defend oneself or the moral obligation to protect another. Dr. Samuel Johnson (cited by Boswell) comments on "the casuitical question – whether it is allowable at any time to depart from the truth" and, while acknowledging the general rule not to speak falsely, insists (against his contemporary Kant and the tradition of Augustine) that this edict is not inviolable:

> There must, however, be exceptions. If, for instance, a murderer should ask you which way a man is gone, you may tell him what is not true, because you are under a previous obligation not to betray a man to a murderer. (Boswell 1791: 426; cf. Newman 1865: 279)

Lies may be justified in defense of others in one's group (as reinforced by evolutionary and economic survival). Thus, Shalvi & de Dreu (2014) describe how "oxytocin promotes group-serving dishonesty," Norris (2014) observes that in the business world, corporate lies don't count, and West Virginia University football coach Dana Holgorsen, on behalf of his coaching fraternity, acknowledges in an August 2014 press conference that lying is part of recruiting, an admission that was mysteriously "scrubbed" from the video and transcript the university posted of Holgorsen's remarks (http://tinyurl.com/nysksu8).

Is lying permissible for the (perceived) good of society? Police or FBI agents represent themselves as drug-dealers or gang members, animal rights activists infiltrate slaughterhouses to expose wrongdoing, investigative journalists seeking to expose corruption or cults conceal their identity from targets. While none of these misrepresentations necessarily involves lying per se, the circumstances may induce lies in support of the deception. Less subtly, there is a widely condoned practice of police officers' "testilying," testifying falsely under oath to help win a conviction (http://wordspy.com/index.php?word=testilying).

On a higher plain, lies can aim at *shalom bayit*, the preservation of household harmony. While the Devil is "the father of lies" (John 8:44; cf. also "Tell the truth and shame the devil"), even God can lie to preserve domestic tranquility, as related in Genesis 18:12-13. When God promises Sarah that she will have a son, she laughs to think that Abraham could give her pleasure and father a child at *his* age, but God tells Abraham that Sarah laughed at the prospect that she could conceive at *her* age. Talmudic commentaries refer, with delicate euphemisms, to God's "making a variation" or "changing the truth" to ensure *shalom bayit* (*Babylonian Talmud*, Baba Metzia 87a; Yevamot 65b; Vayikra Rabba 9:9).

Given the tension between the principles "Do not lie" and "Do no harm," it has been argued that Quality can – and should – be overridden by the Hippocratic oath. Traditionally, as advanced in the influential dicta of Grotius (1625), one may freely "say what is false" to those incapable of judgment, including children (to shield them from the truth about the Tooth Fairy or the stork) and the insane, along with others who don't "deserve" the truth (accused criminals, soldiers wavering in battle). The practice of patients being lied to "for their own good" is embodied in the classical proverb "mentiris ut medicus" – lie like a doctor. Similar exceptions are made for lying to an adopted child, deceived spouse, or elderly parent, shielding each from the presumably devastating effect of the truth; one complex but humorous example forms the basis for the 2003 film "Goodbye Lenin," in which the family of a loyal East German Communist, who falls into a coma just before the fall of the Berlin Wall, must go to great lengths to protect her from the truth that the regime has evaporated.

While some would still defend what Jauhar (2014) – "When Doctors Need To Lie" – calls "soft paternalism," this is no longer generally accepted by doctors, ethicists, or civilians, as can be witnessed by the outraged comments in response to Jauhar's column. The question once again is *Cui bono?* Is the *medicus mendax* sparing the deceived, or the deceiver? (Cf. Bok 1978 for an excellent chronology of shifting views on this question.) Perhaps the best we can do is adopt what we might term the *Dickinson-Dumbledore strategy*, in honor of our epigraph from the poet and the related wisdom imparted to Harry Potter below:[6]

> Harry said, "Sir, there are some other things I'd like to know, if you can tell me [...] things I want to know the truth about."
>
> "The truth," Dumbledore sighed. "It is a beautiful and terrible thing, and should therefore be treated with great caution. I shall answer your questions unless I have a very good reason not to [...] I shall not, of course, lie.
> – J. K. Rowling, Harry Potter and the Philosopher's Stone

That is, (i) Tell the truth but tell it slant; (ii) Never lie.

But what of the speaker who intentionally misleads or deceives the hearer without satisfying (**C1**) and thus without actually lying? I would maintain,

---

[6] Compare also the celebrated exchange (https://www.youtube.com/watch?v=UXoNE14U_zM) from the 1992 film *A Few Good Men:*
Col. Jessep (Jack Nicholson): "You want answers?"
Lt. Kaffee (Tom Cruise): "I want the truth!"
Col. Jessep: "You can't handle the truth!"

following Saul (2012), that while the misleader is not intrinsically on higher ethical ground than the liar, the distinction between the two is crucial, especially in forensic contexts where a premium is placed on what counts as having been said (rather than merely implicated).

9 The statutory status of (Quantity) implicature, from Madison to Bronston

Implicated truths and falsehoods have figured in a variety of ways within legal discourse and policy. A good starting point is provided by implicatures associated with the observance or exploitation of the first Quantity submaxim: "Make your contribution as informative as is required (for the current purposes of the talk-exchange)" (Grice 1989: 26).

When it comes to acknowledging the overt or covert role of Quantity implicature, legal tradition has responded in different ways depending on the local goal and the overall context. In the first place, the tendency to recover unwanted implicatures can be *recognized* and *taken into account*, for example by cancelation. This can be seen in James Madison's 1789 letter to the House of Representatives on the need for the Ninth Amendment to the Constitution – "The enumeration in the Constitution of certain rights shall not be construed so as to deny or disparage others retained by the people":

> It has been objected also against a bill of rights, that, by enumerating particular exceptions to the grant of power, it would disparage those rights which were not placed in that enumeration; and *it might follow by implication, that those rights which were not singled out, were intended to be assigned into the hands of the General Government*, and were consequently insecure. This is one of the most plausible arguments I have ever heard against the admission of a bill of rights into this system; but, I conceive, that it may be guarded against.
> (http://constitution.findlaw.com/amendment9/amendment.html)

Since then, judges have often explicitly reasoned based on inferences from what wasn't said:

> In an amendment to the Public Health Service act, Congress in 1981 said that clinics receiving Federal funds for contraceptive services should, "to the extent practical," encourage family participation in their activities. *If Congress had wanted to require parental notification*, Judge Edwards said, *it could have used more explicit language*.
> (N.Y. Times 5/10/83, http://tinyurl.com/pvgqrev)

Quantity implicatures can also be explicitly *conventionalized* and incorporated into what is said, as in what might be dubbed the precedent of *California v. Grice*:

> The courts recognize that employers do not have any duty to disclose information about their employees. However, if an employer chooses to provide a reference or recommendation, the reference giver must include factual negative information that may be material to the applicant's fitness for employment in addition to any positive information. Campus managers and supervisors who provide employment references on current or former employees must be aware that untrue, incomplete or misleading information may cause a different liability – negligent referral. The court in *Randi M. v. Livingston Union School District*, 1995 Cal. App. LEXIS 1230 (Dec. 15, 1995), found that, "A statement that contains only favorable matters and omits all reference to unfavorable matters is as much a false representation as if all the facts stated were untrue."
> (http://shr.ucsc.edu/procedures/reference_check/index.html)

In California, then, conversationally implicated meaning can count as part of what is said, but only because statutory language makes it so. Another instance in which the scalar upper bound is explicitly built into propositional content is in the forensic treatment of criminal attempt as an "inchoate" offense, one committed "without actual harm being done." While Grice (1989: Lecture 1) makes a compelling case for why trying merely implicates not succeeding – among other considerations, this inference is largely restricted to past tense clauses and is eminently cancelable by the linguistic or extralinguistic context – in the legal domain, to try (or attempt) is necessarily to fail. This is to assure the "merging" of offenses: a murder isn't (ipso facto) an attempted murder, and acquittal of the former charge immunizes one against a subsequent charge for the latter. Thus, "To say that someone has *tried* (past tense) is just a more positive way of saying that he *failed* in what he set out to do," notes Imlay (1967: 125–126), citing New York Penal Law, Art. 1, Para. 2: an attempt to commit a crime is "an act, done with intent to commit a crime, and *tending but failing* to effect its commission." Similarly, a prosecutor aiming to convict someone of attempted murder must prove that he or she took at least one direct *but ineffective* step towards killing someone.

At the same time, implicature can be *exploited* and distinguished from what is said in forensic contexts as well as everyday life. We have encountered one case of such exploitation, Chisholm & Feehan's "My leg isn't bothering me *too* much today" as uttered by someone whose leg bothers him not at all. For a more elaborate real world example, we turn to the fate of Picasso's "Guernica," the celebrated and moving canvas of the horrors of the Spanish Civil War, exiled to New York Museum of Modern Art during Franco's dictatorship but a target for repatriation once a democratic regime had been installed in Spain. Here is the New York Times account of how that repatriation was accomplished:

> Since the long-exiled "Guernica" finally came to Madrid on Sept. 10 [1981], Rafael Fernández Quintanilla, the witty diplomat who dealt with the Museum of Modern Art in New York and Picasso's heirs, has felt free to disclose some of the secrets of his protracted negotiations. One is *an elaborate bluff*. To demonstrate that the Spanish Government had in fact paid Picasso to paint the mural in 1937 for the Paris International Exhibition, Mr. Fernández Quintanilla had to secure documents in the archives of the late Luis Araquistain, Spain's Ambassador to France at the time. But Araquistain's son, poor and opportunistic, demanded $2 million for the archives, which Mr. Fernández Quintanilla rejected as outrageous. He managed, however, to obtain from the son photocopies of the pertinent documents, which in 1979 he presented to Roland Dumas, the Paris lawyer named by Picasso to determine when "public liberties" had been re-established in Spain, permitting delivery of the "Guernica" to the Prado.
>
> "This changes everything," a startled Mr. Dumas told the Spanish envoy when he showed him the photocopies of the Araquistain documents. "You of course have the originals?" the lawyer asked casually. "*Not all of them*," replied Mr. Fernández Quintanilla, *not lying but not telling the truth, either*. (Markham 1981)

What makes the diplomat's move an "elaborate bluff" rather than a lie is his exploitation of Quantity implicature to convey a falsehood that he did not utter.[7]

10 False implicature, (non-)perjury, and case law

Fernández Quintanilla's ploy is part of a distinguished, or at least long, tradition. An important legal precedent in this domain is the landmark case *Bronston v. United States*, 409 U.S. 352 (1973) (https://supreme.justia.com/cases/federal/us/409/352/case.html). Here is the crucial exchange:

> *Bronston v. United States*, 409 U.S. 352 (1973)
> https://supreme.justia.com/cases/federal/us/409/352/case.html
> BANKRUPTCY HEARING, JUNE 10, 1966
> "Q. Do you have any bank accounts in Swiss banks, Mr. Bronston?"
> "A. No, sir."
> "Q. Have you ever?"
> "A. The company had an account there for about six months, in Zurich."

---

7 While the tendency to infer from *not all* to *some* is the locus classicus for scalar implicature (Horn 1972: 96; see Oxford English Dictionary, s.v. *scalar implicature*), Chierchia (2004: 69) takes this to be an instance of "indirect" implicature as against the inverse move from *some* to *not all*. For counterarguments, see Horn 2009: 12–13.

As Chief Justice Burger notes for the majority in overturning an earlier perjury finding against Bronston for his responses here, the movie magnate's answers, while intentionally misleading given the personal account he had previously maintained at the International Credit Bank in Geneva, were nonetheless "literally truthful" at the time he was interrogated under oath:

> It is undisputed that, for a period of nearly five years, between October, 1959, and June, 1964, petitioner had a personal bank account at the International Credit Bank in Geneva, Switzerland, into which he made deposits and upon which he drew checks totaling more than $180,000. It is likewise undisputed that petitioner's answers were *literally truthful*.
>
> (a) Petitioner did not at the time of questioning have a Swiss bank account.
>
> (b) Bronston Productions, Inc., did have the account in Zurich described by petitioner.
>
> Beyond question, petitioner's answer to the crucial question was not responsive if we assume, as we do, that the first question was directed at personal bank accounts. *There is, indeed, an implication in the answer to the second question that there was never a personal bank account; in casual conversation, this interpretation might reasonably be drawn.* But we are not dealing with casual conversation, and the statute does not make it a criminal act for a witness to willfully state any material matter that implies any material matter that he does not believe to be true.
>
> – majority opinion written by Chief Justice Warren Burger (Page 409 U.S. 357–8)

Around the same time that Bronston and his lawyers prevailed on appeal, a similar verdict came down in a case emerging from the outer ripples of the Watergate scandal. As related in various news reports (see e.g. http://tinyurl.com/mf8tvyx), Texas attorney Jake Jacobsen was interrogated on May 3, 1974 concerning a $10,000 bribe he had allegedly offered to then Treasury Secretary John Connally on behalf of the lawyer's milk producer clients. A grand jury had determined that Jacobsen had lied, but U.S. District Judge George Hart Jr. dismissed the indictment because the "lie" denying the bribe was literally true. Prosecutor Sidney Glazer had prefaced his question "And is it your testimony that...," and Jacobsen had responded "That is correct." This led to the following exchange:

> Judge Hart: "Jacobsen in this case gave a literally true answer to your question... You only asked 'is it your testimony?' You didn't ask him if it is true or false."
>
> Glazer: "You don't have to ask him if his testimony is true or false when he's before a grand jury."
>
> Judge Hart: "Not unless you're later going to indict him for perjury."

But it was the precedent established in *Bronston v. U.S.* in 1973 that was cited extensively by all sides during President Clinton's interrogation and subsequent impeachment hearings two decades later. Extensive discussion is provided by Tiersma (2003, 2005) and Solan and Tiersma (2006: 212–235), who stress that Bronston's violation concerned what is implicated (via the Gricean Quantity and Relation maxims) rather than what is literally said and posit the *"Literal Truth Defense"* against perjury charges, in contexts where lawyers fail to fulfill their responsibility of ascertaining the whole truth.

Bill Clinton's finesse at "parsing the truth" by misleading his accusers (on the meaning of *sexual relations* or of *is*) without actually lying was evidently passed on to an adept pupil. When Monica Lewinsky was asked under oath by Rep. Ed Bradley (R-TN) in a 1999 Congressional hearing whether portions of her affidavit in the Paula Jones case had been false, she responded "Incomplete and misleading," thereby (falsely) implicating that no portions of it were false. In reporting this exchange in the Times (http://tinyurl.com/n9xcp8t), Frances X. Clines commends Lewinsky's "Clintonian way with the meaning of words," but the tradition of exploiting the difference between what is implicated and what is said when in durance is much older, as captured in the recommendations of the 17th century Jesuits (to whom we return below) on how to "hide the truth" without actually lying.

Macintyre (1994: 336–337) cites Kant's position "that my duty is assert only what is true and that the mistaken inferences that others may draw from what I say or what I do are, in some cases at least, not my responsibility, but theirs." In a tale retold both by Macintyre and Newman (1865) illustrating the same point, St. Athanasius is accosted on the Nile by his persecutors in the employ of Emperor Julian who demand to know "Is Athanasius close at hand?" "Yes," replies Athanasius, "he is not far from here," and off they go in vain pursuit.

The Literal Truth Defense proves exceptionally useful for seedy producers, crafty Texas lawyers, parsing presidents, sneaky Alexandrian bishops – and handsome Georgian cads, as exemplified by the reprehensible but not actionable misbehavior of Marianne's erstwhile beau Willoughby, resulting in this exchange between Elinor and Marianne Dashwood, "Sense" and "Sensibility" respectively (Austen 1811: Chapter 29):

"But he told you that he loved you?"

"Yes – no – never absolutely. *It was every day implied, but never professedly declared.* Sometimes I thought it had been, but it never was."

If we are tempted to regard the action of non-lying deceivers like Willoughby, Bronston, or Clinton as especially sleazy, even compared to the behavior of overt liars who simply and directly declare the false, this may reflect our sense of how to apportion responsibility for the deception. If I lie to you, the blame is entirely mine for the illocutionary act performed; if I intentionally mislead you, the deception is jointly constructed, with responsibility shared between speaker and hearer. This distinction, and its consequences in the courtroom and out, risks being effaced in accounts like Meibauer's (2005, 2011, 2014a,b) that conflate the two modes of intentional deception and that regard false assertion and false implicature to be different routes to the same destination.

But how are we to determine what is asserted? Does the speaker's intention suffice? What role is played by linguistic convention? For one approach to these questions, we turn to the Jesuit doctrine of radical intentionalism and its discontents.

11 Mental reservations required

The 17th century marked the peak of a vigorous debate over the nature of lies, as seen in the passages cited by Pascal 1656, Roussel de la Tour 1762, and Fauconnier 1979. Jesuit tracts explored the boundary between lying and merely the encouragement of false inferences, an exploration Pascal deftly mocks in the ninth of his Provincial Letters (here and below, the translation (based on the 19th c. rendering of Thomas M'Crie) is mine). Here, for example, is Pascal's rendering of the recipe for dealing with those "embarrassing cases [...] when one is anxious to avoid lying while inducing a false belief," in the (actual) words he puts into the mouth of a helpful (but fictitious) Jesuit monk (Pascal 1656: 101–102; see Roussel de la Tour 1762 for a collection of the original texts on which Pascal draws):

> In such cases, our doctrine of equivocations has been found of admirable service, according to which, as our Father Sanchez has it, it is permitted to use ambiguous terms, leading people to understand them in another sense from that in which we understand them ourselves.

But what if there are no equivocal words?

> Here is something new: the doctrine of mental reservations. A man may swear, as Sanchez says in the same place, that he never did such a thing (though he actually did it), meaning within himself that he did not do so on a certain day, or before he was born, or understanding any other such circumstance, while the words he employs have no such sense as would discover his meaning. And this is very convenient in many cases, and quite innocent, when necessary or conducive to one's health, honor, or advantage."

"Indeed, Father! Is that not a lie, and perjury to boot?"

"No," said the Father; "Sanchez proves it is not, and our Father Filiutius as well, because, he says, 'It is the intention that determines the quality of the action'. And he suggests a still surer method for avoiding falsehood, which is this: After saying aloud, 'I swear that I have not done that, to add, in a low voice, 'today'; or after saying aloud, 'I swear', to interpose in a whisper, 'that I say', and then continue aloud, 'that I have done that.' This, you perceive, is telling the truth."

"I grant it," said I; "it might possibly, however, be found to be telling the truth in a low key, and a lie in a loud one; besides, I should be afraid that many people might not have enough presence of mind to make use of these methods."

"Our fathers," replied the Jesuit, "have taught, in the same passage, for the benefit of such as might not be expert in finding these reservations, that no more is required of them, to avoid lying, than simply to say that they have not done what they have done, provided they have, in general, the intention of giving to their language the sense that a clever man would give to it."

As Sanchez's fellow Jesuit puts it (Casnedi 1719 in Roussel de la Tour 1763: 471): "La manière de *cacher la verité* doit être à la portée de tout le monde, même les gens les plus grossiers." ('The means of hiding the truth should be at the disposal of everyone, even the coarsest among us'). Note in particular the key contrast between lying and (not just slanting but) hiding the truth.

Let us turn to the "whisper" Pascal's Jesuit companion counsels as a way of rendering the entire discourse true. The actual passage is given below (Filiutius 1633 in Roussel de la Tour 1763: 421, translation mine):

> [L]orsqu'on commence à dire *je jure*, il faut ajouter tout bas cette restriction mentale, *qu'aujourdhui*, & continuer tout haut, *je n'ai pas mangé telle chose*. [...] Car tout le discours est vrai de cette manière.
>
> When you begin to say '*I swear...*', you must add under your breath this mental restriction, '*that today...*', and continue out loud, '*I have not eaten such and such.*' [...] For the entire discourse will be true in this way.

The key here for Filiutius is the implicit allusion to what would now be called pragmatic enrichments of propositional content, affecting what is explicitly said (according to Carston 2002, Recanati 2004, and other contextualist analysts) or what is communicated, including "implicitures" or implicit components of what is said (according to Bach 1994, 2001; cf. Horn 2009, Saul 2012, and Meibauer 2014a for applications to the lying/misleading distinction). The consensus view endorses the "contextualist platitude" (Bach 2005: 15):

> Linguistic meaning generally underdetermines speaker meaning. That is, generally what a speaker means in uttering a sentence, even if the sentence is devoid of ambiguity, vagueness or indexicality, goes beyond what the sentence means.

Thus, the speaker uttering the non-bracketed material in each example in (5) will tend to be taken to have communicated the full sentences indicated, enriched by the bracketed addenda.

(5) a. I haven't had breakfast {today}.
 b. John and Mary are married {to each other}.
 c. They had a baby and they got married {in that order}.
 d. Robin ate the shrimp and {as a result} got food poisoning.
 e. Chris is ready {for the exam}.

Thus, we might say that Fillutius was merely anticipating Bach's platitude: "I swear that {today} I have not eaten breakfast/committed the crime." And similarly for a fellow casuist (Tolet 1601, in Roussel de la Tour 1763: 385), the accused can truthfully swear "*Je ne l'ai pas fait*" as long as "la pensée soit de dire qu'il ne l'a pas fait *depuis qu'il est en prison*" – I have not killed anyone {since I've been in prison}. Only the speaker's intention counts: such utterances, Tolet explains, "must be considered not according to the intention of the judge but according to that of the accused." Translating into the terms of Recanati (2004), the judge hears what what is said$_{MIN}$ (based on what the speaker says out loud) but God hears what is said$_{MAX}$ (based on what the speaker intended).

12 *Cacher la verité* in everyday life (and its representations)[8]

The ways of hiding the truth extend from the criminally accused seeking refuge from their Jesuit counselors to contemporary figures in the real and constructed worlds. One example of a mental restriction pronounced "tout bas" is provided by a scenario developed in the 29 Sept. 2006 episode of the ABC medical drama "Grey's Anatomy." Benjamin, a young patient who has a brain tumor causing him to blurt out his thoughts without restraint, is undergoing an examination by Dr. Meredith Grey, the intern whose smoldering glances toward neurologist Derek Shepherd (a.k.a. "Dr. McDreamy") he has earlier detected.

> *Benjamin:* Did you have sex with that brain surgeon?
> *Benjamin's sister:* Benjamin!
> *Dr. Grey:* It's OK. *Nope, I haven't.* [PAUSE.] *Not today, anyway.*

---

[8] An earlier version of the material in this section appears in Horn 2009: §5.

We can assume that Dr. Grey alludes here to the influential discussion of Taylor (2001: 46) on the pragmatic nature of the distinction between having sex and having breakfast:

> (1) I haven't had breakfast.
>
> (2) I haven't had sex.
>
> Taken on its own, independently of context and of the speaker's communicative intentions, (1), for example, expresses neither the question "have you ever in your life eaten breakfast?" nor the question "have you eaten breakfast yet this morning?" Moreover, neither the meaning of the word 'sex' nor the meaning of the word 'breakfast' forces one rather than the other temporal import on the relevant question. Indeed, without changing the meanings of either word, we can cook up contexts in which an utterance of (1) amounts to an 'ever' question and contexts in which an utterance of (2) amounts to a "so far today" question.

Teleporting from *eros* in Seattle to *thanatos* in New Jersey, we enter the domain of "House" (FOX-TV, 21 Nov. 2006). Once more we find a young (but doomed) male patient, his young (but precocious) sister, and an examining surgeon (House's associate Dr. Foreman). Kama is grilling Dr. Foreman about her brother Jack's serious but as yet undiagnosed mystery disease from which is suffering.

> *Kama:* Is he gonna die?
> *Dr. Foreman: No, no one's gonna die.*
> *Kama: In the whole world? Ever?* That's so great!
> *Dr. Foreman:* I meant...
> *Kama:* I know what you meant.

If Dr. Grey was operating under the tacit influence of Taylor (2001) and the Jesuits, the dialog in 'House' was clearly informed by the commentary in Bach (1994: 135):

> The proposition being communicated is a conceptually enriched or elaborated version of the one explicitly expressed by the utterance itself. So, for example, if a mother utters (1) to her crying son upset about a cut finger,
>
> (1) You're not going to die.
>
> she is likely to mean that he is not going to die from that cut, not that he is immortal.

Dipping into the cultural well one more time for a lesson in how artfully the truth can be not just slanted but successfully hidden, we travel back in time to the Celtic legend of Tristan and Iseult as recounted by the troubadours of the 12th century. Having unknowingly consumed the love potion, Tristan and Iseult – the latter wed to King Mark, Tristan's uncle – are the quarry of the jealous

Cornish lords Denoalen, Andret, and Gondoïne, who plot to expose the two lovers in adultery and betray them to King Mark. The three "felons," seizing their chance when Tristan is (supposedly) abroad in service to the King of Frisia, convince Mark to subject his queen to the Ordeal by Red-Hot Iron, as a result of which she will either clear her name forever or – as the miscreants anticipate – burn to death for falsely swearing marital fidelity. Before the day King Mark and his retainers are to put her to the Ordeal, with King Arthur and his knights as warrantors, Iseult secretly sends word to Tristan instructing him to appear at the muddy riverbank garbed as a miserable pilgrim. Everything transpires according to plan, and now – after the ragged vagabond carries her safely to shore and then stumbles and falls in the mud – Queen Iseult addresses the nobles assembled by the river:

> – Roi de Logres, et vous, roi de Cornouailles, et vous, sire Gauvain, sire Ké, sire Girflet, et vous tous qui serez mes garants, par ces corps saints et par tous les corps saints qui sont en ce monde, *je jure que jamais un homme né de femme ne m'a tenue entre ses bras, hormis le roi Marc, mon seigneur, et le pauvre pèlerin qui, tout à l'heure, s'est laissé choir à vos yeux.* Roi Marc, ce serment convient-il?
>
> – Oui, reine, et que Dieu manifeste son vrai jugement!
>
> – Amen! dit Iseut.
>
> Elle s'approcha du brasier, pâle et chancelante. Tous se taisaient; le fer était rouge. Alors, elle plongea ses bras nus dans la braise, saisit la barre de fer, marcha neuf pas en la portant, puis, l'ayant rejetée, étendit ses bras en croix, le paumes ouvertes. *Et chacun vit que sa chair était plus saine que prune de prunier.* Alors de toutes les poitrines un grand cri de louange monta vers Dieu.
>
> "King of Logres and King of Cornwall, and you, Sir Gawain, Sir Kay, and Sir Girflet, and all of you that are my guarantors, by these holy things and all the holy things of earth, *I swear that no man born of woman has ever held me in his arms but my lord King Mark and that poor pilgrim who just now fell down before your eyes.* King Mark, will that oath stand?"
>
> "Yes, Queen," he said, "and let God manifest his true judgment."
>
> "Amen," said Iseult.
>
> Pale and stumbling, she approached the brazier. All were silent; the iron was red hot. She thrust her bare arms into the coals and seized it, and took nine steps holding it. Then she cast it from her and stretched her arms out in a cross, with the palms of her hands up, and *everyone saw her flesh was as healthy and sound as a plum from a plum tree.* And from all the chests a great cry of praise climbed toward God.
>
> (Bédier 1901; translation mine)

And this cry of praise is heard by a God who is clearly a semantic minimalist with a keen appreciation for the distinction between lying and misleading.

13 Lies and (other) broken promises:

To lie is to break an implicit promise to tell the truth.
– Carson 2006: 292, citing W. D. Ross

According to (**C1** + **C2**) and the edicts of Aquinas, to lie is necessarily to say what you do not believe. But while lies involve the assumed falsity of at-issue material, what is said need not involve assertion; anyone who promises insincerely is rightly viewed as having lied. Not every unsatisfied sincerity condition yields a lie; for example, if I issue an order or request that I do not genuinely want you to comply with, my utterance is insincere (following Searle 1969) but is not a lie. Only in the cases of representatives (e.g. assertions) and commissives (e.g. promises, threats, vows) does the speaker commit herself to the truth of the propositional content of the speech act, and if this commitment is undertaken insincerely, a lie ensues.

But as with assertions, casuistry offers ways to promise with mentally crossed fingers. Suarez (1614) explains how someone can evade the query "Have you promised, or contracted yourself?" (Roussel de la Tour 1763: 397): "Il peut simplement dire que non; parce que cela peut avoir un sens légitime, savoir: *'Je n'ai pas promis d'une promesse qui m'oblige'.*" Or, in the seductive words of Pascal's Jesuit priest,

> "Listen, then, to the general rule laid down by Escobar: Promises are not binding, when the person in making them had no intention to bind himself... so that when one simply says, I will do it, he means that he will do it if he does not change his mind; for he does not wish, by saying that, to deprive himself of his liberty."
>
> "My dear Father," I observed, "I had no idea that the direction of intention had the power to render promises null and void."
>
> "You see," he said, "what facility this affords for the business of life."
>
> (Pascal 1656: 101; see also Filiutius 1633 in Roussel de la Tour 1763: 419)

An alternate device is what might be dubbed the hidden argument trick, equivocating on the identity of the implicit indirect object. Sanchez (1614, in Roussel de la Tour 1763: 407) advised that one can promise to pay a certain sum, with the mental reservation *"soit à vous, soit à un autre"* ('to you, or to someone else', i.e. your confederate). This ploy proves equally useful for other speech acts as well, e.g. apologizing. Here is young Oliver, a florist in a Jean a reimagining of *Der Rosenkavalier* as a comedy of manners set in modern Manhattan, impulsively heading to Columbia University to set things right with his older lover Marian with whom he has quarreled, only to run into Sophie, a graduate student of

Marian's, the flowers for whose upcoming wedding he has neglected to supply. So now poor, distracted Oliver must make small talk with Sophie:

> Oliver looks at her. [...] "I'm sorry," he hears himself say, "I feel terrible about what happened" [...]
>
> "You came all the way up here?" Sophie asks, "To apologize?"
>
> "Yes," Oliver says, with some relief, and truthfully enough. He has in fact come all the way up here to apologize, albeit not to her.
>
> (Korelitz 2005: 296; see Horn 2009: 24 for full context)

What is said is true (Oliver did in fact come "all the way up" (to Columbia) to apologize, albeit to someone else); *what is communicated* is (knowingly) false (viz. that Oliver went to Columbia to apologize to Sophie).

14 Equivocation

As Pascal learned from his (apocryphal) Jesuit tutor, the twin doctrines facilitating hiding the truth are those of mental reservation, which we have surveyed, and of equivocation (or amphibology). For the moral theologian Peter Scavini (cited in Newman 1865), what licenses equivocation is that in invoking it *"we do not deceive our neighbor, but allow him to deceive himself."* The OED glosses equivocation (sense 2a) as 'The use of words or expressions that are susceptible of a double signification, with a view to mislead; *esp.* the expression of a virtual falsehood in the form of a proposition which (*in order to satisfy the speaker's conscience*) is verbally true. We are thus back in the realm of the literal truth defense, or what Lewis calls *minimal truthfulness:*

> Take a sentence σ which is assigned multiple interpretations by [Language] *L* on an occasion *o* of its utterance. One can be minimally truthful in *L* with respect to σ on *o* by taking any one of those interpretations and doing whatever one would have to do to be truthful in *L* if that interpretation were the only one assigned to σ on *o* by *L*. A trickster is being truthful in this minimal way if, knowing that Owen is going to the shore of the river, he says "Owen is going to the bank" during a conversation about Owen's lack of cash. (Lewis 1969: 193)

St. Raymond de Peñafort (perhaps not coincidentally the patron saint of lawyers) was celebrated for his deft exploitation of the fortuitous homonymy between two 3rd person singular forms of the Latin verbs *esse* 'be' and *edere* 'eat'. To protect your confederate from the hit man at the door, advises this 13th century Dominican friar, simply swear of the would-be victim "Non est hic." This will ideally be understood as the false or virtual claim 'he is not here' but it happens to be "verbally true" in the alternate sense 'he does not eat here' (Cavaillé 2004; cf. also Cardenas 1702 in Roussel de la Tour 1763: 464).

In the department of *plus ça change*, consider in the same vein the summary in The Murphy Report of the cover-up of clerical sexual abuse in the Irish church in what has come to be known as The Dublin case, invoking both mental reservation and equivocation (Malloy 2009).⁹

> John calls (on) the parish priest to make a complaint about the behavior of one of his curates. The parish priest sees him coming but does not want to see him because he considers John to be a troublemaker. He sends another of his curates to answer the door. John asks the curate if the parish priest is in. The curate replies that he is not. This is clearly untrue but in the church's view it is not a lie, because, when the curate told John that the parish priest was not in, *he mentally reserved to himself the words 'to you,'* the report said. [...] It continued that Cardinal Desmond Connell had explained the concept to the commission as follows: "The general teaching about mental reservation is that you are not permitted to tell a lie. On the other hand, you may be put in a position where you have to answer, and there may be circumstances in which you can use an ambiguous expression *realizing that the person who you are talking to will accept an untrue version of whatever it may be – permitting that to happen, not willing that it happened, that would be lying.* [...]
>
> Cardinal Connell emphasised he did not lie to the media about the use of diocesan funds for the compensation of clerical child sexual abuse victims. He explained to [abuse victim Andrew] Madden *he had told journalists that diocesan funds are not used for such a purpose; that he had not said that diocesan funds were not used for such a purpose.* By using the present tense he had not excluded the possibility that diocesan funds had been used for such purpose in the past. According to Mr Madden, Cardinal Connell considered that there was an enormous difference between the two.

Those across the pond from the Cardinal may be reminded of a secular counterpart of his legerdemain with tense: President Bill Clinton's defense of his lawyer's testimony at a deposition that "there is absolutely no sex of any kind in any manner, shape or form" between Clinton and Monica Lewinsky" and of an earlier claim of his own that "there is no improper relationship." Clinton famously defended the veracity of these claims on the grounds that "it depends upon what the meaning of the word *is* is"; on the present tense reading, the protestation of innocence was literally true (cf. Tiersma 2005 for discussion).

---

9 The relevance to our quarry is indicated by the labels under which the story has been discussed: "When is a lie not a lie?", "Church 'lied without lying'" (cf. http://enlightenedcatholicism-colkoch.blogspot.com/2009/11/reservations-about-this-notion-of.html).

An alumnus of Georgetown University, the oldest Jesuit institution of higher learning in America, Bill Clinton is a son of his Jesuit fathers; his skill at equivocation and the domain narrowing of indexicals ("it depends on what the meaning of the word *is* is"; "it depends on how you define *alone*") has a rich historical lineage. Counsels Fegeli (1750, in Roussel de la Tour 1763: 489), "Asked if the thief has come by this road, one seeking to hide the truth can put his foot on a paving stone and reply, 'He didn't pass by here', i.e. on this paving stone."

Neither the 17th and 18th century Jesuits nor their 20th century disciples in church or state can claim the patent on devices for shading the truth without actually lying. Aquinas (*Summa Theologica* II.II, q. 110, ad 3,4) concurs with Augustine on Genesis 20:12 regarding Abraham's identification of Sarah as his sister: "*It is lawful to hide the truth prudently*, by keeping it back, as Augustine says." But what of Genesis 27:18, where Jacob brings food to his blind father Isaac who asks him who he is and Jacob replies, "*I am Esau, your firstborn*"? This tends to strike the naïve reader as a lie. No problem, Aquinas assures us somewhat unconvincingly,

> Jacob's assertion that he was Esau, Isaac's first-born, was spoken in a mystical sense, because, to wit, the latter's birthright was due to him by right: and he made use of this mode of speech being moved by the spirit of prophecy, in order to signify a mystery, namely, that the younger people, i.e. the Gentiles, should supplant the first-born, i.e. the Jews.

A different, though ultimately no more persuasive, explanation is offered by the 11th century Jewish sage Rashi: What Jacob actually asserts in Gen. 27:18 is not "I am Esau, your first-born" but rather "**I AM** [the one who is bringing you the savory meats, whereas] **ESAU** [is] **YOUR FIRST-BORN**" (Friedman & Weisel 2003).

There are, however, limits to how remotely the truth can permissibly be concealed. For Fegeli, despite his recommended equivocation on indexicals, "*la restriction purement mentale n'est jamais licite*," and even the means for hiding the truth are constrained:

> Si l'intention est bonne, la cause juste, et même grave lorsqu'on joint le serment au témoignage, il est licite d'employer toutes ces manières de cacher la vérité non pas dans l'intention expresse de tromper les autres, mais seulement de les laisser se tromper eux-mêmes.

> If the intention is good, the cause is just, and even grave when one testifies under oath, it is permitted to employ all these means of hiding the truth, not with the express intention of deceiving others, but only of letting them deceive themselves.

In 1679, Pope Innocent XI condemned most forms of strict mental reservation, but equivocation and related strategies of hiding the truth remained on the table. Even mental reservation continues to be exploited on occasion, but the motives for invoking it matter. Doctors and nurses in Catholic hospitals may be counseled to reassure their feverish patients by telling them "Your temperature is normal," mentally reserving the codicil "for someone in your condition" (Bok 1978, Coulter et al. 2012). Even more pardonably, the Jesuit martyrs Robert Southwell and Henry Garnet, authors of treatises on the doctrine in Elizabethan England, refused to up the names of those who practiced or attended mass and were drawn and quartered after refusing to give up the names of those who practiced or attended mass. But there is mental reservation and mental reservation:

> Southwell and Garnet practiced mental reservation to save innocent victims while sacrificing themselves. The Irish prelates practiced mental reservation to save themselves while sacrificing innocent victims. And that difference makes all the difference.
> (Kaveny 2010)

15 Concluding remarks: lies, damned lies, and pragmatics[10]

I have maintained, following a natural extension of the Thomist position and the basis of the views formulated by Chisholm & Feehan (1977), Adler (1997), and Saul (2012), that to lie is to say something, in the relevant sense of say, that commits the speaker to the truth of what you believe to be false. By lying in an assertion or promise, the speaker directly violates a sincerity condition on the relevant speech act, but not all insincere utterances are lies. We noted in §13 that a directive (order, request) cannot be a lie even it is made insincerely, by one who does not truly wish one's interlocutor to comply. But further, if the sincerity condition is presupposed rather than at issue, no lie is committed, although the utterance will be infelicitous. If I apologize for an act I do not regret (the "un-apology apology") or if I express gratitude without actually feeling grateful, I am insincere but not a liar.

---

10 With apologies to Twain et al.; cf. http://en.wikipedia.org/wiki/Lies,_damned_lies,_and_statistics.

What of conventional implicatures, lexically or structurally encoded aspects of an utterance that fall outside what is said?[11] Contra Meibauer (2005, 2011, 2014a,b), I maintain that falsity of what is implicated – conversationally or conventionally – never yields a lie, a point that underlies both theological and forensic approaches to lying and perjury and is borne out by intuition. Whether a conventional implicature (e.g. unexpectedness or noteworthiness for *even*, contrast for *but*, intimacy or familiarity for T vs. V second person pronouns (e.g. Fr. *tu*, Ger. *du*), expressive content for *bastard* and slurs) is part of the literal meaning of an expression is a terminological question, but it's clear these aspects of meaning are indeed conventional (encoded), and it's also relatively clear (at least to me) that they don't have truth conditional repercussions. "That's false" (or "You're wrong") is not a natural response to an utterance of "She's poor but honest" (if she's both), of "Even Hercules can lift that rock" (if he can), of Fr. *"Tu es gentil"* (if you're nice) or of "That bastard got tenure" (if he did), rejecting the utterance in question purely on the grounds that the putative conventional implicature fails. And if nothing has been said that's false (or that the speaker believes to be false), there is no lie.

We have argued that speakers do not lie by *conversationally* implicating something they believe to be false as a route to getting their hearers to deceive themselves. On the strong contextualist position, a speaker who implicates a proposition may be responsible for its truth:

> [In implicating propositions] I take as much responsibility for their truth as for the truth of the proposition I have explicitly expressed [...]. The speaker is committed to the truth of all determinate implicatures conveyed by her utterance, just as much as if she had expressed them directly.
> (Sperber & Wilson 1986: 384)

But what would Aquinas say? It's hard to reconcile the thesis that a speaker is committed to the truth of what she implicates in the same way that she is committed to what she says (= explicitly asserts or promises). The long-standing distinction between lying (via false assertions) and intentionally misleading or deceiving (via false implicatures) buttresses our intuitive skepticism toward this thesis, as Jonathan Adler (1997: 452) points out, "A lies-deception distinction corresponding to an assertion-implicature one is rational for us to want (for purposes of social harmony, lessening the strains of commitment, and facilitating the exchange of information.)" And this is the case regardless of "the moral asymmetry favoring deception to lies" happens to apply in a particular case (cf. also Saul 2012).

---

11 On the relevant notion of conventional implicature and its Fregean precursors and applications of these notions to a variety of linguistic phenomena, see Grice 1989, Barker 2003, Potts 2007, and Horn 2007, 2013.

From Abraham to Pascal's Jesuits and from Fernández Quintanilla to Bronston, Clinton, and Lewinsky, we have reviewed a variety of instances of successful indirect verbal deception – "telling it slant" with a vengeance but without actually lying. For Meibauer (2005, 2011, 2014a,b), however, a speaker who intends to lead her addressees into a false belief via conversational (or, a fortiori, conventional) implicatures does indeed lie: "The case of falsely implicating should be included within a general definition of lying" (Meibauer 2005: 1373). Meibauer (2014a: §4.5) provides for a defense of this position that asserting a true statement while implicating a false one counts as "lying while saying the truth." On the account we have defended, this is not lying but "lying," with scare quotes. Meibauer's approach risks the blurring of important conceptual (and legal) distinctions; it strikes me as sounder to describe the properties that related categories have in common than to efface a distinction between categories that must be recovered in some – arguably most – contexts. To subsume knowingly false *assertions* and knowingly false *implicatures*[12] under a single banner would be akin to branding all types of intentional killing as first degree murder and then having to reconstitute the category of manslaughter when we need it.

But if lies really do result from the assumed falsity of what is asserted, how are we to rule out cases of irony (where the speaker seems to assert something she believes to be false) without also ruling out bald-faced lies (where the speaker doesn't intend to mislead the hearer)? For Fallis (2009), the crucial point is that assertion is possible only when Grice's maxim of Quality is in effect; in cases of irony or sarcasm – or metaphor, winking, play-acting, banter (Leech 1983), or the like – Quality is "turned off." But in fact on Grice's view irony works not by *turning off* the maxim of Quality but precisely by *flouting* it; the maxim must be in effect for this to happen (Stokke 2013a: 35–39). Further, if Fallis were right, bald-faced lies couldn't count as lies, or indeed as assertions of anything, since in that case (as in that of bullshit; cf. footnote 1) the maxim of Quality really is turned off.

---

[12] The correlation we have drawn between the assertion/implicature distinction and the lying/misleading distinction implicitly takes conversational implicatures to form a homogeneous class. A recent experimental investigation of this issue by Weissman and Terkourafi (2016) largely supports the view defended here and in the tradition represented by Adler (1997) and Saul (2012). Contra the predictions of Meibauer's "extended definition" of lying on which false implicatures are assimilated to lies – instances of "lying while telling the truth" – subjects tend not to regard true statements with false (conversational) implicatures as lies. Furthermore, as I have argued (Horn, to appear), in those cases in which Weissman and Terkourafi's subjects deem a speaker who utters a true sentence with a false "implicature" to have lied, the "implicature" in question is (as can be shown on independent grounds) not an implicature at all. Indeed, the determination of what counts as a lie and of what counts as an implicature inform each other.

Rather, following Stokke, an assertion *warrants the truth* of the asserted content (cf. also Carson 2006, 2010) and counts as a proposal to *change the common ground* in the sense of Stalnaker (2002):

> You lie when [and only when – LH] you assert what you believe to be false. Asserting that p is to say that p and thereby propose that p become common ground.
> (Stokke 2013b: 60)

Irony and its relatives do not satisfy these conditions. In sarcastically praising your banal observation O as "brilliant," I do not warrant the truth of my claim or attempt to add the proposition "O was a brilliant observation" to the common ground. (Along similar lines, cf. Pagin 2007 and Camp 2013 – and for complications see Meibauer 2014a: §3.)

If an understanding of asserting, promising, and what is said is vital for delineating lies from what lies beyond, the reverse is also true: knowing what it is to lie is an essential step toward knowing what it is to assert.

Acknowledgments

To avoid any silent lie or deception, I express my gratitude to, while removing any responsibility from, those who attended and commented on presentations of subsets of this material in Rochester, Sheffield, Leysin, Vancouver, and Mainz, in my Yale pragmatics seminars, and to Barbara Abbott, Mira Ariel, Kent Bach, Elitzur Bar-Asher, Betty Birner, Emma Borg, David Braun, Tom Carson, Ben Farkas, Gilles Fauconnier, Bill Ladusaw, Jörg Meibauer, Jennifer Saul, Roger Shuy, Larry Solan, Roy Sorensen, Marina Terkourafi, and Gregory Ward. Thanks too to Dieter Stein and Janet Giltrow for their organizational acumen and their editorial patience.

References

Adler, Alfred. 1931. *What life should mean to you.* Boston: Little, Brown.
Adler, Jonathan. 1997. Lying, deceiving, or falsely implicating. *Journal of Philosophy* 94. 435–52.
Aquinas, St. Thomas. c. 1270. *Summa theologica, Part II-II.* http://tinyurl.com/plgglrc.
Augustine, Saint. 420. Against lying. http://www.newadvent.org/fathers/1313.htm.
Austen, Jane. 1811. *Sense and sensibility.* https://books.google.com/books?isbn=0192811800
Austin, John L. 1962. *How to do things with words.* Cambridge: Harvard U. Press.
Bach, Kent. 1994. Conversational impliciture. *Mind and Language* 9. 124–62.
Bach, Kent. 2001. You don't say? *Synthese* 127. 11–31.

Bach, Kent. 2005. Context *ex machina*. In Zoltán G. Szabó (ed.), *Semantics vs. pragmatics*, 15–44. Oxford: Clarendon.
Baldwin, William. 1571. Treatice of morall philosophie: Contaynynge the sayinges of the wise, wherin you may see the woorthy and pithy sayings of philosophers, emperors, kynges, and oratours: of their liues, their aunswers, of what linage they came of, and of what countrey they were... London: In Fleetestrete within Temple barre, at the signe of the hand and starre, by Richard Tottyll.
Bédier, Joseph. 1901. *Le roman de Tristan et Iseut, renouvelé par Joseph Bédier*. Paris. Project Gutenberg, http://www.gutenberg.org/files/42256/42256-h/42256-h.htm.
Bok, Sissela. 1978. *Lying: Moral choice in public and private life*. New York: Pantheon Books.
Bond, Charles & Michael Robinson. 1988. The evolution of deception. *Journal of Nonverbal Behavior* 12. 295–307.
Boswell, James. 1791. *The life of Samuel Johnson*. London: Hutchinson & Co. Available as e-book, https://books.google.com/books?id=RJJNAAAAYAAJ.
Brown, Penelope & Stephen Levinson. 1987. *Politeness*: Cambridge: Cambridge U. Press.
Camp, Elisabeth. 2013. Insinuation, indirection, and implicature. Talk at Rutgers Semantics Workshop, September 2013.
Carson, Thomas. 2006. The definition of lying. *Noûs* 40. 284–306.
Carson, Thomas. 2010. *Lying and deception: Theory and practice*. Oxford: Oxford U. Press.
Carston, Robyn. 2002. *Thoughts and utterances: The pragmatics of explicit communication*. Oxford: Blackwell.
Cavaillé, Jean-Pierre. 2004. *Non est hic:* Le cas exemplaire de la protection du fugitif. http://dossiersgrihl.revues.org/300?lang=en.
Chierchia, Gennaro. 2004. Scalar implicatures, polarity phenomena, and the syntax/pragmatics interface. In Adriana Belletti (ed.), *Structures and Beyond*, 39–103. Oxford: Oxford U. Press.
Chisholm, Roderick & Thomas Feehan. 1977. The intent to deceive. *Journal of Philosophy* 74. 143–59.
Coleman, Linda & Paul Kay. 1981. Prototype semantics: The English word *lie*. *Language* 57. 26–44.
Coulter, Michael, Richard Myers, and Joseph Varacalli. 2012. Mental reservation. Entry in *Encyclopedia of Catholic Social Thought, Social Science, and Social Policy*, Volume 3, 205–7. Lanham, MD: Scarecrow Press.
Fallis, Don. 2009. What is lying? *Journal of Philosophy* 106. 29–56.
Fallis, Don. 2010. Lying and deception. *Philosophers' Imprint* 10: 1–22.
Fauconnier, Gilles. 1979. Comment contrôler la vérité. *Actes de la Recherche en Sciences Sociales* 25. 3–22.
Frankfurt, Harry. 2005. *On bullshit*. Princeton: Princeton University Press.
Frege, Gottlob. 1892. On *Sinn* and *Bedeutung*. In Michael Beaney (ed.), *The Frege Reader*, 151–71. Oxford: Blackwell.
Friedman, Hershey & Abraham Weisel. 2003. Should moral individuals ever lie? Insights from Jewish law. http://www.jlaw.com/Articles/hf_LyingPermissible.html.
Grice, H. Paul. 1989. *Studies in the way of words*. Cambridge: Harvard University Press.
Grotius, Hugo. 1625. *On the law of war and peace*, trans. F. W. Kelsey. Reprinted. New York: Bobbs-Merrill, 1925.
Horn, Laurence. To appear. What lies beyond: Untangling the web. Ms., Yale University.
Horn, Laurence R. 1972. *On the semantic properties of logical operators in English*. UCLA dissertation. Distributed by Indiana University Linguistics Club, 1976.

Horn, Laurence. 2007. Toward a Fregean pragmatics: *Voraussetzung, Nebengedanke, Andeutung*. In Istvan Kecskes and Laurence R. Horn (eds.), *Explorations in pragmatics: Linguistic, cognitive, and intercultural aspects*, 39–69. Berlin: De Gruyter Mouton.

Horn, Laurence. 2009. WJ-40: Implicature, truth, and meaning. *International Review of Pragmatics* 1. 3–34.

Horn, Laurence. 2013. *I love me some datives:* Expressive meaning, free datives, and F-implicature. In Daniel Gutzmann and Hans-Martin Gärtner (eds.), *Beyond expressives: Explorations in use-conditional meaning*, 153–201. Leiden: Brill.

Imlay, Robert. 1967. Do I ever directly raise my arm? *Philosophy* 42. 119–27.

Jauhar, Sandeep. 2014. When doctors need to lie. *New York Times*, Feb. 22, 2014. http://www.nytimes.com/2014/02/23/opinion/sunday/when-doctors-need-to-lie.html.

Kant, Immanuel. 1799. On a supposed right to lie from altruistic motives. http://tinyurl.com/l528vof.

Kass, Leon. 1994. Why the dietary laws? *Commentary*, June 1994. http://www.commentary-magazine.com/article/why-the-dietary-laws/.

Kaveny, Cathleen. 2010. Truth or consequences: In Ireland, straying far from the mental reservation. *Commonweal*, Jan. 11, 2010. https://www.commonwealmagazine.org/truth-or-consequences.

Korelitz, Jean Hanff. 2005. *The white rose*. New York: Miramax Books.

Lackey, Jennifer. 2013. Lies and deception: An unhappy divorce. *Analysis* 73. 236–48.

Lasersohn, Peter. 1999. Pragmatic halos. *Language* 75. 522–51.

Leech, Geoffrey. 1983. *Principles of pragmatics*. London: Longman.

Lewis, David. 1969. *Convention: A philosophical study*. Cambridge, MA: Harvard U. Press.

Macintyre, Alasdair. 1994. Truthfulness, lies, and moral philosophers: What can we learn from Mill and Kant? *The Tanner Lectures*. At http://tinyurl.com/k224o5p.

Mahon, James. 2008. The definition of lying and deception. In E. Zalta (ed.), *Stanford Encyclopedia of Philosophy*. http://plato.stanford.edu/entries/lying-definition.

Malloy, Cian. 2009. Dublin abuse report asks: 'When is a lie not a lie?' *National Catholic Reporter*, 1 Dec. 2009. http://tinyurl.com/l5ahbfv.

Markham, James. 1981. For Spain, 'Guernica' stirs memory and awe. *New York Times*, Nov. 2, 1981. http://tinyurl.com/omlwl8a.

Martin, Clancy. 2015. Good lovers lie. *New York Times* column, February 14, 2015. http://www.nytimes.com/2015/02/08/opinion/sunday/good-lovers-lie.html.

Meibauer, Jörg. 2005. Lying and falsely implicating. *Journal of Pragmatics* 37. 1373–1399.

Meibauer, Jörg. 2011. On lying: intentionality, implicature, and imprecision. *Intercultural Pragmatics* 8. 277–292.

Meibauer, Jörg. 2014a. Lying at the semantics-pragmatics interface. Berlin: De Gruyter Mouton.

Meibauer, Jörg. 2014b. A truth that's told with bad intent: Lying and implicit content. *Belgian Journal of Linguistics* 28. 97–118.

Newman, John Henry. 1864. *Apologia pro vita sua*. http://www.newmanreader.org/works/apologia/.

Norris, Floyd. 2014. Corporate lies are increasingly immune to investor complaints. *New York Times* March 21, 2014. http://tinyurl.com/kp4vbd2.

Pagin, Peter. 2007. Assertion. In Edward N. Zalta (ed.), *Stanford encyclopedia of philosophy*. http://plato.stanford.edu/entries/assertion/.

Pascal, Blaise. 1656. *Les lettres provinciales*. Manchester: The University Press, 1920. English translation by Thomas M'Crie in *Pensées* [and] *The Provincial Letters*, New York: Modern Library, 1941.

Potts, Christopher. 2007. The expressive dimension. *Theoretical Linguistics* 33. 165–98.
Recanati, François. 2004. *Literal meaning.* Cambridge: Cambridge University Press.
Roussel de la Tour. 1763. Extraits des assertions dangereuses et pernicieuses en tout genre, que les soi-disans jesuites ont, dans tous les tems & perseveramment, soutenues, enseignées & publiées dans leurs livres. (Tome Second, Cap. XII: Parjure, Fausseté, Faux Témoignage.) Paris: Pierre-Guillaume Simon.
Saul, Jennifer. 2006. Lying, misleading, and accidental falsehood: The role of what is said. Unpublished manuscript, University of Sheffield.
Saul, Jennifer. 2012. *Lying, misleading, and what is said.* Oxford: Oxford University Press.
Searle, John. 1969. *Speech acts.* Cambridge: Cambridge University Press.
Shalvi, Shaul & Carsten de Dreu. 2014. Oxytocin promotes group-serving dishonesty. *PNAS* 10.1073. http://www.pnas.org/content/early/2014/03/25/1400724111.
Solan, Lawrence and Peter Tiersma 2005. *Speaking of crime: The language of criminal justice.* Chicago: University of Chicago Press.
Sorensen, Roy. 2007. Bald-faced lies! Lying without the intent to deceive. *Pacific Quarterly* 88. 251–64.
Stalnaker, Robert. 2002. Common ground. *Linguistics and Philosophy* 25. 701–21.
Stokke, Andreas. 2013a. Lying and asserting. *Journal of Philosophy* 110: 33–60.
Stokke, Andreas. 2013b. Lying, deceiving, and misleading. *Philosophy Compass* 8. 348–59.
Taylor, Kenneth. 2001. Sex, breakfast, and descriptus interruptus. *Synthese* 128: 45–61.
Tiersma, Peter. 2003. Did Clinton lie? Defining "sexual relations." 79 *Chi.-Kent L. Rev.* 927 (2004). Available at http://papers.ssrn.com/sol3/papers.cfm?abstract_id=470645.
Tiersma, Peter. 2005. The language of perjury (focusing on the Clinton impeachment). Available as download, http://www.languageandlaw.org/PERJURY.HTM.
Twain, Mark. 1880. On the decay of the art of lying. Available as download, http://www.gutenberg.org/ebooks/2572.
Updike, John. 1976. *Marry me.* New York: Knopf.
Weissman, Benjamin and Marina Terkourafi. 2016. Are false implicatures lies? *An experimental investigation.* Ms., University of Illinois.
Wilson, Deirdre & Dan Sperber. 1986. Inference and implicature. Reprinted in S. Davis (ed.), *Pragmatics: A reader,* 377–94. Oxford: Oxford U. Press, 1991.

Meizhen Liao & Yadi Sun
3 Cooperation in Chinese courtroom discourse

1 Introduction

In this chapter, we will examine the cooperative phenomenon in Chinese courtroom trial discourse. Cooperation is a very important issue in communication and the courtroom trial is a process of communication which takes place at a particular place, is participated in by particular people, follows particular rules and pursues particular goals (Liao 2004) and also because the cooperative phenomenon is rarely addressed in forensic linguistics. We will, first of all, briefly introduce the Cooperative Principle as well as some of our important assumptions and claims about the CP. Secondly, we will outline the aims, the methodology, and the framework for analysis. In the third part, we will carry out our descriptive analysis of the phenomenon based on our data and framework, focusing on the degrees of cooperation among different interactive relations. The fourth part is our explanation of the results of the description by means of our "Goal-driven Principle." Finally, we will present and discuss our conclusions.

2 A brief review of CP and its studies

As Grice (1975: 45) observed:

> Our talk exchanges do not normally consist of a succession of disconnected remarks, and would not be rational if they did. They are characteristically, to some degree at least, cooperative efforts; and each participant recognizes in them, to some extent, a common purpose or set of purposes, or at least a mutually accepted direction. This purpose or direction may be fixed from the start (e.g., by an initial proposal of a question for discussion), or it may evolve during the exchange; it may be fairly definite, or it may be so indefinite as to leave very considerable latitude to the participants (as in a casual conversation). But at each stage, some possible conversational moves would be excluded as conversationally unsuitable. We might then formulate a rough general principle which participants will be expected (ceteris paribus) to observe, namely: Make your conversational contribution such as is required, at the stage at which it occurs, by the accepted purpose or direction of the talk exchange in which you are engaged. One might label this the Cooperative Principle (Hereafter abbreviated as CP).

Meizhen Liao & Yadi Sun, Central China Normal University

Under the principle there are the following maxims (Grice 1975: 45–46):
(1) Maxim of Quantity: (a) Make your contribution as informative as is required (for the current purposes of the exchange). (b) Do not make your contribution more informative than is required.
(2) Maxim of Quality: Do not say what you believe to be false. Do not say that for which you lack adequate evidence.
(3) Maxim of Relation: Be relevant.
(4) Maxim of Manner: (a) Avoid obscurity of expression. (b) Avoid ambiguity. (c) Be brief (avoid unnecessary prolixity). (d) Be orderly.

Ever since the CP came into being, the literature about it has been characterized by the following. First, everyday conversation was predominantly used as data with CP rarely applied to institutional discourse. Secondly, reductionism seems to be the trend. As a matter of fact, criticism seems to have centered on the number of the maxims. Harnish (1976) combines "maxim of quantity" and "maxim of quality" into one maxim; Horn (1984) holds that there should be only two maxims: "maxim of relevance" and "maxim of quantity"; Sperber & Wilson (1986, 1995) believe that only the "maxim of relevance" is enough. This activity around the concept indicates that most researchers think that CP applies. Thirdly, some linguists, among whom Leech (1983) is the representative, have proposed some new principles ("Politeness Principle," for example) in an attempt to rescue CP from trouble. There are also those who doubt the overall application of CP. S.K. Sarangi and S. Slembrouk (1992) found enormous uncooperative phenomena in communication. For a more comprehensive and detailed review refer to Sarangi and Slembrouk (1992) and Davies (2000, 2007).

However, our main claims in this paper are that, despite the fact that there is much dispute over Grice's cooperative principle which is apparently about everyday conversation, it has the potential to account for and explain discourse in institutional contexts, but in order to achieve this, due attention has to be paid to factors of a societal kind. For the present author, this means examining the correlations between participants' socioeconomic interests (embodied as goals in our model of analysis), their social identities, the social and situational powers they (do not) possess, their expectations about activities, etc.

Secondly, while implicature solving or a distinction between speaker meaning and sentence (semantic) meaning is very important for Grice's formulation of the CP, it is not the main business of a Chinese courtroom trial. Rather, the degree of cooperation and the ways to obtain each other's cooperation are the main focus, at least in a Chinese courtroom trial.

Thirdly, we reject the idea of cooperation as social goal-sharing as an overarching presumptive feature in interactions. In reality, it makes more sense to talk about goal adoption, goal imposition, goal resistance, etc. As properties of interaction and social action; these categories, in their application, depend on individual and group social relations as well as pre-constituted social role relations within an Activity Type (Levinson 1979), as will be discussed in the explanatory part of this paper and we also hold that cooperation is rational and so is non-cooperation while the former is what we call "unmarked or preferred rationality" and the latter "marked or dis-preferred rationality," which constitutes the foundation for our descriptive model of degrees of cooperation in the following.

3 The research questions, methodology and framework

3.1 Research questions

The brief review suggests that CP is rarely applied in institutional discourse study and that disputes about application of CP abound. Hence the aim of this chapter is to present a picture of Chinese courtroom discourse from the perspective of cooperation and we will try to answer the following two major questions: How does CP apply in Chinese courtroom trial discourse as a special kind of institutional discourse which is governed by special procedures and rules as situated in a different legal culture and ideology of China? How do we explain the peculiarities of the cooperative phenomenon as shown in the Chinese courtroom interaction? A successful answer to the first question entails a successful description of the phenomenon while an adequate answer of the second question entails an adequate explanation of the phenomenon.

3.2 Methodology

This paper is a data-based qualitative research. Transcripts of lawfully obtained situated tape-recordings of five courtroom trials (of three criminal and two civil cases) out of a corpus of Chinese courtroom discourse ranging in time from 1999 to 2015 were used as data for analysis[1]. The trials were conducted in lower courts in Beijing and Jiangsu. Here is a brief description of the cases involved.

A. The first trial involved a charge of fraud. Five defendants were charged with defrauding some senior citizens of their money or jewelry by purporting to predict their future. Four of the defendants were farmers and one was an unemployed woman. Three of the defendants had received some primary-school education, one had received middle-school education, and one was

---

[1] The transcriptions were made by both the present author and some of his PhD and MA students.

illiterate. All the defendants pleaded guilty. The trial took place in 2000 in a lower court in Beijing, where the crime allegedly had occurred.

B. The second trial involved a charge of destruction of private property. The defendant, a farmer of Fangshan District of Beijing, ran a coal mine originally independently with his elder brother, but was later made to run it jointly with the victim in the case with the defendant as the legal representative of the mine. The defendant and the victim signed a new contract with the production team[2] according to which they should share their fees due to the production team. It turned out that the defendant was made to pay everything and the victim did not pay their share at all. The defendant complained to the leaders of the production team and also talked directly to the victim about the problem but failed in his efforts to correct the situation. The defendant's brother was so enraged when he saw the victim bought a new fancy car that he, out of revenge, committed the act of blowing up the victim's car after considerable preparation in the vein of a dark night, in which he himself was killed. The defendant was accused of being involved in the conspiracy. The trial took place in 2001 in a lower court of Fangshan District, Beijing.

C. The third trial involved a charge of bigamy. A farmer in a Beijing suburban area was accused of maltreating his mentally sick wife and living with a divorced woman unlawfully. The trial took place in 2001 in a lower court in Pinggu, a suburban county, Beijing.

D. The fourth trial is of a civil case involving a charge of environmental pollution, in which residents of a community accused a coal-mining company of polluting their environment. The trial took place in 2001 in a lower court of Fangshan District, Beijing.

E. The fifth trial is also of a civil case involving a dispute over the quality of a computer software. The trial took place in 2002 in a suburban court of Wuxi, Jiangsu Province.

The data were chosen simply because of their being relatively more representative in terms of the nature, the type or complexity of cases, the number and gender of the participants in spite of the fact that they are more characteristic of our earlier work in the corpus construction. The data are not equally used in the analysis and those parts which were chosen as examples for analysis were translated into idiomatic English by the present author[3].

---

[2] The production team is a work unit, or a labor organization, in the countryside of China, the lowest or the basic in the structure of rural economical administration and often formed according to the natural location.

[3] In consideration of academic ethics, most of the trial participants and the places involved were renamed.

3.3 The analytic model and the theoretical framework

3.3.1 Model for descriptive analysis

It seems that previous research on cooperation proceeded on the assumption of a dichotomy of the phenomenon: when it comes to the discussion of cooperation, it is either cooperative or not. This is actually not the case. Analysis of cooperation along that line does not reflect the real situation of the phenomenon. "Rules are either adhered to or broken, whereas the upholding of principles is a cline: they can be obviously upheld and obviously broken, but there is a large gray area in between" (Davies 2000: 5). Here in this paper we propose and employ a model in terms of the degree of cooperation. In social communication, it's definitely not a simple or clear-cut situation where the interaction is characterized as either cooperative or not. Even if a conversation is cooperative, very few people perfectly obey the CP and its maxims. Cooperation is a matter of degrees, a continuum. Following is our model of cooperation in terms of degrees.

Cooperative continuum

Negative pole:
(1) Flouting flagrantly or defiant, without saying anything: no conversational contribution at all;
(2) Saying nothing, or merely silent, but not defiant: no conversational contribution at all;
(3) Declaring non-cooperation, expressions of non-cooperation (Such as "I don't know," "I won't say anything," etc.): no conversational contribution;
(4) Saying things irrelevant, providing formal cooperation, but no substantial cooperation: no conversational contribution;
(5) Low-degree cooperation: lowest degree of conversational contribution, least or minimum satisfaction for conversation;
(6) Middle-degree cooperation: basically satisfactory but not sufficient;
(7) Sufficient contribution: enough or maximum contribution to conversation;

Positive Pole:
(8) Excessive cooperation: contribution more than necessary

Being a qualitative continuum, cooperation cannot be accurately represented with quantitative rank scales, and we can only make a rough generalization. In the continuum, what the first two situations share is the characteristic of no utterance. Defiance (gestural, without saying anything) means flouting, hostility and is hence more aggressive than mere silence. The measurement of the degree is mainly in terms of quantity and quality (or relevance), expressed through choice of words, tone, and speech act forms etc. And we will use this model in analysis of the degrees of courtroom cooperation and interaction. As cooperation is an interpersonal phenomenon, our description of the degrees of cooperation will be conducted in terms of the typical interactive relationships. In the traditional Chinese courtroom trial, where the inquisitorial system was practiced, the judge dominated the trial by performing both the procedural and substantial duties. Beginning in early 1990's, part of the trial system featuring Anglo-American law was introduced, but it did not replace the original system. So now we are actually practicing a mixed trial system. For example, we do not have any jury system, although we do have a people's assessor who sits together with three or five other professional judges. The judge performs both the procedural and substantial duties. We also practice cross and direct examinations, but very rarely do we see any witness appear at court to testify and most of the time it is the defendant who is subject to the examinations. This makes the interactive relationships in China's courtroom trial much more complicated. Typically, there are mainly the following kinds of courtroom interactive relationships (with the double arrow indicating interactive relationship).

(1) In civil trial
Judge ↔ Lawyer (or the party concerned)
Judge ↔ Witness
Plaintiff (lawyer) ↔ Defendant (lawyer)

(2) In criminal trial
Judge ↔ Defendant
Judge ↔ Witness
Judge ↔ Prosecutor
Judge ↔ Defense lawyer
Prosecutor ↔ Defendant
Prosecutor ↔ Defense lawyer
Prosecutor ↔ Witness (in direct-examination)
Prosecutor ↔ Witness (in cross-examination)
Defense lawyer ↔ Defendant
Defense lawyer ↔ Witness (in direct examination)
Defense lawyer ↔ Witness (in cross-examination)

3.3.2 The theoretical framework for explanatory analysis

Having completed our descriptive analysis, we would like to go one step further and try to explain the features revealed. Again we will apply our Goal-driven Principle in order to accomplish the work. The "Goal-driven Principle" is formulated as follows:

> Every act of rational human communication carries the guarantee that it is goal-oriented (Liao 2004a, 2004b, 2005, 2009a, 2010a, 2012, and 2015).

According to this principle, speaking or communication is an activity of expressing, pursuing, negotiating and realizing one's goals. Thus, the most important aspect of communication study is goal analysis, including how those goals are expressed, pursued, negotiated, or realized. The corollaries of this principle are as follows: (1) Utterance meaning is related to or resides in the goal or goals expressed, negotiated and pursued; (2) any text or talk should be seen as a hierarchical system of goals, which are interrelated or supported; (3) coherence of a text or talk is assessed by whether the utterances are related with the super goal(s) of the text or talk; (4) the interpersonal relationship in which the language occurs should be examined or evaluated in terms of whether the participants' goals are shared or convergent, conflicting or divergent, or neutral.

3.4 Cooperation defined

There is confusion as well as dispute pertaining to the notion of "cooperation" (Sarangi & Slembrouk 1992; Davies 2000). In this chapter we follow Grice in our use of the term "cooperation," that is, acting in accordance with the maxims in the CP. Thus silence counts as an example of non-cooperation because here there is no conversational contribution made at all, while excessive information or contribution will be regarded as cooperative. Any communication through implicature is cooperative. Degrees of cooperation will also be evaluated in terms of the maxims of the CP.

4 Cooperation examined in terms of degree

Analysis of our data shows that there are substantial differences in the utterance forms, content and structures by different interactive participants. In other words, cooperation varies a great deal with the interactive relations. Following is a description of cooperation in line with the main interactive relationships.

4.1 Between prosecutor and defendant

In criminal trials, in spite of the fact that the prosecutor and the defendant cooperate most of the time, the degree of their cooperation is generally the lowest, especially when the defendant does not plead guilty. Cases characterizing the first 5 situations in our model of degrees abound in the interaction between the prosecutor and the defendant.

(a) Non-cooperation

Example 1

PP: OK. I mean... you, on this March 3, on this, this day, before setting the car on fire, what did you take with you, I mean, before setting the car on fire?
D: I don't know what we brought with us.

Here an explanation is in order in terms of the defendant's answer. From this passage alone we could hardly say that he was not cooperative, because he might really not know the answer. However, we say that the defendant was not cooperative because according to the later investigation, he knew very well what he and his partner brought with them when they went out to start that fire.

(b) Formal cooperation or non-cooperation in substance or no substantial cooperation

In the following interaction, the defendant said something, but what he said fails to provide any information the questioner wants. In other words, the defendant seems to be cooperative, but in reality he is not.

Example 2

PP: When did he grind the tool?
D: Whatever he grinds he comes to my house.

(c) Low-degree cooperation

Below the answer "long before" is far from being an adequate answer to the questioner's question "when." But "long before" is aimed at the question, so it is cooperative, though not satisfactory.

Example 3

PP: When did you buy this?
D: I bought that long before, and I don't remember how many months I have kept that. —

In many cases, in the process of the interaction between prosecutors and defendants, if there is any cooperation, the level of cooperation varies from low to high. In other words, defendants are generally reluctant to contribute to the conversation on their own initiative; rather, they cooperate passively under prosecutors' pressure of insistent interrogation and repeated requirements. (This is also a feature of forensic interaction.) For example:

Example 4

PP: Who used it?
D: Miners also used it this way. *(The least informative, the lowest level of cooperation)*
PP: Who were they?
D: Those from Hebei Province. *(More informative, increased contribution, higher level of cooperation)*
PP: Who exactly? What are their names?
D: Mr. Liu and Mr. Sang both used this. *(Sufficiently informative, maximum cooperation)*
PP: All of them?
D: Yes.

(d) Ways of soliciting cooperation prominent

Ways of soliciting cooperation are important indicators of cooperation. In the interaction between the prosecutor and the defendant, the former is always asking the latter for cooperation or making the maxims of cooperation explicit. The prosecutor has a very strong awareness of meta-pragmatic devices, which are frequently resorted to to make the defendant cooperate. Some of the most resorted-to meta-pragmatic strategies include:

(1) Expressing a clear request for the quality of the answers

This strategy was employed in the examination of the defendant by the prosecutor or the questioning of the plaintiff, the defendant or the witness by the judge. And more often than not it is used prior to the questioning proper.

Example 5

P: Defendant Bei, I hope you will tell the truth in court today, and you, today, should cherish this opportunity in court today. A few more questions, I want to ask you, just a few questions. Please answer them truthfully.
D: Yes.

(2) Indicating that cooperation will benefit the defendant

This is also a method often resorted to by the prosecutor or the judge. They repeatedly stress that the cooperation will be good for the defendant while non-cooperation will be not.

Example 6

PP: Wait a minute, Defendant Bei. I have just told you that…
D: Ah.
PP: I hope you can cherish the opportunity today.
D: Yes.
PP: You don't have many opportunities.
D: Yes.
PP: You have to tell us the truth.
D: Yes, I am telling the truth.

In the opinion of the prosecutor, cooperation means opportunities for the defendant.

(3) Emphasizing the defendant should take a correct attitude

Before the examination begins, the prosecutor is always emphasizing the importance of a correct attitude.

Example 7

PP: Defendant Li, today we are going through the public trial of your fraud case in accordance with the law. It is hoped that you take a correct attitude, and answer the questions by the prosecutor truthfully and tell the truth. Is it clear?
D: Yes, I will cooperate with you.

(4) Criticizing the uncooperative attitude of the defendant

This usually happened when the defendant did not provide or refused to provide the information requested.

Example 8

PP: You can't remember the other things? Looking at what you said in court today, it seems you have hardly confessed anything. How is it that you remembered everything when we examined you in the public security station and also in the procuratorate's office? So what's wrong with your attitude today in the court?
D: My attitude is indeed a good one. Things have gone thus far, you know. That's all.

(5) Praising the defendant for cooperation

This method is often used at the beginning of the questioning process when the prosecutor tries to encourage the defendant to behave well by praising the defendant for his/her previous cooperation.

Example 9

PP: *Defendant Du, today we are going to try your case in court in accordance with the law. It is hoped that you take a, ah, correct attitude as you did in the public security station and the procuratorate's office and tried to be as co-operative in court today.*
D: *Yes, yes.*

(6) Repeating the question

When the defendant did not offer the information required, the public prosecutor would repeat his or her question. For example:

Example 10

PP: *What things did you take along with you when you went there?*
D: *I, I didn't know.*
    (2 seconds' pause)
PP: *What did you take along with you?*
D: *It was only after the crime act was committed that I got to know that – we took along with us a crowbar, gasoline ‖*
PP: *‖ Wait! After the crime act?*

4.2 Between judge and defendant

Since in courtroom trials in China judges not only perform procedural duties, but also participate in substantial investigation, the interaction between judges and others can be either procedural or substantial. The degree of cooperation in their interaction varies with the nature of their interaction.

(a) In procedural interaction

Procedural interaction demonstrates nearly perfect cooperation in terms of the four maxims of CP. For instance, in the beginning of the trial, the judge asks the defendant for the relevant information about their identity. The interaction is as follows:

Example 11

J: Now the trial commences. What is the defendant's name?
D: My last name is Zhang Wenwang.
J: Have you ever used any other names?
D: No.
J: How old are you?
D: 49.
J: What's your date of birth?
D: May 18, 1951.
J: What is your nationality?
D: The Han nationality.

(b) In substantial interaction

Substantial interaction can be cooperative or not, as shown in the following example.

Example 12

J: At that time you two were quite intimate, right? Can you describe your relationship then? Hmm?
D: (Silent for 3 seconds) (No contribution, non-cooperative)
J: If other people did not know the truth, what would they think of you, or your relationship? Of course, for those who knew the truth, they were aware of what happened; but for those who did not, how would they look at your relationship? You should tell the truth.
D: (Silent for 8 seconds) (No contribution, non-cooperative)
J: Have you ever thought about it?
D: (Silent for 8 seconds) (No contribution, non-cooperative)
J: ‖ Luo Shuixia?
D: ‖ I just thought... (Beginning to contribute or to cooperate)
J: What?
D: I thought that I had my divorce certificate. I was divorced. And he told me that he and his wife had not lived together for more than a year. I thought that separation over half a year without sex life could be regarded as divorce. So I began to live with him. (Making contribution, beginning to be cooperative)

(c) Ways of soliciting cooperation

In the interaction between the judge and the defendant, especially during the substantial investigation, the maxims of CP were also resorted to frequently.

For example, in the following the judge reminded the defendant that he should have a good attitude.

Example 13

J: *I remind you that your attitude in your confession of guilt in the court will directly affect your penalty (sentencing). When asked, you have to answer the questions actively and speak loudly. This is the last time that I remind you.*
D: *I didn't go to Lishui Bridge.*
J: *Louder!*
D: *I didn't go to Lishui Bridge.*

In the procedural interactions, the judge also resorted to the maxims of the CP. For example, in the following interaction, the judge explicitly indicated that the defendant should not offer more information than required.

Example 14

J: *What was the date of your arrest?*
D: *In November, on November 25th last year, I was arrested, being suspected of misappropriating the public funds. Er, in the first hearing on August 3rd this year, I was arrested being suspected of misappropriating the public funds* ▲
J: ▼ *I didn't ask you for that much, ah? I just asked you, that is, concerning the embezzlement, for what, what reason, say, that you were put into prison*

When the defendant offered more information than required, the judge was unsatisfied and explicitly stated that the information the defendant offered was more than required.

4.3 Between lawyer and defendant

The cooperation between the defense lawyer and the defendant basically follows the maxims of CP. For example, in the following interaction, the defendant is fully cooperative in his responses to all the questions posed by the defense lawyer.

Example 15

L: *Eh, Zhang Wenwang, I would like to ask you a few questions. You and – Zhang Didong, you two families jointly opened this coal mine – What did the village authority tell you about the issue of handing in fees?*
D: *The village authority – Originally we two families ran our own separate mines. Later the production team merged the mines, and they told me that I would be the legal person of the new mine group. The party secretary told me*

that I would be the legal person. Eh, each family would hand in half of the profit to the brigade.
L: Just now you told the prosecutor that it was 280,000 Yuan?
D: Yes
L: It means each family would hand in half of 280,000 yuan, i.e. 140,000 yuan?
D: Right.
L: Is that what you mean?
D: Yes.
L: Here is another question. Did the village authority rule that the two of your families would provide without any compensation 300 tons of coal to the villagers (?) Is this true?
D: Yes.
L: Did your family provide the 300 tons of coal?
D: Yes, we did.
L: What about Zhang Didong's family?
D: Zhang Didong – It seems they did not.
L: They did not.
D: Yes. It was all provided by me.
L: All provided by you?
D: Yes.
L: Now you answer my third question. When you found that Zhang Didong did not hand in his share of fees and still ran the mine, did you talk about this with Zhang Didong face to face?
D: Yes, we did. I said to him, "let's go and hand in the profit together," but he said he would quit.
L: He said he would quit?
D: Yes
L: Did you tell the village authority that he continued running the business but did not hand in their fees?
D: I told the party secretary about it.
L: You told the party secretary about it?
D: Yes
L: OK. Please answer the next question. Regarding the issue of blowing up the car, did you ever discuss it with your brother beforehand?
D: No.
L: No?
D: No.
L: Another question. When did you get to know that you were going to burn the car?
D: I got to know it only on that same day we went to destroy the car.

L: You got to know it on that same day?
D: Yeah.
L: Why didn't you leave the scene and terminate the crime?
D: I didn't hear you clearly. Would you please repeat it?
L: I mean since you already knew that ... that you were going to burn the car, eh, to destroy the guy's property, why didn't you, eh, turn back and, eh, end the plan?
D: Before we started my brother said to me, "We should not be so cowardly and be bullied by others. He ran our mine but we paid the fees for him. That's not fair. You just follow me, and I will be responsible for whatever happens. You really need not be worried. All you need to do is to watch over these guys."
L: Uh.
D: He asked me to come to him if anything happened.
L: Answer the next question. What did you actually do when you arrived at the crime scene?
D: I was just in charge of watching over those other guys for him.
L: How far was the car – away from you?
D: It – was 30 or 40 meters.
L: 30 ‖ or 40 meters?
D: ‖ Well, I had never been there before and I had been there only twice in my life.
L: Only twice?
D: Yeah.
L: I have another question for you. Why did you run away after the crime happened?
D: At that moment, I was terribly scared and said to myself that things had got serious. (A 1.5 second pause) Since my brother died and situation went bad, I ran away because I was terrified.
L: Well. (A pause for 4 seconds) After you were arrested, did you, uh, honestly tell all this to the public security department?
D: Yes.
L: Well, did you pay for the car when the public security department and the procuratorate began to investigate this case?
D: I went to my prison instructor many times and asked him to call you, so that my family members could discuss the issue of compensation with you and make up for the victims' losses as soon as possible.
L: Uh, what do you think about your problem?
D: My problem, as for me myself, since I committed the crime, I will simply listen to the court and accept whatever the court will do to me.

4.4 Between plaintiff and witness (in cross examination)

In civil trials, the interaction (in cross examination) between the plaintiff and the defendant's witness is also characterized by a low degree of cooperation. In the interaction in the case below, instead of cooperating, the two parties assume a taunting and hostile tone towards each other, and the judge had to intervene.

Example 16

P: What are the units in between?
W1: You mean the ash yard?
P: Of course, the ash yard you just mentioned.
   (A burst of laughter from the audience)
W2: You, you mean ‖ which ash yard?
W1: ‖ Which do you mean? There are quite a few of ash yards in between.
P: Quite a few? So would you please name all of them one by one? (A pause for 2 seconds)
W2: Name all of them one by one? Why should I?
P: Because you think that ‖ that all these ash yards are polluting sources...
J: ‖ All right. Well, plain ‖ tiff, about this...
W1: ‖ You, the one you are accusing is the Jing Coal Group ⊥ the Di Coal Group ‖ [...]
W2: ‖ You should direct your questions at them.
W1: ‖ What we did was to come and intervene and investigate ‖
J: ‖ That's enough.   ‖ You two, well, listen to me, uh, plaintiff, the questions you asked the witnesses just now were irrelevant, you should have asked questions that are relevant to the pollution caused by the Di Coal Group.
P: OK. Well, I'd like to ask you another question. Uh, when was the factory built? (2s) I mean the time.
W2: About the 1950s.
W6: No, no. We are not clear about the specific time of the building of the factory ‖ What we did was to come and investigate after we received the complaint about it.
J: ‖ This question you witnesses need not answer. Your question (−) is unrelated to the witnesses, right?
   ‖ Witnesses are here to testify the pollution.
W6: ‖ When we received the complaint, we came to solve the problem, eh, we took the problem in hand during that period. (Plaintiff: Well) Uh, you were talking of things dating back to the Japanese Puppet Regime Period. It's certainly none of our business

(Defender's witness 5 laughs). Even the Communist Party can not straighten out what exactly happened during the Japanese Puppet Regime Period, right? Don't ask such questions. Ask questions about what happened after we looked into this case [...]), won't you?

4.5 Between plaintiff (lawyer) and defendant (lawyer)

The cooperation in the interaction between the plaintiff (lawyer) and defendant (lawyer) is similar to that between the plaintiff and the defendant, which is also characterized by a low degree of cooperation. We can see this from how the judge intervened in the following.

Example 17

PL: Well, Judge, I want to pose some questions to the defendant.
J: Yes, you may.
PL: Well, my first question to the defendant is whether the software, the media and the 8 disks presented by the plaintiff just now were provided to the defendant by the plaintiff, uh, provided by the defendant to the plaintiff? In other words, were these media, including the floppy discs and the dongles, given to the plaintiff by the defendant?
DL: Just now we saw the floppy disc had not been inserted into the computer after I gave it to him. Instead, it was placed on the table, but he said the computer had been fixed. We can envisage the whole process, as it was quite clear. On the face of it, the disk was what we sold them, but, em, who knows whether the disk has been changed or not. Also, whose computer is this? Was it moved here from your company or from somewhere else? And you did not follow the correct method or procedure for the software installation.
PL: Em... What I wanted to ask was, I just wanted, I just wanted the defendant to give a direct answer to this question, that is, "Is this floppy disk shown in the court the same one that he provided to the plaintiff according to the contract?" I did not ask you about the computer program nor the software in this floppy disk; I only wanted to know whether the disk itself was the one which was delivered to the plaintiff by the defendant?
DL: This question is connected with the question raised by us just now. Because just now, you see, the process of testifying included the presentation, but in your presentation you did not follow the rules, the standard procedure. So, under this condition, you cannot very well ask us to give a definite answer.
PL: Em... We request the collegiate panel rule about this. We just wanted to know whether these 8 disks are the same ones given by the defendant. If the

presentation did not follow the procedure, we can delete the programs in this computer, and redo it with another demonstration. (3s)
J: Defendant!
DL: Yes.
J: I request that you give a direct answer to the question raised by the accuser just now.
DL: Em, we did answer his question directly. Why did we need a presentation? The presentation was a part of the question of the plaintiff, and the presentation also reflects our concern: whether the floppy disks had been used or not? Or you used it with it already installed before? What does the presentation do?
J: Defendant, I do not think the court needs to explain what a direct answer means.
DL: Of course not. I have already given a direct answer to the plaintiff's question.
J: The question of the plaintiff was the software ▲ you gave to the defendant
PL: ▼ Floppy disk
J: In this disk, is it the carrier of the software you gave to the defendant, em, the plaintiff? Is it the same disk? Please give a direct and clear answer.
DL: OK. Let me repeat (1.5s) the answer I have already given you. On the face of it, the disk is what we provided them, but as this article is something special, something that can be read and written, and as can be seen from the presentation and the witness testimony, the form is the same, but the content in the disks is different.

The judge repeatedly asked the defendant's lawyer to give a direct answer to the plaintiff's question. The so-called "direct answer" means to give direct and clear information to plaintiffs' lawyer. Not giving a direct answer means non-cooperation.

5 Cooperation explained

5.1 The goal(s), the goal relationship and cooperation

As can be seen, the CP seems to be inadequate in its explanation of some of the courtroom cooperation phenomena. We believe the unique features represented above in terms of cooperation relate to the institutional goal of the courtroom trial and in particular to the different goals of different trial participants and the nature of the goals. The relevance of the goal and the goal relationship to cooperation lies in the fact that the nature of the diverse goals and goal relationships determines whether the interaction will be cooperative or not. In other words, whether to cooperate or not primarily depends on the goal(s) and the goal relationships of the interactants. In the CP it is presumed that both sides have the common goal(s) or a common direction (Grice 1975). The CP works on this premise. But in reality, especially in a courtroom trial, the goals of the participants of the trial are diverse and, most of the time, different right from the very beginning. When the goal(s) is shared, cooperation will be expected or taken for granted; when the goal or goals are conflicting, lower degree of cooperation is expected; and when the goals are neutral to each other, the interaction is normally cooperative; and if the nature of the goal(s) is unknown, cooperation varies. The CP seems to work very well when the goals are shared but turns out to be somewhat inadequate where conflicts of the goal(s) dominate. Therefore, we propose that "The goal-driven principle of" (Liao 2004 and 2005) apply first in analysis of interaction, esp. when the CP is in trouble. In other words, an analysis of the goal(s) and the goal relationship is prior to the analysis of the cooperative phenomena. Or an analysis of cooperation entails an analysis of the goal(s) and the relationship of the participants in terms of the nature of their goals.

The goal analysis model proves to be adequate in Chinese courtroom discourse study in the following ways. First of all, a courtroom trial is prominently goal-oriented, where all the parties involved have their own clearly defined goals. Secondly, goal relationship of the courtroom interaction is not simple or one way but complex and we can identify at least three types of relations in terms of the goal(s): (a) sharing of the goal(s), typically represented in the interaction between the defender and the defendant as well as in the direct examination; (b) conflict in the goal(s), typically exemplified in the interaction between the public prosecutor and the defendant (who does not plead guilty) in the criminal trial, or in the interaction between the plaintiff (lawyer) and the defendant (lawyer) in the civil trial, or in the interaction in the cross-examination, and (c) the goal(s) being neutral. These relationships are most of the time predetermined. Based on the goal-driven principle, we interpret the court trial cooperative phenomena as follows.

5.2 The goal relationship and the degree of the courtroom cooperation

Whether to cooperate or not depends on the goal relationship of the interactants, so does the degree of cooperation. In the cases of sharing of the goal(s), both sides will be cooperative and the degree of cooperation inclines to the positive pole of the continuum formulated above. For example, in questions and answers between the defense lawyer and the defendant, since the lawyer's questions are for the sake of the defendant, the lawyer naturally expects the defendant to be cooperative; and since the defendant knows that the defense lawyer is arguing for his or her interests, he or she will try to be as cooperative as possible. In the cases of neutral goal(s), where the goal of an utterance is harmless, the degree of cooperation leans towards the positive pole of the continuum. In the Chinese courtroom trial, one's attitude is very important, and the court attaches great importance to one's attitude. Cooperation or not is an indicator of a good or bad attitude; therefore in a neutral goal relationship it is unnecessary for the questioned not to cooperate and my data also support this conclusion. For example, in the pretrial inquiry of the witness by the judge we can see perfect cooperation.

Example 18

J: The criminal division of People's Court of Fangshan District of Beijing is now in session. Defendant Zhang Wenwang, do you have any other names?
D: No.
J: How old are you?
D: Thirty.
J: Your date of birth?
D: July 1st, 1971.
J: Your nationality?
D: Han.
J: Your native place? (After 5 seconds' pause) That is, your birthplace, where is it?
D: It is Wangwu Village, Lujiaying Town, and Fangshan District of Beijing.
J: Your education?
D: Junior middle school.
J: Your occupation?
D: Farmer.
J: Your address?
D: Wangwu Village, Lujiaying Town, and Fangshan District, Beijing.

The question-answer interaction is very cooperative whether in terms of quantity, quality, relation or manner of the CP. Obviously on matters of no important interest, it is not necessary for the defender to be uncooperative.

In case of goal conflicts, that is, when the question penalizes the replier, non-cooperation is normal and expected. If there is any cooperation, the degree tends to be very low, leaning towards the negative side of the continuum. Let us take the interaction between the public persecutor and the defender as an example.

Example 19

PP: Well, I continue to ask you. (2s) Over the problem of the contract fee, did your brother Zhang Wenwang (1.5s) have any complaints? Because your partner Zhang Didong did not pay his contracted due, did your brother have any grudges against him?
D: Yes.
PP: What did he tell you about it?
D: He said that the guy was somebody, and he used some tricks and made us pay his due.
PP: Then what would your brother decide to do?
D: He never told me what he would do. He only said he was angry, extremely angry.
PP: What did he want to do while he was angry?
D: He did not ▲
PP: ▼ What ideas did he have then?
D: He did not say anything about it. He never told me about it. At that time, I did not meet him very often, only once a month or half a month. But I heard from my wife that he came to my house nearly every day. He was especially angry as we had been made to pay his share.
PP: What would he do then? What else did he say, when he was extremely angry?
D: Nothing else. No, no other words.
PP: What would he do when he was angry?
D: When angry, what could he do? That is, ah, he said nothing. Nothing else, at that time, anyway. But later, after the Spring Festival, he said, that guy bought a Buick.

In order to prove that the defender's elder brother had the motivation of revenge against the business partner, the public persecutor asked the defender what his brother thought, what he said and what he planned. Obviously, the defendant knew very well why the public persecutor asked this question. He knew his answer to this question would have a decisive effect on the case, so he parried the question again and again and only said his brother was especially angry. But the public persecutor did not give up, but instead, repeated the question six times until finally the defendant had no choice but to admit that his elder brother had planned to burn the car. On the most important question, the defendant adopted the least cooperative way of answering, but under the pressure of the insistent and successive questions of the public persecutor, the defendant had to move from the minimum cooperation to the maximum cooperation, which is further illustrated in the following.

Example 20

PP: Was this tool also used in other mines in your village?
D: It was very common in the mines.
PP: Was it used?
D: Yes.
PP: Who used it?
D: Workers all used it. Because it was slippery when the feet sweated, the workers had to ▲
PP: ▼ Was it used in your mine?
D: Yes, it was also used in my mine.
PP: Who used it? Who?
D: Miners also used it in this way.
PP: Whoever?
D: Miners from Hebei Province, not local people.
PP: Who exactly? What were their names?
D: Liu XX and Sang XX, both of them used it.

Our research indicates that public prosecutors (and judges as well) all tried and sought the maximum cooperation from the defendants, while the defendants were always reluctant to (or refused to) provide the maximum cooperation. Therefore, quite often, it took many turns for a single question of the public prosecutor to get its proper answer, which is a typical structural characteristic of the Chinese courtroom discourse.

5.3 The focus of research on cooperation in Chinese courtroom with the goal-driven principle

Having observed many courtroom trials and analyzed the transcripts of the situated recordings carefully, we conclude that since cooperation varies a great deal with the different relationships in terms of their goals, the focus of research on cooperation will also differ. When the goal(s) is shared, cooperation is assumed and the CP applies. So the focus will be the ways of cooperation, i.e., whether it is direct or indirect. When the goal(s) are conflicting, the study of cooperation will be focused on how one side makes the other side adopt their own goal(s), or how to make the other side cooperate. For instance, in the following the meta-pragmatic strategies used by the public persecutor should be the focus of study.

Example 21

PP: *Defendant Zhang Wenwang, I hope you will tell the truth in court today and today and cherish this chance of appearing in court. I will ask you several questions. Please answer them honestly.*
D: *Sure.*

Traditionally, in trials in the Chinese courtroom great emphasis was placed on the oral confession of the defendant, and the way of obtaining the oral confession was of vital importance as it concerns the procedural justice. In other words, the unjust or illegal ways in which to get the defendant's cooperation may cause serious problems in the way of the judicial justice. Therefore, in the trial discourse in the courtroom, the way public prosecutors (judges) manage to obtain cooperation of defenders (witnesses) is the most important question. For example, when the public prosecutor cross-examined the opponent's witness, there was such a conversation:

Example 22

PP: *Did the defendant hand the money over to the enterprise?*
D: *Yes. He did.*
PP: *Where were you at that time?*
D: *I was at Yuhuan.*
PP: *Then how could you see what happened in Lanhua, a place far away from you? You should be careful of your own problem. Give much thought to what you say! Think it over before you say anything.*

As what the witness said in his answer was in favor of the defendant, the public prosecutor became very angry and flagrantly threatened the witness, which was obviously illegal. When the defense lawyer noticed this, he put up his hands immediately and said to the chief judge: "Your Honor, when the public prosecutor questions the witness, he should let the witness say what is the case. Some of the prosecutor's words just now were inappropriate."

However, when a neutral goal is negotiated, the focus will be on whether the interaction is cooperative or not and why. Therefore, we cannot randomly use the CP without any discrimination. As conflict and confrontation is predominantly the theme of judicial activities, research on cooperation in courtroom discourse should focus on how the opposing sides make each other cooperate, that is, how one side makes the other side adopt the other side's goal(s).

6 Conclusion

This chapter focuses on the phenomenon of cooperation in courtroom discourse. We have found that cooperation is not simply a binary issue, but a continuum, that is to say, a matter of degrees. For this reason, it is of great theoretical and practical value to study cooperation in terms of degrees. The cooperative performance of various interacting participants differed significantly. For example, in a criminal trial, the defender and the accused tend to cooperate, with the degree of cooperation inclining to the positive pole of the cooperative continuum. In the interaction between the prosecutor and the accused, non-cooperation is pervasive, with the degree of cooperation approaching the negative pole of the non-cooperative continuum. In the interaction between the judge and the accused, both cooperation and non-cooperation exist. These phenomena could not well be explained with the CP. As courtroom discourse is predominantly goal-oriented with goals varied, participants talk for their own benefits, so that the goal-driven principle and the goal analysis can better explain the courtroom cooperation. As the prosecutor and the accused do not normally share their goals, where goal imposition is the rule, the degree of cooperation between them is low and non-cooperation or goal resistance is pervasive. As the defender and the accused share their goals, they tend to be cooperative with the degree being very high and goal adoption is the rule. The concurrence of both cooperation and non-cooperation between the judge and the accused is due to the fact that the judge plays two roles in the courtroom trial: the executor or the administrator of the trial procedure and the investigator of the substantial facts of the case. As the executor of the trial proceeding, the goals of the speech acts of the judge are neutral to the defendant as well as the other participants. In other words, his speech acts in this role do not affect the interests of the accused. This is why the accused is cooperative in most cases. However, when the judge switches his role as the investigator of the facts of the case, his speech acts are often detrimental to the interests of the accused. Once his speech acts are in conflict with the interests of the accused, non-cooperation emerges or abounds. So in study of cooperation, the goals of the parties should be taken into consideration.

Bethan Davies (2000: 23) is definitely right in saying "It is clear that Grice's work has two major limitations: it is based on introspection rather than data, and take no account of interpersonal factors." Theories must be supported by real data and tested in practice. In addition, interpersonal factors are essential to cooperation. We believe that goal factors and goal relations are the most important and fundamental ones among various interpersonal factors. To be cooperative or not is the choice of the conversation participants, made under the guidance of their goals. As a result, a study of cooperation should start with the analysis of the goals and goal relations between the interactive parties. We do not intend to replace the CP with our GP, but supplement the CP with our GP and try to rescue the CP where it is in serious trouble.

Courtroom discourse is notoriously known as "a war-like discourse" and the theme is conflict. Quite often non- or low degree of cooperation prevails. As the CP mainly applies in the interaction where there is a common goal or direction, in a conflict-led interaction, the CP is in the cart. Many scholars who have studied institutional discourse (courtroom discourse in particular) have indicated this (Sarangi and Slembrouck 1992, Harris 1995).

Last but not least, in study of courtroom trial discourse very important issues such as fairness, justice, power, rights and life and property interests are involved. It seems that non-cooperative phenomena are more worthy of studying than those cooperative phenomena, because non-cooperation represents conflicts and contradictions, which are the main tasks for the court to address and the areas for linguists to study. In cooperative interactions, the focus should be on how the dominating parties of the discourse (the judge, the prosecutor and the lawyer) try and obtain cooperation from their interactants. Traditionally, criminal court trials in China stress the confession from the defendants, and how the court tries and obtains the confession is a vital legal issue. Quite often, the ways of obtaining the defendants' confession by the judges or the prosecutors is controversial and there has been a lot of complaint about them. Our study on cooperation can help facilitate the solution of these legal issues and contribute to the realization of justice pursued by law.

All in all, where there is cooperation, there is non-cooperation. Cooperation entails non-cooperation. Human beings are being rational in being cooperative and they are also rational in being not cooperative. Choice of being cooperative or not is determined, most importantly, by their goals.

References

Davies, Bethan. 2000. Grice's Cooperative Principle: Getting the meaning across. In D. Nelson & P. Foulkes (eds.), *Leeds working papers in linguistics and honetics* 8. 1–26.

Davies, Bethan. 2007. Grice's Cooperative Principle: Meaning and rationality. *Journal of Pragmatics* 39. 2308–2331.

Grice, H. P. 1999. Logic and conversation. In Adam Jaworski and Nikolas Coupland (eds.), *The discourse reader*. Routledge, London and New York.

Gu, Yueguo. 1996. Doctor-patient interaction as goal-directed discourse in Chinese social-cultural context. *Journal of Asian Pacific Communication* 7(3 & 4).

Harnish, R. M. 1976. Logical form and implicature. In S. Davis (ed.) *Pragmatics: A reader*. 1991. Oxford: Oxford University Press.

Horn, L. R. 1984. Toward a new taxonomy for pragmatic inference: Q-based and R-based implicature. In D. Schiffrin (ed.), *Meaning, form, and use in context: Linguistic applications.*
Habermas, Jürgen. 1979. *Communication and the evolution of society.* Toronto: Beacon Press.
Habermas, Jürgen. 1987. *The theory of communicative action, vol. 2: Life world and system: A critique of functionalist reason* (T. McCarthy, trans.). Boston: Beacon Press.
Leech, Geoffrey. 1983. *Principles of pragmatics.* Harlow: Longman.
Liao, Meizhen. 2004. The goal-driven principle and cooperation in Chinese courtroom discourse. *Foreign Language Research* 5. 43–52.
Liao, Meizhen. 2005. The goal-driven principle and goal analysis: A new way of doing pragmatics. *Rhetorical Learning* 3. 1–10. *Rhetorical Learning* 4. 5–11.
Liao, Meizhen. 2009. The goal-driven principle and communication. *Foreign Language Research* 4. 62–64. *Foreign Language Research* 6. 101–109.
Liao, Meizhen. 2010. The goal-driven principle and dynamics of context. *Journal of PLA University of Foreign Languages* 33(4).
Liao, Meizhen. 2012. The goal-driven principle and construction of context. *Journal of Hubei University: Philosophy and Social Science* 39(5). 108–112.
Liao, Meizhen. 2015. Speech or silence: Within and beyond language and law. In Lawrence M. Solan, Janet Ainsworth & Roger W. Shuy (eds.), *Speaking of language and law*, 127–130. Oxford: Oxford University Press.
Searle, John. 1969. *Speech acts: An essay in the philosophy of language.* Cambridge: Cambridge University Press.
Searle, John. 1983. *Intentionality: An essay in the philosophy of mind.* Cambridge: Cambridge University Press.
Sarangi, S. K. & S. Slembrouk. 1992. Non-cooperation in communication: A reassessment of Gricean pragmatics. *Journal of Pragmatics* 17. 117–154.
Sperber, D. & D. Wilson. 1986. 1995. *Relevance: Communication and cognition.* Oxford: Basil Blackwell.

Notes for transcription symbols and abbreviations

(1) "▲▼" for simple interruption
(2) "|| ||" for overlap interruption
(3) "-" for drawling
(4) (–) for utterance not clear
(5) —— for omission of words
(6) PTL for "particle"
(7) "PP" for public prosecutor
(8) "D" for defendant
(9) "J" for judge
(10) "P" for plaintiff
(11) "PL" for plaintiff lawyer
(12) "DL" for defense lawyer
(13) "W" for witness

Nicholas Allott and Benjamin Shaer
4 Inference and intention in legal interpretation

1 Introduction

In this paper we argue that the interpretation of statutes and other legal texts is of a piece with utterance interpretation more generally, where this variety of interpretation is best understood as a species of inference to the best explanation. Such an explanation of an utterance's meaning treats the text produced by the utterer as a clue to the "speaker's meaning" or "utterance content" – that is, in the general case, what the utterer intended to communicate.

This view of legal interpretation is controversial in legal scholarship, as demonstrated in two notable recent discussions, by Andrei Marmor and John Perry, which advance claims that are in some tension with it. The claim advanced by Marmor (2008: 425) is that the content prescribed by the legislature is nearly always exactly "the content which is determined by the syntax and semantics of the expression uttered." That advanced by Perry is the "meaning-textualist" view that what is conveyed by the use of a particular word or words in a legal text is (at least generally speaking) an "ordinary" or "conventional" meaning of the word-type.

To pursue our argument, we first briefly review the basic ingredients in an "inferential-intentional" approach to utterance interpretation, then take up the two claims just described. In a nutshell, our point about Marmor's claim is that it incorrectly characterizes the content prescribed by the legislature. This is because what normally determines this content is what is explicitly meant by the speaker, and this differs systematically from "the content which is determined by the syntax and semantics of the expression uttered" as Marmor defines the latter (2008: 425). Our point about the meaning-textualist view is that it cannot be right either, because in many cases words and sentences in statutes and other legal texts, as in other utterances, are used to convey meanings other than the conventional or dictionary meaning of the word-type.

In challenging these two claims, we will be offering an "inferential-intentional" alternative, based on the work of the philosopher H. Paul Grice. Like most work in linguistic pragmatics since Grice, this alternative develops his view of an

Nicholas Allott, University of Oslo
Benjamin Shaer, Carleton University, Ottawa

utterance's meaning as (in normal cases) constitutively determined by a complex "utterer intention," applying it to the legal domain. To clarify the nature of this intention, we can say that it is the intention to modify the addressee's thoughts so that the addressee grasps the utterer's intention to modify the addressee's thoughts. Crucially, this "intention-to-mean" is, like other intentions, constrained by rational expectations – in this case, by what the speaker can rationally expect the intended addressee to take the speaker to have meant. In the interpretation of statutes and other legal texts, this constraint is (for various reasons and in various ways) tighter than it is in face-to-face conversation. Yet, it does not follow – nor, we will argue, is it actually the case – that the process of interpreting legal utterances is non-inferential. It is likewise not the case that words in legal texts can express only their ordinary or conventional meanings.

Our efforts to advance these claims will involve taking a leaf from Wilson's (2011) approach to literary interpretation and arguing that the interpretation of legal texts "draws on the same basic cognitive and communicative abilities used in ordinary, face-to-face exchanges." We claim that "theoretical notions which apply to the interpretation of ordinary utterances – the notion of inferential communication itself, the distinction between explicit and implicit communication, [...] expressions of attitude, and so on – should carry over" to legal interpretation, just as they should, in Wilson's view, to literary interpretation. The basic assumption guiding both inquiries, then, is that neither literary nor legal texts "are [...] entirely *sui generis*, but exploit at least some of the same abilities used in other varieties of verbal communication" (Wilson 2011: 70).

The distinctive features and goals of legal interpretation have led at least some legal scholars (e.g. Greenawalt 2010) to express skepticism of the explanatory utility of assimilating this form of interpretation to others. In particular, the fact that "legal interpretation," in this expression's common use by jurists, frequently describes activity that goes beyond simply ascertaining the meaning of, say, a contentious provision in a statute and extends to the task of determining how this provision applies to the case at issue strongly suggests that the complex activity of interpretation in the legal context is not congruent with its counterpart in other domains.

We agree that the term "legal interpretation" has this broad sense. However, it does not follow that the interpretation of legal texts is entirely different in kind from utterance interpretation more generally. We claim that a clearer understanding of legal interpretation requires factoring out certain aspects that, we will argue, following Endicott (1994, 2012) and others, fall outside the ambit of utterance interpretation proper. As we will also be pointing out, this exclusion holds up even if their inclusion by jurists within the rubric of "legal interpretation" is justifiable on grounds internal to the legal domain. In excluding these aspects of legal interpretation, we will be appealing to Endicott's (2012: 109) distinction between "interpretive" and "creative" activities in legal interpretation; and to a further distinction between the content of a statute as an utterance and the content of the law.

In making our case for an "inferential-intentional" approach to legal interpretation, our general strategy will be to demonstrate the limits of alternatives that do not exploit these processes in their own approaches to interpretation. This will involve demonstrating, through examples drawn from legal texts, just where the linguistic or conventional meaning of an expression in a legal text underdetermines speech act (and legal) content. Our textual focus will be statutory and regulatory provisions, and we will be drawing our examples from international law as well as common law contexts. Granting important differences between these legal contexts, we believe that our claim applies across these and others, given the general nature of the interpretative principles at the heart of our claim. We also take this point to hold for legal texts other than legislation. Although important differences again exist in the respective principles involved in interpreting statutes, regulations, constitutions, contracts, wills, and other legal documents, we see the recovery of the utterer's "intention-to-mean" as playing a central (if not necessarily identical) role in the interpretation of all of these legal texts. For this reason, we will be using the umbrella term "legal interpretation" throughout our discussion in referring mostly to the interpretation of statutes, regulations, and other legislative "speech," with the idea behind this usage being that our remarks should be applicable to a wider variety of legal texts.

The rest of our discussion will proceed as follows. Section 2 will offer a brief summary and motivation for the "inferential-intentional" approach to utterance interpretation that we will be defending in the rest of the paper. Section 3 will introduce two key distinctions into our analysis: between "investigative" and "creative" processes in the phenomenon of "legal interpretation" broadly construed, and between the content of a legal speech act and the content of the law itself. With this groundwork done, we will investigate Marmor's (2008) claims about the content of legal texts in section 4 and certain of Perry's (2011) claims about the legal doctrine of "textualism" in section 5. Section 6 will offer a summary and some conclusions.

2 "Inferential-intentional" theories of meaning and communication

In linguistic pragmatics, the dominant view of utterance content, and one traceable to two seminal papers by Grice (1957, [1967] 1989), is that it is constitutively determined by certain speaker intentions; accordingly, interpretation is a matter of the hearer inferring those speaker intentions. In other words, in order to understand an utterance, the hearer infers what the speaker has intended to convey, using the linguistic material uttered as a clue. Although we cannot offer a full defense of these assumptions here,[1] we can explain some of the rationale behind them.

Let us start by asking why it might be useful to think of meaning as dependent on speaker intentions. We can shed some light on this question with a non-linguistic example: someone pointing to something. When we see this action and want to know what the person pointing means by it, what we are, in fact, interested in is in finding out what she has intended to point to. In other words, while there will be, for example, many objects, parts of objects, and activities in the direction in which the pointer has pointed, what matters for determining the meaning of the pointing gesture is the one that the pointer has had in mind – and, crucially, has wanted her audience to come to have in mind.

The same observations can be made about determining the relevant meaning of indexical, or "pointing," expressions, such as *he*, *it*, *here*, and *later*. Consider, for example, a speaker's utterance of (1):

(1) It'll be here later.

On the view just described, what *it*, *here*, and *later* signify in this utterance depends on what the speaker has intended to refer to.

To further clarify this point about intention, consider another example of non-verbal communication: raising an empty glass in the pub (Sperber and Wilson 2008: 89). What makes it the case that I am communicating that I would like another drink is simply my performing this action intending you to see it and to infer that this was my intention and that I intended you make this inference. If I raised my glass for some other reason, such as to check whether the speck in the dregs is a fly, then intuitively I did not mean to ask for another drink – nor to communicate anything at all – and that is *because* I lacked an intention to convey something.

What emerges from these examples, and from the juxtaposition of examples of both verbal and non-verbal forms of communication, is not only that they all appear to require explanation in terms of speaker intentions, but also that verbal and non-verbal communication might have a unified explanation in these terms.

Grice's work on speaker meaning provided the basic framework for such an explanation. His key innovation, however, was the claim that since speaker

---

[1] But see, e.g., Allott (2013).

meaning is a function of certain speaker intentions, if the hearer can infer these intentions, then communication succeeds.[2]

So far, though, it is not clear why we should think of utterance content as needing to be inferred. A simple answer is that a hearer does not have any direct access to a speaker's mind and thus has to work with available evidence of the speaker's behavior, in particular, what the speaker says and does, which serve as (no more than) clues to what the speaker means. The action itself may, as in the glass-raising case just discussed, underwrite or not underwrite a communicative intention. This indicates that the determination of speaker meaning cannot simply be a matter of decoding. Generally speaking, a particular gesture or a spoken sentence does not communicate the same content whenever or by whomever it is used.

A ready objection to this claim as it applies to verbal communication is that in using words and sentences, we do not merely provide clues to our meaning; instead, we say what we mean. Therefore, someone listening to us can in fact decode our meaning and does not need to infer it. Yet, there are at least two compelling reasons not to accept this objection.

One is that there are many ways in which the contribution made by the basic, stable meanings of the words uttered – what some linguists call their "encoded meaning" and (roughly) what many philosophers call their "conventional meaning" – falls short of what the speaker has intended to communicate.

When one considers, in particular, actual instances of verbal communication, it becomes clear that an analysis in terms of coding and decoding that makes no appeal to inferential processes cannot be the whole story. Strong evidence for this already emerged in our consideration of one type of interpretative process, that of assigning a referent to indexical expressions like *it*. In these cases, a simple decoding of this word in the sentence determines at most that there is some inanimate entity being referred to, with the hearer still left to infer what that entity is. Many other types of interpretative processes exist, including resolution of ambiguity and polysemy and what have been called "completion," "saturation," "enrichment," "narrowing," and "broadening" in the pragmatics literature. The crucial point that we will be making in the discussion to follow is that such processes must also figure in legal interpretation.

A subtler, but no less important, response to the objection that in verbal communication you simply say what you mean is one offered by Bach (2006: 24). This is that even if the message that the speaker intends to communicate by uttering some sentence corresponds exactly to the semantic content of that

---

[2] For this claim that this was Grice's great innovation, see Sperber and Wilson (1986: 25).

sentence, the hearer still needs to infer that this is the case. In other words, the hearer must still determine that the speaker means precisely what she has said and thus must rule out other possibilities, such as that the speaker has been speaking ironically or metaphorically, or rehearsing a line from a play.[3]

The response just offered to the "say what you mean" objection can also be couched in somewhat more technical terms. In these terms, arriving at the semantic content of an utterance and inferring that this is what is meant by the speaker involve – at least on what is arguably the consensus view of utterance interpretation among linguists – two kinds of analysis and processing, seen not only as conceptually distinct but even as subserved by distinct mental architectures.

The first, or "lower" level, of the two processes, which is "linguistic" narrowly construed, takes as its input the stream of sounds coming from the speaker, segmenting this stream into linguistic units and assigning a syntactic structure to these units. The second, or "higher" level, process, that of pragmatic inference, is a conceptually distinct process (or processes) that takes material that has undergone linguistic processing and arrives at utterance content – that is, (in general) what the speaker has intended to convey. However, this process makes use of far more than just linguistic input. It also needs to take account of information pertaining to the particular circumstances and manner of a sentence's utterance, and other available clues such as relevant background knowledge.

On this view of utterance interpretation, linguistic processing is clearly a crucial input, yet only one among others, to what is in essence an inferential process of utterance interpretation proper.[4] These sources of information come together in helping the hearer to arrive at the best available explanation of the speaker's utterance. This typically consists of a proposition expressed as well as

---

[3] Marmor's view may be that, although legal utterance interpretation rarely deviates from the linguistically encoded meaning, it is inferential for Bach's reason (Hrafn Asgeirsson, personal communication 2017). A more fundamental question raised by Marmor's claim is whether a speaker *can* intend to communicate precisely the semantic content of the sentence she utters, given doubts expressed in the linguistics and philosophy literature about whether the linguistic meanings of words and sentences are plausible candidates for speaker meanings or components of these meanings. We will briefly take up this point later in the discussion.

[4] However, we might recognize certain cases of linguistic communication where very little linguistic processing is required of the hearer, such as that illustrated in (i): (see Sperber and Wilson 1986: 227, ex. 98)

A: Do you speak Japanese?

B: Banshun, kaze tachinu, oku no hosomichi, fūshikaden, nantoka nantoka.

Here, just determining that B is speaking Japanese, rather than fully processing B's utterance, is sufficient to work out the gist of B's answer to A. Of course, cases of non-verbal communicative activities such as pointing, miming, or nodding involve no linguistic processing at all.

any implicatures and other utterance content. Returning to the "what you say is what you mean" objection, we can see it in terms of this two-level analysis of utterance interpretation as simply failing to distinguish two conceptually distinct, and perhaps even mentally distinct, processes.

3 The activities of "legal interpretation"

Having sketched what we see as a very well-motivated approach to utterance interpretation, we will show how this view can be applied to legal interpretation – that is, to the interpretation of legal speech acts such as (provisions in) statutes.[5] Admittedly, the move from one to the other may strike many jurists and others as unhelpful or even misguided, relying on a glossing over of crucial details and differences to achieve any apparent explanatory success. While sensitive to this concern, we hope to show that the "inferential-intentional" view does indeed provide a compelling framework for analysing all forms of purposive human communication, and sufficient ancillary means to capture distinctive aspects of legal interpretation.

Before arguing for our thesis, we need to do some of the ground-clearing alluded to earlier regarding what reasonably counts as legal utterance interpretation. The basic idea here is that that not everything called "legal interpretation" is utterance interpretation, in the sense of investigation into the meaning of a speech act.

3.1 "Investigative" versus "creative" processes

As noted earlier, scholars such as Endicott (1994, 2012) have observed that the term "legal interpretation" has been used to refer to activities that are (as we will describe them) "creative" as well as those that are "investigative." One activity, legal utterance interpretation, consists in attempting to understand the utterance content of legislative speech. This is a variety of utterance interpretation, which, we claim, is an attempt to infer what the utterer intended to convey by her utterance.

---

[5] We leave open here the question of whether the enactment of a statute is a single speech act or a series of speech acts corresponding to the various provisions in it. For one response to this question, see Allott and Shaer (to appear).

The second activity is a kind of creative decision-making. Endicott has convincingly argued that what is called legal "interpretation" can be creative in part: for instance, when the rule that the statute sets up does not determine an action in the matter in question.[6] To see this, consider one of the cases that Endicott discusses, *Bankovic v. Belgium* (2001), heard by the European Court of Human Rights. The case revolved around a rocket strike conducted as part of the NATO bombing of Belgrade, which hit a radio and television station, killing 16 people. The question at issue was whether, as the victims' families had argued, the European NATO countries had, by this action, violated the victims' right to life as given in the *European Convention on Human Rights* (ECHR) or whether, as the defendant countries had argued, the military operation was an extraterritorial one outside their jurisdiction, to which the Convention did not apply.

Endicott observes that the Court presented the task before it as that of determining the interpretation of the word *jurisdiction* in Article 1 of the ECHR, as given in (2):

(2) "The High Contracting Parties shall secure to everyone within their jurisdiction the rights and freedoms defined in Section I of this Convention."

On this question, the Court concluded that the meaning of the term in this provision was "primarily territorial," thus ruling in favor of the defendant countries. Yet, as Endicott emphasizes, the Court's "interpretative" activity narrowly understood actually would have ended with the conclusion that the ECHR's framers had not established any territorial limits to a member state's jurisdiction as referred to in Article 1 (2012: 113). In other words, the content of this provision in the Convention, in the sense of what the framers meant by what they uttered, encompassed the establishment of an obligation on member states to secure certain rights within the sphere of their legal authority, leaving open this sphere's actual extent.

We agree with Endicott that "legal interpretation" as generally understood includes many instances of what are more perspicuously described as legal decision-making. On Endicott's (perhaps mischievous) description, judges have a tendency to see their decision-making activities as merely interpreting previous decisions, so that understanding the utterance content of, say, a statutory provision that is at issue is a part, but only a part, of legal "interpretation" in this broader sense:

---

[6] Endicott (2012: 111) actually makes the stronger claim that "most legal reasoning is not interpretative" and that "[m]uch of what is commonly called 'interpretation' can be done with no interpretation at all." We address this claim in more detail in Shaer and Allott (to appear).

> Judges, instead of claiming authority to invent a resolution to a dispute, have a natural inclination to see what they are doing as interpreting what others have decided (the parties, the legislature, framers of a constitution, states that signed a treaty, previous courts...). Conversely, when judges are moved (legitimately or illegitimately) to depart from what others have decided, they have a natural inclination to see what they are doing as interpreting what those others have done. (Endicott 2012: 110)[7]

It is worth noting, however, that even decomposing "legal interpretation" broadly construed into these distinct components does not resolve the question of what the characteristics of "legal interpretation" narrowly construed actually are. Endicott and others, for example, offer a view of interpretation in the legal context as necessarily involving reasoning about the meaning of the law – that is, of finding and presenting reasons for a conclusion – the chief merit of which seems to be its highlighting of the deliberative aspect of determining legal meaning.

Yet, it is unclear how far highlighting this deliberative aspect of legal interpretation can take us. Unless legal interpretation is a *sui generis* phenomenon that does not involve the same basic cognitive and communicative abilities used in ordinary, face-to-face exchanges – and, as we have already noted, we do not believe it is – then this form of interpretation, like literary and utterance interpretation, among others, must involve at least some spontaneous and intuitive processes and not just voluntary and reflective ones.[8] This is, in particular, because utterance interpretation itself is widely understood to be mostly fast and free from conscious effort, albeit with greater effort sometimes required given various contingent factors such as the familiarity of the utterance to be interpreted and the accessibility of the information required to do so. We do not believe that scholars like Endicott have offered sufficient reason to depart from a similar understanding of legal interpretation.

It is also worth noting that Endicott's placing of explicit reasoning about meaning at the heart of legal interpretation properly understood likewise prejudges the outcome of many ongoing debates about the nature of inferential and reasoning processes. One of these debates concerns whether either process is necessarily conscious (whether in the sense of occurrently conscious or available to consciousness – on this, see Grice 2001; Boghossian 2014: 2).

---

[7] Cf. Raz (2001: 419): "One kind of discretion, or context of discretion, enjoyed by courts is the discretion to make law, either by repealing existing law, or by making a rule where there was a gap in the law. One case in which they have such discretion is where the law is vague."

[8] We might speculate further that while most episodes of utterance interpretation are spontaneous and intuitive, even those episodes that are to some degree reflective, labored, or occurrently conscious involve interpretative work that is still mostly performed subliminally and automatically.

Another concerns whether intuitive and reflective inferential processes – the latter of which "involves attending to the reasons for accepting some conclusion" (Sperber et al. 2010: 377, n. 4; see also Mercier and Sperber 2009) – should be distinguished and if so, whether utterance interpretation is better captured in terms of one or the other. A third concerns whether activities of utterance interpretation are "personal" or "sub-personal" (that is, respectively operating at or below a level to which the notion of personhood applies; e.g. Dennett 1969: 90–96) and "central" or "modular" (that is, respectively having access to central memory, in the form of beliefs and the like and operating in an "encapsulated" manner without such access).[9]

For our purposes, the relevance of these debates is simply this: given our current understanding of what cognitive processes are involved in any form of interpretation, it seems best to remain neutral on such questions. Accordingly, we will claim only that legal interpretation narrowly construed includes all of the cognitive processes involved in determining the utterance meaning to a legal text and excludes further "creative" processes of decision-making that take this utterance meaning as input and are aimed at reaching a conclusion on the matter at issue.

3.2 The content of utterances and the content of the law

In the previous section, we conducted a ground-clearing effort to distinguish, in the broad phenomenon called "legal interpretation," between what we take to be its interpretative or "investigative" aspect and its more "creative" or "decision-making" aspect. The result was the emergence of a process that more clearly resembles utterance interpretation. Here we will conduct a second ground-clearing effort, revealing an additional distinction within the former aspect itself.

What we wish to distinguish here is activity targeting the content of an utterance and that targeting the content of the law itself. In other words, "utterance interpretation," in our view, is an investigation into utterance content; but this investigation is analytically distinct from one into the law beyond or distinct from the meaning of the utterance of a legal text.[10]

---

9 For some opposing views on these questions, see e.g. Recanati (2004) (arguing that the interpretation of implicatures is personal, consciously available, and reflective) and Sperber et al. (2010) (arguing that utterance interpretation as a whole is modular, sub-personal, and intuitive).
10 We do not see this claim of the occasional splitting apart of legal speech act content and the content of the law as original, but see it as reflected, for example, in Raz's (2001: 418) observation that "[t]he law is systemic, and each of its rules derives its meaning not only from the utterance that created it but from other parts of the law." However, we make finer distinctions here than Raz's point requires.

Since this step in our argument is important but may sound very puzzling to some, it is worth clarifying. The basic idea is an obvious one: that the utterance of a legal text has content by virtue both of being a kind of utterance, of having legal content in and of itself, and of interacting with a larger body of law; accordingly, various splits between speech act and legal content may arise. In particular, the speech act content of the statute might fall short of determining the legal content of the statute.

Similarly, a statute's legal content may not determine by itself the content of the law, which may instead emerge from a court's consideration of the statute itself together with the relevant case law and perhaps other statutes. Moreover, the court may need to determine what priority to give to one or another source of law under consideration in making a conclusion about the current state of the law. One famous illustration of this divergence between a statute's legal content and broader legal content is the 1889 American case *Riggs v. Palmer*. In that case, the court decided that a murderer could not inherit from his victim, even though the relevant "local wills legislation was silent on the issue" (Holland and Webb 2003: 101). Although it is possible to understand this result, following Holland and Webb, as involving the court's discovery of implied statutory meaning, we think that it is more plausible to see this ruling as involving the court's recognition that the law applicable to this case did not end with the speech act meaning of the statute, nor with the legal content of the statute *itself*. Rather, it encompassed an important principle of common law, that a wrongdoer should not benefit from his own wrong.

Admittedly, the distinctions just outlined between the content of a legal speech act and that of the law may seem highly abstract ones that can be easily glossed over. Our point in offering them here, though, is simply to allow us to further restrict the ambit of our claim. In this way, we can avoid the charge that our analysis seeks to address everything that has been or could be called "legal interpretation," and advance a view of legal interpretation as a matter of working out the speech act content of legal speech acts. This will prove to be crucial as we confront two recent, and prominent, claims about legal interpretation, those of Andrei Marmor and John Perry. We do so in the following sections.

4 Legal interpretation and linguistic underdetermination

In the previous section, we arrived at a highly circumscribed claim about legal interpretation, after further restricting the scope of our analysis. This is that this form of interpretation is of a piece with utterance interpretation generally and thus a species of inference to the best explanation for the utterance. Our thesis is *prima facie* at odds with two recent claims by prominent scholars, the legal philosopher Andrei Marmor and the philosopher of language John Perry. These claims are, respectively, that the content the legislature prescribes is determined by the syntax and linguistically encoded meaning of the expressions uttered; and that the kind of meaning that is key to legal interpretation is "the meaning the words and phrases used in the text had at the time the text was written." In what follows, we will explore these claims and what we believe to be the compelling evidence against them.

4.1 Marmor's (2008) claims about legislative content

In his (2008) study of legal language, Marmor says "that what a speaker *says* on an occasion of speech is the content which is determined by the syntax and semantics of the expression uttered" (425; his emphasis). He later qualifies this statement by granting that there may be "some cases in which it is quite obvious that the content the legislature prescribes is not exactly what it says," although speculating "that such cases would be very rare" (429).

Taken together, these remarks can be seen to produce the following claim about legal interpretation: This is that the content prescribed by the legislature is (but for rare exceptions) exactly the content determined by the syntax and linguistically encoded meaning of the expressions that the legislature has uttered. Accordingly, this is content that the hearer could arrive at by linguistic decoding alone, by taking the meanings that the words stand for and combining them according to the relevant syntactic rules.

As we noted earlier, such a position seems to reflect the common-sense view of legal interpretation whereby legislative texts say what they mean and the task of the interpreter is simply to decode this meaning from the text. Given what we have already argued, it should be clear that we see this claim as oversimplifying the activity of legal interpretation. To be sure, we do take the content prescribed by the legislature to be (nearly always) exactly what it *says*, in that what matters here is *explicit* rather than *implicit* utterance content – that is, the proposition expressed, with its direct illocutionary force, and not implicatures. Yet, as we have already argued, what the legislature "says" in this sense must quite often go beyond the decoded (or linguistic, or compositional, or conventional) meaning of the sentence and thus be inferred.[11]

---

[11] We do think that there is a way of understanding "semantic" that might make Marmor's claim compatible with ours: If lexical words (e.g. nouns and verbs) encode Kaplanian characters rather than concepts, the proposition expressed is a matter of the composition of the concepts determined by those characters in context, and "semantic" refers to the level of the concepts,

Note that the distinction just appealed to between implicit and explicit utterance content is a mainstay of modern pragmatics and a key part of Grice's insight that when speakers produce an utterance, they can mean more than the meaning of the sentence-type that they utter. Grice made use of the notion of implicit utterance content to give a unified account of such diverse cases as indirect answers to questions and ironic utterances, as illustrated in (3), in which at least part of what speakers mean is something quite different from what they say:

(3) a. Mary: Have you changed the litter tray?
         John: I've only just got in from work.

     b. What delightful weather! [said in a downpour]

More specifically, what speakers mean in such cases includes something that the speakers intentionally imply by (or in) making their utterances. Such intended implications of an utterance are now known as "implicatures."

As Searle (1975) pointed out, this account naturally extends to "indirect" speech acts, as illustrated in (4), in which the speech act force must be inferred:

(4) A cup of tea would be really nice just now.

Although a sincere utterance of (4) is a statement (and accordingly might receive a response like "That's true" or "That's not true"), such a sentence may simultaneously be used as a request – that is, with directive illocutionary force. Such examples are also standardly considered to be cases of implicature.

Now, we should emphasize that we take as eminently reasonable Marmor's claim that legal instruments rarely if ever have implicatures as part of their utterance content, which we ourselves have pursued in another context (Allott and Shaer, to appear).[12] Marmor's claim, however, is a broader one: that in the case of legal instruments, it is very rare for the propositions expressed to be

---

then it will be the case that what a speaker says on an occasion of speech is the content determined by the syntax and semantics of the expression uttered (as Marmor claims) and that what is said goes beyond the decoded (linguistic, compositional) meaning of the sentence (as we claim). However, what Marmor (2008) says about non-legal utterances, as we have quoted in the text, shows that this is not his view.

12 In that work, we argue that the illocutionary force of statutory provisions is just that of enactment, bringing into effect a new state of affairs, and is explicitly encoded in the enactment formulae that often introduce statutes. In particular, they do not (pace Marmor 2011b; Searle 1976: 22) function as implicit directives, as does the sentence in (4).

linguistically underdetermined in these texts. Now, there is considerable agreement among scholars of communication that the proposition expressed by an utterance is in general, as Marmor himself puts it, "not fully determined/explicable by the meaning (and syntax) of the sentence uttered" (Marmor 2008: 425). The question that Marmor's claim about legal interpretation raises is whether legal texts are different in kind in this respect. We do not believe that they are, and in what follows, we will provide substantial evidence against Marmor's claim and in favor of our own. This will take the form of numerous legislative examples of various kinds of linguistic underdetermination of legal speech act content, as described in Carston (2002), Allott (2016), and elsewhere. The idea, then, is that whenever the linguistic material uttered does not encode a single proposition, there remains inferential work for the hearer to do.

Before we do so, however, it is worth briefly revisiting an earlier remark we made about the ability of sentences to encode propositions. This is that the claim that sentences are even able to do so has been challenged by a number of researchers (e.g. Chomsky 2000; Carston 2002: 359–360; Recanati 2004, 2010; Pietroski 2005; Rayo 2013; Sperber 2014). There are at least two bases for this challenge, to which we ourselves are very sympathetic (see e.g. Allott and Textor, to appear). These are that words may not encode concepts and that it is speakers and not linguistic expressions that are plausibly seen as referring to individuals and expressing propositions. Yet, the assumption that sentences typically encode propositions remains the standard one among linguists and philosophers of language, and is, moreover, compatible with the claim that we are defending: namely, that inference plays a major role in the elaboration of a proposition. Since we do not wish to proceed on the basis of an assumption that entails the conclusion that we wish to argue for and is also a non-starter for many linguists and philosophers, for the purposes of the following discussion we will instead adopt the assumption that sentences may encode propositions, examining ways in which explicit speech act content goes beyond what is unambiguously encoded by the sentence.

One form of underspecification already mentioned earlier is that reflected in the use of indexical expressions such as *it*, *she*, *over there*, and *that time*. These expressions do not encode their referent – compare, for example, the indexical *then* with the phrase *28 March 2015* – but nevertheless allow a speaker to refer to different people, places, times, and other entities. That the speaker may do so is, of course, dependent on the hearer's ability to infer what or whom the speaker has intended to refer to.[13]

---

[13] Arguably, some uses of indexicals do not point to a specific referent, e.g. *I* used to indicate the speaker, whoever that happens to be (see Korta and Perry, to appear). We put this possibility aside in our discussion.

Indexical expressions are not difficult to find in statutes; the following provisions in British statutes provide some examples:[14]

(5) a. "This Act may be cited as the London Development Agency Act 2003 and shall come into operation at the end of the period of two months beginning with the date on which **it** is passed."
(London Development Agency Act 2003 (UK))

b. "Every copy of a consolidated statute or consolidated regulation published by the Minister under this Act in either print or electronic form is evidence of that statute or regulation and of **its** contents and every copy purporting to be published by the Minister is deemed to be so published, unless the contrary is shown."
(Legislation Revision and Consolidation Act (Canada), s. 31(1))

Although the referent of the indexical in (5a) is certainly easier to determine than that in (5b), this determination in each case nevertheless requires the hearer to make inferences in order to do so, given the number of potential antecedents that each indexical has in its respective sentence.

These cases clearly show, then, that linguistic meaning encoded in a statute may not fully determine what the statute prescribes; this supports our claim that further inferential processes are then necessary to derive the fuller legal speech act content. Admittedly, though, it remains possible to account for the resolution of indexicals while still maintaining Marmor's claim that the legal speech act content does not go beyond the syntax and semantics of the words uttered. This involves adopting a common view of pronoun meaning, whereby their encoded meaning is something like a Kaplanian character and their contribution to utterance interpretation is their content – typically their referent, which may be an object, time, event, or situation. On this view, the resolution of indexicals does not go beyond working out the syntax and semantics of what has been uttered, consistent with Marmor's claim.

Similar remarks apply to the resolution of ambiguity. Again, instances of this turn out to be fairly common in legal texts, further buttressing our contention that legal speech act interpretation must be inferential. Yet, these are again compatible with Marmor's claim, since the process of disambiguation can be reasonably described as a matter of inferring which one of two or more (homographic or homophonous) words or phrases was uttered rather than of inferring meaning beyond what is linguistically encoded.

---

14 In these and subsequent examples, we indicate the expressions at issue in bold.

Before examining some examples, we should note that our understanding of the term "ambiguity" here, based on its use in linguistics, is much narrower than its ordinary or legal use. We will say that an utterance is ambiguous only if it corresponds to a string (of graphemes or phonemes) that bears more than one linguistic meaning. This ambiguity may be "lexical," involving the meanings associated with a particular word, as is the case for both *case* and *bat* in (6a); or structural, involving the meanings associated with a particular phrase, as is the case for the phrase *those fleeing ISIL terrorists* in (6b):

(6) a. I've made the **case** for your **bat**.

b. "I welcome President Obama's pledge to [...] get aid to **those fleeing ISIL terrorists**."

(David Cameron, 8 August 2014)

= 'I welcome President Obama's pledge [...] to get aid to those who are fleeing ISIL terrorists'; or

= 'I welcome President Obama's pledge to [...] get aid to those ISIL terrorists who are fleeing'.[15]

From our own investigation of legal texts, we have found both forms of ambiguity to be quite common. It is easy to find statutes that make use of lexically ambiguous expressions, such as *banking*, as in (7):

(7) "An Act to make provision about **banking**" (*Banking Act* 2009)

And while there is very little doubt in this and many other cases about the relevant sense of the word in question, it is still true that the word *banking* in (7) can in principle mean 'the business conducted or services offered by a bank'; 'an embankment or artificial bank'; 'the tilt of (e.g.) a plane in making a turn'; or 'the act of providing additional power for (a train) in ascending an incline' (*Oxford English Dictionary*). The absence of doubt about the likely meaning of (7) just shows that the inference involved in eliminating the other meanings from consideration is performed easily and automatically.

Instances of structural ambiguity, while perhaps just as common in legal texts as those of lexical ambiguity, may often go unnoticed, just as they do

---

15 There also appears to be a further restrictive/non-restrictive ambiguity associated with the phrase *those fleeing ISIL terrorists*. Moreover, Cameron's actual statement, which we have shortened for the sake of simplicity, was "I welcome President Obama's pledge to help the Iraqi government tackle this crisis and get aid to those fleeing ISIL terrorists," which admits of still further readings, which we leave for interested readers to determine.

in ordinary speech – until they result in different understandings of the same utterance. In the legal context, this, of course, often gives rise to a lawsuit. This was true in the case of *Maersk Drilling USA, Inc. v. Transocean Offshore Deepwater Drilling, Inc.* (2012),[16] which revolved around two different interpretations of the phrase in an American statute, as given in bold below:

(8) "Except as otherwise provided in this title, whoever without authority **makes, uses, offers to sell, or sells any patented invention, within the United States** or imports into the United States any patented invention during the term of the patent therefor, infringes the patent."
(35 USC § 271(a))

Because the sale was negotiated in Scandinavia, the question came down to whether "offers to sell" fell within the scope of "within the US."

Such instances of structural ambiguity, which typically come to light only when a disagreement arises as to which reading of a phrase should prevail, certainly indicate that determining utterance meaning involves inferential work and not merely linguistic "decoding." This is true whether the authors of a given legal text have actually been aware that two or more meanings are available and have intended to convey only one or have simply been unaware of the availability of more than one meaning; this is because in either case the hearer must still infer which of the available meanings the authors have intended.[17]

---

16 This case is discussed by Liberman (2013).
17 Alternatively, the authors of a legal text might have no specific intention regarding which of the two meanings is to govern. This could arise, for example, as a way of reaching a compromise on a contentious provision. (Such cases might be seen to involve the phrasal counterparts of deliberately vague single-word expressions like *jurisdiction*, as described earlier.) Such strategic considerations are arguably a common aspect of the drafting of legislation, contracts, and other legal texts, raising the question of whether the goal of the interpreter of an ambiguous legal utterance is always to infer the intended speaker meaning.

There are certainly cases where this is not the goal. One is the interpretation of ambiguous contracts, where the common law "*contra proferentem*" ('against the offeror') rule applies to resolve ambiguities in favor of the party that did not draft a contract. As Sorenson (2001: 412) points out, this rule applies "even if the speaker proves that he intended" the other reading. Another is (at least some instances of) "dynamic" statutory and constitutional interpretation, such as *Re B.C. Motor Vehicle Act* (1985). In this case, the Supreme Court of Canada disregarded parliamentary committee evidence of the intended meaning of the expression "fundamental justice" in the *Canadian Charter of Rights and Freedoms*, arguing that legislative intent related to the Charter was "a fact which is nearly impossible of proof" (para. 52) and that relying on such historical evidence might "stunt [the] growth" of the "newly planted 'living tree' which is the *Charter*" (para. 53).

Nevertheless, as we have already noted, such cases can still be thought to revolve around determination of the linguistically encoded meaning of the sentences uttered and thus as consistent with Marmor's claim.

However, many other kinds of underspecification, to be described in what follows, appear to be incompatible with Marmor's claim in that their resolution requires the interpreter of a legal text to make inferences that cannot plausibly be seen as determining meaning that goes beyond what is linguistically encoded. One such form of underspecification is that involving "missing constituents," as illustrated by the sentences in (9), which look as though they are missing a constituent relative to the logical form of the proposition they are understood to express:

(9) a. Paracetamol is suitable.
　　b. He is ready.
　　c. This milk is sufficient. (see Carston 2002: 22)

Thus, in interpreting (9a–c), the hearer must infer, respectively, what it is that paracetamol is suitable for, what he is ready for, and what the milk is sufficient for. According to our own (informal) investigations, occurrences of words like *suitable*, *ready*, and *sufficient* with "missing constituents" appear to be quite rare in legal texts. When these words occur, they typically have a complement that specifies what the subject is suitable for, ready for, and the like, as is the case in (10), where *for immediate maneuver* is the complement of *ready*:

(10) "Every vessel shall proceed at a safe speed adapted to the prevailing circumstances and conditions of restricted visibility. A power-driven vessel shall have her engines **ready** for immediate manoeuvre." (*Collision Regulations*, Schedule 1: *International Regulations for Preventing Collisions at Sea, 1972*, with Canadian Modifications)

It is possible, however, to find examples in which the intended complement is implicit and thus must be inferred. These include the following examples from

---

The existence of such cases might, however, be reconciled after all with our claim that the process of inferring speaker meaning is central to legal interpretation. This would involve appealing to the distinction between interpretation proper and "creative" decision-making and seeing such rulings as involving departures from the results of the former process for the purpose of advancing certain institutional goals in the latter. Since further discussion of the complex issues involved here would take us too far afield, we will leave this for another occasion.

the Canadian *Criminal Code* of *suitable* and *adequate*, as is given in (11); and *sufficient*, as given in (12):

(11) "Every one commits an offense who (a) by wilful neglect causes damage or injury to animals or birds while they are being driven or conveyed; or (b) being the owner or the person having the custody or control of a domestic animal or a bird or an animal or a bird wild by nature that is in captivity, abandons it in distress or wilfully neglects or fails to provide **suitable and adequate** food, water, shelter and care for it." (s. 446(1))

(12) a. "Except where otherwise expressly provided by law, a court, judge, justice or provincial court judge before whom anything that is seized under this section is brought may declare that the thing is forfeited, in which case it shall be disposed of or dealt with as the Attorney General may direct if no person shows **sufficient cause** why it should not be forfeited." (s. 199(3))

b. "If an accused alleges that he or she believed that the complainant consented to the conduct that is the subject-matter of the charge, a judge, if satisfied that there is **sufficient evidence** and that, if believed by the jury, the evidence would constitute a defense, shall instruct the jury, when reviewing all the evidence relating to the determination of the honesty of the accused's belief, to consider the presence or absence of reasonable grounds for that belief." (s. 265(6))

In the provision given in (11), clause (b) makes it is an offense to fail to provide food, water, shelter, and care that is suitable and adequate for (roughly) the well-being of the animal in question. That is, *suitable and adequate* must be "enriched" to (something like) 'suitable and adequate for the reasonable maintenance of the pet's well-being'.[18] In the provisions given in (12a) and (12b), the expressions *sufficient cause* and *sufficient evidence* are respectively understood as something like 'sufficient cause to provide a legal basis' and 'sufficient evidence to establish that the accused had a reasonable belief in the complainant's consenting to the conduct'.

---

[18] Of course, it is fair to ask just what this provision requires in order avoid contravening it: must the food, water, shelter and care be sufficient only to keep the animal alive, or in good condition, or something else? Presumably the legislature intended to leave this somewhat open (as in the case of *jurisdiction* discussed earlier) and further determined through judicial interpretation. Regardless of the ultimate answer to such questions, the intended content of the law clearly goes beyond the linguistic meaning of the words *suitable* and *adequate* themselves and accordingly must be inferred.

As regards *sufficient cause* in (12a), it might be argued this expression is a kind of legal shorthand, which in practice involves a "short-circuiting" of the inferential process. While this might be true, it actually supports the claim that the expression was originally the result of a full-fledged inference. However, even if we grant such a "short-circuiting" analysis for the occurrence of *sufficient cause* in (12a), such an analysis is a rather implausible one for *sufficient evidence* in (12b), where a full-fledged inference is clearly necessary. This is because the "sufficiency" of evidence in question – that is, its kind, quality, and quantity – is quite specific to this provision, and is even further specified to be of a kind such "that, if believed by the jury [...] would constitute a defense." This means, then, that the sufficiency of the evidence in question is relative to these specific purposes and must be worked out on the basis of the information provided in this provision and elsewhere, including the case law (as well as ordinary "common sense"). This, it should be noted, is also true of *sufficient cause* in (12a).

In sum, what is communicated in these "missing constituent" examples obviously goes beyond the linguistically encoded meaning of the words uttered. However, like the "indexical" examples described earlier, these examples are considered by most pragmatics researchers to involve no more than a "filling in" of values (or "saturation") that is necessary for the sentences associated with them to express a proposition.[19] As it happens, there are many other cases of linguistically underdetermined legislative content that provide even more compelling evidence of the need for inference in legal interpretation. These are ones, as we will illustrate below, in which the words of a legislative provision might unambiguously encode a proposition, but not the one intended by the speaker. Thus, arriving at the latter must involve inferential enrichment of the encoded proposition.

Such cases include those in which a sentence contains a quantifier expression such as *all*, *some*, *most*, *somewhere*, and *nothing*, which indicate what proportion of some class of entities under consideration a claim applies to. More technically speaking, this class of entities is the "domain" that a quantifier "ranges over," and the "entities" in question may be individuals, places, and times, among others. Arguably, most uses of quantifier expressions in ordinary

---

[19] As it happens, this claim about the necessity of such "saturation" for a proposition to be expressed has been challenged by some researchers, who have claimed that the decoded words of the utterance themselves suffice for a minimal proposition; on this, see Korta and Perry (to appear) as the claim applies to indexicals, and the work of semantic "minimalists" such as Borg (2004) as it applies to "missing constitutents." Even if these researchers are right that decoding alone can result in a minimal proposition, the "indexical" and "missing constituent" cases in statutes strongly suggest that the proposition expressed can (and, we speculate, generally does) go beyond the content of the decoded words of the utterance.

speech, such as *nothing* in (13), involve an implicit "restriction" of the quantifier's domain, so that the speaker's assertion that she has nothing to wear is implicitly "restricted" – for example, to things suitable for wearing to job interviews (or perhaps a particular job interview) – and does not range over absolutely all things.

(13) I've got nothing to wear.

However, Parmenides' claim in (14) reminds us that quantifiers may sometimes be intended and interpreted as unrestricted and as ranging over absolutely all types of things:

(14) Nothing comes from nothing.

If we return now to legislative texts, we can easily find cases of explicit quantifier domain restriction, such as that given in (15), from a Canadian provision:

(15) **Every motor vehicle** with a GVWR of 4 536 kg or less [...] and **every tire rim** manufactured for use on those vehicles shall conform to the requirements of Technical Standards Document No. 110, Tire Selection and Rims for Motor Vehicles With a GVWR of 4,536 kg or Less (TSD 110), as amended from time to time.
(Motor Vehicle Safety Regulations (Canada), s. 110(1))

Yet, further investigation reveals many examples of quantifier expressions that plausibly involve implicit domain restriction. These include very clear cases, such as the following one (from the same regulations just quoted):

(16) "A System A mirror and a System B mirror shall be tested as follows: [...]
(b) **every mirror** shall be adjusted in accordance with the manufacturer's recommendations to the driver's eye position and is not to be moved or readjusted during testing for that eye position but may be readjusted for subsequent tests for different eye positions [...]"
(Motor Vehicle Safety Regulations, s. 111(25))

Here the intended domain of the quantifier is not all mirrors in the world, but "System A" and "System B" mirrors installed on school buses. Although that can be worked out from the linguistic context here – what is sometimes called the "co-text" – it still needs to be inferred.

Other cases of implicit domain restriction include ones like *every one* in the following provision, which cannot be inferred on the basis of a provision's immediate co-text:

(17) "**Every one** is a party to an offense who
 (a) actually commits it;
 (b) does or omits to do anything for the purpose of aiding any person to commit it; or
 (c) abets any person in committing it." (Canadian *Criminal Code*, s. 21(1))

At first sight, this provision might seem to apply to absolutely all people. Yet, on further reflection, we can see that it applies only to those subject to the criminal laws of the jurisdiction that enacted them, in this case Canada, and thus as restricted with respect to jurisdiction, geography, and even age.[20] Such cases of implicit domain restriction might in turn lead us to recognize it as a feature not only of examples like (17) but also of examples like (15), since in each case there must be an implicit geographical restriction on the entities subject to the provision.

These examples of implicit quantifier domain restriction provide additional evidence in favor of our claim that inference is a key part of legal interpretation, since the intended restriction is not given and must therefore be inferred. Do they also tell against Marmor's claim? We believe that they do, on the view that such cases are best handled as ones in which the logical form of the proposition expressed has a constituent, namely, the restrictor, with no corresponding constituent in the syntactic structure of the sentence uttered. However, Marmor's claim would be compatible with these examples of implicit quantifier domain restriction on the alternative analysis (e.g. Stanley 2000) according to which every quantifier brings to the linguistic structure a covert "slot" or variable corresponding to the domain, and that inferring the restriction is a matter of filling in this "slot."

There has been a great deal of debate in the pragmatics literature about the analysis of various kinds of sentences that lack any overt linguistic material corresponding to certain understood constituents. These, even more clearly than the cases of implicit domain restriction just described, make our point against Marmor's claim. They include cases like (18), which involves what has been called "free enrichment":

---

[20] More specifically, the *Criminal Code*, s. 13 provides that "[n]o person shall be convicted of an offence in respect of an act or omission on his part while that person was under the age of twelve years."

(18) I've often been at the Korean ambassador's parties, but I've never had kimchi. (based on Wilson and Sperber 2002: 611)

An utterance of (18) might convey either that the speaker has never had kimchi in her life or that she has never had kimchi at the Korean ambassador's parties; in the latter case, the proposition expressed seems to have been "freely enriched," indicating a place of eating for which the sentence itself has no corresponding constituent.

The analysis of sentences like (18), like those involving implicit domain restriction, remains a matter of debate between the same two positions, which treat them, respectively, as lacking corresponding constituents in linguistic structure and as having such (albeit unpronounced) constituents, which must be assigned values. In the latter case, this idea would mean that, for example, the pronounced [have had kimchi] would be accompanied by unpronounced variables for time, place, and perhaps manner of eating. There are, however, good reasons to think that this "variable" approach cannot be right for all cases (Carston 2000: 36; Wilson and Sperber 2002: 611ff.; Recanati 2012: 186). Generally, we believe, following Pietroski (2010: 267), that while linguistic expressions may encode such implicit variables, their occurrence is not sufficient "to track all the ways in which truth can depend upon context." What nevertheless remains true regardless of which of the two approaches is correct is that the hearer must infer the interpretation intended, given that the information needed for interpretation does not occur explicitly in the speaker's utterance.

Two other kinds of case where the sentence uttered lacks overt linguistic material corresponding to certain understood constituents involve what have been called "narrowing" and "broadening" in the pragmatics literature. These are illustrated in (19a) and (19b), respectively:

(19) a. John's a man.
b. France is hexagonal. (Wilson 2003: 345; Austin 1975: 143)

In certain contexts, the more likely reading of (19a) is one that involves "narrowing": that John has some property more specific than that of being an adult male human being, namely, that of being a (stereo)typical or ideal male adult. As this example shows, "narrowing" involves arriving at a more specific concept than the lexically encoded sense of some term such as *man*, so that the extension of the occasion-specific sense is, as a proper subset of the extension of the lexically encoded concept, narrower than the latter extension. The standard reading of (19b), exemplifying the converse process of "broadening," is that whereby

France is more or less hexagonal, so that the property being predicated of it is "broader" or less specific than hexagonal shape as strictly construed.

Of course, the phenomena of free enrichment, narrowing, and broadening are of interest to us here because of their possible occurrence in legal interpretation. As we will see, they both turn out to figure crucially (if perhaps not commonly) in the interpretation of legislation, again providing compelling evidence for the role of inference in such interpretation. Although these phenomena have been treated as distinct in the pragmatics and philosophy of language literature, both are cases in which underdetermination of the proposition expressed is purely pragmatic. In other words, in neither case can the hearer determine the speaker's intended proposition merely by resolving linguistic ambiguities through a choice of one or another available linguistic structure, or by assigning referents to indexical elements and filling in "slots" in a linguistic structure (cf. Neale 2004 on "pragmatic ellipsis"). A further reason for treating these types of case together is that they are difficult to distinguish in the legal examples that we will be considering.

Arguably, free enrichment or narrowing are institutionalized in legal interpretation in the technique of "reading down," which Sullivan (2008: 165) describes as "add[ing] words of restriction or qualification" to legislation. Of course, this technique does not involve literally adding words to legislation but rather interpreting it as if such words had been added. A clear illustration of this technique is given in the Canadian case *Montreal (City) v. 2952–1366 Québec Inc.* (2005), which hinged on the following provision in a city by-law:

(20) [T]he following noises, where they can be heard from the outside, are specifically prohibited:
(1) noise produced by sound equipment, whether it is inside a building or installed or used outside. (Montreal *By-law concerning noise*, art. 9(1))

In this case, the court interpreted *noise* in clause (1) as meaning "noise that interferes with the peaceful enjoyment of the environment" (Sullivan 2008: 166). This can be seen as an instance of either free enrichment, where a constituent is added whose meaning pertains to the effect of the prohibited noise; or narrowing, whereby the phenomenon expressed by *noise* is understood in a more restricted manner as a more specific kind of noise in accordance with the court's description. On either analysis, the proposition expressed is underdetermined by the words used and must be inferred by the interpreter of the text.

The same kind of inferential process – which can again be understood as either as free enrichment or narrowing – can be seen in instances of the application of traditional principles of legal interpretation such as *noscitur a sociis* ('it is known from its associates'). According to this principle, the meaning conveyed by a particular word may be determined from the words accompanying it, where all of these words typically occur in lists. For example, in *Pengelly v. Bell Punch Co Ltd* (1964), the word *floors* in the following provision was understood as (something like) 'floors used for passage' and excluded a floor used solely for storage (Powell and Simmonds 2006: 143):[21]

(21) "floors, steps, stairs, passageways and gangways" (*Factories Act* 1961 (UK))

Legal instances of "broadening," whereby a meaning of an expression "broader" or less specific than its standard meaning is understood to be what the legislature itself meant (and not reached by a more creative act that serves, for example, to make the law constitutional), seem far rarer than cases of "narrowing," although plausible cases of this process do still emerge. One such case, a well-known application of the "Golden Rule" (whereby a court departs from the ordinary meaning of an expression in order to avoid an absurd result) is the British case *R v. Allen* (1872), which considered the following statutory provision in determining whether Allen, who was already married, had committed bigamy in engaging in a marriage ceremony with a woman called Harriet Crouch:

(22) "whosoever being married shall marry any other person during the lifetime of his spouse" (*Offences Against the Person Act 1861* (UK))

Allen's defense was that he had not succeeded in marrying Crouch, since someone who is already married cannot marry, and so had not committed bigamy by the terms of the statute. Of course, on this argument no bigamous "marriage" would ever be illegal, and the statute would become a dead letter. The court's solution was to construe *marry* as 'go through the marriage ceremony' (Holland and Webb 2003: 216). Worth noting here is that the court's "broadened" interpretation of *marry* can plausibly be seen as respecting not just the purpose of the law but also the legislature's intention-to-mean – which involved understanding, and intending, the use of *marry* in the provision in such a way as to make it an offense for people who were already married to engage in a marriage ceremony. After all, it is unclear how else the statute could make any sense.[22]

---

[21] Another legal example of "narrowing" is that at the heart of the Canadian "Persons" case, which hinged on the interpretation of the word *qualified Persons* in the *British North America Act*, s. 24. For discussion, see Shaer (2013: 289).

[22] Another case in which what the legislature meant by its legislation is plausibly understood as broader than the legislation's linguistic meaning is the interpretation of *speech* in the US constitution as something like self-expression, which notably includes such acts as flying (and perhaps burning) flags (Lawrence Solum, personal communication 2015).

The cases of free enrichment, narrowing, and broadening that we have just discussed are all clear examples of pragmatic inference in legal interpretation. They are also clear counterexamples to Marmor's claim, since they indicate the need of the legal interpreter to venture well beyond the syntactic and semantic features of the linguistic material itself in interpreting *noise, floors,* and *marry* as respectively conveying 'noise that interferes with the peaceful enjoyment of the environment', 'floors used for passage', and 'go through the marriage ceremony'.

Note that one who still wished to defend Marmor's claim would not be left without arguments to do so. One argument, in particular, would involve appealing to the distinction, introduced earlier, between "investigative" and "creative" processes in legal interpretation broadly construed, and claiming that these cases of free enrichment, narrowing, and broadening reflect creative acts of legal reasoning rather than investigations into what the legislature intended to communicate.

Yet, there is good reason to doubt the plausibility of this move, at least for some of the cases that we have discussed. As pointed out by many commentators, including Marmor (2011a), the legislature and the courts engage in a kind of strategic dialog. This means that what the legislature intends to communicate is constrained by how it expects its utterance to be interpreted – which includes its recognition that courts interpret what legislatures say in such a way that their interpretation extends beyond the strictly linguistic meaning of legislative utterances, and in particular by appealing to *noscitur a sociis*, "reading down," and other "extralinguistic" rules of legal interpretation. The text that a legislature creates thus reflects its members' anticipation of that fact; and the courts, in turn, take it as read that legislatures will know that the courts will interpret in this way, and so on.[23] This suggests that the inferential processes of free enrichment, narrowing, and broadening are, at least in some cases, better seen not as part of a court's creative decision-making but as part of its basic interpretative work, which it undertakes in the reasonable anticipation that a legislature, in crafting legislation, is responding to interpretative decisions that courts have previously made.

---

23 An obvious parallel can thus be drawn between this "dialogic" interaction between legislatures and courts and Grice's schema for working out conversational implicatures, which he formulates as follows:

'He has said that p; there is no reason to suppose that he is not observing the maxims, or at least the [Cooperative Principle]; he could not be doing this unless he thought that q; he knows (and knows that I know that he knows) that I can see that the supposition that he thinks that q *is* required; he has done nothing to stop me thinking that q; he intends me to think, or is at least willing to allow me to think, that q; and so he has implicated that q.' (Grice [1967] 1989: 31)

That such a "dialogic" interaction between legislatures and courts may indeed figure in legal interpretation is highlighted in *R. (Evans) v. Attorney General* (2015), a recent UK Supreme Court decision that dealt with the expression *reasonable grounds* in a provision of the *Freedom of Information Act 2000*. As Lord Neuberger pointed out in the decision's leading judgment, this statute was passed after two court decisions had ruled out as inappropriate certain grounds for making executive decisions, "[s]o it [was] not as if the[se] grounds [...] could have been unforeseen by Parliament" (para. 88), which would therefore not have counted them as "reasonable grounds." In other words, the legislature could, and indeed should, have anticipated how a court would interpret this expression given previous court decisions on closely related matters.

We can conclude this section, then, by reiterating its main point: namely, that there are very clear cases in which syntactically and semantically encoded content does not fully determine what the legislature has communicated, and a process of inferring this additional content is thus a necessary part of legal interpretation.

5 Inference and textualism

In the previous section, we presented detailed evidence in favor of our claim that the task of legal interpretation crucially involves inferring various aspects of author (or speaker) meaning. We considered this claim in relation to Marmor's claim that the content of legislative texts is determined by their linguistically encoded structure and meaning; and found that, taken as a whole, the evidence we presented cast substantial doubt on Marmor's claim.

In this section, we push our "intentional-inferential" claim further by investigating how it relates to (Perry's [2011] characterization of) the doctrine of legal interpretation known as "textualism." Before we do so, however, we might offer two caveats about "textualism" and Perry's analysis of it. One is that, for the purposes of legal as well as pragmatic analysis, this doctrine should probably be recognized as a moving target, which exists in a profusion of versions and which has also given rise to rather different understandings of even some of its main tenets – facts about it highlighted by studies with such titles as Tutt's (2013) "Fifty Shades of Textualism" and Nelson's (2005) "What is Textualism?."[24]

---

24 See, e.g. Shaer (2013) for some discussion about these and other difficulties in characterizing and understanding textualism.

The other caveat is that textualism, at least in most of its varieties, is best understood in normative terms, as a prescription about how legal interpretation *should* work, rather than a claim about how legal interpretation generally *does* work.

We will be addressing the first caveat simply by focussing on Perry's characterization, which is admirably clear, in the hope that the various other versions and understandings available do not significantly affect our conclusions. The second caveat may seem a more serious one, since it suggests that we and advocates of textualism may simply be talking past each other. We can, however, address this caveat, too, by observing that in order for textualism to be worthy of serious consideration as a doctrine of legal interpretation, it must be consistent with what we know about how interpretation actually works. Otherwise, it can hardly offer much insight into the interpretation of legislation or much guidance to jurists about how such interpretation should proceed.

About Perry's study itself, we might note that, in addition to clarifying and motivating textualism as a legal doctrine, it also shows how this doctrine can underwrite progressive interpretations of certain disputed expressions in the US Constitution, in particular, the Eighth Amendment's prohibition of "cruel and unusual punishments."

For our purposes, what is important about Perry's discussion is what it claims about the role in textualist doctrine of speaker intention and hearer inference and whether the doctrine is compatible with our own claims about these. Perry envisages a very limited role for hearer inference about speaker intention in legal interpretation, rehearsing textualism's emphasis on "ordinary" meaning without probing the ways in which this and other encoded legal content come to be shaped and elaborated in the process of legal interpretation.

5.1 "Meaning-textualism" and "conception-textualism"

A key result of Perry's examination of textualism is the distinction he draws between two understandings of the doctrine; these he dubs "meaning-textualism" (which he endorses) and "conception-textualism" (which he rejects). He defines the former as follows:

> the view that the content of a statute is determined by the words in the text of the statute, given the meaning that those words had at the time of enactment or ratification, or, in the case of ambiguity, those meanings or senses, among those the words had at the time, which the enactors intended to exploit and the ratifiers understood the text as written to be using. (2011: 106)

The latter, "conception-textualism," Perry defines as follows:

> the view that the conceptions that the enactors had of the states, conditions, phenomena, and the like referred to by their words, used with their commonly understood meanings, in the operative senses, are determinative [of the statute's content].
>
> (Perry 2011: 106)

As Perry (2011: 107) points out, for the former variety of textualism, "it is the *sense* of the words that was originally operative [...] that is at issue" for the enactors of legislation, whereas for the latter variety it is the enactors' conceptions of what is "referred to by their words."

This difference between meaning-textualism and conception-textualism is reflected, in turn, in what Perry calls the "functional" and "fixed" varieties of interpretation respectively licensed by them. Perry explains these varieties of interpretation by considering the example of the following (fictitious) legislative prohibition:[25]

(23) "Endangered species shall not be hunted." (Perry 2011: 114)

On a functional interpretation of *endangered species,* the particular set of species that this expression picks out may vary over the time the legislation in question is in force. Accordingly, "hunting for minks might be prohibited, by the original meaning of the statute, even though at the time it was enacted it did not outlaw the hunting of minks, and was even part of legislation that licensed hunting for them" (Perry 2011: 114). By contrast, on a fixed interpretation of this expression, what the expression would mean is that it is "the set of species that are endangered at the time of the legislation that cannot be hunted, even if they cease to be endangered, or if other species come to be endangered" (Perry 2011: 114). It is on the basis of such considerations that Perry concludes that conception-textualism is "confused, implausible, and unworkable" as an approach to legal interpretation.

Perry's rejection of conception-textualism is consistent with our own claims about utterance content. According to modern inferential-intentional views of communication, including ours, what is expressed by the use of a word is (in normal cases) the concept that the speaker intends to convey by that use of the word or words used. Other mental representations of the speaker – which might include beliefs about what might be in that concept's extension – are not the target of utterance interpretation. In the legislative examples of the expressions

---

25 This is based on an example from Dworkin (1997: 121).

reasonable grounds and *noise* that we discussed earlier, we can say that an interpreter arrives at the relevant meanings of these expressions by working out the legislature's intended sense of these expressions. Now this task *may* include assessing whether a particular event or thing indeed falls under the intended sense. It is worth emphasizing, though, that on our view, this assessment is primarily the task of the interpreter and not the legislator: legislators may well have certain referents of an expression in mind when they enact legislation, but these are not determinative of the legislation's utterance content.

Also consistent with our view of legal interpretation – in particular, that it "exploit[s] at least some of the same abilities used in other varieties of verbal communication" (Wilson 2011: 70) – is Perry's assertion that meaning-textualism "seems to apply to statutes the same apparatus we use to determine what some individual says when they are talking to us" (Perry 2011: 107). We also agree with Perry that a statute's legal speech act content is (in general) precisely what it *says* – that is, "statutes prohibit or allow what the person who uttered the words, at the time they were enacted, said was prohibited or allowed" (Perry 2011: 107).

Where we part company with Perry, however, is in the role that we see for speaker intentions in fixing this legal utterance content. Perry restricts this to selecting among preexisting senses of ambiguous expressions, that is, to disambiguation. He claims that the kinds of word meanings relevant to legal interpretation "will typically be among the meanings a good dictionary of the time will explain"[26] and that what thus guides legal interpretation "is what we learn about a word in a specific text by looking up the meaning of the word in a dictionary, and, if more than one meaning is given, by figuring out which one is employed" (Perry 2011: 107).

As we have discussed earlier, speaker intentions (and their inferential recovery by interpreters) appear to play a much broader role than this, in cases such as the use of *noise* to express 'noise that interferes with the peaceful enjoyment of the environment', *floors* to express 'floors used for passage', and *marry* to express 'go through the marriage ceremony'. If we are right about these cases, then Perry's meaning-textualism must be wrong.

The problem for Perry is simply this: that the picture of interpretation that he has sketched allows for no departure from the assignment to words of their "ordinary" meanings save for "special meaning[s]" indicated for terms "in the text itself" (Perry 2011: 106) or, Perry might have added, in the case law and doctrinal statements. However, as we have noted, there are many varieties of

---

[26] We take it that the hedge "typically" is intended to allow for the possibility that even good dictionaries may fail to record all the conventional senses of ambiguous words.

textualism, and the late Justice Antonin Scalia himself, one of the chief architects of textualism, allowed for departures both from "what is said" and from the dictionary meaning of statutory language. Since Perry's analysis of textualism addresses Justice Scalia's understanding of this doctrine specifically (see Perry 2011: 105–107), it seems only reasonable to consider Justice Scalia's own exceptions to textualist dictates.

Justice Scalia's writings about textualism recognize, for example, that "context is everything" and in particular that constitutional interpretation involves "giv[ing] words and phrases an expansive rather than narrow interpretation," thereby licensing the interpretation of the words *speech* and *press* "as a sort of synecdoche for the whole" of "communicative expression" (Scalia 1997: 37–38). This suggests – notwithstanding Perry's view – that some form of textualism might be compatible after all with the kinds of pragmatic enrichment of word meanings described in the previous section.

Justice Scalia's writings also recognize a need for the correction of "scrivener's errors" "where on the very face of the statute it is clear to the reader that a mistake of expression [...] has been made" (Scalia 1997: 20). Such cases can be seen as analogous to those of misspeaking in ordinary conversation, as illustrated in (24), where the speaker has clearly meant to say *pigeons* but has said *penguins* instead:

(24)   Those penguins we were feeding yesterday are back.

Of course, it might be objected that admitting such exceptions into textualist doctrine renders the doctrine incoherent, since they contradict the textualist tenet that "[t]he text is the law, and it is the text that must be observed" (Scalia 1997: 22). In response, one could say that the same objection that applies, for example, to the correction of scrivener's errors would also apply to the recognition of misspeaking in conversation, since here, too, the interpreter apparently disregards the speaker's words in favor of an intention-to-mean inconsistent with these words. Yet, in each case, the inference that the speaker has intended to say what she has in fact said is defeasible; this fact allows the hearer to make additional inferences in order to reconcile the *prima facie* incompatibility between the speaker's words and what the speaker most plausibly intended to convey.

It must still be recognized, however, that a tension does exist in textualist doctrine between accommodating such mismatches between what legislation says and what it is intended to convey, on the one hand, and maintaining the authority and predictability of the legal system, on the other, including the delicate balance that this system seeks to strike between legislative and judicial authority. This tension may account both for the discomfort expressed by Justice Scalia and other textualists for "certain presumptions and rules of construction that load the dice for or against a particular result," such as the "rule of lenity" (which resolves ambiguities in criminal statutes in a defendant's favor), and for the debates that continue to surround the treatment of such matters as scrivener's errors and the "Absurdity Doctrine" (e.g. Manning 2003; Doerfler 2016). Arguably, this tension exists not only within textualism but very generally in jurisprudence that addresses such tensions, such as the treatment of different categories of "error," which allow the "correction" of some but not other kinds of "error."[27]

The upshot of these considerations is that while textualist doctrine may draw no clear line between permissible and impermissible pragmatic enrichments of linguistically encoded meaning, the more it permits such enrichments, the less sure its commitment becomes to preventing judicial encroachment on the legislative domain. Yet, if the pragmatic processes of enrichment that we have described are an inevitable part of legal interpretation cognitively speaking, then restraining such judicial encroachment by ruling out such processes would be misguided in any case.

6 Conclusion

We think that we have shown in this study that the interpretation of both legal speech acts and the speech acts in ordinary conversation are of the same general kind – or that we have at least shifted the burden onto anyone who would claim otherwise.

Our discussion began with an explanation of the role of speaker intentions in standard approaches in pragmatics, whereby certain speakers' intentions normally determine what the speaker means by an utterance. Since intentions are not available to hearers, these intentions, which (in general) constitute the meaning of the utterance, must be inferred by the hearer from the material that the speaker utters.

We argued that this position applies straightforwardly to legal interpretation. In particular, we pointed out that legal texts, like virtually all verbal utterances, contain linguistically ambiguous expressions and that some of these expressions

---

[27] For example, as Sullivan (2008: 177) observes, courts have historically distinguished between "drafting errors" and "gaps in a legislative scheme" and have the authority to "correct" the former but not to "cure" the latter.

are clearly intended to convey one sense and not another, a fact that must therefore be inferred. We also adduced several types of counterexample to Marmor's (2008) claim that legal speech act content is determined by what the linguistic material uttered encodes. These counterexamples included ones involving the resolution of indexical expressions and of "missing constituents," "free enrichment" and "narrowing" (which in their legal guises took the form of "reading down" and the application of the *noscitur a sociis* rule), and "broadening." The logic of our argument was that if any of these kinds of counterexamples do exist, then Marmor's claim could not be correct; and we took the *noscitur a sociis* and broadening cases to be particularly good counterevidence to his claim.

We next investigated the implications of our claims about the role in legal interpretation of speaker intention and hearer inference for the legal doctrine of textualism as described in Perry (2011). What we argued was that the role of these went far beyond the limited one that Perry has envisaged, and thus that textualism, at least as he has characterized it, does not sufficiently recognize the importance in legal interpretation of various processes of pragmatic enrichment of encoded linguistic content.

We believe, then, that we have offered a very compelling case for rejecting the idea of legal interpretation as a *sui generis* phenomenon and for treating it as a variety (albeit a rather distinctive one) of verbal communication. Admittedly, though, we might not have dispelled the doubts of some readers that we have ignored substantial differences between legal utterance interpretation, on the one hand, and both face-to-face and various kinds of written communication, on the other.

We have said that the utterance content of legal instruments rarely if ever includes implicatures, and have argued elsewhere (Allott and Shaer, to appear) that legislative provisions do not have the implied speech act force of orders, contra Searle (1975), Marmor (2008), and others. Moreover, we have noted in this study that implicitly restricted quantifiers and "missing constituent" cases, though common in normal talk, are relatively rare in legislative texts, although we did not offer any explanation of these differences.

Although we must leave a detailed explanation for another occasion, we can briefly offer some reasons for these differences. One of these is that the interpretation of legislative and other legal texts relies less on information from context than do other forms of speech, including – indeed, in particular – face-to-face conversation. In other words, legislators know that they create laws for addressees who will often be distant from them in both space and time. Yet, this lesser reliance on inference cannot be plausibly attributed entirely to a lesser availability of shared context than in face-to-face conversation. Consider the interpretation of literary texts, where there is often little physical context shared by author and reader but where texts are nevertheless rich in implicatures and in such figures of speech as metaphor and irony.

We suggest that legislators are aware not just that the rich context typical of personal interactions is not available to guide interpretation but also that the stakes are high, and that they as speaker are a corporate entity rather than individuals. For these reasons, they seek to achieve a high level of explicitness and thus to minimize or perhaps even eliminate implicated content and implicit domain restrictions, among other such departures from encoded content. That legislators might thus seek to minimize or eliminate these elements from their texts cannot, however, be taken to suggest that they might also seek to entirely eliminate, for example, indexicals and ambiguity, since the elimination of the latter elements would not obviously be consistent with the use of natural language. Despite whatever efforts legislators do make, then, to minimize appeal to non-encoded content, there nevertheless remains, as we have suggested, a considerable amount of content that must be inferred by the legal interpreter.

References

Allott, Nicholas. 2013. Relevance theory. In Alessandro Capone, Franco Lo Piparo & Marco Carapezza (eds.), *Perspectives on linguistic pragmatics*, 57–98. Cham: Springer.

Allott, Nicholas. 2016. Misunderstandings in verbal communication. In Andrea Rocci & Louis de Saussure (eds.), *Verbal communication*, 485–507. Berlin: Walter de Gruyter.

Allott, Nicholas & Benjamin Shaer. To appear. The illocutionary force of laws. *Inquiry*.

Allott, Nicholas & Mark Textor. To appear. Lexical modulation without concepts: Introducing the derivation proposal. *Dialectica*.

Asgeirsson, Hrafn. 2012. On the possibility of non-literal legislative speech. *Monash University Faculty of Law Legal Studies Research Paper No. 45* (available at SSRN).

Austin, John L. 1975. *How to do things with words*, 2nd edn. Oxford: Clarendon Press.

Bach, Kent. 2006. The top 10 misconceptions about implicature. In Betty J. Birner & Gregory L. Ward (eds.), *Drawing the boundaries of meaning: Neo-Gricean studies in pragmatics and semantics in honor of Laurence R. Horn*, 21–30. Amsterdam: John Benjamins.

Boghossian, Paul. 2014. What is inference? *Philosophical Studies* 169(1). 1–18.

Carston, Robyn. 2000. Explicature and semantics. *UCL Working Papers in Linguistics* 12. 1–46.

Carston, Robyn. 2002. *Thoughts and utterances: The pragmatics of explicit communication*. Oxford: Blackwell.

Carston, Robyn. 2012. Word meaning and concept expressed. *The Linguistic Review* 29(4). 607–624.

Chomsky, Noam. 2000. *New horizons in the study of language and mind*. Cambridge: Cambridge University Press.

Doerfler, Ryan. D. 2016. The scrivener's error. *Northwestern Law Review* 110(4). 811–857.

Dworkin, Ronald. 1997. Comment. In Antonin Scalia, *A matter of interpretation: Federal courts and the law*. Princeton: Princeton University Press.

Endicott, Timothy. 1994. Putting interpretation in its place. *Law and Philosophy* 13(4). 451–479.
Endicott, Timothy. 2012. Legal interpretation. In Andrei Marmor (ed.), *Routledge companion to philosophy of law*, 109–122. Oxford: Routledge.
Greenawalt, Kent. 2010. *Legal interpretation: Perspectives from other disciplines and private texts*. New York: Oxford University Press.
Grice, H. Paul. 1957. Meaning. *The Philosophical Review* 66. 377–388.
Grice, H. Paul. 1989 [1967]. Logic and conversation: William James lectures. In *Studies in the way of words*, 1–143. Cambridge, MA: Harvard University Press.
Grice, H. Paul. 2001. *Aspects of reason*. Oxford: Clarendon Press.
Holland, James A. & Julian S. Webb. 2003. *Learning legal rules: A students' guide to legal method and reasoning*, 5th edn. Oxford: Oxford University Press.
Korta, Kepa & John Perry. 2006. Pragmatics. In Edward N. Zalta (ed.), *The Stanford encyclopedia of philosophy*, Summer 2006 edn. http://plato.stanford.edu/entries/pragmatics/ (accessed 7 May 2015).
Korta, Kepa & John Perry. To appear. Full but not saturated: The myth of mandatory primary pragmatic processes. In Sarah-Jane Conrad & Klaus Petrus (eds.), *Meaning, context, and methodology*. Berlin: De Gruyter Mouton.
Liberman, Mark. 2013. Legal scope again. *Language Log*. http://languagelog.ldc.upenn.edu/nll/?p=8161 (accessed 7 May 2015).
Manning, John F. 2003. The absurdity doctrine. *Harvard Law Review* 116(8). 2387–2486.
Marmor, Andrei. 2008. The pragmatics of legal language. *Ratio Juris* 21(4). 423–452.
Marmor, Andrei. 2011a. Can the law imply more than it says? On some pragmatic aspects of strategic speech. In Andrei Marmor & Scott Soames (eds.), *Philosophical foundations of language in the law*, 83–104. Oxford: Oxford University Press.
Marmor, Andrei. 2011b. Truth in law. *University of Southern California Legal Studies Working Paper Series*, 11-3. Reprinted as ch. 3 of Marmor (2014).
Marmor, Andrei. 2014. *The language of law*. Oxford: Oxford University Press.
Mercier, Hugo & Dan Sperber. 2009. Intuitive and reflective inferences. In Jonathan S. B. T. Evans & Keith Frankish (eds.), *In two minds: Dual processes and beyond*, 149–170. Oxford: Oxford University Press.
Perry, John. 2011. Textualism and the discovery of rights. In Andrei Marmor & Scott Soames (eds.), *Philosophical foundations of language in the law*, 105–129. Oxford: Oxford University Press.
Pietroski, Paul M. 2005. Meaning before truth. In Gerhard Preyer & Georg Peter (eds.), *Contextualism in philosophy: Knowledge, meaning, and truth*, 255–302. Oxford: Oxford University Press.
Pietroski, Paul M. 2010. Concepts, meanings and truth: First nature, second nature and hard work. *Mind & Language* 25(3). 247–278.
Powell, Amanda & Tony Simmonds. 2006. *Legal method*, 4th edn. London: College of Law.
Rayo, Agustin. 2013. A plea for semantic localism. *Noûs* 47(4). 647–679.
Raz, Joseph. 2001. Sorensen: Vagueness has no function in law. *Legal Theory* 7(4): 417–419.
Recanati, François. 2004. *Literal meaning*. Cambridge: Cambridge University Press.
Recanati, François. 2010. *Truth-conditional pragmatics*. Oxford: Oxford University Press.
Recanati, François. 2012. Compositionality, flexibility, and context-dependence. In Markus Werning, Wolfram Hinzen & Edouard Machery (eds.), *The Oxford handbook of compositionality*, 175–192. Oxford: Oxford University Press.
Scalia, Antonin. 1997. *A matter of interpretation: Federal courts and the law*. Princeton: Princeton University Press.

Searle, John R. 1975. Indirect speech acts. In Peter Cole & Jerry L. Morgan (eds.), *Speech acts*, 59–82. New York: Academic Press.
Searle, John R. 1976. A classification of illocutionary acts. *Language in Society* 5(1). 1–23.
Shaer, Benjamin. 2013. Toward a cognitive science of legal interpretation. In Michael Freeman & Fiona Smith (eds.) *Law and language: Current legal issues*, 259–291. Oxford: Oxford University Press.
Shaer, Benjamin & Nicholas Allott. To appear. Legal speech and the elements of adjudication. In Brian G. Slocum (ed.), *The nature of legal Interpretation: What jurists can learn about legal interpretation from linguistics and philosophy*. Chicago: University of Chicago Press.
Sorensen, Roy. 2001. Vagueness has no function in law. *Legal Theory* 7(4). 387–417.
Sperber, Dan. 2014. What scientific idea is ready for retirement? The standard approach to meaning. http://www.edge.org/response-detail/25378 (accessed 19 March 2014).
Sperber, Dan, Fabrice Clément, Christophe Heintz, Olivier Mascaro, Hugo Mercier, Gloria Origgi & Deirdre Wilson. 2010. Epistemic vigilance. *Mind & Language* 25(4). 359–393.
Sperber, Dan & Deirdre Wilson. 1986. *Relevance: Communication and cognition*. Oxford: Blackwell.
Sperber, Dan & Deirdre Wilson. 2008. A deflationary account of metaphors. In Raymond W. Gibbs (ed.), *The Cambridge handbook of metaphor and thought*, 84–108. New York: Cambridge University Press.
Sullivan, Ruth. 2008. *Sullivan on the Construction of Statutes*, 5th edn. Markham, Ontario: LexisNexis.
Wilson, Deirdre. 2011. Relevance and the interpretation of literary works. *UCL Working Papers in Linguistics* 23. 69–80.
Wilson, Deirdre & Dan Sperber. 2002. Truthfulness and relevance. *Mind* 111(443). 583–632.

Legislation and cases cited

35 USC § 271 – Infringement of patent.
Banking Act 2009 (UK), 2009, c. 1.
By-law concerning noise (Montreal), R.B.C.M. 1994, c. B-3.
Collision Regulations (Canada), C.R.C., c. 1416.
Constitution Act, 1867, 30 & 31 Victoria, c. 3 (UK).
Criminal Code (Canada), R.S.C. 1985, c. C-46.
Factories Act 1961 (UK), 1961, c. 34.
Freedom of Information Act 2000 (UK), 2000, c. 36.
Legislation Revision and Consolidation Act (Canada), R.S.C., 1985, c. S-20.
London Development Agency Act 2003 (UK), 2003, c. 1.
Montréal (City) v. 2952-1366 Québec Inc., 2005 SCC 62.
Motor Vehicle Safety Regulations (Canada), C.R.C., c. 1038.
Offences Against the Person Act 1861 (UK), 1861, c. 100.
Bankovic v. Belgium, 52207/99 [2001] ECHR 890.
Pengelly v. Bell Punch Co Ltd [1964] 1 WLR 1055.
R. (Evans) v. Attorney General [2015] UKSC 21.
R v. Allen (1872) LR 1 CCR 367.
Re B.C. Motor Vehicle Act [1985] 2 SCR 486.
Transocean Offshore Deepwater Drilling, Inc. v. Maersk Drilling USA, Inc., No. 11-1555 (Fed. Cir. 2012).

Brian G. Slocum
5 Pragmatics and legal texts: How best to account for the gaps between literal meaning and communicative meaning

1 Introduction

There are various ways to answer the constituent question of how to characterize the meaning of a legal text. At one extreme, the meaning of a legal text is synonymous with its literal meaning.[1] At the opposite extreme, the communicative meaning of a legal text is exogenous to its legal meaning. Instead, the legal meaning is determined in accordance with some other standard, such as the purpose of the provision, its intended meaning, or some notion of public good or morality. Between these two extremes reside numerous variations of how communicative meaning contributes (or does not) to legal meaning. In order to address the role of pragmatics in the interpretation of legal texts, this paper will first reject the notion that the meaning of a legal text can be constituted without its communicative meaning generally being (at the least) a constraint on permissible interpretations. The importance of this point is that if the communicative meaning of a legal text serves (at least) as a constraint on permissible interpretations, the components of communicative meaning, including the applicability of pragmatic theories of meaning, which involve inferential processes of reasoning that sometimes deviate from an utterance's conventional meaning, are of crucial importance to legal interpretation.

To be sure, the communicative meaning of a legal text is not always determinative of legal meaning. Even in situations not involving ambiguity or vagueness, where communicative meaning cannot be coextensive with legal meaning, the communicative meaning of a text may differ from its legal meaning. Flanagan (2010) argues that a particular case will always contain some circumstance not covered by the enactment, where that omission alone cannot determine the

---

[1] Talmage (1994) indicates that literal meaning is commonly identified with the conventional meaning of language. For the purposes of this paper, the term is used in a similar way that is essentially synonymous with the linguistic meaning of the relevant sentence that is conventional and context-independent.

Brian G. Slocum, University of the Pacific

DOI 10.1515/9781501504723-005

circumstance's relevance to whether the relevant interest should prevail. Thus, the text alone is never decisive because the circumstance, not contemplated by the enactment's meaning, may be controlling. Some of these circumstances have been formalized by courts, creating interpretive principles that are systematically recognized and which result in a legal text being given an interpretation that differs from its communicative meaning. For example, a legal text may otherwise mean p, but a judge will feel justified in believing that p was not intended if that interpretation would produce absurd results.[2]

Notwithstanding the non-decisive nature of communicative meaning, it should be readily accepted that, in general, the communicative meaning of a legal text serves (at least) as a constraint on permissible interpretations. Although various definitions are possible, for purposes of this paper the communicative meaning of a legal text is, roughly, synonymous with what an appropriate hearer would most reasonably take a speaker to be trying to convey in employing a given verbal vehicle in the given communicative-context.[3] Although they often correspond, communicative meaning is distinct from literal meaning, which is typically described as being a compositional one that accords with the primary or strict meanings of the words and is not figurative or metaphorical.[4] With legal texts, figurative or metaphorical meanings are obviously not applicable, but the literal meaning of an utterance can differ from its communicative meaning in ways other than through figurative language or metaphor. As will be seen, the distinction between communicative meaning and literal meaning is crucial to the proposition that pragmatic processes are relevant to legal interpretation.

In Part 2, I use Hart's (1958) famous vehicles in the park hypothetical to illustrate that legal interpretations are generally constrained by the communicative meaning of the relevant provision. The discussion is not meant to conclusively establish that legal interpretations are constrained by the linguistic meaning of the relevant provision but, rather, to offer an illustration of this paper's

---

[2] See Manning (2003) for a discussion of the absurdity doctrine.
[3] Communicative meaning is defined here as relying on an objective notion of intent, where the meaning is the one the appropriate hearer would most reasonably take the speaker to be expressing, which may differ from the meaning the speaker intends to express. In an earlier paper, (Slocum 2014), I rejected the intentionalist argument that the meaning of a legal text is constituted by the actual intentions of the draftor(s). Elaborating further on the distinction between communicative meaning and intentionalism is not essential to this paper, which seeks to examine different accounts of the gap between literal meaning and communicative meaning.
[4] "The principle of compositionality states that the meaning of a complex linguistic expression is built up from the meanings of its composite parts in a rule-governed fashion" (Murphy and Koskela 2010: 36).

assumption that legal interpretations are so constrained.[5] If such a proposition is accepted, it follows that identification of the components of communicative meaning is of crucial importance to legal interpretation. It should also follow that, absent some exceptions, the components of the communicative meaning of a legal text are similar to the components of communicative meaning generally. If so, it is often the case that the communicative meaning of a legal text is not synonymous with its literal meaning, as Part 2 discusses. In these situations, some linguistic phenomenon can be said to operate which can be described as pragmatic in character. As a consequence, it must be conceded that pragmatic processes are relevant to the interpretation of legal texts. As Part 2 discusses, contrary to the claims of some legal scholars, there are no good reasons to believe that these pragmatic processes do not include conversational implicatures in some cases. Part 3 describes the different approaches that can be taken when considering the relevance of pragmatic processes, such as conversational implicatures, to legal texts. Part 4 concludes that theories that provide default, ordinary meanings should be preferred to reductive approaches that attempt to explain linguistic phenomena in terms of deeper, underlying processes.[6] Rather than conclusively prove any of these arguments, this paper instead is meant only to offer a conceptualization of such issues and how they might best be analyzed.

2 Accounting for gaps between literal meaning and communicative meaning

2.1 Communicative meaning as a constraint on legal meaning

Using Hart's (1958: 607) famous hypothetical, consider a legal rule that "forbids you to take a vehicle into the public park." The word *vehicle*, like most other

---

[5] If one doubts that legal interpretations are, as a general matter, constrained by the linguistic meaning of the relevant provision, any gaps between literal meaning and communicative meaning would be of little interest, as the meaning given to a provision by a court would bear no necessary relationship to the conventional or specialized meanings of the words in the relevant text.

[6] The ordinary meaning doctrine stands for the concept that language in legal texts should be interpreted on the basis of general principles of language usage that apply equally outside of the law (Slocum 2014). Legal texts are widely viewed as a form of communication (McCubbins and Rodriguez 2011; Van Schooten 2007). Ideally, assuming that successful communication is the goal in most cases, these texts should be understood by different people in the same way. One aspect of this broad requirement is that legal texts should be understandable to the general public, as well as to judges and sophisticated practitioners. As Cappelen (2007: 19) explains, "[w]hen we articulate rules, directives, laws and other action-guiding instructions, we assume that people, variously situated, can grasp that content in the same way."

natural language terms, has a fuzzy extension, and questions will inevitably arise regarding the scope of the prohibition (Slocum 2015). Consider cases involving citations given to individuals for taking a motorized wheelchair and scooter into the park.[7] Suppose that the court deciding the cases believes that the 'purpose' of a legal provision should be the main criterion on which to base an interpretation. The court, reasonably, determines that the purpose of the provision is to enhance the safety of people using the park. The court concludes that a motorized scooter is a vehicle but a motorized wheelchair is not.[8] The court's decision would undoubtedly be controversial to some commentators but could be defended as being consistent with the communicative meaning of the legal text. The communicative meaning of a legal utterance often underdetermines its legal meaning, especially when vagueness is an issue. In situations where the extension of a concept (such as *vehicle*) must be determined, a borderline case presents a situation where there is no linguistic fact-of-the-matter to discover (Slocum 2015). A judge might determine that motorized scooters and motorized wheelchairs are at the borderline of the vehicle category and that either might be said to fall within or outside of the category. Thus, the judge might reasonably determine that the semantic meaning of the concept cannot determine the proper categorization of the object being considered (such as a wheelchair). Instead, the categorization decision must be based on other grounds, such as the purpose of the provision.

Suppose that a new case involves a citation given to a person for riding through the park on roller skates. The court learns that there have been several incidents where people riding through the park on roller skates have injured pedestrians. On the basis that the purpose of the provision is to enhance the safety of people using the park, the court determines that roller skates fall within the scope of the provision. Even more so than the two examples above (involving a motorized wheelchair and a scooter), many commentators would no doubt strongly criticize such a ruling. One objection would be that roller skates are not even borderline cases of vehicles and that the ordinary meaning of the term clearly does not include them. Such an objection might be correct, but even in such a situation the court, if it so desired, would be able to offer a linguistically based rationale for its decision (even if it is motivated by the purpose of the provision). The court, as often happens, could point to a broad

---

[7] In his paper, Hart (1958: 607) similarly asserts, "Plainly this forbids an automobile, but what about bicycles, roller skates, toy automobiles? What about airplanes?."
[8] Of course, there could be a number of characteristics that could change the result in a particular case, such as the size of the scooter, its use, etc.

dictionary definition (i.e., "any means in or by which someone travels or something is carried or conveyed; a means of conveyance or transport") and treat the definition as though it sets forth necessary and sufficient conditions for the concept.[9] Such an approach has been rightly criticized by scholars, including Solan (2010), because using the dictionary definition in such a way would be inconsistent with the ordinary meaning of the term. Nevertheless, the court's decision at least requires a non-minimal degree of semantic analysis to address its deficiencies.

Suppose that a later case involves a citation given to a person walking his dog through the park. There have been several dog attacks in the park (some might even say that it has been an epidemic), and the dog at issue is a member of the breed that has been responsible for the majority of the attacks. The court, considering purpose at a high level of generality, decides that the purpose of the provision, protection of park users, dictates that certain dangerous breeds of dogs fall within the scope of the provision. Similar to the roller skating case, the court's decision, even if well-meaning, would likely be harshly criticized by many commentators. Many of the objections to the decision, though, would be of a different character than those directed towards the decisions described above. Chiefly, commentators would allege that the court's decision fails to adhere to important rule of law principles, and these criticisms would be made even if the case did not involve a citation where notice would be particularly important. The commentary would reveal the widespread belief that the communicative meaning of a legal text generally constrains its possible interpretations (Duarte 2011). A dog (of any breed) is clearly not a vehicle, and there is no plausible argument that dogs are even borderline cases of vehicles.[10] This line of criticism would likely hold even if the court could find some evidence that the legislative intent was that "vehicle" in the provision should have a very broad meaning, perhaps even extending to things like dogs.

Even those advocating a purposive approach to interpretation that would reject textualist arguments about the primacy of communicative meaning agree that purposive reasoning is, in most cases, constrained by communicative meaning. The debates between purposivists and textualists generally focus on *motorized scooter*, *wheelchair*, and maybe even *roller skate* type cases, where commentators argue about whether there is linguistic uncertainty and, if so, how it should be

---

9 vehicle. Dictionary.com Unabridged. Random House, Inc. http://www.dictionary.com/browse/vehicle (accessed: May 02, 2016).
10 Of course, the issue might be closer if the dog was transporting someone (perhaps a small child) on its back. Nevertheless, it is not a controversial claim that there exist objects that clearly are not vehicles.

resolved. In such cases, those arguing in favor of the validity of the citations can at least make language-based arguments that the objects in question present borderline cases that should be resolved in favor of inclusion under the provision. In contrast, the *dog* case does not present such an opportunity for language-based argument, and in general this is sufficient to conclude that a citation is inappropriate.

As the above discussion illustrates, the communicative meaning of a sentence in a legal provision constrains in some way the legal meaning of the sentence. Notwithstanding that the literal meaning of a text is never by itself decisive of legal meaning, in determining the legal content of a text it must still be acknowledged that the communicative meaning is influential, if not decisive, in that determination. Courts in fact consistently purport to interpret plain and unambiguous statutory language according to its terms (Slocum 2014). An assertion that the court's decision in the *dog case* would be widely condemned should, therefore, not be controversial.

2.2 The three levels of meaning

If, as was illustrated above, the communicative meaning of a legal text is influential in the determination of its legal meaning, the components of communicative meaning are of significant importance to legal interpretation. In order to examine the components of communicative meaning, it is necessary to consider the distinctions made by scholars between *sentence meaning*, *what is said*, and *what is implicated* (Recanati 2004). Doing so implicates the distinction between *semantics* and *pragmatics*. There is considerable debate regarding the respective definitions and where the semantics/pragmatics borderline crosses for specific linguistic expressions. A long-standing view is that semantics accounts for linguistic phenomena by relating, via the rules of the language and abstracting away from specific contexts, linguistic expressions to the world objects to which they refer (Ariel 2010). Under this account, semantics is compositional and convention based, and sentence meanings are derived from a null context. A semantic meaning is thus one based on decoding and not intent-determining (Ariel 2010). In contrast to semantics, pragmatics is not compositional, accounts for linguistic phenomena by reference to the language user (producer or interpreter), and involves inferential processes (Ariel 2010). Context is thus centrally involved in explaining how pragmatics complements semantics. Pragmatics takes account of contextual factors, such as the mutual knowledge shared by the speaker and addressee, and the relevant unit is a sentence-context pair. Pragmatics is concerned with whatever information is relevant to understanding an utterance, even if such information is not reflected in the syntactic properties of the sentence.

Scholars disagree about the components of *sentence meaning, what is said* and *what is implicated*, but such disagreements are not relevant to the points raised in this paper. In any case, the terms can be put in a hierarchy of communication, as follows:

sentence meaning
vs.
what is said
vs.
what is implicated

Sentence meaning is conventional and context-independent. In contrast, one theory of *what is said* is that it corresponds to the primary truth-evaluable representation made available to the subject as a result of processing the utterance (Recanati 2004: 17). In turn, *what is communicated* involves what can be secondarily derived from *what is said*.

In order to fill in the details of *what is said* and *what is communicated*, Recanati (2004) distinguishes between two sorts of pragmatic processes.[11] The first, *primary pragmatic processes*, are contextual processes which are subpersonally (i.e., not the result of conscious processing) involved in the determination of *what is said*. Thus, they involve situations where the speech participants themselves are not distinctly aware of the processes through which the context-independent meanings of the expressions used are enriched or otherwise adjusted to fit the situation of use. In contrast to *primary pragmatic processes*, *secondary pragmatic processes* are *post-propositional*. *Secondary pragmatic processes* cannot take place unless some proposition p is considered as having been expressed, for they proceed by inferentially deriving some further proposition q (the implicature) from the fact that p has been expressed. *Primary pragmatic processes*, however, are *pre-propositional* because they do not presuppose the prior identification of some proposition serving as input to the process. *Secondary pragmatic processes* are conscious in the sense that normal interpreters are aware both of what is said and of what is implied and are capable of working out the inferential connection between them. They are ordinary inferential processes that take the interpreter from *what is said* to *what is communicated*, which is something that

---

[11] Some of the linguistic phenomena discussed below could be given a semantic rather than a pragmatic explanation (Slocum 2015). For the purposes of this paper, though, it is not necessary to address whether a given linguistic phenomenon should be given a semantic or pragmatic explanation. Rather, the paper assumes that the linguistic phenomena should be given pragmatic explanations and focuses on which pragmatic accounts are most explanatory. The reason for this treatment is that giving a semantic explanation of any of the linguistic phenomena would be consistent with the arguments in this paper.

"(under standard assumptions of rationality and cooperativeness) follows from the fact that the speaker has said what she has said" (17). The inferences thus correspond to further conscious representations inferentially derived from what is said. As such, the hearer must be able to recognize what is said and what is implied by saying it. *Primary pragmatic processes* are not conscious in that sense. Normal interpreters need not be aware of the context-independent meanings of the expressions used, nor of the processes through which those meaning are enriched or otherwise adjusted to fit the situation of use.[12]

2.3 Communicative meaning and primary pragmatic processes

Some linguistic phenomena, considered pragmatic by some, should uncontroversially be considered part of the communicative meaning of a legal text. Consider one of Recanati's (2004) examples below:

(1) Everybody went to Paris.

Literalism holds that universal quantifiers such as *any*, *everybody*, and *most* quantify over everything (Stojanovic 2008). Therefore, the literal meaning of (1) is that every existing person went to Paris. Even with little contextual evidence, though, the literal meaning of (1) is different from that which "untutored conversational participants" would ascribe to it (Recanati 2004: 11). Likely, the audience for (1) would restrict the application of the predicate by making it more contextually specific than its literal meaning. Consider, for example, that the speaker of (1) might have made the statement in a context that clearly indicates a reference to a subset of people, such as a class, club or family. Stojanovic (2008, 2012) notes that empirical data shows that the majority of speakers understand the restricted meaning of utterances such as (1) to be true. In Recanati's view, quantifier domain restriction is a pragmatic process because it involves the application of conditions on predicates that are not linguistically encoded. Furthermore, it is a *primary pragmatic process* because, unlike *secondary pragmatic processes*, it is *not* a conscious process in the sense that normal interpreters

---

[12] The arguments made in this paper do not strictly depend on distinguishing between primary and secondary pragmatic processes, as the arguments made do not depend on the distinction. Nevertheless, explaining the distinction helps to illustrate that the interpretation of legal texts depends on a variety of pragmatic processes, some of which (the primary pragmatic processes) are not typically the result of conscious processing.

are aware both of what is said and of what is implied and are capable of working out the inferential connection between them.[13]

Like the case generally, quantifiers are frequently used in legal texts. Unsurprisingly, considering the frequent inappropriateness of interpreting quantifiers consistently with their literal meanings, interpretive questions have been raised regarding their scope. At times the Supreme Court has exhibited a poor understanding of quantifiers, especially the linguistic reality that quantifier phrases have a certain domain that is typically restricted. One recent case illustrating this lack of linguistic understanding is *Ali v. Federal Bureau of Prisons*,[14] which involved the Federal Torts Claims Act. In § 1346(b)(1), the FTCA authorizes

> claims against the United States, for money damages [...] for injury or loss of property [...] caused by the negligent or wrongful act or omission of any employee of the Government while acting within the scope of his office or employment.[15]

The FTCA exempts from this waiver certain categories of claims, including an exception in § 2680(c) which provides that § 1346(b) does not apply to

> [a]ny claim arising in respect of the assessment or collection of any tax or customs duty, or the detention of any goods, merchandise, or other property by any officer of customs or excise or *any other law enforcement officer* (emphasis added).

The Supreme Court, with Justice Thomas writing the opinion, interpreted § 2680(c) as encompassing all law enforcement officers. The Court began its opinion by noting the expansive meaning of *any* and quoting a dictionary definition (via one of its previous decisions) that defined *any* as "one of some indiscriminately of whatever kind."[16] The Court believed that it gave an unrestricted scope to the phrase "any other law enforcement officer," indicating that the phrase means "law enforcement officers of whatever kind."[17]

Whether the Court interpreted the relevant provisions correctly is debatable, and a close examination of the issue is beyond the scope of this paper. Even a relatively cursory examination, though, reveals that it is not at all unusual for the literal meaning of a legal text to differ from its communicative meaning. In fact, it is often obvious that the literal meaning of the text is not coterminous with its communicative meaning. Despite the Court's language in *Ali*, it was of course implicitly restricting the domain of "any other law enforcement officer." The Court would undoubtedly reject any interpretation that would include

---

13 According to Recanati (2004), normal interpreters (i.e., not linguists) are aware only of the output of the primary processes involved in contextual adjustment.
14 552 U.S. 214 (2008).
15 Id.
16 552 U.S. 214, at 219.
17 *Id.* at 220.

foreign law enforcement officers or even state law enforcement officers (or any "law enforcement officer" in existence, either on earth or otherwise), even though they would fall within the literal meaning of the 'other' clause. These situations are not, however, likely to be part of a litigated interpretive dispute. Considering that the related provision, § 1346(b)(1), to which § 2680(c) is the exception, authorizes claims against the United States only for acts of employees of the federal government, including foreign or state law enforcement officers in § 2680(c) would obviously be nonsensical. Precisely because such an interpretation is so obvious, and pointless to challenge, it would not be litigated. Thus, judicial decisions, which generally resolve (relatively) close interpretive disputes, do not reflect the variety of obvious ways in which the literal meaning of legal texts differs from their communicative meanings.

As indicated above, Recanati (2004) views quantifier domain restriction as being wholly pragmatic in nature. In contrast, Stanley (2000) offers a semantic account of quantifier domain restriction that emphasizes compositionality and the systematic nature of language. It is not necessary here to decide whether quantifier domain restriction is properly viewed as pragmatic. Rather, at this stage of the discussion, a few points should emerge. First, and most importantly, linguistic phenomena like quantifiers illustrate that literal meaning and communicative meaning can differ. When an utterance includes a quantifier, literal meaning and communicative meaning will typically differ, even when the utterance is found in a legal text. Second, deciding the scope of a quantifier involves a judgment about the influence of co-text rather than merely the determination of a convention of meaning. The judgment, though, relates to the communicative meaning of the words used, not some external restraint on the 'true' meaning of the language. Finally, like the case with borderline issues of vagueness, the relevant domain will restrict the scope of the quantifier so that it clearly excludes some cases (such as the foreign law enforcement officers example above), clearly includes some cases (such as an officer of customs or excise) and neither clearly excludes nor clearly includes other cases (i.e., the cases likely to be litigated). In borderline cases there will thus be uncertainty and disagreement regarding the scope of the quantifier.

2.4 Secondary pragmatic processes and the *ejusdem generis* canon

2.4.1 A description of the *ejusdem generis* canon

As the discussion of quantifiers illustrated, a primary pragmatic process such as quantifier domain restriction is an aspect of the communicative meaning of a legal text, and there are good reasons to believe that at least some secondary pragmatic processes are also aspects of the communicative meaning of a legal text. To illustrate this point, consider so-called 'textual canons', which "set forth inferences that are usually drawn from the drafter's choice of words, their grammatical placement in sentences, and their relationship to other parts of the 'whole' statute" (Eskridge and Frickey 1995: 634). Like quantifier domain restriction, the application of a textual canon will tend to narrow the scope of an utterance. One paradigmatic canon, the *ejusdem generis* canon, will be the focus of the discussion. One description of the canon provides that "if a series of more than two items ends with a catch-all term that is broader than the category into which the proceeding items fall but which those items do not exhaust, the catch-all term is presumably intended to be no broader than that category" (Dickerson 1975: 234). The motivation for the *ejusdem generis* canon is straightforward and intuitive. Simply put, legislatures often use general terms at the end of lists of specifics that intuitively must be narrower in meaning than the literal meaning of the general term would suggest. Furthermore, any indeterminacy relating to the canon concerns not whether there is typically a gap between the literal meaning and communicative meaning of the general term but instead the multiple ways in which the general catch-all term (usually an 'other' phrase) can be given a limited meaning.

Application of the *ejusdem generis* canon will result in an interpretation that narrows the scope of the provision from its literal meaning. In that respect, it is similar to quantifier domain restriction (discussed above). It is not difficult to conceive of examples where the application of the *ejusdem generis* principle is intuitively correct. For example, a law concerning the regulation of

(2)   gin, bourbon, vodka, rum and other beverages

would not likely (absent some unusual context) be interpreted as including Coke (the soda) even though it is a *beverage.* Due to the predilection that legal drafters have for general 'other' phrases following lists of specific items, courts frequently apply the *ejusdem generis* canon in order to narrow the meaning of the 'other' phrase. By doing so, they of course recognize another gap between literal meaning and communicative meaning.

Like quantifier domain restriction, the *ejusdem generis* canon often operates to narrow the domain of a statute from its literal meaning even if the restriction is not relevant to the particular interpretive dispute before the court. For example, Scalia and Garner (2012) consider the following utterance that is placed on a sign at the entrance of a butcher shop:

(3)   No dogs, cats, pet rabbits, parakeets, or other animals allowed.

The authors (212) argue that "no one would think that only domestic pets were excluded, and that farm animals or wild animals were welcome." The authors reason that "when the context argues so strongly against limiting the general provision, the canon will not be dispositive" (*ibid.*). Note, though, that even with this example there is a gap between literal meaning and communicative meaning. No one would argue that, for example, the prohibition would include humans.

2.4.2 The *ejusdem generis* canon and conversational implicatures

Ejusdem Generis, and perhaps other textual canons, can be defended as aspects of communicative meaning by appealing to Grice's theory of *conversational implicature*. If so, these principles would fall under Recanati's (2004) third level of meaning, *what is communicated*, which, according to Recanati, is similar to Grice's theory of conversational implicature. Recall that *what is communicated* concerns what Recanati terms *secondary pragmatic processes*. In contrast to *primary pragmatic processes*, which are included in *what is said* (the second level of meaning), *secondary pragmatic processes* are *post-propositional*. *Secondary pragmatic processes* cannot take place unless some proposition p is considered as having been expressed, for they proceed by inferentially deriving some further proposition q (the implicature) from the fact that p has been expressed. They are ordinary inferential processes that take the interpreter from *what is said* to *what is communicated*, which is something that "follows from the fact that the speaker has said what she has said" (17).

Grice's conversational implicatures are oriented towards everyday conversation where people often convey information that goes beyond *what is said*. What is conversationally implicated is not coded but, rather, is inferred on the basis of assumptions concerning the Cooperative Principle and its constituent maxims of conversation, which describe how people interact with each other. The *Cooperative Principle* is the following:

> Make your contribution such as is required, at the stage at which it occurs, by the accepted purpose or direction of the talk exchange in which you are engaged (Grice 1989: 26).

The Cooperative Principle works in both directions in the sense that speakers observe it and listeners assume that speakers are observing it.

In fleshing out the Cooperative Principle, Grice proposed four maxims of conversation, which describe specific rational principles observed by people who obey the cooperative principle. There is a maxim of quality ("Try to make your contribution one that is true"), a maxim of relation ("Be relevant"), a maxim of quantity ("Make your contribution as informative as is required (for the purposes of the exchange)" and "Do not make your contribution more informative than is required") and various maxims of manner ("Be perspicuous") (Grice 1989: 26-27). The maxims enable effective communication and are a way of explaining the link between utterances and what is understood from them. Conversational implicatures arise on the basis that the maxims are being preserved. A conversational implicature is defined by Grice (1989: 30-31) as follows:

> A man who, by (in, when) saying (or making as if to say) that p has implicated that q, may be said to have conversationally implicated that q, provided that (1) he is presumed to be observing the conversational maxims, or at least the Cooperative Principle; (2) the supposition that he is aware that, or thinks that, q is required in order to make his saying or making as if to say p (or doing so in those terms) consistent with this presumption; and (3) the speaker thinks (and would expect the hearer to think that the speaker thinks) that it is within the competence of the hearer to work out, or grasp intuitively, that the supposition mentioned in (2) is required."

It might seem quite intuitive that the *ejusdem generis* canon (and perhaps other textual canons) is an aspect of communicative meaning and can be given a Gricean-type explanation. As Carston (2013), a leading pragmatic theorist, notes, textual canons look very similar to the principles/heuristics formulated by theorists of pragmatics for general communication and interpretation. Some prominent scholars, though, have criticized the idea that conversational implicatures are applicable to legislation. Marmor (2008), for instance, seems to take a very aggressive position, arguing that, unlike ordinary conversations, it would be "very rare" for there to be cases in which the content the legislature prescribes is not exactly what the text says. In Marmor's (429) view, the reason is that "[a]n essential aspect of what enables parties to an ordinary conversation to express content that is not exactly what their expressions mean, consists in the fact that an ordinary conversation is, typically, a cooperative activity." In contrast, legislation is typically a form of complex strategic behavior and cannot be considered a cooperative activity. Poggi (2011) similarly argues against the applicability of conversational implicatures to legal texts. His main reasons concern the "conflictual behavior of the addressees and, above all, to the insurmountable indeterminacy of the contextual elements" (21).[18]

A full defense of the applicability of conversational implicatures to legal texts is beyond the scope of this paper. Nevertheless, such a defense would, as

---

[18] Asgeirsson (2012) disagrees with some of Marmor's (2008) analysis, particularly with Marmor's claim that a speaker succeeds in asserting something other than what she literally says only if it is obvious that she cannot be intending to assert the literal content of her remark. However, he agrees with Poggi (2011) that the legislative context is typically equivocal and rarely supports the application of conversational implicatures.

outlined below, focus on the kind of cooperation between speaker and audience relevant to the application of some implicatures. At the outset, it is important to note that quite often it *is* obvious that the literal content of a legal text must differ from its legal meaning. Even when application of an implicature would leave a degree of interpretive discretion regarding the meaning of the text, this would (contra Poggi's [2011] position) constitute a normal aspect of interpretation and not a reason to reject the applicability of implicatures. Lumsden (2008: 1900) explains that the Cooperative Principle can concern "some constrained form of cooperation, a kind of cooperation within the conversation, as opposed to cooperation generally." Similarly, Pavlidou (1991: 12) distinguishes between *formal cooperation* and *substantial cooperation*. *Formal cooperation* is cooperation in the Gricean tradition, which involves acting according to, or contrary to, the conversational maxims. In contrast, *substantial cooperation* refers more broadly to the sharing of common goals amongst the communication partners that go beyond the maximal exchange of information. In some cases an extra-linguistic goal determines linguistic cooperation, but in other situations an extra-linguistic goal of one of the participants is clearly not shared by the other. In fact, Lumsden (2008) describes situations in which no significant extra-linguistic goals enter into the relevant conversation at all, so the issue of the goals being shared or not does not arise. The extra-linguistic goal, if any, thus does not determine the linguistic goal. Yet, the cooperative principle is still applicable.

The cooperative principle therefore should be viewed as only requiring linguistic cooperation, as there is no common non-linguistic goal in some cases where implicatures are applicable. Furthermore, the linguistic cooperation required is itself relatively narrow. The principle thus "does not say anything about the speaker's extralinguistic goals, but is a theory of the ways in which speakers maximize the efficiency of information transfer" (Capone 2001: 446–447). The cooperation expected allows the speaker to rely on the audience to interpret the implicatures, thereby allowing the speaker to communicate more briefly. Thus, the linguistic goal itself can be imprecise and does not require that the linguistic purposes be shared or mutual, but only that the purposes be mutually modeled. As Lumsden (2008) argues, critics should be open to a range of cases displaying variation in the form and nature of the cooperation. Marmor and Poggi thus overstate the requirements of the cooperative principle. There is no obvious reason to think that a legislature and the judiciary, the body primarily responsible for giving statutes authoritative interpretations and thus the most relevant cooperative partner, do not engage in the kind of *formal cooperation* that is sufficient to warrant the application of conversational implicatures. Textual canons are based on generalized beliefs about how drafters and others use language. If such beliefs are generally unwarranted in lieu of specific evidence of legislative intent that a regularity of language was intended, a court would be equally warranted in refusing to give a word its conventional meaning absent specific evidence that it should do so. If linguistic cooperation is not sufficient to establish drafting regularities, it is not sufficient to establish conventional meaning.

3 Competing accounts of pragmatic processes

3.1 A scalar implicature approach to the *ejusdem generis* canon

As the above discussion indicates, strong arguments exist that both primary and secondary pragmatic processes are relevant in determining the communicative meaning of a legal text. Certainly, many commentators have argued in favor of interpreting legal texts according to their literal meaning or against the relevance of certain pragmatic theories such as conversational implicatures. If, though, one agrees that the literal meaning of a legal utterance often underdetermines its communicative meaning, a range of possibilities exists for capturing how the gap between literal meaning and communicative meaning should be characterized. The two approaches discussed below encapsulate the significantly different ways in which the gap might be conceived. The first attempts to capture the systematicity of language, focuses on particular linguistic phenomena, and offers accounts that may sometimes blur the line between semantics and pragmatics. The second, discussed in the next Part, offers a wholly pragmatic account of meaning and attempts to identify a deeper underlying principle underlying communication that can explain all linguistic phenomena.

An example of the first approach uses Levinson's (2000) analysis of scalar implicatures as a way to conceptualize the *ejusdem generis* canon. Consider the utterance

(4) Some of the students did well.

The literal meaning of (4) is that some, and perhaps all, of the students did well. In contrast, the intuitive interpretation, of course, is that not all of the students did well. This interpretation can be based on the theory of a scalar implicature, the central notion of which is a contrast set, or linguistic expressions in salient contrast, which differ in informativeness (25). Relevant to the interpretation of (4), there is a scalar contrast set <some, all>, such that saying (4) implicates the rationale that the speaker would have chosen the stronger alternative if she was in a position to do so. Thus, for sets of alternatives, use of one (especially a weaker) implicates rejection of another (especially an otherwise compatible stronger alternate).

Pursuant to Horn's (1972, 1989) account, scalar implicatures come about through a constrained set of relevant alternatives. In typical cases, they are lexically constrained by items of the same category whose entailments line them up in a scale of increasing informativeness. Using positive quantifiers, an example of a Horn scale would be the following: some, many, most, all. The scales are characterized by the increasing strength of the items going from left to right. If, for example, all of the students did well, then *most, many* and *some* of them did. The process for other scales works similarly, and according to Chierchia, *et. al.*, (2012: 2303), "Horn's suggestions can be extended to other seemingly more volatile/ephemeral scales."

Similar to other scales, the *ejusdem generis* canon can be seen as being based on salient contrasts. A generic scale, as considered by a draftor of a legal text, might look as follows: <specific list, list + 'other' clause, general term>. For example, a prohibition might be phrased as a specific list, like the following

(5) No dogs, cats, or birds allowed.

In (5), the scope of the provision is constrained and does not allow (at least explicitly) for prohibitions outside of *dogs, cats* or *birds*.

Suppose, though, that the drafter believes that *dogs, cats* and *birds* are the known and primary targets of the prohibition but that other, similar targets exist, even if they cannot all be known at the time of drafting. The drafter might then redraft (5) as follows:

(6) No dogs, cats, birds or other animals allowed.

Compared to (5), (6) is a stronger statement. In addition to *dogs, cats* and *birds*, *other animals* are prohibited. Of course, the literal meaning of (6) is broad, and can be said to include all animals, but its ordinary meaning is narrower. This is illustrated by the option on the far right of the scale, as illustrated below.

Suppose that instead of (5) or (6) the drafter has the following prohibition:

(7) No animals allowed.

The scope of the literal meaning of (6) and (7) is the same. Both would seem to prohibit all animals, and (6) would seem to include unnecessary surplusage (i.e., "dogs, cats, birds"). When considering scalar implicatures, though, the ordinary meanings of (6) and (7) may differ. While (6) has a list of specifics followed by an 'other' clause, (7) has a general prohibition. In comparison to (5) and (6), (7) is the stronger statement. The comparison between (5) and (7) is obvious. The list of specifics in (5) is narrower in scope than the category *animals* in (7). The comparison between (6) and (7) while less obvious, also reveals that the scope of (7) is broader than the scope of (6). The drafter of (6) understands that (7) is more succinct than (6), if the intent is for (6) to carry its literal meaning. There is reason, though, to believe that (6) should not carry its literal meaning. Contrary to the analyzes of some commentators, a broad catch-all 'other' phrase is not due to infelicitous drafting, but, rather, because the simple language has a conventional meaning that is stereotypically exemplified through the other items on the list. Otherwise, the drafter could simply use the catch-all, as in (7), without the list of specifics. By not explicitly defining the classification, the drafters leave courts with the flexibility to frame the classification in light of the variety of cases (some of them undoubtedly unexpected by the legislature) that come before the court.

As illustrated above, certain views of scalar implicatures provide a way of conceptualizing the role of the *ejusdem generis* canon. Furthermore, as Levinson and others have shown, there is a level of systematicity to generalized conversational implicatures like scalar implicatures such that the semantics/pragmatics distinction is implicated. Where scalar implicatures fall on the semantics/pragmatics divide is not important for present purposes. Instead, considering scalar implicatures to be a systematic aspect of language usage establishes their relevance to the interpretation of legal texts and explains and justifies the continuing relevance of the *ejusdem generis* canon.

3.2 A Relevance Theoretic approach to conversational implicatures

The second approach to linguistic phenomena is exemplified by Relevance Theory (RT), which assumes that communication is essentially an inferential process grounded in a general property of human cognitive systems. The theory relies on a technically defined notion of relevance that operates as a potential property of any input to any perceptual or cognitive process. Relevance is assessed in terms of processing effort and cognitive effects (Wilson and Sperber 2004). An input is relevant to an individual when it yields a positive cognitive effect as a result of being processed in a context of available assumptions. Positive cognitive effects include contextual implications, and strengthening and/or eliminating of existing assumptions (Falkum 2007: 224). The greater the cognitive effects of an input to an individual who processes it and the smaller the processing effort required to derive those effects, the greater the relevance of that input to that individual at that time.

Relevance is defined according to the following two principles: The *Cognitive Principle of Relevance* and the *Communicative Principle of Relevance*. The *Cognitive Principle of Relevance* provides that human cognition tends to be geared to the maximization of relevance. This principle predicts that hearers will aim at deriving as many cognitive effects as possible for as little processing effort as possible (Falkum 2007: 224). In turn, the *Communicative Principle of Relevance* provides that every act of ostensive communication communicates a presumption of its own relevance. The speaker, by the very act of addressing the hearer, is communicating according to the following presumption of optimal relevance:
(a) The ostensive stimulus is relevant enough for it to be worth the addressee's effort to process it.
(b) The ostensive stimulus is the most relevant one compatible with the communicator's abilities and preferences.

It is assumed that, at every stage of the process of developing the linguistic meaning into a complete proposition, the hearer will choose the solution involving the least processing effort, and the solution will be abandoned only if it does not yield an interpretation consistent with her expectations of relevance (Sperber and Wilson 1995).

Under RT, the fact that utterances carry a presumption of relevance licenses a particular comprehension procedure, which, in successful communication, reduces the many logically possible interpretations to a single warranted interpretation. According to Carston (2013: 28), the RT comprehension procedure is as follows:
a. Follow a path of least effort in computing cognitive effects (contextual implications): Test interpretive hypotheses (disambiguations, reference resolutions, lexical adjustments, implicatures, etc.) in order of accessibility.
b. Stop when your expectations of relevance are satisfied.

Carston (2013) indicates that the above procedure is automatically applied in the online processing of verbal utterances. The schematic decoded linguistic meaning is taken as input, and processes of pragmatic completion and enrichment at the explicit level occur in parallel with the derivation of the contextual implications of the utterance. Central to the procedure is a subprocess of mutual parallel adjustment of explicit content and intended contextual implications, which is guided and constrained by expectations of relevance. An input may deliver a variety of different types of cognitive effects to the system. For example, contextual implications follow (inferentially) from the new input in combination with a context of existing assumptions, but not from either alone. Thus, new information is only relevant if it connects up productively with contextual information.

3.3 Relevance Theory theorists vs. alternative approaches to language

One of the arguments of RT is that Grice's maxims either conflict or lead to erroneous predictions of meanings when applied to some utterances, and neo-Gricean theories, such as Levinson's (2000), suffer from the same problems. Such a claim may be accurate, especially if a carefully chosen, elaborated context is supplied in the hypothetical. Consider Carston's (1998) hypothetical below, involving a scalar implicature, meant to illustrate how RT is superior to neo-Gricean theories in predicting correct interpretations:

> B: Are some of your friends Buddhist?
>
> A: Yes, some of them are.

Carston (1998: 220-21) notes that, contrary to a Gricean analysis, "[t]here is no reason to suppose that A is (scalar) implicating that not all of her friends are Buddhist" and offers Green's (1995) analysis on the hypothetical:

> [...] suppose that A knows that B, in spite of only asking whether some of A's friends are Buddhist, would also be interested to know if in fact all, or most, of A's friends are Buddhist [since, let us suppose, B is gathering data about interactions amongst people of different religious groups]. And suppose that B is aware of the fact that A knows this. In this situation a stronger assertion such as 'Yes, in fact all of them are', would be relevant. But it does not follow that in giving only the weaker answer, 'Yes, some of them are Buddhist', A is implicating that she is not in an epistemic position to make a stronger claim. It would be more generous for A to make the stronger remark – that all of her friends are. Yet A might have some reason for diffidence concerning this stronger point, such as fear of being considered a Buddhist-groupie. Such a reason might prevent A from being as generous with her information as she might [...]

Carston (221) then offers the following commentary:

> Let us see how the Communicative Principle of Relevance [...] fares with this sort of example. First, it is clear that A's response meets the requirement of the first clause of the presumption: A's utterance certainly does have sufficient effects for it to be worth the addressee's effort to process it, since it gives exactly the information B has asked for. Now, in the context that

Green sketches, it is evident that there is a more relevant response that A could have given, concerning whether all or most of her friends are Buddhist; this would have more contextual effects for the hearer (B) and would cost him negligible further processing effort. Since A has chosen not to utter this, doesn't it follow that she must be communicating that only some (that is, not all or most) of her friends are Buddhist? This would follow from a presumption of maximal relevance (just as it would follow from a maxim of maximal informativeness, i.e. volubility). However, Green's context makes it plain that while the speaker has the ability to make the stronger statement, she prefers not to (she is afraid of being considered a Buddhist-groupie) and the hearer is aware of this. Hence the relevance principle correctly predicts that the speaker is not implicating that not all of her friends are Buddhist and that the hearer recovers no such assumption as part of what is communicated.

Note that Carston is correct that RT predicts the correct interpretation and other theories which emphasize default meanings may not. It is unclear, though, whether RT can offer a persuasive analysis when the relevant context is sparse, as it often is in legal cases. Consider the following statute, 18 U.S.C. § 924(c)(1)(A), that provides for enhanced punishment if the defendant "uses" a firearm "during and in relation to [...] [a] drug trafficking crime." Although the statute specifies the subject or agent (the defendant), the direct object (the firearm), and requires a connection to a drug trafficking crime, it is underspecified regarding the event; how the defendant must "use" the firearm within the meaning of the provision.[19] This underspecification, a paradigmatic example of underspecificity due to ellipsis, has challenged courts in their efforts to give the ordinary meaning to the statutory language. In *Smith v. United States*,[20] an infamous case for legal commentators, the Supreme Court held that exchanging a firearm for drugs "can be described as 'use' within the everyday meaning of that term."[21] The Court consulted two dictionaries regarding the word 'use' and concluded that it means "to employ" or "to derive service from."[22] The Court rejected the argument that "uses" has a reduced scope in § 924(c)(1)(A) because it appears alongside the word "firearm."[23] The Court reasoned that "it is one thing to say that the ordinary meaning of 'uses a firearm' *includes* using a firearm as a weapon," "[b]ut it is quite another to conclude that, as a result, the phrase also *excludes* any other use."[24]

---

[19] An "event" is defined as a type of situation "in which something happens" (Murphy and Koskela 2010: 156).
[20] 508 U.S. 223 (1993).
[21] Id.
[22] *Id.* at 229.
[23] See id.
[24] *Id.* at 230.

The *Smith* case is similar to the following example (which has been extensively discussed in the literature):

(8) Mary began a book.

Slocum (2012) explains how the verb *begin* selects for an event as its complement type. In cases where this requirement is not directly satisfied by the surface syntactic structure, as in (8), an inference about the systematicity of language can be made. In brief, one possibility is that the process specified by the verb phrase is made apparent from the context of the other lexical items in the sentence (namely, the direct object *book*) in order to change the type of the complement NP into an event. This process results in the interpretation *began reading*. Of course, such an interpretation is a default one that could be canceled by indications from the broader context.

In contrast to the above approach, under RT the relevant event associated with *began a book* would be supplied entirely on pragmatic grounds. It would be considered a case of "free pragmatic enrichment," "where a conceptual constituent which is not articulated in the linguistic form of the utterance is contextually derived, as a result of the hearer's trying to figure out which proposition the speaker has explicitly expressed" (Carston 2002: 323; Falkum 2007: 226). Consider the following scenario offered by Falkum (2007), relating to the hypothetical in (8):

> Let us imagine a context where John, Mary and Sue have been given the job of cleaning their late grandmother's house before it is advertised for sale. The bookshelves haven't been dusted for years, and, because they are completely covered in dust, each book has to be dusted individually. After they have been cleaning for a while, John asks if they should all take a break and go for coffee, and Sue replies[ ]: Let's wait for a couple of minutes. Mary just began a book.

In such an enriched context, Falkum is of course correct that 'Mary just began [DUSTING] a book' would clearly be the most relevant, accessible interpretation. It undoubtedly involves the least processing effort on the part of the hearer and offers a superior premise for Sue's conclusion that they should wait before leaving for coffee. Falkum is also correct that at no stage in the interpretive process did the RT analysis assume that a 'default' interpretation is computed and then canceled by context.

Returning to the *Smith* case, various accounts that address how some systematicity of language, such as focusing on how sentential (i.e., sentence level) context gives meaning to a verb like *use*, can suggest a correct meaning for the statutory provision (Slocum 2012, 2015). These accounts can be useful in further critiquing the Supreme Court's decision in *Smith* and explaining how the Court approached the interpretive question in an incorrect manner. In contrast, it is not clear that without the sort of enhanced context that would reveal the underlying motivations of the authors of the statute (like that referenced in the *Mary began a book* hypo), RT, or some similar theory, can offer a persuasive account of how the "uses a firearm" provision should be interpreted. That is, it is not clear that RT could offer an account that, if followed, would enhance a court's ordinary interpretive process.

4 Conclusions about the most useful approach to pragmatic processes in legal texts

It is beyond the scope of this paper to explicate fully the constituent question of how the meaning of a legal text should be characterized. It suffices for present purposes to aver that the communicative meaning of a legal text is not determinative of its legal meaning, yet it typically acts as a constraint on permissible interpretations. Courts often consider non-textual evidence such as drafting history and purpose when determining the meaning of a text, and such considerations are understandably controversial for various reasons (e.g., the unreliability of legislative history and subjectivity of considerations of purpose). Two important, and related, aspects of interpretation should be uncontroversial, though. One is that pragmatic processes are relevant to legal interpretation. The second is that the communicative meaning of a legal text is not always synonymous with its literal meaning, and various linguistic phenomena, seen as pragmatic by many, operate so that the intended meaning of a legal text often differs from its literal meaning. Quantifier domain restriction is one such example, and under one theory it is an aspect of *what is said* and a primary pragmatic process.

The relevance of secondary pragmatic processes, such as conversational implicatures, to legal texts has been questioned by some scholars. A complete defense of their applicability is beyond the scope of this paper, but those scholars arguing against their applicability face the difficult task of establishing that the draftors of legal texts, particularly statutes, do not use language in the same ways as do others, and that these differences preclude the applicability of conversational implicatures. If one agrees that secondary pragmatic processes may be applicable to legal texts, the next step is to decide whether any particular theory offers a persuasive explanatory theory of one or more of the linguistic phenomena. In considering such claims, two issues should be considered: 1) whether a particular theory of a linguistic phenomenon is, as a general matter, explanatory and persuasive; and 2) whether the theory is explanatory and persuasive as applied to a legal text. Theories that offer accounts of specific linguistic phenomena offer advantages over more reductive theories that seek to identify deep underlying principles of communication. Importantly, it is not clear that the latter sort of theories, such as RT, offer insights into the ordinary meaning of language (an important aspect of legal interpretation), and they consequently fail to meaningfully contribute to the sequential process of legal interpretation (explained below).

As illustrated above, RT advocates claim that the theory provides a more unified, often simpler, account of meaning that avoids problems of misinterpretation (Falkum 2007: 224). It purports to represent a deeper underlying principle from which Gricean maxims follow as more specific heuristics whose application is limited to particular subdomains of linguistic interpretation. Certainly, the theory seems to make more accurate predictions of meaning than do other competing theories. It is not clear, though, that RT provides a useful framework for theorizing about the interpretation of legal texts. First, unlike other theories that create default interpretations based on limited context (typically no more than sentential context), RT hypotheticals seem to depend on an enriched context. In a sense, then, RT does not use the same data as do other theories. Second, legal texts do not always (or even typically) involve the kind of enriched contextual environment that RT seems to rely on for accurate interpretations. A legal text is not a contextualized, lengthy conversation, and some contextual evidence such as legislative history is controversial in any case. When interpreting legal texts, the specific provisions themselves are typically of paramount importance to courts, and often the only evidence considered by the court. Certainly, courts consider the purpose of the provision at issue, and Carston (2013: 21) indicates that "considerations of 'purpose', when they fall within the communicative relevance of a word's use, can reasonably be recruited in the pragmatic inferential process." It is not clear, though, that RT offers any novel insights into how the proper consideration of purpose leads to accurate interpretations.

Furthermore, for scalar implicatures, as well as other linguistic phenomena, theorists have shown how salient interpretations are determined without the necessity of consideration of the context of the particular situation in which the utterance was made (Jaszczolt 2005). These sorts of default interpretations are useful to courts, which uniformly purport to interpretation language according to its 'ordinary meaning' (Slocum 2014). A sequential process where ordinary meaning is first determined and then accepted as the legal meaning of the text or, conversely, rejected in favor of some other meaning, is preferable to an alternative where the communicative meaning is decided without considering the ordinary meaning of the text. Determining the ordinary meaning of the text provides an important methodological commonality amongst judges that would not otherwise exist. A frequent comment about legal interpretation is that there is no generally agreed upon methodology of interpretation (Rosenkranz 2002). The two main methodologies of interpretation, textualism and intentionalism, differ in various important ways.[25] Furthermore, judges do not agree on which contextual aspects of meaning are relevant, or their persuasive value in general or in any given case. Even generally accepted interpretive principles are often haphazardly applied by judges, or ignored altogether. Yet, both intentionalist and textualist judges use the ordinary meaning concept, establishing an area of agreement regarding a fundamental principle of interpretation. Unlike some other linguistic theories of meaning, RT does not provide default, ordinary meanings, and does not address the issue other than to show that such meanings are sometimes inaccurate.

Carston (2013: 32) recognizes that the relevance of RT to legal texts is still underdeveloped, particularly the "question of whether the RT account of ordinary everyday utterance interpretation can, perhaps with certain provisos and/or modifications, be carried over to the case of legal interpretation." Such caution is well-founded. RT claims that it has the capacity to account for a wide range of linguistic phenomena, but it is questionable whether the reductive nature of the theory can provide productive new insights into the interpretation of legal texts. For instance, if RT is applied to an interpretive question, it is not clear what independent role other well-established interpretive principles, such as *ejusdem generis* and textual canons, would have in the interpretation. Such concerns suggest that other linguistic theories, which have the ability to generate default meanings based on relatively limited context, offer accounts of language that more directly and precisely relate to current problems in legal interpretation.

References

Ariel, Mira. 2010. *Defining pragmatics*. Cambridge: Cambridge University Press.
Asgeirsson, Hrafn. 2012. On the possibility of non-literal legislative speech. Unpublished manuscript or Social Science Research Network. Consulted 8/1/14. PDF file.
Capone, Alessandro. 2001. The semantics/pragmatics interface from different points of view. *Journal of Linguistics* 37(2). 445–50.

---

[25] The details of the divergencies between textualism and intentionalism are not necessary to detail in this paper. It suffices to note that two methodologies disagree about whether a court should seek to effectuate legislative intent (intentionalism) or the public meaning of the text (textualism).

Cappelen, Herman. 2007. Semantics and pragmatics: Some central issues. In Gerhard Preyer & Georg Peter (eds.), *Context-sensitivity and semantic minimalism*, 3–22. Oxford, England: Clarendon Press.
Carston, Robyn. 1998. Informativeness, relevance and scalar implicature. *Pragmatics and Beyond New Series*. 179–238.
Carston, Robyn. 2002. *Thoughts and utterances: The pragmatics of explicit communication*. Oxford: Blackwell.
Carston, Robyn. 2013. Legal texts and canons of construction: A view from current pragmatic theory. In Michael Freeman & Fiona Smith (eds.), *Current legal issues: Law and language*, 8–33. Oxford: Oxford University Press.
Chierchia, Gennaro, Danny Fox & Benjamin Spector. 2012. Scalar implicature as a grammatical phenomenon. In Claudia Maienborn, Klaus von Heusinger & Paul Portner (eds.), *Semantics: An international handbook of natural language meaning, Volume 3*, 2297–2331. Berlin: De Gruyter Mouton.
Dickerson, Reed. 1975. *The interpretation and application of statutes*. Boston, MA: Little, Brown and Company.
Duarte, David. 2011. Linguistic objectivity in norm sentences: Alternatives in literal meaning. *Ratio Juris*. 24(2). 112–139.
Eskridge, William & Frickey, Philip. 1995. *Cases and materials on legislation: Statutes and the creation of public policy*. St. Paul: Thomson West.
Falkum, Ingrid. 2007. Generativity, relevance and the problem of polysemy. *UCL Working Papers in Linguistics* (UCLWPL) 19. 205–234.
Flanagan, Brian. 2010. Revisiting the contribution of literal meaning to legal meaning. *Oxford Journal of Legal Studies* 30. 255–271.
Green, Mitchell. 1995. Quantity, volubility, and some varieties of discourse. *Linguistics and Philosophy* 18. 83–112.
Grice, Paul. 1989. *Studies in the way of words*. Cambridge, MA: Harvard University Press.
Hart, H. L. A. 1958. Positivism and the separation of law and morals. *Harvard Law Review* 71. 593–629.
Horn, Laurence. 1972. *On the semantic properties of logical operators in English*. Mimeo, Indiana University Linguistics Club. Bloomington, IN.
Horn, Laurence. 1989. *A natural history of negation*. Chicago, ILL: University of Chicago Press.
Jaszczolt, K.M. 2005. *Default semantics: Foundations of a compositional theory of acts of communication*. Oxford, England: Oxford University Press.
Lumsden, David. 2008. Kinds of conversational cooperation. *Journal of Pragmatics* 40. 1896–1908.
Manning, John. 2003. The absurdity doctrine. *Harvard Law Review* 116. 2387–2486.
Marmor, Andrei. 2008. The pragmatics of legal language. *Ratio Juris* 21(4). 423–452.
McCubbins, Mathew D. & Daniel B. Rodriguez. 2011. Deriving interpretive principles from a theory of communication and lawmaking. *Brooklyn Law Review* 76. 979–95.
Murphy, M. Lynne & Anu Koskela. 2010. *Key terms in semantics*. New York: Continuum International Publishing Group.
Pavlidou, Theodossia. 1991. Cooperation and the choice of linguistic means: Some evidence from the use of the subjunctive in Modern Greek. *Journal of Pragmatics* 15(1). 11–42.
Poggi, Francesca. 2011. Law and conversational implicatures. *International Journal for the Semiotics of Law* 24. 21–40.

Scalia, Antonin & Brian Garner. 2012. *Reading law: The interpretation of legal texts*. St. Paul, MN: Thomson/West.
Recanati, François. 2004. *Literal meaning*. Cambridge, England: Cambridge University Press.
Rosenkranz, Nicholas. 2002. Federal rules of statutory interpretation. *Harvard Law Review* 115. 2085–2157.
Solan, Lawrence. 2010. *The language of statutes: Laws and their interpretation*. Chicago, IL: The University of Chicago Press.
Slocum, Brian. 2012. Linguistics and 'ordinary meaning' determinations. *Statute Law Review* 33(1). 39–83.
Slocum, Brian. 2014. The ordinary meaning of rules. In Michał Araszkiewicz, Paweł Banaś, Tomasz Gizbert-Studnicki, Krzysztof Płeszka (eds.), *Problems of normativity, rules and rule-following*, 295–317. Springer.
Slocum, Brian. 2015. *Ordinary meaning: A theory of the most fundamental principle of legal interpretation*. Chicago, IL: The University of Chicago Press.
Sperber, Dan & Deirdre Wilson. 1995. *Relevance: Communication and cognition*. Oxford: Blackwell.
Stanley, Jason. 2000. Context and logical form. *Linguistics and Philosophy* 23. 391–434.
Stojanovic, Isidora. 2008. The scope and subtleties of the contextualism-literalism-relativism debate. *Language and Linguistics Compass* 2(6). 1171–1188.
Talmage, C. J. L. 1994. Conventional meaning and first meaning. *Erkenntnis* 40(2): 32. 213–25.
Van Schooten, H. 2007. Law as fact, law as fiction: A tripartite model of legal communication. In Anne Wagner, Wouter Werner & Deborah Cao (eds.), *Interpretation, law and the construction of meaning: Collected papers on legal interpretation in theory, adjudication and political practice*, 3–20. AA Dordrecht: Springer.
Wilson, Deirdre & Dan Sperber. 2004. Relevance theory. In Laurence Horn & Gregory Ward (eds.), *The handbook of pragmatics*, 607–632. Oxford: Blackwell.

Lawrence M. Solan
6 One ambiguity, three legal approaches

1 Introduction

In this article I examine how different areas of law resolve a particular type of semantic ambiguity that occurs in various legal contexts. The law resolves this ambiguity in different ways for different contexts. The very fact that the law adjusts to the legal context at hand in resolving ambiguity demonstrates that there is no escaping pragmatic considerations in legal interpretation, whether the document in question is a law, regulation, contract or something else. One may contrast this to situations in which the legal system develops canons of construction, i.e., rules intended to apply across different contexts.

The ambiguity is the one that occurs in the following sentence, taken from a text on linguistic semantics, Chierchia and McConnell-Ginet (1996: 245).[1]

> Bond believes that the author of this letter is a spy.
>
> The sentence is ambiguous between the following two readings.
>
> (1) The speaker reports that Bond believes that a particular individual, say, McIntosh, is a spy. The definite description, "the author of this letter," is really the speaker's longhand for "McIntosh." Notice that this reading is silent with respect to whether Bond knows anything about the letter.
>
> (2) Perhaps judging from the style of the letter's writing, or perhaps from its reference to facts that only a spy would know, Bond believes that some spy wrote the letter, but does not know who that spy might be.

Philosophers sometimes call the first reading "transparent" and the second "opaque." Linguistic contexts that create this ambiguity are called "opaque contexts." The "transparency" reflects the ability to identify "the author of this letter."

Acknowledgment: Don Forchelli Professor of Law, Brooklyn Law School. My thanks to Janet Giltrow, Dieter Stein, Stephen Neale, Christopher Serkin, Emmon Bach, and Barbara Partee for advice and discussion. I am also grateful to Elliott Siebers for his help as my research assistant. This project was supported by a Dean's Summer Research Stipend from Brooklyn Law School.

---

[1] Legal contexts in which this ambiguity occurs have been the subject of two important articles by Jill Anderson (2008, 2014). I return to Anderson's work below.

Lawrence M. Solan, Brooklyn Law School

DOI 10.1515/9781501504723-006

The law is not uniform in its treatment of opaque contexts. Nor should it be. If the best understanding of what someone intended to leave in his will requires one interpretation, and the best understanding of what conduct a particular criminal law was intended to ban requires another, so be it. In the realm of statutory interpretation, the law resolves the ambiguity every which way, sometimes quite obviously along political lines, sometimes reasoning from the purpose of the statute, sometimes not recognizing the ambiguity at all. The law of wills resolves it as a sensible default rule. It presumes that a person leaving a sum to "my grandchildren" means "whoever my grandchildren happen to be at the time of my death," as opposed to the grandchildren alive at the time the will was drafted. The law governing contracts acknowledges the ambiguity, but in doing so creates doctrinal problems. The law has developed a preference for opaque contracts, in which a party can "consent to the terms" of an agreement without knowing what they are.

The lesson to be derived from these differing approaches is that linguistics and the philosophy of language can contribute a great deal towards explaining why it is that efforts to write clear contracts or clear statutes fail as a result of ambiguities well-known to those who study linguistics. But the decisions on how to resolve those linguistic indeterminacies rest solely within the legal system itself, based on each legal situation at hand. (See Bix 2003, 2012, Patterson 1995).

2 Opaque contexts language

Let us return to James Bond. Consider the following syllogism, also taken from Chierchia and McConnell-Ginet 1996):

> Bond believes that the author of this letter is a spy.
> McIntosh is the author of this letter.
> Therefore, Bond believes that McIntosh is a spy.

This syllogism holds only for the first of the two readings presented above, in which the speaker uses "the author of this letter" as longhand for "McIntosh." That is, Bond indeed believes that McIntosh is a spy, but not by virtue of his having written the letter. In fact, Bond may not even know that McIntosh wrote the letter. As for the second reading, if Bond believes that some spy whose identity is unknown to him wrote the letter, then it is not true that by virtue of believing that the author of this letter is a spy that Bond believes that McIntosh is a spy if McIntosh actually wrote the letter.

The examples discussed above point to an observation made by Bertrand Russell (1905): definite descriptions (e.g., "the author of this letter") are not the same as names (e.g., "McIntosh"). Philosophers Peter Ludlow and Stephen Neale (1991: 173) develop this point further: "So on Russell's account, where we have a thought *about* a particular individual, we entertain a singular proposition; where we only have a thought to the effect that a unique individual satisfies some description, we entertain a general proposition." Ludlow and Neale develop the point further. Referring to observations made by Saul Kripke (1979), they argue that the ambiguity of definite descriptions (including "the author of this letter") is itself a matter of pragmatic inference, rather than sentence semantics. The literature contains a great deal of discussion about the interface between semantics and pragmatics (see, e.g., Bach 2002, Bach and Bezuidenhout 2002).

Russell's characterization contains an important point relevant to the interpretation of contracts and other authoritative legal documents. The expression "the author of this letter" is a definite description. A definite description describes something unique, but not necessarily specific, unless the speaker has something specific in mind.[2] In all of the legal cases discussed in this chapter, the decision revolves, in some way, around specificity. Did the parties agree to specific terms, or just to abide by the terms of the written contract, whatever they may happen to be? Does the grandmother's will leave assets to the particular grandchildren she had in mind, or to the members of the set of grandchildren at the time of her death, whoever they may happen to be? Returning to our original terminology – opacity versus transparency – we can say that one interpretation is transparent to a specific referent that the speaker had in mind, while the other reading is opaque to a specific referent. Thus, although the legal examples discussed below may not all share exactly the same linguistic properties, they do share the uncertainty as to whether the legal document identifies a specific individual (or event, or thing).

3 Opacity in legal contexts

3.1 Statutory interpretation

As noted, the kind of ambiguity discussed in this section does arise in various legal contexts. Statutes, for example, are sometimes subject to both specific and nonspecific readings, and sometimes even to the three-way state of mind

---

[2] There is some controversy about the relationship between definiteness and specificity. For a view that relates the two more than do Ludlow & Neale, see Enç (1991).

ambiguity discussed above, in which, returning to our James Bond example, it would matter not only whether Bond believed that McIntosh is a spy, but also whether Bond knew that McIntosh had written the letter. I discuss below several examples from U.S. law.

First consider *Circuit City Stores v. Adams*.[3] An exception to the Federal Arbitration Act, which requires the enforcement of arbitration agreements, says that the law does not apply "to contracts of employment of seamen, railroad employees, or any other class of workers engaged in foreign or interstate commerce [...]."[4] At the time the law was enacted, transportation workers, such as those listed in the exception, were the only class of workers deemed to be engaged in foreign or interstate commerce. Currently, interstate commerce is understood much more expansively, and the class of workers engaged in interstate commerce includes a person like Saint Clair Adams, who was a sales counselor for Circuit City Stores, a now defunct national chain of electronics stores. Should Adams have been forced to arbitrate his discrimination claim against his employer?

A majority of five justices (the Court's conservative bloc) said yes. Although the case has many nuances (see Solan 2010 for discussion), the decision ultimately hinged on the resolution of the kind of ambiguity discussed above. Under one interpretation – corresponding to the first of our James Bond readings – the legislature had in mind a specific list of workers who constitute those engaged in interstate commerce, namely the transportation workers listed in the statute, and any other transportation workers who are doing similar kinds of work. A principle of statutory interpretation, *ejusdem generis*, calls for general words on a non-exclusive list, in this case, "any other class of workers engaged in foreign or interstate commerce," to be construed in light of the specific items in the list, which in this case are various subcategories of transportation workers. The majority opinion relied on this interpretive principle.

The other reading – the nonspecific one – would construe "other workers engaged in foreign or interstate commerce" in accordance with the opaque reading of the James Bond story. In essence, under this reading the statute contains a definite description whose interpretation does not pick out any specific groups of workers, but rather, whoever is engaged in interstate commerce at the time that a subsequent dispute arises. This reading does not have the advantage of *ejusdem generis*, but it does have the advantage of being more consistent with what seemed to be the purpose of the exception to the arbitration statute when it was originally enacted (see Breyer 2005). The case thus boiled down to a conflict between whether a canon of construction should be applied as a proxy

---

[3] 532 U.S. 105 (2001).
[4] 9 U.S.C. § 1 (2012).

for legislative intent, or whether the Court should engage in specific inquiry into the history of the law's enactment. In this case, the former prevailed.

This sort of statutory ambiguity is not limited to one case. Jill Anderson (2008, 2014) has written two extremely interesting articles, demonstrating how this ambiguity has gone unnoticed in judicial interpretations of statutes. In one (Anderson 2008), she discusses the Americans with Disabilities Act. The act in an earlier version prohibited certain kinds of discrimination based on a person's disability. Prior to a recent amendment, the Act defined disability as follows:

> (A) a physical or mental impairment that substantially limits one or more of the major life activities of such individual; (B) a record of such an impairment; or (C) being regarded as having such an impairment.[5]

The first two parts of the definition refer to actual disabilities or records of actual disabilities. But the third prong refers only to "being regarded" as having such an impairment." The word "such" refers back to subpart (A). Substituting that language for "such that" the provision includes: "being regarded as having a physical or mental impairment that substantially limits one or more of the major life activities of such individual."

"Being regarded" creates the same kind of opaque context as does "believe." Consider someone who may or not have an actual disability, but appears to an employer to have something wrong with him. The employer refuses to hire the person because he does not want to be saddled with the responsibility of dealing with a disability. Such conduct would violate the statute in its opaque reading. Here again, the ambiguity is between a specific reading in which the mental impairment is identified, and the nonspecific reading in which it is not.

Anderson (2014) discusses many more examples of this phenomenon, including the famous nineteenth century English case, *Whiteley v. Chappell*,[6] in which an appellate court reversed the conviction of a person who used the identity of a dead neighbor to cast a fraudulent vote in an election. The law made it a crime to "[im]personate any person entitled to vote." As Anderson points out, the court locked on to the transparent reading of the statute, in which "any person entitled to vote" is intended to identify a specific person within that category. Since the dead neighbor was not entitled to vote because he was dead, the court held that Whitely did not violate the statute by taking on his identity. Had the court noticed the opaque interpretation, however, it may have come to the opposite decision, Anderson notes. Like the second reading of our James Bond sentence in which the speaker refers generally to spies without

---

5 42 U.S.C. § 12102(2)(A)-(2)(C).
6 (1868) 4 L.R.Q.B. 127.

having any particular spy in mind, it is possible to understand the voter fraud statute as including anyone who attempts to falsely represent himself as being in the category of a person entitled to vote, regardless of whether such a person exists or who it is.

In both articles, Anderson focuses on cases in which courts miss the fact that the opaque reading exists at all. Thus, the opinions tend to be justified on the grounds of "plain language," when, in fact, the language is not at all plain. In common law countries, this mistake may become a precedent binding on lower courts, and presumptively settled in a higher court that missed the opaque interpretation in the earlier case, entrenching the error for indefinite periods of time. High courts are generally reluctant to change their minds about an issue of statutory interpretation, even though they have the right to do so (see Solan 2016). Anderson describes situations in which this resistance, known as "horizontal stare decisis," precludes future courts from recognizing the legitimate opaque reading of a statute, including some bizarre cases in which impersonating a government officer is construed transparently (see Schauer 2012).

It is difficult to find cases of statutory interpretation in which the court understands the opaque reading as the only possible one. Perhaps this is because language has many uniquely transparent expressions (e.g., "the worker was engaged in interstate commerce"), but does not have uniquely opaque ones. Yet, it would be a serious overstatement to conclude that courts typically ignore the opaque reading of a statute. For example, there are many cases in which appellate courts uphold convictions for impersonating a government official, when there is no particular official being impersonated.

To take a recent case, in 2014 a U.S. federal court of appeals upheld the conviction of a tax consultant who used the letterhead of a member of the U.S. House of Representatives that she had received in correspondence to identify herself falsely as an aide of that legislator in order to misrepresent her activities to her own client.[7] The court had no trouble holding that her "fictional" identity violated the statute. The law punishes a person who "falsely assumes or pretends to be an officer or employee acting under the authority of the United States or any department, agency or office thereof, and acts as such."[8] Here, there was no officer or employee that that the defendant pretended to be. Rather, the defendant pretended only to be a member of the class of government employees, assuming a fictitious name. As noted earlier, this reading is nonspecific, but still unique. The opaque reading is the only one that makes sense in these circumstances, and courts often adopt it. From the beginning, courts have said that it

---

7 *United States v. Tomsha-Miguel*, 766 F.3d 1041 (9th Cir. 2014).
8 18 U.S.C. § 912.

is not necessary to identify a particular official of the United States who is being impersonated.⁹

Verbs like *intend, attempt* and *try*, which are at the core of inchoate crimes, create opaque contexts. Cases involving attempts to commit a crime are notoriously incoherent with respect to the resolution of this ambiguity (see Yaffe 2011). In one, *People v. Jaffe*,¹⁰ a 1906 case from New York, the defendant thought he had received 20 yards of stolen cloth. As it turns out, the cloth he received was not stolen. He was tried for and convicted of attempting to receive stolen property. He could not be tried for receiving stolen property, because he did not receive stolen property. "Receive" does not create an opaque context. The conviction was later reversed by New York's highest court. The court reasoned: How can he have committed a lesser included offense of attempting to commit a crime, when the consummated act was not itself a crime? But this interpretation, as Gideon Yaffe notes (in somewhat different terminology), misses the fact that one can attempt to consummate a crime and fail at it not only by reason of incompetence (shooting and missing), but also by reason of having gotten the attendant circumstances wrong. In this case, Jaffe indeed attempted to receive a member of the category "stolen goods" although he did not attempt to receive any specific "stolen goods" because the actual goods he attempted to receive were not stolen. A brief dissenting opinion recognized the failure to acknowledge this understanding. This case, then, is very much like the Americans with Disabilities Act cases discussed above.

Compare *Jaffe* to another New York case discussed by Yaffe: *People v. Dlugash*,¹¹ decided in 1977. Dlugash shot bullets into a person who might have been already dead because he had also just been shot by another in the room. Dlugash could not properly be convicted of murder because the prosecutor could not prove beyond a reasonable doubt that Dluglash had killed a living person and it is not murder to shoot a corpse: it is a lesser crime.

Here, though the court upheld the conviction, notwithstanding the argument that it could not be proven that Duglash had intended to kill any particular living person, only that he had attempted to kill a member of the category, "living people." In fact, New York's statute governing attempted crimes now covers this situation: "If the conduct in which a person engages otherwise constitutes an attempt to commit a crime [...], it is no defense to a prosecution for such attempt that the crime charged to have been attempted was, under the attendant circumstances, factually or legally impossible of commission, if such crime could

---

9 See Brafford v United States, 259 F. 511 (6th Cir. 1919).
10 185 N.Y. 497 (1906).
11 41 N.Y. 725 (1977).

have been committed had the attendant circumstances been as such person believed them to be."¹² Thus, the legislature was aware that the opaque reading was available and wanted to ensure that courts not miss it.

Now consider *Fowler v. United States*,¹³ a 2011 decision of the U.S. Supreme Court. Fowler and his confederates were planning a bank robbery in Florida, when they were discovered by a police officer, whom Fowler shot and killed. Bank robbery is a federal offense. Ordinarily, a murder in Florida is a matter for the Florida police and courts, not the federal criminal justice system. However, Congress passed a federal witness tampering statute to make it a federal crime to kill someone to obstruct a federal investigation or prosecution. The statute reads as follows:

> Whoever kills or attempts to kill another person, with intent to [...] prevent the communication by any person to a law enforcement officer or judge of the United States of information relating to the commission or possible commission of a Federal offense [...] shall be punished [...] ¹⁴

Fowler was convicted of having violated this law. He had killed another person in order to prevent the communication by that person to a law enforcement officer of information relating to the commission or possible commission of a federal offense. What he did not take into account was whether the person he killed was going to report the crime to a federal official, or some state official. He had no intent with respect to that issue, he simply didn't think of it.

Another part of the statute seems to take care of this issue:

> In a prosecution for an offense under this section, no state of mind need be proved with respect to the circumstance − [...] that the law enforcement officer is an officer or employee of the Federal Government [...]¹⁵

Thus, not only can the federal officer be understood nonspecifically, but any dispute about how much the defendant knows about the relationship between state and federal law enforcement activities is also taken off the table.

The principal statute, as applied to Fowler, has three readings, which correspond to the possible understandings of our James Bond story. The legal question is what Fowler was required to have intended with respect to the likelihood that the person he killed would report the crime to a federal officer. First, if the

---

12 N.Y. Penal Law § 110.1.
13 131 S.Ct. 2045 (2011). Thanks to Jeffrey Kaplan for his discussion of this case in the 2013 West Coast Roundtable on Law and Language, Simon Fraser University, July 2013.
14 18 U.S.C. § 1512(a)(1)(C).
15 18 U.S.C. § 15112(g).

defendant has a particular federal officer in mind, he is uncontroversially guilty. This corresponds to the first, transparent reading of the James Bond story, in which the speaker and Bond both know that McIntosh wrote the letter and is a spy. Second, if the defendant had an officer in mind, and that officer happens to be a federal officer although the defendant was unaware of that fact, then he would also be guilty. This also corresponds to the transparent reading of the James Bond story, but this time the speaker knows that McIntosh wrote the letter, but Bond knows nothing about the letter itself – only that McIntosh is a spy. Third, if Fowler had a generalized sense of there being a federal officer that would be contacted, but knew no more than that, Fowler would be guilty under the nonspecific, or opaque reading of the statute.

Because of the added provision, however, there is a fourth reading. Even if Fowler had no idea that the person to be contacted would be a federal officer, as long as it was some kind of officer, Fowler would be guilty. Fowler, as noted above, had this fourth state of mind – the one that would not follow from a natural reading of the principal statute, but which does follow from the added provision, which says that no proof is needed on the issue of whether the officer that the murdered person would have contacted is actually an employee of the federal government. But this leads to another question: To what extent, if any, must the government prove that, regardless of Fowler's state of mind, the person who was murdered would have communicated with a federal officer?

Note that this is not a relevant question under the first three readings: If Fowler had a particular federal agent in mind, or a particular person in mind that was in fact a federal officer but Fowler didn't know it, or a generalized sense of preventing communication with any federal officer, it really would not matter if the person he killed would not have communicated with any such federal officer. In all three instances, he would have killed a person for the purpose of preventing him from communicating with a federal officer, whether he was right or wrong about the need to do so. But once the added provision comes into play, it would be strange to conclude that not only is it irrelevant whether Fowler knew that the officer deprived of the information would be a federal officer, but that it is equally irrelevant whether communication with a federal officer would have occurred absent the murder. If that were so, then it would be a federal crime to kill a person whom the defendant thought would convey information to a state law enforcement officer, even if the victim had no plans to do that. This has nothing to do with the federal government at all, and is not likely what Congress intended to accomplish.

Of the nine justices, it was Justice Scalia whom this fact disturbed the most. Notwithstanding the provision that absolved the government of the need to prove that Fowler knew that the officer that the murdered person would contact was actually a federal officer, Scalia noted:

> But removing the 'federal officer' requirement as an element of the statute's mens rea does not remove it as an element of the actus reus – that is, as an element of the facts that must be proved for conviction. It must be proved, and proved beyond a reasonable doubt, that the communication intended to be prevented was communication to a federal officer.[16]

Scalia's opinion was a concurrence: The majority held that the government need prove only that there was a *reasonable likelihood* that had the murder not occurred, the individual would have reported the crime or attempted crime to a federal officer.[17]

Yet nothing in the statute establishes such a standard, as both Scalia and the dissent pointed out. While Scalia would have imposed a requirement that the government prove with certainty that a federal officer would have been informed of the crime, the dissent took the opposite position: Since the statute mentions no such requirement, none should be imposed. For the dissenters, killing a person violates the statute if the defendant believed that he would be preventing information about a crime from being transmitted to any law enforcement officer – state or federal. Period.

The dissent's reading is the most loyal to the statute's actual language (at least in my opinion), but it makes little sense in practice because it takes the federal requirement out of the statute altogether, as both the majority and concurrence noted. As between the majority and concurring opinions, both have inserted into the statute some requirement that the murder did indeed block the communication with a federal officer. They differed only in how strong the evidence of such a hypothetical communication must be. Since both have added this requirement to the statute's language, they have engaged in a policy choice, not an interpretive one.

The justices all agreed that all three possible readings of the principal statute could lead to conviction. They thus recognized the opaque context. The interpretive problem with the statute is in the expression, "with intent to prevent a communication." The verb *prevent* typically requires that an event that would have occurred was headed off:

> Toyota prevented even more deaths by recalling the cars.
> Regular exercise prevents heart attacks.

---

16 131 S.Ct. at 2053 (Scalia, J. concurring).
17 131 S.Ct. at 2052.

These sentences are true if, respectively, there were fewer deaths as a result of the recall, and there are fewer heart attacks (generically) as a result of regular exercise. Typically, one has prevented something from happening only if the event is actually thwarted. Note that there need not be any state of mind attached to this success:

> The teacher's having forgotten his keys prevented the class from entering the auditorium.

However, once *prevent* occurs within the context of a state of mind verb, all of this changes. If we say,

> Toyota intended to prevent even more deaths by recalling the cars.

we have no commitment to the plan having succeeded. We have instead a commitment to a state of mind: the state of intent. But whether fewer people died or not has not been expressed. Returning to *Fowler*, the statute only requires that he intend to prevent communication with a federal officer. Fowler killed a witness, intending to prevent that witness from talking to some officer or employee of some government – state or federal. He should have been found guilty and the guilty verdict upheld.

I discuss this case at such length here because it illustrates how the three-way ambiguity that deals both with a hearer's knowledge and at the same time with specificity can cause enormously difficult interpretive problems for the legal system. It also demonstrates how situational statutory interpretation can be and, consequently, the central role that pragmatic inference plays in resolving problem cases. In this case, as in *Circuit City Stores*, discussed above, the choice among various interpretations that concern opacity is clear, since different justices voted to support one or the other interpretation. Yet there is no consensus. Cases like *Fowler* and *Circuit City Stores* demonstrate that resolving semantic ambiguity is only a first step. Politics and legal analysis, on a case by case basis, is the second (see Bix 2003, 2012, Patterson 1995, Anderson 2014). The cases discussed by Anderson, in which courts do not notice the opaque reading at all are disturbing because they do not even allow the starting point for substantive debate to become realized.

Anderson (2014) suggests that a cognitive bias in favor of transparent readings is at work. She may well be correct to some extent, although the opaque reading is sometimes recognized, as it was in *Fowler*, and is actually the default interpretation in some areas of law, as we shall see below.

3.2 Class gifts in wills

Now, consider the following scenario. A person leaves in his will:

$50,000 to be divided among my grandchildren; or
$20,000 to the members of the Real Madrid Football Club

The problem is one of "class gifts" in the law of wills. In the first example, let us say that there were four living grandchildren at the time the will was made, and a fifth is born between the time that the will is made and the time that the person who wrote to the will dies. Or, in the second example, there is a turnover of personnel on Real Madrid, so that the membership of the team at the time of the will differs from the membership at the time of death.

This ambiguity here is exactly the same as the ambiguity in *Circuit City Stores*. Expressions like "grandchildren" and "members of the real Madrid Football Club" are definite descriptions, which are understood either as shorthand for the list of members at the time, or as a general description, as per Bertrand Russell's account.

But the law of wills differs somewhat from the approach taken by courts in statutory cases. The statutory cases discussed above were more or less a hodgepodge of opinions reflecting ad hoc efforts to divine which possible reading(s) the legislature intended, combined with the inescapable inference that the justices' individual politics play at least some role. In both *Circuit City* and cases decided under the Americans with Disabilities Act, courts preferred the reading in which the term in question referred to a particular set of individuals. In *Fowler*, by contrast, all nine justices were happy enough to permit all three readings to come within the statute.

The law of wills attempts to be more uniform than that. It sets a presumption that the author intended the nonspecific reading – the reading in which members of the class at the time of the testator's death share equally in the bequest. Below is the language from a leading American legal treatise on this subject, the American Law Institute's (2011) *Restatement (Third) of Property*, relating to Donative Transfers (ALI 2011):

(a) A class gift is a disposition to beneficiaries who take as members of a group. Taking as members of a group means that the identities and shares of the beneficiaries are subject to fluctuation.

(b) A disposition is presumed to create a class gift if the terms of the disposition identify the beneficiaries only by a term of relationship or other group label. The presumption is rebutted if the language or circumstances establish that the transferor intended the identities and shares of the beneficiaries to be fixed.

(ALI 2011, Wills and Other Donative Transfers § 13.1).

The presumption is that a gift worded this way is a class gift rather than a gift intended for the members of the class at the time of the gift because that is more likely what someone writing a will this way would have intended.[18]

The case by case resolution of opaque context, including cases in which one of the readings (the opaque reading) goes unnoticed entirely, is totally absent in the domain of the interpretation of wills. The law of wills acknowledges both readings, and chooses one of them – the opaque reading – as presumptively valid, subject to evidence that the person who wrote the will had intended the transparent reading. The difference lies in the fact that, at least in the United States, statutes are enacted individually, with all kinds of legal purposes, making a uniform presumption untenable.

Thus, while people write individual wills, just as legislatures write individual statutes, there is one difference: All wills are intended to provide instructions concerning the disposition of property after death. Consequently, if practitioners know from experience that just about everyone who makes a class gift using language that can be construed either transparently or opaquely intends the opaque reading, the law can create a presumption that will, in the main, enforce the wishes of the testator, leaving room for evidence of a contrary intent.

3.3 Specificity and generality in contracts

Now, let us turn to the law of contracts. When people agree not to the particular terms of a contract, but rather to a definite description of the terms of the contract, the ambiguity under discussion in this chapter holds: On one reading, they have agreed to the specific terms themselves, on the other, they have agreed only to a category without regard to what the terms actually are. Let us turn to the following syllogism:

> Max agreed abide by the terms of the contract.
> The contract requires Max to arbitrate any disputes in Guam.
> Max agreed that he would arbitrate any disputes in Guam.

Under one interpretation of "Max agreed to the terms of the contract," the transparent one, Max indeed agreed to arbitrate any disputes in Guam. If Max read and understood the contract before signing it, noticed the arbitration clause, and agreed to it (perhaps because he did not think anything important would depend upon it), then he agreed to arbitrate in Guam. But there is another

---

18 Comment b to the same section of the Restatement makes this clear: *"Question of intent."* Whether or not a disposition creates a class gift is a question of the transferor's intent. . . .

reading – the reading in which Max agreed only generally to the terms of the contract, perhaps without knowing what the terms were. Again, the terms to which he agreed are unique, but his agreement is not specific. He may well be legally bound to arbitrate in Guam by virtue of having said that he agreed to the terms of the contract, but in this transparent sense he did not agree to arbitrate in Guam. He did not even know that such a clause existed. For that matter, he may not know what arbitration is. All consent clauses in which an individual is asked to agree to a general description (e.g., "the terms of the user agreement") are ambiguous in that they have both specific and nonspecific readings.

Were we to approach this situation as we did the ambiguity in the law of wills, we would ask which of the two interpretations is the more likely to have been intended by the contracting parties, and make that one the default interpretation. Or, as in the cases governing statutory interpretation, we might not assign a default interpretation at all, on the theory that contracts differ from each other enough that we cannot determine in advance which interpretation the parties to the contract most likely had had in mind. Were we to take that path, it would be up to a court to determine the intended interpretation separately for each case.

As currently formulated, however, contract law makes the ambiguity between the specific and the general largely irrelevant: opacity wins. The reason is that, at least as a formal matter, contract law does not care whether a person actually consented to the particular terms of an agreement, but rather whether the person exhibited "a manifestation of assent."[19] In fact, the American Law Institute's (1981) *Restatement (Second) of Contracts* makes it clear that actual assent is not required: "Neither real nor apparent intention that a promise be legally binding is essential to the formation of a contract, but a manifestation of intention that a promise shall not affect legal relations may prevent the formation of a contract."[20] Once the manifestation has occurred, it counts, subject to a specific manifestation that it was intended not to form a contract.

Signing a document is ordinarily thought to constitute adequate manifestation of the required state of mind, and courts so hold, consistent with the objective approach to evaluating the events leading to contract formation. Thus, it should not be surprising that agreeing to the terms of a form contract – even if one agreed only in the general sense – binds one to the specific terms of the contract, that is, to the terms in a specific sense.

---

[19] See Restatement (Second) of Contracts §§ 3, 17, 26.
[20] Restatement (Second) of Contracts § 21.

This stance requires us to subscribe to the proposition that it does not matter whether one has consented generally or specifically.[21] As far as the law is concerned, they both amount to the same thing, because they both constitute adequate manifestations of assent. When the contract itself refers to a particular item or service, the transparent reading is the only one available, and the problem goes unnoticed:

> I agree to buy your Toyota Camry for $2,000.
> I agree to paint your house if you pay me $2,000.

There is no question here about the terms agreed to, since the terms are individually stated as terms in the agreement itself.

When we substitute "the terms" for "buy your Toyota Camry for $2000," this transparency evaporates because we have substituted a definite description for the thing itself. As in the examples discussed earlier, the question arises as to whether "the terms" is a shorthand for the specific terms agreed to, or a category in its own right. And as we have also seen (see Anderson 2014), one cannot always substitute the category for the specific terms without changing meaning.

To some extent, such a stance is inevitable. How can the law possibly require that the terms of, for example, your internet service not be binding unless you took and passed a comprehension test at the time you subscribed to service? The commodification of the provision of goods and services may come at the cost of being kept on hold for long periods of time as one waits for the music to stop and a person to answer the phone, but it has also resulted in the provision of inexpensive and largely efficient services, including at-home internet shopping in a competitive marketplace.

My argument here is not, then, that the notion of consent should be limited to transparent consent. If that were the law, then a party could avoid all obligation simply by not reading the terms of a contract, even when those terms are reasonable and even when that party is happy to take advantage of the favorable terms unless and until something goes wrong.

Rather, I suggest here that contract doctrines in general developed under the assumption that consent to terms means specific consent to terms, and that the

---

21 Of course, we can make it matter by embedding into the contract a second issue of transparency by including definite descriptions within the contract's terms, as in "I agree to pay $100,000 to your grandchildren in five years, divided equally among them." We now have an issue as to whether the party agreed to this term at all if he did not read the contract, and if he did, whether "your grandchildren" means those alive at the time of contracting or those alive in five years when the payment is due.

shift from specific to general consent invites a reexamination of a number of doctrines within the law of contract. In a world where you know that the used car you bought from your neighbor for $800 is a clunker, it is reasonable for contract law to set the bar high for undoing the transaction based on the subsequent claim that you overpaid. U.S. law enforces contracts unless the terms are unconscionable, agreed to under duress or undue influence, or fraudulently induced, which are very difficult burdens to meet. In such a legal regime, claims of unfairness based on price are especially unlikely to succeed. But in a world in which you have no real understanding of what you've committed to – nor could you without not only reading and understanding a very long document but then subsequently presenting yourself with a series of hypotheticals about what might go wrong to your disadvantage – unconscionability may be too forgiving a standard. Nor may some of the equitable defenses, such as duress, be strong enough.

Some have argued that opaque consent is no consent at all (see, e.g., Meyerson 1993: 1265; White and Mansfield 2002). I do not agree with that position (see Solan 2015 for further elaboration). Rather, commercial life has changed, with so many of our transactions now occurring online as click-through contracts, or on the phone, agreeing to certain core terms (i.e., a two-year commitment to lock in cell phone service at an agreed price), subject to the terms of user agreement that we have never seen, but which we can find on the internet if we wish. As this has happened, the law has adjusted inadequately. A good argument can be made that the ambiguity in the concept of consent is largely to blame. While legal doctrine has always required consent, just about all legal doctrines traditionally assumed consent in transparent transactions. As commercial life has changed, it has appeared that traditional legal doctrines can continue to apply, creating a seamless transition from one sort of economy to another without requiring any serious change in the law.

Thus, I agree with Radin's (2012: 96–97) characterization of opaque consent as "normatively degraded" consent. The problem with opaque consent is simply that it is inadequately responsive to the economic reality of a world in which we sign complicated legal documents without reading them, and we would not understand the consequences of all the provisions even if we did read them. American judges have reacted by ridiculing those who do not read the documents, instead of by stepping up the regulation of the sorts of terms that are permissible in situations in which reading and understanding the terms is unreasonable (see Solan 2015 for further discussion). In this regard, Europe has done a better job.

4 Conclusion

It is not unusual for legal terms to have specialized meanings that apply to particular situations. One literally sees thousands of cases in which a court says, "For purposes of x, y means...." Sometimes the definitions are contained in the statutes themselves. In other cases, the statute contains a word that had earlier been construed by a court, and the word retains its context-sensitive definition.

Consider, for example, a federal law prohibits the transportation of stolen vehicles:

> Whoever transports in interstate or foreign commerce a motor vehicle, vessel, or aircraft, knowing the same to have been stolen, shall be fined under this title or imprisoned not more than 10 years, or both.[22]

What does "stolen" mean in the statute? In *United States v. Turley*,[23] decided in 1957, the question was whether "stolen" should be limited to acts that would constitute larceny under the common law. The defendant in that case had obtained the automobile in question by embezzlement – not by ordinary theft. The U.S. Supreme Court decided that "stolen" has a broader meaning than does common law larceny, so that some activities that would not count as a theft under common law would violate the stolen vehicle statute: "'Stolen' as used in 18 U. S. C. § 2312 includes all felonious takings of motor vehicles with intent to deprive the owner of the rights and benefits of ownership, regardless of whether or not the theft constitutes common-law larceny."[24]

This kind of reasoning is common, and demonstrates that in law, even the formal is pragmatic. The problem arises from a recurring ambiguity in how we understand definite descriptions, a question of interpretation discussed by linguists and philosophers of language for more than a century. The solution in each instance is pragmatic: generally a matter of informed speculation as to the meaning that the speaker (or drafter) intended. What is different about the ambiguity discussed in this chapter is that it describes a general interpretive principle, rather than particularized word meaning, which is the dominant issue in the legal interpretive literature. Courts, though, have been of two minds about both. With respect to word meaning, the "Whole Act Rule" and the "Whole Code Rule" tell courts to assume that a legislature intends to use a word to convey a

---

22 18 U.S.C. 2312.
23 352 U.S. 407 (1957)
24 *Id.* at 417.

uniform meaning, especially within the same statute, but even across statutes within the same code, where "code" may even be construed so broadly as to include all of federal statutory law, which is embedded in the United States Code (see Scalia and Garner 2012 for discussion and defense of the Whole Act Rule; see Eskridge 2016 for some discussion of its limits). On the other hand, as we just saw in connection with the Stolen Vehicle Act, courts are frequently willing to give words specialized meanings in different contexts.

The examples discussed in this chapter suggest that the same ambivalence applies when it comes to the interpretation of larger linguistic structures. On the one hand, courts continue to apply canons of construction, such as *ejusdem generis*, notwithstanding that courts are notoriously inconsistent in their application, a fact pointed out colorfully by Karl Llewellyn (1949) long ago. This practice is part of a formalist trend in U.S. law, through which it is hoped that the application of a set of well-defined procedures can reduce the amount of discretion that judges exercise in making decisions. On the other hand, we have phenomena like the one discussed in this chapter. In some ways it is unusual, for most ambiguities (as distinct from vagueness, see Poscher 2012) permit interpretations sufficiently remote from each other that there is not likely to be regular confusion. Chomsky's (1965) example, "flying planes can be dangerous" is a classic example.

When it comes to opaque contexts, however, it is not unusual for both meanings to make sense in context, which makes the formalist turn more difficult. Yet the pragmatic turn is not an all or nothing affair. In the three areas of law discussed in this chapter (statutes, wills and contracts), we saw a distinctively formalistic approach to contract formation; a pragmatic approach to the law of wills, namely the establishment of a default rule based on actual experience; and in the law governing statutory interpretation, what we saw is a legal mess, with courts sometimes appearing formalist by not acknowledging the ambiguity at all, while at other times presenting sophisticated analysis. Perhaps this messiness is no more than a reflection of language being able to bear the burden of rule of law values only up to its own breaking point.

References

American Law Institute. 1981. *Restatement (second) of contracts*. Washington, D.C.: American Law Institute.

American Law Institute. 2011. *Restatement (third) of property*. Washington, D.C.: American Law Institute.

Anderson, Jill C. 2008. Just semantics: The lost readings of the Americans with Disabilities Act, *Yale Law Journal* 117. 992–1069.

Anderson, Jill C. 2014. Misleading like a lawyer: Cognitive bias in statutory interpretation. *Harvard Law Review* 127. 1521–1592.
Bach, Kent. 2002. Seemingly semantic intuitions. In Joseph Keim Campbell, Michael O'Rourke, & David Shier (eds.), *Meaning and truth: Investigations in philosophical semantics*, 21–33. New York: Seven Bridges Press.
Bach, Kent & Anne Bezuidenhout. 2002. Distinguishing semantics and pragmatics. In Joseph Keim Campbell, Michael O'Rourke, & David Shier (eds.), *Meaning and truth: Investigations in philosophical semantics*, 284–309. New York: Seven Bridges Press.
Bix, Brian. 2003. Can theories of meaning and reference solve the problem of legal determinacy? *Ratio Juris* 16. 281–295.
Bix, Brian. 2012. Legal interpretation and the philosophy of language. In Peter M. Tiersma and Lawrence M. Solan (eds.), *The Oxford handbook of language and law*, 145–155. Oxford: Oxford University Press.
Breyer, Stephen. 2005. *Active liberty: Interpreting our democratic constitution*. New York: Basic Books.
Chierchia, Gennaro & Sally McConnell-Ginet. 1996. *Meaning and grammar: An introduction to semantics*. Cambridge, Mass.: MIT Press.
Chomsky, Noam. 1965. *Aspects of the theory of syntax*. Cambridge, MA: MIT Press.
Enç, Mürvet. 1991. The semantics of specificity. *Linguistic Inquiry* 22: 1–25.
Eskridge, William N., Jr. 2016. *Interpreting law: A primer on how to read statutes and the constitution*. St. Paul, MN: Foundation Press.
Kripke, Saul. 1979. Speaker's reference and semantic reference. In Peter A. French, Theodore E. Euhling, & Howard K. Wettstein (eds.), *Contemporary perspectives in the philosophy of language*, 6–27. Minneapolis, MN: Univesity of Minnesota Press.
Llewellyn, Karl. 1949. Remarks on the theory of appellate decision and the rules or canons about how statutes are to be construed. *Vanderbilt Law Review* 3. 395–406.
Ludlow, Peter & Stephen Neale. 1991. Indefinite descriptions: In defense of Russell. *Linguistics and Philosophy* 14. 171–202.
Meyerson, Michael. 1993. The reunification of contract law: The objective theory of consumer form contracts. *University of Miami Law Review* 47. 1263–1333.
Patterson, Dennis. 1995. Against a theory of meaning. *Washington University Law Quarterly* 73. 1153–1157.
Poscher, Ralf. 2012. Ambiguity and vagueness in legal interpretation. In Peter M. Tiersma and Lawrence M. Solan (eds.), *The Oxford handbook of language and law*, 128–144. Oxford: Oxford University Press.
Radin, Margaret. 2012. *Boilerplate: The fine print, vanishing rights, and the rule of law*. Princeton: Princeton University Press.
Russell, Bertrand. 1905. On denoting. *Mind* 14. 479–493.
Scalia, Antonin & Bryan A. Garner. 2012. *Reading law: The interpretation of legal texts*. St. Paul, MN: Thompson/West.
Schauer, Frederick. 2012. Precedent. In Andrei Marmor (ed.), *The Routledge companion to the philosophy of law*, 123–136.
Solan, Lawrence M. 2010. *The language of statutes: Laws and their interpretation*. Chicago: University of Chicago Press.
Solan, Lawrence M. 2015. Transparent and opaque consent in contract interpretation. In Susan Ehrlich, Diana Eades & Janet Ainsworth (eds.), *Coercion and consent in the legal process: Linguistic and discursive perspectives*. Oxford: Oxford University Press.

Solan, Lawrence. 2016. Precedent in statutory interpretation. *North Carolina Law Review* 94. 1165–1234.

White, Alan & Cathy Mansfield. 2002. Literacy and contract. *Stanford Law and Policy Review* 13. 233–266.

Yaffe, Gideon. 2011. Trying to kill the dead: *De dicto* and *de re* intention in attempted crimes. In Andrei Marmor & Scott Soames (eds.), *Philosophical foundations of language in the law*. 184–216. Oxford: Oxford University Press.

II **Horizons of inference: Extending the context of interpretation**

Angela Condello and Alexandra Arapinis
7 Between similarity and analogy: Rethinking the role of prototypes in law and cognitive linguistics

1 Introduction

Like ordinary common-sense reasoning, legal decision-making connects particular instances or cases with general principles in order to reason about them and make inferences from them. This in turn relies on classificatory operations of the elements making up the situations at hand, grouping particular instances and referents under general terms or concepts (legal or extra-legal). For instance, the classification of a term in a contract as a 'condition' will depend on various aspects, among which: *i.* the general and abstract characterisation of a 'condition' conventionally accepted; *ii.* the cases where the classification of that term has been at issue; *iii.* the role that conditions play within the contract and within contractual liability; *iv.* the interrelation with other concepts and with other aspects of contract law.

Legal practitioners can follow various mechanisms in order to decide whether the terms of a legal norm apply to a specific situation. These mechanisms could be organized under two main categories: one rests on comparison with precedents to establish whether a case is *similar enough* to past cases in order to be judged according to the same norm (typical of Common law systems). The other involves *analogical reasoning* to settle whether more remote cases *should* be judged according to the same norm (typical of Civil law systems). In the former, similarity is generally considered as a matter of fact checking, tied to the material features and circumstances of the compared cases. The latter goes beyond similarity comparison, involving inference making from more general principles dealing with the values and interests at stake in the specific case.

Against this background, we aim to show how similarity comparison and analogical reasoning are much more deeply intertwined, playing very intricate roles both in classification of legal reality and in legal reasoning. In particular, we intend to underline how this intertwinement between similarity and analogy is informed and influenced by the necessity and the pressure produced by the

---

Alexandra Arapinis, LOA Trento
Angela Condello, University of Roma Tre and University of Torino

DOI 10.1515/9781501504723-007

legal decision-making process. To do so, we will draw new insights from prototype theory, a theory of cognitive and linguistic classification which also builds on the fundamental cognitive role of similarity-based and analogy-based mappings. In particular, we will argue that similarity recognition in law, like analogy, involves a kind of structural alignment. This parallel will shed new light on the general and fuzzy notion of *relevant* similarity. We will then discuss the idea of a material theory of inference, according to which legal analogical reasoning should always ultimately seek its ground in material similarities between the analogical base and the analogised case, their facts and context. Pursuing our parallel with prototype theory, this will open the way for a solution to the problem of the over-generation of analogy that has been raised against analogy-driven prototype theories. In conclusion, through this confrontation of the use of prototypical instances in law and cognitive linguistics we aim to establish that similarity and analogy are not complementary, but rather take root one in the other. This means that the way we divide and classify reality drives the way we reason about it, and *vice versa*.

2 Analogy, precedent and classification in the legal decision-making process

2.2 Classificatory similarities and precedents

When connecting particular cases with rules and principles, both in the case of comparison with precedents and of reasoning according to general and abstract norms, legal practitioners deal with legal categorization (we will use the terms 'classification' and 'categorization' interchangeably). Legal reality does not always correspond to ordinary reality.

Legal cases are considered similar when they are not identical, nor are they completely different: when they have aspects that would support their placement within a category as well as aspects that would support placing them outside that category, i.e., when their characteristics are hybrid and somewhat indeterminate. What makes a new case similar to an existing case depends in part on why the courts in the earlier cases related a particular concept or a particular category to the facts of the earlier case (or refused to do so). The features that the court highlighted as contributing to the classification, and those that it regarded as unimportant, provide points of comparison for the classification of new cases. In some cases, the similarity to existing cases will provide very strong support for adopting the classification in dispute. In other cases, the similarity will provide only weak or partial support.

Similarities between cases are not always difficult to detect: obviously, no case is *exactly like* any other case. Every case is unique, but legal history is full of non-hard cases that were easily decided according to comparisons and similarities on which there was no doubt at all. Let us think of the First Amendment to the US Bill of Rights: the right to free speech has, intrinsically, a very broad realm of application; as a matter of fact, under the First Amendment right to free speech judges decided cases involving false speech (*Debs v. US*, 1919), "fighting words" (*Cantwell v. Connecticut*, 1940), freedom of assembly and public forums (*Schneider v. New Jersey*, 1939), symbolic speech (*US v. O'Brien*, 1968), compelled speech (*Wooley v. Maynard*, 1977), school speech (*Morse v. Frederick*, 2007), obscenity (*US v. Stevens*, 2010) *et cetera*. Not only all these cases fell in the semantic frame of the First Amendment quite ordinarily, but all the similar cases involving similar actions like, for instance, organizing labor meetings in public places (*Hague v. C.I.O*, 1939) and distributing handbills on public streets or door-to-door (*Schneider v. New Jersey*, 1939), were not problematic as to the category those activities should fall into.

The thesis we intend to develop is that the classification of legal reality, both in hard cases and in more "ordinary" cases, is related to decision-making processes. Unlike ordinary language, legal language connects general rules and particular events, actions and objects in order to solve conflicts through a process of decision.

When it comes to deciding more complex cases like those analysed in this chapter, legal decision-making processes relate to some basic aspects of legal systems like (i) the *fragmentary* nature of legal materials and (ii) the *plurality* of decision-making bodies. Legal materials – precedents, statutes, conventions, principles – are the work of many different hands at different times and with different outlooks. As a result, legal systems tend to exhibit only contextual and relative coherence.

Given the fragmentary nature of legal systems and the plurality of legal decision-makers, there is considerable scope for disagreement when decision-makers are faced with novel questions. The use of analogies in law serves to compensate for some of the indeterminacy which flows from fragmented materials and the pluralism of decision-makers. That a relevant similarity exists usually provides a good reason for deciding the case the same way, since it renders the law more replicable than it would otherwise be, and enables lawyers to predict more accurately how a situation will be treated by the law.

In Common law, individual decisions by a court are *binding* for that court and on lower courts; the reasoning applied in an individual decision, referred to as the *ratio decidendi*, can function as a precedent for future cases involving similar conflicts. In practice, of course, the situation is complex. The *ratio* must be understood in the context of the facts of the original case, and there is considerable room for debate about its generality and its applicability to future cases. If a consensus emerges that a past case was wrongly decided, later judgments will *distinguish* it from new cases, effectively restricting the scope of the *ratio* to the original case.

Since courts are bound to apply the law, and since earlier decisions have practical authority over the content of the law, later courts are bound to follow the decisions of earlier cases. This is commonly known as the *doctrine of precedent*, or *stare decisis* (i.e., standing by things decided). The practice of precedent involves later courts being bound to either follow or not follow the earlier decision, but only if the facts of the later case fall within the terms of the *ratio*. The *ratio* plays an indispensable role in fixing the scope of the later court's duty to follow or distinguish. The *ratio* represents the view of the court that those facts spoke in favor of the outcome, and that they were not defeated by any combination of the other factors present in the case. The *ratio* of a precedent case is constructed through a process of comparison and balance of similarities and differences that are evaluated contextually. Outside the law, analogies are not binding *per se*. The normative force of a similarity, on which an argument by analogy is based, is always contextual and bound to the decision-making process.

2.3 Classificatory analogies in law

The *force* of an argument by analogy is different from that of precedent. An indistinguishable precedent must be followed unless the court has the power to overrule the earlier decision and does so. By contrast, arguments by analogy vary in their strengths: from very 'close' analogies (which strongly support a result) to more 'remote' analogies (which weakly support a result). Analogies do not bind *per se*: they must be considered along with other reasons in order to reach a result. That an analogy is rejected in one case does not preclude raising the analogy in a different case.

In law analogies might carry a weight additional to the merits of the case although it is not easy to state if and how an analogy can be preferred to another one. The approach of courts is complex: some decisions and doctrines are regarded as mistakes and have no analogical weight. Other doctrines may be regarded as imperfect but they do have analogical weight. Other still may be regarded as simply correct, and their existence provides further support for adopting the view in the novel case. There are a number of possible indirect benefits that accrue from the practice of analogical reasoning, such as exposing judges to a wider variety of fact situations than the particular set before them, making them consider the views of other judges in previous cases and exerting a conservative pressure on individual decision-makers.

Legal systems are constituted by elements profoundly interconnected, but no two cases are identical. The *ratio* of each case must be understood in the context of the facts, and there is often considerable room for debate about its generality and its applicability to future cases. What makes two cases similar is a matter of considerable debate, and goes to the root of the question of the nature of *precedent* in legal reasoning. In saying that two cases are the same, we can never say that they are *identical*: even if the interests or values at stake are similar, the conditions, the timing, the places, the spaces and the individuals involved in the case will never be exactly identical. No two situations are identical in every respect: they must differ at least in having occurred at different times and/or different places. For this reason, lawyers speak of two cases being the same in "all relevant respects." Which of course raises the question of what makes two cases "relevantly" similar. As a matter of fact, identifying a related case relevantly similar to the case at stake is the first step in the use of analogies. The second step is how that case bears on the issue in the current case. That depends not on the fit between the issues in the two cases, but on the *rationale* for the resolution of the issue in the first case, namely on the "proportionality" between the two situations. Unlike similarity judgments, analogical reasoning entails a more complex judgment on the coherence between two different situations that, at first stake, do not look *plainly* similar as, for instance, in the First Amendment examples aforementioned. Even though generalization has a central role also in detecting similarities (two characteristics are *alike* by reference to a more general one), we can say that analogical reasoning proceeds from the recognition of some differences and then works on the relevance of the similarities and irrelevance of the differences between two situations.

Against the background of this arbitrary distinction we are drawing between similarity and analogy, we can say that in law both similarity and analogy are informed by the necessity to decide conflicts. The main philosophical problems raised by similarity and analogy are thus: (1) when are two cases the "same" for the purposes of precedent? (2) when are two cases "similar" for the purposes of analogy? and (3) in both situations, why should the decision in the earlier case affect the decision in the later case? The linguistic debate on prototypes can help clarifying these issues and, at the same time, can earn perspective and depth from the legal examples and the "conflictuality" of legal categorization (which would not exist outside the necessity to decide who is right and who is wrong according to and coherently with a conventionally built normative system).

3 The analogical force of *relevant* similarities: insights from the linguistic debate on prototypes

3.1 Relevant similarity in the standard prototype theory

As we will now see, there is a natural and, we believe, insightful parallel to be drawn between the way similarity and analogy are used in legal reasoning to decide whether the terms of a norm apply in a particular situation (or in more than one), and the role they play, according to prototype theories, in our everyday processes of categorization (cognitive and linguistic) of the world. Indeed, following the original version of the prototype theory (also known as "*standard* prototype theory"), which was developed in psycholinguistics under the impulse of Eleanor Rosch's work (1973), similarity is the motor of our general common sense ability to classify things under concepts, and the best explanation of linguistic meaning, pretty much in the way similarity is shown to operate in legal classification and reasoning by precedent. This view of categorization is indeed supported by developmental studies of the way children master new categories based on examples, as well as by language acquisition and understanding. Based on psycho-developmental and ethnological studies, prototype theory argues that, contrary to a widely shared view, linguistic concepts and general categories are not definable in terms of necessary and sufficient satisfaction conditions. In other words, there is no fixed set of conditions that can possibly determine a priori what belongs to a concept or a linguistic category, and what does not. More precisely, two main theses distinguish prototype theory of categories from the standard on: 1) categories are not conceived in terms of definitions encompassing necessary and sufficient conditions, but rather in terms of prototypes (most representative exemplars of the category), or of combinations of traits, attributes and properties that are typical of a category; 2) categorization is not an activity of verification of satisfaction conditions but rather a measurement of degrees of similarity of an object to the prototype of the category.

The flexibility of the prototypical conception allows it to account for the fuzziness of its referential applicability, the non-homogeneity of categories, and the adaptability to the changing conditions of reality (allowing to incorporate new instances in the existing categories), while preserving its structural stability. For instance, there is no fixed set of traits (e.g. having feathers, having a beak, being able to fly, etc.) that defines what a bird is. Rather, each community (linguistic or cultural), retains certain exemplars (those that are more "exemplary") as prototypical of a category (best exemplars) and others as more peripheral instances, depending on their degree of proximity with the exemplary instances, that is, on their similarity. So while a robin might be considered as a prototypical example of a bird, most people would consider that an ostrich or a penguin is less representative of this category. Categories are thus not well-delimited sets of instances with clear-cut boundaries and determinate tests for deciding what falls in or out. Rather, they have an internal gradient structure and fuzzy boundaries. And the features that we commonsensically tend to use to characterize instances of a certain class are prototypical but in no way necessary or sufficient.

As pointed out by Charnock, "In his presentation of open texture Hart used the term 'penumbra' to refer to what in prototype theory is called the periphery. In this he followed a tradition found in American jurisprudence (see *Olmstead v US* and *Griswold v Connecticut*, 1965). He thus presents roller skates (among other things) as penumbral instances of vehicles. Even more unlikely examples have been envisaged in both English and American cases. In *Garner v Burr*, a poultry shed was accepted as a vehicle, while in *McBoyle v US* (per Justice Holmes) an aircraft was not" (Charnock 2013: 131). In law as in psycholinguistics, this relationship between a clearer semantic "center" and a periphery (where various objects that might be similar can be listed) opens the question of what constitutes a *relevant similarity*, and thus drives the inclusion under a given category. As we will see in the next section, the notion of alignment can provide a more rigorous explanation of the intuitively fuzzy idea of relevance. But before we turn to it, let us first note that, in both spheres of categorization under discussion, relevance is acknowledged as context-dependent. In law, different norms that include the same term allow for a divergence in the similarities that are judged relevant. In the same way, psycholinguistic studies have shown that different linguistic/cultural communities classify very different objects under the same concept, based on different sorts of similarity judgments. In discussions on the role of similarity in the prototype model of categorization, many scholars have pointed out, for example, that, while bats share many features with birds, they nevertheless fall out of this category in Indo-European languages. In these communities, similarity in the way animals reproduce (viz. laying eggs) is more important than similarities concerning the capacity to fly. But this is not true of all cultures. For example, in the Australian language Nunggubuyy, the category that comes closer to our category of bird does include bats as well (Heath 1978: 41). So the dimensions along which degrees of similarity are measured tend to vary among groups, even in cases where the traits that are considered as prototypical are the same. Indeed, even for us, prototypical birds do fly.

In this respect, the examples chosen by Charnock are particularly interesting, as they further highlight the context sensitivity of legal objects such as *vehicle*. Indeed, in the case of *Garner v Burr*, a farmer had added iron wheels to a poultry shed and pulled it with his tractor on the highway. He was prosecuted, and finally acquitted, for the accusation of violation of the British Road Traffic Act of 1930, which stipulates that any "vehicle" traveling on a public highway must be fitted with pneumatic tires. The reason that motivated this decision was that 'vehicle' was understood as a means of transportation on wheels or runners and used for the carriage of persons or goods. However, the farmer wasn't carrying anything at the time. So the feature that was primarily used to judge membership to the category of vehicles in the context of the British Traffic Act was that of transportation of goods or people.

While *McBoyle v United States* was also judged in relation to what could be classified as a vehicle, this involved a different contextual criterion for similarity. In the United States, the National Motor Vehicle Theft Act, punishing whoever transports, or caused to be transported – in interstate or foreign commerce – a motor vehicle, knowing it to have been stolen, defined 'motor vehicle' as including "an automobile, automobile truck, automobile wagon, motorcycle, or any other self-propelled vehicle not designed for running on rails." In 1931 the Supreme Court of the United States of America had to decide whether to apply this Act in the case *McBoyle vs. United States*. According to the Supreme Court, the definition "an automobile, automobile truck, automobile wagon, motorcycle or any other self-propelled vehicle" should not apply to aircrafts. The problem was the meaning of the word "vehicle" in the phrase "any other self-propelled vehicle not designed for running on rails." The phrase under discussion recalled the popular concept related to the term 'vehicle'. As the definition explicitly mentioned automobile truck, automobile wagon, and motorcycle, the words "any other self-propelled vehicle not designed for running on rails" meant a 'vehicle' in the popular sense, that is, in the interpretation of the Supreme Court, a vehicle running on land.

Notice finally, that while the relevant similarities differ in the two cases, they nevertheless seem to share the same prototypical example to which all other members of the category are compared, viz. automobiles are considered as prototypical vehicles in both cases.

3.2 *Relational alignment* of similarities and their analogical force

Let us now look at the way scholars in cognitive linguistics have proposed to account for *relevant* similarity, to then show how it can be exported into the legal domain. Indeed, standard prototype theory was faced with the very same question in the 90's, that is, it didn't provide any explanation of what makes certain similarities more relevant than others. It was thus argued that the higher number of shared features with a prototype (viz. higher similarity) does not necessarily imply membership to the represented category (viz. best similarity). By comparing knives with forks and saws respectively, Cornell Way noted:

> It is unclear how similarity to a prototype is sufficient to account for the way we structure our concepts, that is there aren't some similarities more salient than others? [...] For example, if a fork is a prototype of an eating utensil and a saw is a prototypical tool, how can we explain that a steak knife is classified as an eating utensil when its resemblance to a saw is far greater than its resemblance to a fork? (Cornell Way 1991: 212)

In other words, the notion of similarity cannot stand alone as a classificatory principle given that any two things will be similar in some respect or other.

To address this limitation, Gentner and Markman (1997) draw a compelling distinction between similarity and *mere-appearance matches* based on the notion of alignment. Based on empirical developmental studies, they defined mere-appearance matches as involving shared object attributes and nothing else. This is for instance the case when we compare the shape of a coin and that of the moon. However, it was argued that in similarity judgments the attributes that are relevant are of course shared ones, but most importantly, ones that stand in the same relations. Similarity comparison thus involves alignment of the relational structures in which the compared features stand. More precisely, we recognize similarities between two objects because they play *analogous* explanatory or causal roles. The reason we single out similarities in these cases is that they are cognitively easier to notice than the relations in which they stand.

What is interesting with this view is that it overturns the widely shared idea that similarity is just a flat comparison, as opposed to analogy, which involves reasoning and inference making. Indeed, the most *relevant* similarities are in fact the ones that stand in alignable complex systems of relations, including higher-order explanatory relations, that is, in alignable theories of the world. In other words, the conceptualisation of world that involves classification of its entities cannot be dissociated from the corresponding theorising of the world, which supports inferring and reasoning. In this sense, Gentner and Markman rightly point to the close kinship between similarity and analogy. In categorisation, similarity judgment is a goal-oriented or theory-driven activity, just like analogical reasoning. Though left implicit, similarity can be seen as operating, in the process of categorisation, as an analogical "potential," as highlighting the features that are relevant for complex representation or theorisation of the situation at hand, and which can, in less obviously comparable cases, operate to analogically extend the category.

Following this line, one can argue that the choice of some similarities, over others, as driving category membership judgments, also constrains the range of relevant analogies that can be made to extend the category. In general, Gentner and Markman note that: "commonalities gain importance when they are part of a matching system." Extending this from similarity to differences, they highlight that "Just as commonalities gain importance when they are part of a matching system, so too do differences. That is, alignable differences are more salient than non-alignable differences. Intuitively, this focus on alignable differences makes sense, for it leads to a focus on those differences that are relevant to the common causal or goal structure that spans the situation" (Gentner & Markman 1997: 50).

Addressing the criticisms that have been raised against the central role of similarity in categorization, in particular against the standard prototype theory, they argue that recognizing the analogical-like mapping that is operated through similarity recognition, gives the means to understand why certain similarities while numerous might be irrelevant or not salient enough. Indeed, showing examples where similarities are important but things are categorized differently (as with birds and bats), many scholars have prompted to abandon similarity as driving categorization to the benefit of more theory-based judgments. Gentner and Markman argue, however, that "if similarity computation is assumed to be that of structural alignment, then the similarity between two instances will be based not only on object-level commonalities but also on common relations and common origins. Assuming that our representations include information about theory-based relations [...] as well as information about features, then the schism between similarity-based and theory-based categorisation may be more apparent than real" (Gentner & Markman 1997: 54).

3.3 Aligned similarities in legal decision-making: some examples

In order to see how the notion of alignment and of analogical potential of similarities can be "exported" from cognitive linguistics to the legal domain, one has to acknowledge a crucial difference between these two domains. Indeed cognitive and linguistic processes of categorization are essentially descriptive in nature. Correspondingly, alignment and analogical reasoning serve a predictive function. If two domains of experience bear significant similarities, relative to a given system of relations or theory of the domain that is the base of the comparison, then one can predict certain things about the targeted domain of comparison. Legal reasoning, on the other hand, is normative in nature.

Relevant similarities are established against systems of values and interests, and analogical comparison of situations serves a prescriptive purpose. The question to be decided is whether a given situation *ought* to be treated in the same way as a previously decided case.

To use a distinction recently made by Grassen (2009), in reasoning by normative analogy, one makes inferences about what the consequences ought to be in the analogised case: "*A* and *B* ought to lead to the same consequences." On the other hand, reasoning by descriptive analogy leads to predictions about consequences: since *A* and *B* stand in the same *ratio* R to *C* and *D* respectively, everything that follows from R in the first case will also follow in the second. So, from the legal perspective, balancing values and contrasting interests are fundamental processes. These are subject to alignment and actually inform the criteria through which the similar characteristics are evaluated.

In order to evaluate if two situations are similar – in order to apply the same general norm (Civil Law systems) or in order to evaluate if the same *rationale* applies (Common Law systems), the legal interpreter has to consider the actual alignment of the relational structures in the two situations involved. In particular, what is evaluated is whether two cases are similar according to the structure of relations involved in the case, that is, in law, the values and the interests. The single traits of a case are not relevant in themselves. The similarities are functional: we could define them as the common features that help building normative parallels between the base and target situations under comparison. Comparison processes, accelerated by the necessity of the decision, foster insights. By highlight commonalities and relevant differences, comparisons invite new inferences. The process of normative alignment of legal cases shows the importance of how different relational systems can match – and thus which commonalities are salient and which differences are salient. As a matter of fact, not every similarity increases the probability of the conclusion and not every difference decreases it. Some similarities and differences are known to be (or accepted as being) utterly irrelevant and should have no influence on the probability judgments.

To illustrate this point, let us reconsider, in a bit more detail, the decision-making argumentation in the case *McBoyle v. United States* [43 F.2d 273 (10th Cir. 1930)]. The question was: could the airplane fall in the category of "vehicles" as defined by the *National Motor Vehicle Theft Act*? Decision-making process, classification of reality according to legal criteria, evaluation of the relevant similarities and reasoning by analogy: in the answer to that question all these aspects were involved. Counsel for McBoyle contended that the word "vehicle" should include only conveyances that travel on the ground; that an airplane is not a vehicle but a ship; and that, under the doctrine of *ejusdem generis*,[1] the phrase "any other self-propelled vehicle" could not be construed to include an airplane. The evaluation of the similarities was functional to decide on the inclusion or exclusion of an object (airplane) in a category (vehicles). While similarity is generally considered as a comparison of the single traits, and analogy as a type of inferential reasoning, we should underline how the evaluation of the relevant similarities is already informed by the legal decision-making process. Already the evaluation of similarities is driven by reasoning, and thus depends on the structural alignment of the compared cases: similarity, inasmuch as analogy, is not "neutral."

A vehicle is an instrument of conveyance or communication, but it is also that in or on which any person or thing is or may be carried, especially on land, as a coach, wagon, car, bicycle, etc. A more specific definition of 'motor vehicle' could be: a vehicle operated by a power developed within itself and used for the purpose of carrying passengers or materials. Since the term is used in the different statutes regulating such vehicles, it is generally defined as including all vehicles propelled by any power other than muscular power, except traction engines, road rollers, and such motor vehicles as run only upon rails or tracks. Both the derivation and the definition of the word 'vehicle' indicate that it is sufficiently broad to include any means or device by which persons or things are carried or transported, and it is not limited to instrumentalities used for traveling on land. What *is* an airplane, then? It is a self-propelled object, designed to carry passengers and freight from place to place. It runs partly on the ground but principally in the air. It furnishes a rapid means for transportation of persons and comparatively light things. It therefore serves the same general purposes as an automobile, automobile truck, or motorcycle. It is of the same general kind or class as the motor vehicles specifically enumerated in the statutory definition and, thus, considering an airplane to come within the general expression 'any other self-propelled vehicle,' does not offend against the maxim of *ejusdem generis*. The role of the *ejusdem generis* in legal argumentation is analogous to the process of alignment in cognitive linguistics, since they both start from the recognition of the relevant similarities according to a final objective (decision, classification). In the case discussed, it was decided that the phrase "any other self-propelled vehicle" should include an airplane, a motor-

---

[1] The *ejusdem generis* interpretive rule is used in statutory interpretation: this rule implies that where general words are not followed by an enumeration of persons or things or by words with a specific meaning, such general words are not to be construed in their widest extent, but are to be held as applying only to persons or things of the same general kind or class as those specifically mentioned).

boat, and any other like means of conveyance or transportation which is self-propelled, and is of the same general class as an automobile and a motorcycle.

4 Grounding coherent analogies in similarity

4.1 The material theory of induction

Replicability relates to the importance of *coherence* in law (Sunstein 1993: 778–779). Arguments in favor of coherence normally emphasize its instrumental value. This is tied up with the replicability of legal decision-making. The pluralism of decision-making bodies is the reason for the fragmentary nature of legal materials and of the plurality of decision-makers. There is indeed considerable scope for disagreement when decision-makers are faced with novel questions. Analogies in law serve first of all to compensate for the indeterminacy which flows from this. The existence of a close analogy usually provides a good reason for deciding the case the same way, since it renders the law more replicable than it would otherwise be, and it enables lawyers to predict more accurately how a situation will be treated by the law.

At the more general psycholinguistic level, Gentner and Markman highlight the very same requirement of coherence of the process of alignment as it operates in analogy, but also, as we saw, in similarity. This is captured by the authors under the general principle of systematicity:

> The systematicity principle captures a tacit preference for coherence and causal predictive power in analogical processing. We are not much interested in analogies that capture a series of coincidences, even if there are a great many deal of them. [...] Given an alignment of structure, further inferences can be made from the analogy – for aligning of connected systems of knowledge – is crucial here. It is what permits us to generate spontaneous inferences. (Gentner & Markman 1997: 47)

This "formal requirement" of alignment and reasoning is at work both in analogical reasoning and in similarity comparisons. Legal theorists have, however, emphasized that for an analogy to be sufficiently strong, and thus legally efficient, a material grounding has to be further given. Formal requirements alone are too permissive. This in turn emphasizes the need to ground analogy in material comparisons of the situations at stake, that is, on similarity comparisons.

Rules of analogical inference in law would need to be supplemented with considerations of *relevance*, which depend upon the subject matter, historical context and logical details particular to each analogical argument. Searching for a general rule of analogical inference is thus futile.

In order to understand how, in turn, analogy traces back to similarity in law, we can refer to Norton's idea that there is no general theory of induction and that every inductive process is always, necessarily, based on material and contextual criteria ("material theory of induction").

Norton argues that every project of formalizing analogical and inductive reasoning in terms of one or more simple formal schemata is impossible and even wrong. He writes:

> If analogical reasoning is required to conform only to a simple formal schema, the restriction is too permissive. Inferences are authorized that clearly should not pass muster [...] The natural response has been to develop more elaborate formal templates [...] The familiar difficulty is that these embellished schema never seem to be quite embellished enough; there always seems to be some part of the analysis that must be handled intuitively without guidance from strict formal rules. (Norton 2010)

Norton argues that there is no universal logical principle that "powers" analogical inference "by asserting that things that share some properties must share others." On the contrary, each analogical inference is warranted by some local constellation of facts about the target system that could be defined, according to Norton, "the facts of analogy." These local facts are to be determined and investigated on a case-by-case basis. Analogy and similarity are informed and related to their function in the decision making process, as the case studies indicate.

4.2 Analogical selection of relevant similarities: a compelling case study

Most importantly, the use of analogy in law is always supported by highlighting relevant similarities. It is not enough to say that two cases should be treated in the same way. While this may be the drive of the comparison, this needs to be supported and substantiated by highlighting what, in the two cases, makes them similar *with respect* to the norm that is to be analogically applied. It is to this complex relation between analogy and similarity that we will now turn to.

In this respect, an interesting case concerns the use of the trespass to chattels in internet law: in particular, in the cases *Thrifty-Tel* v. *Bezenek* (1996) and *CompuServe* v. *CyberPromotions* (1997). In these cases, some courts applied the Common Law action called "trespass to chattels" in order to decide cases where the plaintiff had received undesired emails. Chattels are material goods and the trespass to chattels is a type of tort whereby the infringing party has intentionally or negligently interfered with another person's lawful possession of a chattel (some kind of movable personal property). The interference can be any physical contact with the chattel in a quantifiable way, or any dispossession of the chattel (whether by taking it, destroying it, or barring the owner's access to it). So the material interference is necessary for the application of the trespass to chattels. In order to apply it, the judges had to use analogical arguments. The action of trespass requires an intentional contact and a concrete interference with the mobile good, the chattel. The problem was that an email account is much less concrete an object than a physical space. In order for it to be as a mobile, material good (which is the necessary condition for the application of the trespass to chattels), an analogy had to be drawn.

The trespass to chattels was used for the first time to decide an internet law case in *Thrifty-Tel v Bezenek*, decided by the Court of Appeals of California. In this specific case, there had been an intrusion (provoked by the action of sending spam continuously) in the email account of the plaintiff. The telephone service provider (plaintiff) lamented an illicit appropriation against the parents of some children that had hacked (through an action called "phreaking") their domains – they had used telephone services without authorisation. The children had entered the informatic system of the society *Thrifty-Tel* by manually creating authorization codes; then they had used the software to search for new codes of access. The Court of Appeals decided to apply the trespass to chattels because of the "tangible" materiality of the electronic particles of which the electronic signals were made. The Court, in order to justify the analogical inference, pointed out that there was a clear similarity between the electronic particles and other types of interference, like that produced by electromagnetic waves (that could also cause damages). *Thrifty-Tel* opened the path to the application of the trespass to chattels also to Internet.

The leading case afterwards became *CompuServe v Cyber Promotions*: the latter, offering commercial services online, transmitted huge volumes of emails to the net that was property of *CompuServe* (despite *CompuServe* was using filters against spam). The Court of Ohio, recalling *Thrifty-Tel*, held that the electronic signals received by CompuServe were sufficiently tangible to justify an action of trespass. The contact was in fact intentional, since the spam email had been sent intentionally. Analogies were drawn with the case of owners of commercial activities forbidding to enter their offices, and with owners forbidding to throw newspapers inside the space of their property.

4.3 Blind analogies in the extended prototype theory: towards a solution

We saw how the developments in psycholinguistics and standard prototype theory could furnish some useful insights to understand the notion of relevant similarity and bring it closer to analogy. Now, this last legal point on the material theory of legal analogical induction can in turn be used to inform and overcome some limitations of the way analogy has been embedded in the extended version of prototype theory, and provide the missing unifying link with its standard similarity-driven version.

The extended version of the prototype theory (there are in fact many versions but they share a common core) effected two related revisions on the standard version. First, it dropped the assumption of one central exemplar situated at the center of each category, and correlatively it abandoned the idea of a periphery made up of non-prototypical. Alongside, the idea that the prototypes are those against which all other instances are compared was also abandoned. This implies that under the extended prototypical view of categories, there is no single trait that is necessarily shared by all the instances of the category (Lakoff 1987: 12; Lakoff and Johnson 1980). Prototypicality is not anymore considered as driving categorization, but as an effect of categorization according to a more general Wittgensteinian principle of family resemblance. Note that this extended version is not incompatible with the standard prototype theory, as similarity with respect to a prototype becomes a particular case of family resemblance.

Crucially, the original theory was extended to include analogy-driven processes of categorization, such as metaphorical mappings. Following this line, Lakoff (1987), who has been one of the central figures of this movement, notoriously defended the view that metaphor was the most central mechanism of lexical meaning extension. According to the fundamental principles of cognitive linguistics, the linguistic role of metaphor was considered as the mirror of the more general, extra-linguistic role of analogical mappings in the way we structure and organize our domains of experience and knowledge:

> Austin turns to what Johnson and I (Lakoff and Johnson 1980) refer to as metaphor, but which Austin, following Aristotle, terms "analogy."
>
> When $A:B=X:Y$ then A and X are often called by the same name, e.g., the foot of a mountain and the foot of a list. Here there is a good reason for calling the things both "feet" but are we to say they are "similar"? Not in any ordinary sense. We may say that the relations in which they stand to B and Y are similar relations. (Austin 1961: 71)
>
> Austin isn't explicit here, but what seems to be going on is that both mountains and lists are being structured in terms of metaphorical projection of the human body onto them. (Lakoff 1987: 19–20)

Note that the above-mentioned use of analogy relies on purely structural principles (also known as formal analogies). This notoriously led extended versions of prototype theory to accept very disparate categories, spanning across domains, and with no cognitive unity beyond the lexically (and highly polysemic) unity.

Following similar concerns to the ones raised by Norton (2003) with respect to legal analogies, Kleiber (1999) (among others) expressed his worry that prototype theory was thus getting astray from cognitive mechanisms of categorization.

> The most spectacular result of abandoning the constraint of similarity to a prototype is [...] the explosion of the category in sub-categories that might have nothing in common anymore. If the prototype [and correlatively similarity], as a unifying entity [principle] of the category, disappears, [...] then the door is open for a referentially exploded conception of categories: a category might conceivably be formed out of different types of referents [...], linked to each other in a way that the one has nothing directly in common with the other [...] In other words categories do not stand anymore for one type of referent. (Kleiber 1999: 161, translation by the authors)

A reply to this criticism, we would like to suggest, can be developed along the lines of Norton's material theory of induction. Tracing analogy back to similarity, at least when it operates as a general cognitive categorisation principle, allows us to avoid the overgeneralisation of the extended prototype theory. As we saw, in legal analogical reasoning, every analogy has to be further supported by, or anchored in, similarity. In the legal domain, analogy cannot stand alone. This is all the more obvious in the extreme cases of *Thrifty-Tel* v *Bezenek* (1996) and *CompuServe* v. *CyberPromotions* (1997) discussed above. The argument does not rest on the mere analogy between physical trespass and the trespass (by receiving unwanted email) of a virtual private space (a personal mailbox). This is further substantiated by a search for actual similarities involving physical intrusion in some private physical space (by particles).

This essential connection between analogy and similarity was absent from the standard prototype theory where similarity is the exclusive operating principle, but also from the extended prototype theory where analogy operates between domains with no common feature at all, as in analogies between concrete and abstract situations (typical of metaphoric uses of analogy). In a way, one can say that the extended version of the prototype theory took a significant step by bringing into focus analogical principles of categorization, emphasising the formal, structural significance of analogical mappings, as a central tool for understanding and comparing different domains and situations of experience. But in doing so it completely left aside the material ground of analogy which refers to shared and typically observable features. Note in passing that in the original Aristotelian theory of analogy we find among others in the *Topics* the proposed criteria for the evaluation of the strength of analogical arguments include both the number of similarities, viz. shared properties, and the shared relations, causes and laws from which the analogy derives. Criteria of evaluation give equal weight to the material and the formal grounds of analogy.

5 Conclusion: the blurry boundaries between similarity and analogy

Looking at the way similarity and analogy operate in legal and in cognitive and linguistic processes of categorization, we argued that the difference between the two is much more a matter of degree than a clear-cut difference in nature. On the one hand, if similarity involves the sharing of features, the relevance of the single feature can only be judged on the basis of the respective roles played in higher order inferential structures and on the basis of their alignment. On the other hand, when applied to reason on real subject matters, in a way that determines or conditions our actions in the world, analogy is not useful in its purest structural form. Its strength and adequacy need to stand on shared features between the analogised situations. This holds whether analogy bears on actions in a normative or a predictive way (viz. what consequences ought to derive from them, or what will be causally entailed).

We claim, in this sense, that categorization processes fulfill parallel purposes in the legal and extra-legal sphere, that is they are intimately linked, oriented towards and driven by, reasoning: normative decision-making in one case, and predictive theorizing in the other. Categorization is never a mere activity of labelling. The categorical labelling that unifies referents as exemplars of a legal or general concept or term is not operated *per se*. It is goal-oriented and is inseparable from the inferential processes it sustains. Such inferences from systems of relations and principles that bear, normatively or descriptively, on reality thus have to be both formally and materially grounded.

Similarity and analogy are always deeply nested in one another.

References

Austin, John L. *Philosophical papers*. J. O. Urmson & G. J. Warnock (eds.), Oxford: Clarendon Press (1961).

Charnock, Ross. 2013. Hart as contextualist? Theories of interpretation in language and the law. In M. Freeman and F. Smith (eds.), *Law and language: Current legal issues*, Vol. 15, 128–150.

Cornell Way, Eileen. 1991. *Knowledge representation and metaphor*. Springer.

Garssen, Bart. 2009. Comparing the incomparable. Figurative analogies in a dialectical testing procedure. In F. H. van Eemeren & Bart Grassen (eds.), *Pondering on problems of argumentation: Twenty essays on theoretical issues*. Dordrecht: Springer.

Gentner, Dedre & Arthur B. Markman. 1997. Structure mapping in analogy and similarity. *American Psychologist* 52. 45–56.

Heath, Jeffrey. 1978. *Linguistic diffusion in Arnhem Land*. Canberra: Australian Institute of Aboriginal Studies.
Kleiber, Georges. 1999. *La sémantique du prototype. Catégories et sens lexical*. Presse Universitaire de France.
Lakoff, George. 1987. *Women, fire, and dangerous things. What categories reveal about the mind*. University of Chicago Press.
Lakoff, George & Johnson, Mark. 1980. *Metaphors we live by*. University of Chicago Press.
Norton, John D. 2010. There are no universal rules for induction. *Philosophy of Science* 77. 765–777.
Norton, John D. 2003. A material theory of induction. *Philosophy of Science* 70. 647–670.
Rosch, Eleonor. 1973. Natural categories. *Cognitive Linguistics* 7. 532–547.
Sunstein, Cass. 1993. On analogical reasoning. *Harvard Law Review* 106(3). 741–791.

Klaus P. Schneider and Dirk Zielasko

8 When is an insult a crime? On diverging conceptualizations and changing legislation

1 Introduction[1]

The amendment of the Public Order Act 1986, section 5 [POA 1986] by the Crime and Courts Act 2013, section 57 in January 2014 has ended a heated public debate on the "legality" of insults in England and Wales. In May 2012, the campaign "Reform Section 5: Feel Free to Insult Me" was launched, supported by a wide range of civic interest groups such as The Christian Institute[2] and the National Secular Society[3]. Its claim was that POA 1986, section 5 unduly restricted citizens' right to free speech. High-profile cases such as the police's confiscation of a placard that read "Scientology is not a religion, but a dangerous cult" at a rally and the issuing of a court summons to the 16-year old pupil who had brought it[4] under the then-current wording of POA 1986, section 5 were taken as evidence that this legislation had what was called "a chilling effect on democracy"[5].

The controversial debate that was channeled by the initiative not only provides insight into diverging opinions on what type of behavior should by criminally prosecuted, but also into what different speakers understand by the term *insulting behavior*. In this contribution, we will look at different interpretations brought forth in the debate and reference dictionary entries as well as corpus data to establish in what different ways speakers can understand the term *insulting* and how this informs the interpretation of the legislation and its enforcement.

As we will try to show under what conditions the issuing of *insulting behavior* is subject to criminal prosecution in general, a broad definition of

---

[1] We would like to thank the editors and an anonymous reviewer for their helpful comments. Any remaining shortcomings are, needless to say, our own responsibility.
[2] http://www.christian.org.uk/section5insult/, accessed Feb 17th, 2015.
[3] http://www.secularism.org.uk/reform-section-5.html, accessed Feb 17th, 2015.
[4] http://www.theguardian.com/uk/2008/may/20/1, accessed Feb 17th, 2015.
[5] http://www.bbc.co.uk/news/uk-politics-18084081, accessed Feb 17th, 2015.

Klaus P. Schneider and Dirk Zielasko, University of Bonn

DOI 10.1515/9781501504723-008

"crime" as provided by the Oxford English Dictionary, third edition – "an action or omission which constitutes an offense and is punishable by law"[6] – will suffice for our purposes.

2 The legislation and its problems

In 2013, 12,019 offenses under POA 1986, section 5 went to trial, with 9,631 convictions[7]. The total of public order offense proceedings stands at 72,027 with 55,680 convictions for the period April 2013 – March 2014[8].

The Public Order Act of 1986 was originally introduced in response to a number of riots and public disturbances (Southall 1979, Brixton 1981, and the Miners' Strike of 1984/1985) (Strickland and Douse 2013: 3) in an attempt to give the police an instrument to better prevent the outbreak of such disturbances. Before the recent amendment, POA 1986, section 5 read:

> "5 Harassment, alarm or distress. (1) A person is guilty of an offense if he – (a) uses threatening, abusive or insulting words or behavior, or disorderly behavior, or (b) displays any writing, sign or other visible representation which is threatening, abusive or insulting, within the hearing or sight of a person likely to be caused harassment, alarm or distress thereby. [...]"

The range of this provision becomes clear when compared to the immediately preceding section 4A, which was introduced in 1995 and describes the more severe offense:

> 4 A Intentional harassment, alarm or distress. (1) A person is guilty of an offense if, with intent to cause a person harassment, alarm or distress, he – (a) uses threatening, abusive or insulting words or behavior, or disorderly behavior, or (b) displays any writing, sign or other visible representation which is threatening, abusive or insulting, thereby causing that or another person harassment, alarm or distress. [...]

Section 4A includes prosecution thresholds that section 5 lacks, namely:

---

[6] While more verbose, the Oxford Dictionary of Law's definition "an act (or sometimes a failure to act) that is deemed by statute or by the common law to be a public wrong and therefore punishable by the state in criminal proceedings" does contain the same essential semantic elements and is therefore dispensable.

[7] Freedom of Information Request 573-14 FOI 92037, July 25th, 2014.

[8] Ministry of Justice Statistics Bulletin: Criminal Justice Statistics Quarterly Update to March 2014 (England and Wales), published August 14th, 2014.

- The suspect's intent to cause the effects that ultimately make their behavior a matter of public order legislation: *harassment, alarm or distress*. The previous wording of section 5 (of the previous Public Order Act of 1936) required a *"breach of the peace*[9] to be intended or likely to occur," creating at least a tenuous connection between the verbal injury and the threat of physical violence that is absent in POA 1986, section 5.
- The actual causation of *harassment, alarm or distress* in another person or even their noticing the offending behavior (*threatening, abusive or insulting words or behavior, or writing*). To commit an offense under section 5 it is sufficient that the suspect showed *insulting behavior*, and that there was an appropriate target in the vicinity whom the police consider likely to be caused *harassment, alarm or distress*. Prosecution under section 5 is possible even if the police officers themselves are the persons that are subject to *harassment, alarm or distress*, although police officers have to tolerate higher levels of offending behavior than ordinary members of the public[10].

A. T. H. Smith, author of a textbook on public order law, sees the potential for abuse rooted in the provision's phrasing: "Because of the potential breadth of the language in which the section is drafted, it affords scope for injudicious policing."[11]

There are several safeguards against prosecution under POA 1986, section 5, but none manage to sufficiently narrow the provision's scope:

Suspects may invoke the defense of *reasonable conduct* [POA 1986, section 5 (3c)], but carry the burden of proof. *Reasonable conduct* is, according to the police manual *Keeping the Peace*, to be judged "objectively" (National Policing Improvement Agency 2010: 31). Since police officers will usually only take action against persons whose conduct they consider unreasonable, it will be difficult to convince them otherwise. Cases where the suspect means to provoke, especially when aimed at members of ethnic or religious groups, are said to be unreasonable conduct (National Policing Improvement Agency 2010: 31). This makes it hard for protesters who voice controversial opinions to rely on this defense, such as in the exemplary case of a protest against Scientology (see the preceding section).

---

9 A breach of the peace is committed when an individual causes harm, or appears likely to cause harm, to a person, or in that person's presence, to his or her property, or puts that person in fear of such harm being done through an assault, affray, a riot, unlawful assembly or other disturbance (R v Howell, 1982 QB 416).
10 DPP v Orum [1989] 1 WLR 88.
11 http://www.telegraph.co.uk/news/uknews/law-and-order/9734919/Lets-do-away-with-this-insult-to-free-speech.html, accessed Feb 19th, 2015.

Apart from the act itself, the European Charter of Human Rights provides basic protection of the freedom of speech in its Article 10:

> (1) Everyone has the right to freedom of expression. This right shall include freedom to hold opinions and to receive and impart information and ideas without interference by public authority and regardless of frontiers. This Article shall not prevent States from requiring the licensing of broadcasting, television or cinema enterprises.

All legislation must be read in a way that is compatible to the ECHR. However, this protection is not absolute and may be restricted by law:

> (2) The exercise of these freedoms, since it carries with it duties and responsibilities, may be subject to such formalities, conditions, restrictions or penalties as are prescribed by law and are necessary in a democratic society, in the interests of national security, territorial integrity or public safety, for the prevention of disorder or crime, for the protection of health or morals, for the protection of the reputation or rights of others, for preventing the disclosure of information received in confidence, or for maintaining the authority and impartiality of the judiciary.

Limitations on the freedom of speech may be imposed by law as long as they are necessary and proportionate (The Law Commission 2013: 12, 15). This can only be judged on a case-by-case basis, so Art. 10 ECHR does not *per se* counter section 5's criminalization of *insulting behavior*. The Joint Committee on Human Rights supported the deletion of *insulting* from section 5 to "remove a risk that these provisions may be applied in a manner which is disproportionate and incompatible with the right to freedom of expression, as protected by Article 10 ECHR and the common law."[12]

The broad applicability of POA 1986, section 5 has been assessed as extending "the criminal law into areas of annoyance, disturbance, and inconvenience" (Strickland and Douse 2013: 3). Its low threshold leads to insecurity in those voicing their opinions in public, potentially causing citizens to refrain from exerting their right to free speech. Linguistically, we can attribute this to the different ways sections 5 and 4A construct cases of punishable *insulting behavior*.

Politeness research has for some time worked to explain the interpersonal mechanics of insults and other types of impolite behavior. Brown and Levinson categorize insults as a threat to a person's positive social *face*, i.e. "the positive consistent self-image claimed by interactants" (1987: 61, 66).[13] Going forward, a

---

[12] Human Rights Joint Committee, Eighteenth Report Legislative Scrutiny: Protection of Freedoms Bill, 7 October 2011, HL 195/HC 1490 2010–11, paras 157–158.

[13] It is complemented by negative face as "freedom from imposition" by other interactants (Brown and Levinson 1987: 61).

general understanding of face as one's public self-image that can be augmented or threatened through conversation is sufficient.

Focusing especially on *im*politeness, Bousfield (2010: 120–124) presents a tentative system of classification of face-threatening events using four parameters:

a) speaker intent [to threaten/damage face]/projectability;
b) speaker awareness of possible face-damaging effects of their utterance(s);
c) hearer perception/construction of the speaker's intent/hurtfulness of their words, leading to;
d) hearer face actually being, or not being, damaged.

In his terminology, Bousfield (2010: 123) distinguishes between *impoliteness* as the "issuing of intentionally gratuitous and conflictive face-threatening acts that are purposefully performed" and *rudeness* as "inadequate levels of, or inexpertly used politeness," i.e. speech events where no face threat is *intended* by the speaker.

Prosecution under section 4A requires all four parameters present, amounting to what Bousfield calls a "successful communication of impoliteness":
- The phrasing "with intent to cause a person harassment, alarm or distress" refers to parameter a);
- "uses threatening, abusive or insulting words or behavior [...]" to b) and c), given that speakers will consciously use words they think will be understood as being face-threatening by the hearer, and that hearers will correctly interpret such words to mean a conscious face attack by the speaker;
- "thereby causing that or another person harassment, alarm or distress" to d), the actual outcome.

Section 5, on the other hand, does not require parameters a) or d); no intent to cause or an actual causation of *harassment, alarm or distress* is necessary. Parameter c) is mandatory, but can be entirely constructed by the hearer, either pertaining to themselves or even others (e.g. a police officer inferring a face threat targeted at someone else). Parameter b) is also required as the "mental element" of the offense, formulated in POA 1986, section 6(4):

> (4) A person is guilty of an offense under section 5 only if he intends his words or behavior, or the writing, sign or other visible representation, to be threatening, abusive or insulting, or is aware that it may be threatening, abusive or insulting or (as the case may be) he intends his behavior to be or is aware that it may be disorderly.

A lack of awareness regarding the face-threatening potential of one's actions prevents prosecution under section 5, but its presence will regularly be inferred by the hearer, similar to the way the defense of *reasonable conduct* will be difficult to prove to police officers who suspect a section 5 offense in the first place.

This means that section 5 covers impoliteness and rudeness events from "successful communication of impoliteness" (as in section 4A) to any situation where impoliteness is only inferred as a result of "speaker insensitivity or hearer hypersensitivity," "cultural misunderstandings" or "inadequate levels of politeness" (Bousfield 2010: 122–123). In fact, hearer perception or construction of impoliteness – parameter c) – is the key to section 5's applicability.

The only events not covered by section 5 are consequently those where parameter c) is absent:
- "failed attempts at impoliteness," i.e. intended impoliteness not inferred as such or misinterpreted as rudeness; (actual) "rudeness" or inexpertly used politeness;
- "incidental face damage," where harassment, etc. are caused without consciously being attributed by the hearer to the speaker's behavior;
- actual politeness, where face-threatening behavior is sufficiently mitigated by the speaker without the hearer noticing.

3 Different opinions = conflicting conceptualizations?

Conflicting opinions on the matter of reform of section 5 need not be based on different political or moral views on the criminalization of insulting behavior, but can simply be informed by different perceptions of what insulting behavior actually is, i.e. the mental concept or *signified* that is evoked by the term. In this section, we will examine the viewpoints of key actors to see whether they refer to the same mental concept when they talk about *insulting behavior*.

Since the debate centered on a proposed new phrasing of POA 1986, section 5, we must take its context into account, in particular the opposition between insulting and *abusive* within section 5, and *(intentionally) insulting* in section 4A. As noted in Smith's textbook on public order offenses (1987: 117), "the point has been made that *abusive* and *insulting* are semantically very similar, and can be used more or less interchangeably."

3.1 Reform supporters

The Reform Section 5 movement wanted to see *insulting* removed from section 5, arguing that it criminalized legitimate critique that was misinterpreted as being *insulting*, either because of semantic ambiguity or recipients' hypersensitivity.

Abusive in section 5, as well as a*busive* and *insulting* [with intent to harass] in section 4A were not objected to. This indicates that *abusive* is considered more severe than *insulting* behavior and the two terms are considered to be partially exclusive: *insulting* is being construed as mainly low-intensity and *abusive* as exclusively high-intensity offensive behavior.

Furthermore we can infer that in the view of the reform campaigners, *insulting* behavior should only be legal if committed without intention to *harass, alarm or distress*. Using Bousfield's terminology, only actual impoliteness should be punishable (under section 4A), and rudeness that is mistaken for impoliteness should only be punishable (under section 5) if its intensity qualifies it as *abusive behavior*.

3.2 The government

The British government wanted to retain the word *insulting* within section 5 based on the assumption that the provision ensured a good level of protection, especially for minorities and religious groups that were frequent victims of verbal abuse. Section 5 was also praised for providing clear boundaries of what kind of conduct was allowed, and that a reform could create ambiguity, leaving "courts in the invidious position of having to decide on a case-by-case basis whether particular words or behavior were criminally 'abusive' or merely non-criminally 'insulting'" (Strickland and Douse 2013: 1). While what is described here is nothing other than the courts' everyday task of applying the legislation to the case at hand, this indicates that although *insulting* is considered lower in intensity than *abusive*, it should still be prosecuted. On this level, their opposition to the reform can be seen as a case of political, not linguistic divergence.

Yet other arguments that were brought forth against a reform indicate a different understanding of *insulting behavior* with regard to its intentionality: Home Secretary Theresa May elaborated that "The Government supports the retention of section 5 as it currently stands, because we believe that the police should be able to take action when they are sworn at, when protesters burn poppies on Armistice day and in similar scenarios" (Strickland and Douse 2013: 14). Additionally, it was argued that a reform could send out the wrong message to the public by suggesting that it was "acceptable" to insult someone in public.[14]

If we assume the typical insult not to be simply a failed attempt at politeness, but an intentional attack on another person's face (examples of which could be the swearing at others or the burning of remembrance poppies), we can

---

14 Home Office (2013: 4; statement by the Police Federation of England and Wales).

conclude that this reasoning does not take the provisions of section 4A into account, which covers insulting behavior that is driven by the *intent to harass, alarm or distress*. This means that either the term *insulting* in section 5 is mistakenly expanded to include its counterpart in section 4A, or that there was reason to doubt section 4A's usefulness to prosecute offenders in the above cases, which was not overtly communicated for political reasons. Section 4A indeed plays a much smaller role in the courts than section 5, with only 111 proceedings and 81 convictions in England and Wales in the year 2013.[15]

Taken at face value, we can say that the two key actors in the reform debate partially differ in their understanding of the meaning of *insulting* in section 5.

3.3 The media

The fear to "communicate the wrong message" was not misplaced, as in the news media, the campaign against section 5 was often narrowed down to whether or not it should be legal to publicly insult someone, without mentioning that section 5 penalizes *abusive behavior* and ignoring the entire section 4A. Headlines such as "Rowan Atkinson and Stephen Fry back campaign to make insults legal"[16] mislead by ignoring the fact that even with section 5 amended, it would still be illegal to *intentionally harass, alarm or distress* someone by *insulting behavior*, and even to unintentionally do so if the conduct can be considered *abusive*. These omissions communicate to the public that high-intensity offensive behavior would be legalized by the reform, which is clearly not the case. In this light, the government's hesitance to initiate a reform of section 5 as to not communicate to the public that "[all kinds of] insults are okay" was somewhat justified, although it is debatable whether possible misinformation is a legitimate reason to oppose legislative reform, especially if the communication of the reform's wider consequences falls into one's own purview.

3.4 The director of public prosecutions

Relating the judicial perspective on this issue, then-incumbent Director of Public Prosecutions Keir Starmer said to be "unable to identify a case in which the

---

15 Freedom of Information Request 573-14 FOI 92037, July 25th, 2014.
16 The Week, Oct. 18th, 2012, cf. also "British 'insult law' to be repealed" (The Commentator, Jan 14th, 2013), "Law banning insulting words and behavior 'has to end'" (BBC News, May 16th, 2012).

alleged behavior leading to conviction could not be characterized as *abusive* as well as *insulting*" (Strickland and Douse 2013: 13) and that the word *insulting* could be safely removed from section 5. His statement implies that in cases where *insulting* behavior did not cross the threshold of *abusive* (or was not likely to cause *harassment, alarm or distress*), the defendant was acquitted, leading to an understanding that *insulting* is to be considered the general term for offensive verbal behavior of all intensities and that *abusive* exclusively refers to higher-intensity behavior.

If we for a moment imagine that in his assertion, the DPP flouted the Gricean maxim of relevance, that is, gave the impression that there were numerous cases in which *merely insulting* behavior did not lead to a conviction (when in fact there were none), he would have meant the exact opposite: that *abusive* covers offensive behavior of any intensity, including that which can be described as *insulting*. With *abusive* being the more general term, the removal of *insulting* would have no effect on the legislation at all. However unlikely, this reading illustrates that given a certain understanding of *abusive*, the proposed amendment would not change the way it is enforced, something we will explore further in the next sections.

4 Intentionalism and textualism

Only an accurate definition of the term *insulting* as it is used in POA 1986, section 5, especially regarding its semantic relationship with *abusive*, allows us to assess the effect that its removal will have on the legislation as a whole. To this end, we will examine the provision as it appears in its context. If the context fails to establish a clear relationship between these terms, the question arises whether they can be given a law-specific (but legislation-independent) definition and be treated as legal terms of art.

But why can there even be doubt that the removal of *insulting* will have the effect the legislator wants it to have? The public and parliamentary debate on the reform of POA 1986, section 5 has yielded a number of exemplary cases where the application of the provision caused public outrage because the charge of *insulting behavior* clearly did not match many peoples' understanding of the term. The ensuing debate could provide courts with copious evidence of exactly what behavior is viewed as being *insulting* and what is not.

To see how this problem can be resolved in court, we have to look at two methods of statutory interpretation (for an informative overview, see Bix 2009, p. 161 ff.): *intentionalism* and *textualism*.

In everyday communication, our understanding of utterances is informed by the conventionalized symbols speakers use to communicate, but also by our knowledge about the speakers themselves and the situation in which the utterance is made. We use our knowledge of both to find out what the speaker intends to convey.

In the case of legal texts, that speaker would be the legislator, that is, the Members of Parliament who drafted and enacted the law. According to the method of *intentionalism*, those who interpret the law may use any available source that helps to clarify the will of the legislator if that will is not unambiguously communicated by the legislation itself, from records of debates and parliamentary hearings to suggestions made by the commission preparing the act.

However, there are arguments against interpreting legislation as one would interpret any other written utterance:
- It is questionable whether one can attribute a single, common intent to the large number of people who constitute the complex speaker that is the legislator, as each might have had a different conceptualization of the same terms.
- More importantly, the binding character of the legislation mandates that those who are subject to it must be able to discern its meaning without having any knowledge of the facts that have led to its instatement.

By contrast, under the paradigm of *textualism*, judges are to treat the legal text as an authoritative source in its own right instead of trying to attribute a communicative intent to the legislator. In this, textualism departs from the inferential model of communication. This eliminates the need for any kind of legal discourse-specific definition of the terms used in legislation apart from an actual *legal definition*, i.e. a definition that is itself part of the statute. Instead, the plain meaning of words is to be taken into account. In terms of politeness research, this can be understood as giving precedence to first-order concepts as "common sense notions" rather than to theoretical models which constitute second-order concepts.[17]

In the words of the Lord Reid (1975):

"We are seeking not what Parliament meant but the true meaning of what they said"[18].

In practice, this means that no sources other than the relevant legislation itself are to be considered, be they records of parliamentary debates or the judges' personal knowledge or even educated guesses of how a particular law came to be. Restricting the interpretation to the conventionalized meaning of the legislation seems to fall one step short of a full linguistic analysis, but is certainly justified

---

[17] cf. Watts/Ide/Ehlich (1992: 3–4); Kádár/ Haugh (2013: 41).
[18] Black-Clawson International Ltd v Papierwerke Waldhof-Aschaffenberg AG [1975] HL.

by the fact that – in theory – the meaning of legal provisions, which can produce tangible consequences for their subjects, needs to be equally accessible to everyone.

Thus, judiciaries who interpret section 5 do not interpret speaker meaning, but word/sentence/text meaning as it is, not at the time of enactment, but at the time of interpretation. As Lord Reid affirms in an earlier decision (1972), "many things otherwise unobjectionable may be said or done in an insulting way. There can be no definition. But an ordinary sensible man knows an insult when he sees or hears it."[19]

This implies that the fact that an insult has been made is objectively discernable by "an ordinary sensible man," revealing an understanding that words have an inherent, if context-dependent, meaning.[20] If we assume judges to be "ordinary sensible men and women" (who have a command of the language of the legislation), they should be able to reliably tell an insult from a mere annoyance. Yet because first-order concepts are heterogeneous, the result of any interpretation by intuition is also highly heterogeneous (cf. Tiersma 1999: 127). Consequently, this approach has been criticized. Bix (2009: 164) argues that "judges are fooling themselves if they think that their access to meaning is different from and better than that of other people." Busse (1992: 183) even suspects that some judges assume to have been given "custodianship over language," and that they even seek to influence the ordinary meaning of terms by readily providing definitions which *pretend to reflect* their common usage.

An intentionalist interpretation of legislation would allow us to extensively define the semantic space of *insulting* in the context of the specific legislation (as second-order concepts of the terms in their *legal sense*) but would conflict with the democratic notion of legal certainty.

Given that the problems of section 5 lie not in its interpretation in the courtroom, but its (mis)application by the police, an analysis of spontaneous first-order interpretations of the term seems sensible in order to pinpoint the reasons for this. The textualist interpretation is based on the ordinary meaning of the words in legislation (first-order concepts), which gives rise to other problems, as we will see in the next section.

5 Contextual constraints on meaning

We have established that the Reform Section 5 campaign, Government representatives, and the Director of Public Prosecutions each conceptualize *insulting behavior* as a gradable antonym to *abusive behavior*, while many press articles in

---

[19] Brutus -v- Cozens; HL 19-Jul-1972.
[20] One of two paradoxa of first-order conceptualizations, cf. Bousfield (2010: 108).

fact imply that *insulting behavior* includes *abusive behavior* and that the former's removal from the legislation would also legalize the latter. Additionally, there is some implicit disagreement on the intentionality of *insulting behavior* in section 5, as opponents of the reform as well as the same superficial media reports suggest that a reform would make intentional, gratuitous insults legal and leave the police unable to intervene.

According to the plain meaning rule, there are no law-specific definitions for the terms used in legislation and "words in a statute have to be given their ordinary natural meaning."[21]

Because of the relative scarcity of context offered by most legal sources, the interpretative frame that the terms provide for one another is crucial:

Within section 5, *insulting words or behavior* is always contrasted with *abusive words or behavior*, as well as *insulting words or behavior with intent to cause harassment alarm or distress* in section 4A. From the latter, we can tell that *insulting* in section 5 refers even to behavior that was made *without* intent to cause harassment etc., even though this is not explicitly mentioned.

The importance of context for the interpretation becomes especially clear in the case of *abusive/abuse*, which has a number of different meanings in English, including:

– improper use,
– physical mistreatment and violence, including sexual violence,
– offensive speech.[22]

The phrases *abusive words or behavior*, and *writing, sign or other visible representation that is abusive* provide some disambiguation, pointing towards the element of "saying or doing something that is offensive." Only this shade of meaning of *abusive* is comparable to *insulting*.

As *insulting* and *abusive* behaviors are co-ordinated within sections 5 and 4A, we can also assume that *insulting* and *abusive* are distinct entities of roughly equal severity. Other readings are possible, however:

Insulting could restrict the interpretation of *abusive* to their common semantic element, as in the sentence "Swearing at someone is what we call abusive or insulting." This would counter-indicate an interpretation of *abusive* in the sense of "used against its purpose/misused" or "physically violent," but leave the relationship between the two terms open, even allowing for synonymy. If this

---

21 Brutus -v- Cozens; HL 19-Jul-1972.
22 The Oxford English Dictionary (2011).

were indeed the case, the phrase "abusive or insulting" would be pleonastic, which is not an uncommon feature of legal language[23].

Insulting could also serve to do the opposite: If we assume that there are no redundancies in the legislation, *insulting* could account for the common element of *offensive speech* on its own, leaving *abusive* to cover other types of behavior, for example one that borders on or is comparable with physical violence.

Finally, still assuming no redundancies, both terms could refer to the same type of behavior (*rude, offensive*), but cover different levels of severity, with *insulting* ostensibly covering the lower end of the scale, as was presupposed by the key actors in the reform debate.

Were the enumeration to contain other terms, for example *violent*, the word *abusive* would be constrained and interpreted in yet other ways. The legislation thus supports different conceptualizations of the relationship between *insulting* and *abusive* and by extension different conceptualizations of their individual meanings.

In the amended legislation, without *insulting* present to constrain it, it is possible that the interpretation of *abusive* will be expanded to cover the whole range of intensity of offending behavior. One would need to refer to section 4A, where *insulting* is still present, to infer that the interpretation of *abusive* in section 5 needs to be restricted.

This demonstrates that first-order concepts of meaning can also conflict with the notion of legal certainty. It is understandable that in interpreting (or *making sense of*) legislation, judiciaries try to find an objective conceptual system behind it to provide reliable and foreseeable results. There is an urge to mimic the perceived precision of technical and legally defined terms. To this end, dictionaries are often consulted to approximate the meaning of the terms in question, which has its own problems.

6 The common meaning of *insulting*

As the legal context allowed for different interpretations of the term *insulting* in relation to *abusive*, we will turn to wider usage contexts in order to find a "default relationship" between the two terms. These contexts are made available by two principal devices: dictionary definitions and linguistic corpus data.

Dictionaries try to formulate the common semantic element across a large number of usage contexts of the same term. They come with the disadvantage

---

[23] See Tiersma (1999: 213–214) for examples.

that they offer no individualized account of actual use; only particularly instructive samples, i.e. examples which are considered (proto)typical, are listed.

The terms *insulting* and *abusive* are peculiar in that they represent categories that are used to describe the nature of a given utterance. Culpeper (2011: 77–78) shows that *verbal abuse* acts as a frequent metalinguistic label for impoliteness in academic texts, despite that, unlike most alternatives (*rudeness, impoliteness*), it needs to be contextually constrained. This indicates that the term encapsulates the notion of impoliteness in interaction especially well.

We have looked at a number of dictionaries to test whether they can help us differentiate the terms in section 5. An analysis of the words *insulting, insult, to insult, abusive, abuse, to abuse* as defined by the Oxford English Dictionary (OED), Merriam-Webster, and the Longman Dictionary of Contemporary English (DCE) shows that it is not easy to establish a difference in semantic intension between *insult* and *abuse*.

The OED readily uses the terms *insult/abuse* to define the other: "to insult: to treat with scornful abuse or offensive disrespect"; "to abuse: to speak insultingly or unkindly of or to"; "abuse: contemptuous or insulting language"; "abusive: insulting, scurrilous."

The DCE uses the terms *rude* and *offensive* to define all terms except *abusive* (*using cruel words*), and even equates *abuse* to *insult*: "to say rude or offensive things to someone [=insult]."[24]

Merriam-Webster, by contrast, differentiates between *insult* as "rude or offensive behavior or showing lack of respect," and to *abuse* as "to attack in words, unjustly condemn or vilify," or *abusive* as "using *harsh* insulting language."

All sources suggest that *insulting* can refer to low-intensity offensive behavior. Furthermore, two out of the three sources point towards synonymy of *abuse* and *insult*. Taken literally, this would mean that the reform of section 5 would not serve to limit its breadth. This result would fit the alternate interpretation of the Director of Public Prosecutions' affirmation that to his knowledge, all convictions under section 5 were for behavior that was *abusive* as well as *insulting*.

Employing corpus data from the British National Corpus (BNC)[25], we have looked at uses of the terms *insulting* and *abusive*. The goal was to establish whether our own interpretation of the dictionary definitions was supported by actual usage.

---

24 It must be borne in mind, however, that the DCE is a learner dictionary in which a restricted defining vocabulary is used that imposes certain restrictions on the precision of the definitions.
25 http://corpus.byu.edu/bnc/.

It is worth noting that a high percentage of occurrences of the two adjectives is taken from the legal discourse (*insulting*: 113/411 = 27%; *abusive*: 103/275 = 37%; cf. *insult*: 30/475 = 6%), and that consequently the two often occur in the same utterance (80 times), particularly where the data is taken from legal sources such as court proceedings which mention the wording of POA 1985, section 5.

While all three major meaning components of *abuse* (misuse, physical, and verbal abuse) appear, in the majority of occurrences it is used in the sense of *offensive speech*.

The results do not support the notion that *abusive* and *insulting* are synonymous. The data suggests a common semantic element, but also that both terms differ in intensity, with *insulting* being the weaker of the two and *abusive* the stronger. This conceptualization differs from the relationship we extracted from two of the three dictionaries.

The following examples illustrate typical usage where in a) *abusive* could be replaced by *insulting*, whereas b) only works with *insulting*:

a) "She had been woken up at one in the morning by Mr Landor and again at four, and both times he had been abusive, calling her 'a bitch as fat and stupid' as his wife."
b) "Nothing more insulting than a non-jealous partner."

We also looked at *insult* [noun] to assess what kind of conceptualization is evoked by the media coverage of the section 5 reform. We found that the noun covers a wide range of intensity and can, especially in the plural, be used interchangeably with *abuse*, as in

c) "And I can't watch football anymore because of the way white fans shout racist insults at the black players."

Across a wide range of contexts, *insulting* and *abusive* can be used synonymously, but usage data from a corpus analysis shows that *abusive* does not readily cover low-intensity offensive behavior. For the reform of POA 1986, section 5 this could mean that the removal of *insulting* would indeed limit the provision's extensive coverage of offending behavior.

7 Summary: When is an insult a crime?

To predict the effect that the amendment of POA 1986, section 5 may have on court decisions and, more importantly, policing, we have looked at the legislation's phrasing before amendment and considered various possible changes in meaning that occur once the word *insulting* is removed.

Key reform supporters and opponents agree on the intensity of *insulting behavior* vis-a-vis its legislative counterpart *abusive*, but differ in their assessment of the intentionality of *insulting behavior* in section 5, while some news outlets completely exaggerated the extent of the contested term by lifting it out of its contextual constraints.

Even with those in place, several conflicting readings of the legislation are possible. The consultation of dictionary definitions of the respective terms also yields conflicting results, from synonymy to stratification by intensity. An analysis of corpus data points towards the latter alternative as the more common one in actual speech events.

Nevertheless, the difficulties in distinguishing the two terms illustrate a major problem of the plain meaning rule and the textualist paradigm of legal interpretation: It is nearly impossible to transfer heterogeneous concepts into a rigid code that is either applicable or not applicable to a given situation.

The textualist paradigm requires that the legislator's intent be evident in the contextual ordinary meaning of the words used. Looking only at a reformed section 5 that punishes *threatening or abusive behavior* does not necessarily leave space for low-intensity *insulting behavior* to be exempt from prosecution. Only a comparison to section 4A combined with the assumption that the legislation contains no redundancies yields a result that is decisively different from section 5's original wording. This interpretation of *insulting* (as not synonymous with *abusive*) mandates a departure from documented usage of the word and thus from its plain meaning. In this, we see that the plain meaning rule can only be formulated in a negative way: "The meaning of words in a statute must not deviate from their ordinary natural meaning."

Under the intentionalist paradigm, judges could use the concepts and cases that surfaced during the reform debate to rule that a reformed POA 1986, section 5 has higher requirements regarding the offending behavior compared to its previous phrasing and to section 4A, bypassing the problems of the plain meaning rule. In this light, it is understandable that judiciaries are tempted to schematize the terminology of the law.

Bousfield (2010: 107) describes a paradox of first-order conceptualizations of politeness in that lay users "tend to have an idealised, socially constructed idea of what constitutes appropriate and inappropriate behavior." The parlance of special language discourses such as law has a great power to influence these assumptions of "correct speech."

Because of the reciprocal influence that the legal language and the common language exert on another, this could well lead to a differentiation of the terms *insulting* and *abusive* in their everyday usage ("criminally 'abusive' vs.

non-criminally 'insulting'"). Then we would witness that the ordinary meaning of words *follows* its use in a special language, validating the plain meaning rule in the process, but with the "tables turned." Busse (1992: 183) has criticized that judicial definitions of ordinary words do find their way into dictionaries without being labelled as technical terms. This could lead to *insulting/insult* shifting into the semantic space of *annoyance* and *inconvenience*. The media coverage that greatly exaggerates the extent of the reform could exacerbate this perception without even mentioning *abusive*.

Regarding the application of the provision in court, there seemed to exist a certain pre-amendment "conviction threshold" that corresponded to the interpretation of *abusive* as *higher-intensity offending behavior*. Hence, *insulting* apparently had no independent meaning in section 5; its function was rather to provide a context for the interpretation of *abusive*.

While removing *insulting* from the legislation will raise the arrest threshold so that it matches the threshold of conviction, it will merely decriminalize insults that are side-effects of the expression of opinions, not (as the press in part implies) gratuitous swearing and other forms of calculated offensive behavior.

Further research into this area could be done as a complete analysis of the public discourse and the different conceptualizations of *insulting* and *abusive* that surface in it. One could also focus on the relationship between the two terms by having speakers classify utterances as *abusive* or *insulting* in perceptual experiments. The results could help us refine the process of interpreting statutory terms.

References

Bix, Brian. 2009. *Jurisprudence. Theory and context*. 5th edn. London: Sweet & Maxwell Thomson Reuters.
Bousfield, Derek. 2010. Researching impoliteness and rudeness: Issues and definitions. In: Miriam A. Locher & Sage L. Graham (eds.), *Interpersonal pragmatics*. 101–134. Berlin: De Gruyter Mouton.
Brown, Penelope & Stephen C. Levinson. 1987. *Politeness. Some universals in language use*. Cambridge: Cambridge University Press.
Busse, Dietrich. 1992. Recht als Text. *Linguistische Untersuchungen zur Arbeit mit Sprache in einer gesellschaftlichen Institution*. Berlin: De Gruyter.
Culpeper, Jonathan. 2011. *Impoliteness. Using language to cause offense*. Cambridge: Cambridge University Press.
A dictionary of law. 2009. 7th edn. Oxford: Oxford University Press.
The Law Commission. 2013. Consultation paper 213: Hate crime: The case for extending the existing offenses.
Longman dictionary of contemporary English. 2009. 5th edn. Harlow: Pearson.

The Lord Macdonald of River Glaven. 2011. *Opinion: A proposed amendment to the Protection of Freedoms Bill.* http://reformsection5.org.uk/download/rs5-macdonald-opinion.pdf [accessed March 5th, 2015].

Merriam-Webster's collegiate dictionary. 2003. 11th revised edn. Springfield, Mass.: Merriam-Webster.

The Oxford English dictionary. 2010. 3rd edn. Oxford: Oxford University Press.

The National Policing Improvement Agency (NPIA). 2010. *Manual of guidance on keeping the peace 2010.* London: The National Policing Improvement Agency.

Strickland, Pat & Diana Douse. 2013. *"Insulting words or behavior": Section 5 of the Public Order Act 1986.* Standard Note SN/HA/5760. House of Commons Library.

Smith, A. T. H. 1987. *Offences against public order.* London: Sweet & Maxwell.

Tiersma, Peter. 1999. *Legal language.* Chicago: University of Chicago Press.

Watts, Richard J., Sachiko Ide & Konrad Ehlich. 1992. Introduction. In Richard J. Watts, Sachiko Ide & Konrad Ehlich (eds.), *Politeness in language: Studies in its history, theory and practice.* 1–20. Berlin: De Gruyter.

Frances Olsen
9 Pragmatic interpretation by judges: Constrained performatives and the deployment of gender bias

1 Introduction

For many years feminists and Critical Legal Studies (CLS) scholars have criticized the tendency of judges, and lawyers generally, to constrict the issues involved in a legal dispute, and have complained about courts' tendency to treat as irrelevant matters that are particularly important to women. For example, it was only after a struggle that courts finally began to find it relevant that a woman charged with a crime against her partner was also the victim of domestic violence, a change in the direction of pragmatic relevance.[1] These critics would be expected to be pleased that a broader range of voices – the judicial pragmatists, including some very powerful and privileged voices – have begun speaking in favor of such a more inclusive approach that takes a larger quantity of relevant information into account before deciding cases.

The pragmatic turn in jurisprudence refers to a normative and descriptive practice that began attracting attention around 1985–1990 and has gradually increased in prominence. It challenges the classic model of legal argumentation that assumes judges should and usually do decide legal disputes through a rational and objective process of interpreting statutes, examining case law to find relevant precedents, and reasoning from analogy to test the applicability of the various precedents to the case at hand.

A more formalist version of the classic model, largely discredited by the legal realists but still holding some sway, assigns a more ambitious task to judges able to live up to it. Instead of just picking the closest precedent and constructing an analogy, a gifted formalist judge distills from the prior precedents a broad, abstract principle of law, sometimes at a fairly high level of generality –

---

[1] That is, inferences of criminal culpability that one draws from underlying assumptions about free will and intention are altered when placed in the context of a defendant suffering chronic intimate violence. See generally Nancy Gertner, In defense of women, 129–154. But see also Ramsay (2013).

Frances Olsen, University of California at Los Angeles

or in the heyday of legal formalism an overarching principle. This principle becomes the major premise, enabling the judge to use the facts of the case at hand to form his minor premise and through a rigorous, logically valid deduction reach the correct decision.

A more modern version of the classic model was constructed and popularized by Ronald Dworkin under the banner of "law as integrity" (Dworkin 1986: 225–228). Legal precedent remains important but not for logical deduction or even for providing analogies. His ideal judge can move the law in the direction of greater justice, but she should struggle to keep law consistent. Judges ought to be and generally are like the author of the next chapter in a chain-novel: they always build upon what has gone before – the previous "chapters" that were written by many other co-authors. A skillful judge can fit her "chapter" into the corpus of legal materials, respecting the content that preceded her just as her decision should be respected and built upon by the next judge. Precedent remains central, and part of the skill of a good judge is to induce or inspire the author of the next chapter to build upon her work (Dworkin 1986: 228–238). Despite the need to adjust each chapter of the cumulative narrative for internal consistency, this process has more flexibility than other iterations of the classic model.

Pragmatic judges repudiate the classic model. The legal pragmatist emphasizes that legal controversies arise in specific and often unique contexts and maintains that such controversies are better addressed with reference to these contexts than by abstract legal principles. Moreover, because legal principles have been abstracted from concrete cases with their own specific contexts, they are unlikely to be applicable beyond their originating context.[2]

Pragmatic jurists claim to be anti-foundationalist, anti-essentialist and anti-authoritarian. There is no solid ground to stand upon, no core principles. Everything is fluid and contingent – messy, open-ended and subject to revision. Instead of placing primary importance upon precedent, the legal pragmatist generally claims to look to the effect the decision is likely to have, which may involve bringing in considerable context as well as engaging knowledge of economics and sociological data. Legal pragmatism, contrasted with its predecessors, offers the promise of resolving the tension between substantive justice and abstract principle by modifying if not abandoning its commitment to the latter and instead offering forward-looking decisions guided "by their conformity to social

---

[2] Cf. *Bush v. Gore*, 531 U.S. 98, 109 (2000). ("Our consideration is limited to the present circumstances, for the problem [...] presents many complexities.").

or other human needs rather than to 'objective,' 'impersonal' criteria."[3] As Richard Posner puts it proudly, the pragmatic judge looks to the future, not to the past. He should always strive to find better solutions to the problems that arise, and these problems can best be addressed in the context in which they arise.

To both feminists and CLS scholars who have worked long and hard for reform, the liberation offered by judicial pragmatism might seem a welcome solution to our problems, but I am very wary of it, and contend that it misrepresents the problems we face and offers no relief from them. To illustrate this, I propose to examine three cases that embody tensions between laws passed by legislatures, their implementation by the courts, and the claims of substantive justice served or denied in terms of a communication model devolving from the normative ideal of the judge as an impartial adjudicator of competing concerns. I believe these cases illustrate that the barriers faced by feminist theorists, and perhaps by those concerned with social justice generally, are the courts' receptivity to the relevant laws, facts, and concerns of substantive justice – communicative defects that reflect deep-seated biases that a pragmatic approach is as likely to empower as to overcome.

In discussing gender bias shown by judges I propose as a useful heuristic to loosely adapt some concepts from J.L. Austin and H.P. Grice – the adaption from Grice being by far the looser – but stopping short of honoring Grice in the breach. It is important to maintain, as does Grice, the distinction between cooperation amongst the parties regarding ends or even cooperation amongst the parties to make the communication easy; and agreement amongst the parties regarding the communicative norms by which those ends are conveyed and discussed. I suspect that Grice's Cooperative Principle is often fundamentally misunderstood because its name falsely suggests cooperation amongst the parties governed by it, at least in trying to make communication clear and simple. I suspect that the elements of this Cooperative Principle (CP) would be better understood as rough Communicative Norms obedience to or seeming deviation

---

[3] Richard A. Posner, "What has pragmatism to offer law?" 63 S. Cal. L. Rev. 1653 (1989–1990). Posner makes plain that he considers the legislators unworthy of and unfit for their responsibilities and feels that many if not most of these tasks should be arrogated by the judiciary.

> The legislative process is buffeted by interest-group pressures to an extent rare in the judicial process. The result is a body of laws far less informed by sound policy judgments than the realists in the heyday and aftermath of the New Deal believed. It is no longer possible to imagine the good pragmatist judge as one who acts merely as the faithful agent of the legislature. Indeed, the faithful-agent conception has become a hallmark of modem formalism – judges as faithful agents despite the perversity of so many of the statutes that they are interpreting. Id at 1658.

from which permits the theoretical "calculability" of the relevant implicature, i.e., what is implied and usually meant by the utterance but is not part of its semantic meaning. These norms permit communication but do not require that it be easy, cooperative, or serve cooperative ends.[4]

Austin introduced the notion that some speech acts did not describe the world, but accomplished things in it; were not constatives, but performatives.[5] Paradigmatic amongst the latter were the familiar, "I promise," "I apologize" "Will you marry me?" (I propose), or "Watch out!" (I warn you of danger) which lacked truth values but had felicity conditions for their success and may be

---

[4] Bethan Davies ("Grice's cooperative principle: Getting the meaning across" in Nelson, D. & P. Foulkes (eds) *Leeds Working Papers in Linguistics* 8 (2000), pp. 1–26) captures what I am avoiding when she writes, "The use of the word 'cooperative' seems to lead to a confusion between Grice's technical notion and the general meaning associated with the lexeme *cooperation*, leading to what we term 'cooperation drift'. ... Our contention is that there is a tendency for Grice's technical term to be confused with a folklinguistic notion of *cooperation*." She continues:

> What Grice (1975) does not say is that interaction is 'cooperative' in the sense which is found in the dictionary. In fact, as we have suggested in Davies (1997), it could be argued that the existence of this pattern of behavior enables the speaker to make the task of the hearer more difficult. Speakers can convey their intentions by a limitless number of utterances, it is up to the hearer to calculate the utterer's intention. It would seem from this that the CP is not about making the task of the Hearer straightforward; potentially, it is quite the reverse. It allows the speaker to make their utterance harder, rather than easier, to interpret: we can omit information or present a non-literal utterance, and expect the Hearer to do the extra work necessary to interpret it.

Davies offers an excellent example:

> To demonstrate the conflict between this non-technical meaning, and the type of technical meaning for 'cooperation' which we would argue is suggested by Grice, it will be useful to consider an example:
>
> (2) A is a member of staff in an English department; B is a new member of staff who has been employed as a poet to teach creative writing. The conversation takes place at a departmental party.
>
> A: What sort of poetry do you write?
> B: Name me six poets. [said aggressively]
>
> This exchange can scarcely be considered 'cooperative' in the non-technical sense: it is evidently unhelpful, and is certainly leading to clarification and repair (in an interpersonal sense). However, the implication is perfectly clear. There is a flout of the maxim of relevance here, and B's reply implicates that A's question is not worth answering because A knows nothing about poetry. So, B's utterance is not 'cooperative', but it fits the model for inte[r]pretation suggested by the CP.

[5] See Austin, J. L., How to do things with words: The William James Lectures delivered at Harvard University in 1955, (J. O. Urmson and Marina Sbisà, eds.), Oxford: Clarendon Press (1962).

considered pure performatives. Some judicial functions seem to be performatives straightaway, "Overruled!" or "You're in contempt," but it is useful, I propose, to conceive of many of them – and even these – such as pronouncing a verdict of guilt or innocence, deciding a complex case, or upholding or overturning an appeal, as *constrained* performatives. Unlike the paradigm examples of pure performatives, where the satisfaction of felicity conditions assures their success *simpliciter*, constrained performatives may satisfy their felicity conditions because the speaker is typically imbued with the relevant institutional authority, yet be faulty or inadequate due to the speaker's failure to meet or uphold the institutional norms fidelity to which is deemed necessary for being endowed with, and continuing to deserve, the requisite authority.

An archetypal proclamation in the performance of a wedding ceremony is "By the authority vested in me by the State of _____, I now pronounce you husband and wife."[6] No such wedding ceremony pronouncement could be felicitous unless the person performing it "is either entitled or authorized to perform the solemnization of marriage by the ordaining entity and the respective state."[7] Yet the bare felicity conditions fail to distinguish between the dull bureaucratic monotony of a Las Vegas wedding chapel and the traditional church wedding attended by friends and family that speaks to the couple's unique values, beliefs and life circumstances and sets them within a sacred or spiritual dimension that rises above mere legal contract. These differences, which reflect commonly held normative notions, might be expressed by saying of the latter that it was "a real wedding" rather than one which merely met the bare requirements of its felicity conditions.

Other institutions carry their own criteria of performative fitness, which we will sketch but not explore in detail. The military, for example, insists that a commanding officer has the authority to give an order which his subordinates are duty-bound to obey, but if the officer exercises that power too poorly – outside the conventionally accepted norms – he may be faced with mutiny from below or court-martial from above. And far short of such extremes lies a range of behaviors that embody norms that lead to an officer being admired and respected by his men, or held in various degrees of disdain or contempt despite his never overstepping his authority. Similarly, an essential part of a police officer's job when faced with a citizen guilty of a minor offense is to decide whether to put the person into the system – burdening both the system

---

[6] The author does not endorse any gender bias conveyed by the proclamation. (Last viewed June 17, 2016).
[7] "How to perform a wedding ceremony," http://www.open-ministry.org/wedding-ceremony.php. (Last viewed June 17, 2016).

and the citizen – or to exercise his authority by letting him go with a performative like, "Get out of here but watch yourself next time!" Both the officer who insisted on enforcing every infraction he observed to the fullest extent of the law, and the one who sat through his coffee and donuts while watching a thief snatch a woman's purse would chafe against norms of adequacy even if the former's "You're under arrest" and the latter's (implicit) "You're free to go" satisfied felicity conditions.

For present purposes I wish to sketch a minimalist account of the internal norms governing the judicial process in terms of judicial communicative access and responsiveness – impartiality – by relying on a very important difference between the observance and enforcement of the rules of baseball and those of judicial procedure. A baseball umpire shouts "Strike three, you're out!" and thus calls the batter out but the umpire is constrained, at least in theory, to basing his performance upon the fidelity of the pitch to the strike zone. An umpire's very bad call of a strike may satisfy its felicity conditions yet remain subject to legitimate reproach. In baseball the custom is for the umpire's performance to be done with sufficient drama, emphasis and alacrity to convey a confidence in his judgment to his audience that sometimes undermines the very accuracy of his decision that the nearly instantaneous decision is designed to convey.[8] In court decisions, by contrast, the custom used to sanctify confidence in judicial accuracy is that of prolonged and weighty deliberations designed, at least in theory, to produce decisions that correctly embody both relevant law and instant facts of the case before it, as well as the consequences of its decision, in which the ideally impartial court at least does its best to operate by means of a non-Gricean Cooperative Principle, perhaps better termed a Principle of Communicative Impartiality. While the parties contend with each other, and while the court may be required to frustrate the goals of the parties as justice demands, the court's communications and decisions should at a bare minimum reflect its fidelity to a Principle of Communicative Impartiality in which it pays attention to and appreciates all legitimate concerns by actively pursuing and attending to relevant communications and considerations. We do not yet reach the issue of how the court should weight these elements, but it must at least listen to them, and when consistent with its obligations, try to accommodate substantive justice. The fundamental difference between the snap decision of the baseball umpire and the ideally cool and deliberative decisions of the courts points to the central advantage in applying the concept of a constrained performative to the latter: unlike the umpire's quick call, almost

---

8 The example of the baseball umpire is taken from Erving Goffman, *The presentation of self in everyday life*, 30.

the entire corpus upon which the court's decision rests, including much of its deliberations, is memorialized and preserved for our inspection and evaluation.

I propose that by conceiving of the courts as engaged in constrained performatives wherein they must as a minimal norm maintain cooperative lines of communication with legislative demands, the facts and arguments put before them, the consequences of their decisions, and substantive justice, we are able to see how deeply and clearly they deviate from such a communicative norm – a Principle of Communicative Impartiality – because they are moved by deep-seated biases that would be bound to determine their decisions if liberated from what pragmatists regard as unnecessary formal constraints.[9]

2 People ex rel. Brooks v. Brooks (1861): child custody

During the middle of the Nineteenth Century, the progressive New York legislature was willing, when pressured by feminists and their allies, to enact legislation undoing the strict hierarchy the common law imposed upon family relations. Under the common law, upon marriage legal title to any property a woman owned was vested in her husband. Wages or other property she acquired during the marriage also belonged to her husband, and any children whom she bore fell under the full and exclusive control of her husband. He was considered their legal father, guardian and custodian and was entitled to their labor and its fruits. New York was one of the first states to document the injustices caused by these rules, and its state legislature enacted one of the earliest Married Women's Property Acts. When the New York courts dragged their feet and demonstrated a reluctance to abide by New York's first Married Women's Property Act, the legislature enacted a second, stronger version of the bill. And as the courts

---

[9] We might well become wary after reading Posner's first of three essential elements of pragmatism, *viz.*, "The first is a distrust of metaphysical entities ('reality,' 'truth,' 'nature,' etc.) viewed as warrants for certitude whether in epistemology, ethics, or politics." (Posner 1989–1990: 1660.) If I were charged with a murder of which I were innocent, I would be more than wary if forced to trial before a judge who failed to appreciate that there was indeed a certain objective determinate underlying *reality*, an objective *truth* to the matter, and that his task was to carefully weigh the evidence and arguments and assess whether they constituted a warrant of certitude beyond a reasonable doubt as to whether I had committed the crime. If this misconstrues Posner, then we may admire his glibness, but have reservations regarding his depth or his clarity.

continued to defy the laws as written, the legislature continued to amend and revise them over the course of some years.[10]

An 1830 statute began tempering the father's exclusive common law rights over his children in cases where he and his wife were living separately without being divorced. The Revised Statutes provided simply that a mother, living in a state of separation, could bring a writ of *habeas corpus* on behalf of her child and "the court, on due consideration, may award the charge and custody of the child [...] to the mother, for such time, under such regulations and restrictions, and with such provisions and directions, as the case may require."[11] The 1830 statute empowered the courts and stated the procedure; it made no reference to the cause of the couple's separation. Because custody was not divisible at that time, the court would either leave the father's common law rights undisturbed or grant full custody to the mother. A challenge to this law led to an 1837 decision by the New York Supreme Court limiting its application to cases where the marital separation was legally authorized, consented to, or caused by execrable behavior by the husband. According to the court, the father still enjoyed superior common law rights, which usually benefited the children, and, in the absence of "good and sufficient reasons, [...] is entitled to their custody, care and education" (Nickerson 1837: 16). The court characterized the "interference of the court with the relation of father and child" as "a delicate and strong measure" that should not be undertaken "except for the most sound and solid reasons" (Nickerson 1837: 19). This tepid interpretation fell short of the reformers' intent, so in 1860 the legislature passed another law granting married women additional rights with respect to their children: "Every married woman is hereby constituted and declared to be the joint guardian of her children, with her husband, with equal powers, rights and duties in regard to them, with the husband" (Laws of New York, 1860, Chap. 90, Section 9). The grant of equal powers and rights was balanced by the imposition of equal duties to gainsay the common law presumption that only the father had such duties, and that these duties entitled him to full rights over the child.

Lydia Brooks left her husband in May of 1858 and obtained custody of her infant son through a writ of habeas corpus. The husband appealed the decision of the county court, and at a special term Justice Mullin upheld the county judge's decision on the basis of the 1860 act. On further appeal to the Supreme Court general term, the court ruled 3–1 in favor of the husband, over the dissent

---

[10] Progressive bills were enacted in 1848, 1849 and 1860. See Norma Basch, *In the eyes of the law: Women, marriage, and property in nineteenth-century New York*. In 1862 the legislature repealed the provision the court had gutted in People ex rel. *Brooks v. Brooks*, 35 Barb. 85 (1861).

[11] The People ex rel. *Nickerson v.* _____, 19 Wend. 16, 18. (N.Y. 1837), citing 2 Revised Statutes, 148, 149, secs. 1, 2 (1830).

of Justice Mullin. The initial paragraph set the tone of the opinion: "Among the many radical changes in the domestic relations attempted by recent legislation, none is more pregnant with grave consequences for good or for evil than the very brief and summary statute which gives rise to this controversy."[12] The majority went on to assert, "a more crude or imperfect law I think can hardly be found upon the statute book," (Brooks 1861: 86) and "I doubt if any effect can be given to the statute, and perhaps in that way it would be less mischievous" (Brooks 1861: 86–87). Thus, from the beginning of the opinion the court warned, using the passive voice, that it might refuse to give "any effect" to the legislation, not because it was unconstitutional but simply because the judge considered the legislation "crude" and "imperfect."

The majority acknowledged that courts had *parens patriae* power to remove children from their parents for good cause and admitted that "cases of extreme hardship have resulted from the jealous care" the common law had taken to enforce fathers' "rights," thus enabling some men of "immoral character" to "embitter the life of the mother by depriving her of the society of her offspring" (Brooks 1861: 88). The opinion asserted that the 1830 statute, empowering courts to award custody to the mother, granted her "an ample remedy, and all that the legislature *have thus far* seen fit to give her" (Brooks 1861: 89 [*emphasis* added]). Thus, shockingly, the court denied that the legislature had even attempted to enlarge her custodial rights.

The majority court decision in *Brooks* quoted with approval language that the 1837 New York court had used in limiting the 1830 act that gave courts jurisdiction and discretion to award the mother custody of a child when the parents were living apart to cases where the separation was legally justified or had been instigated by the husband:

> [I]t may be well doubted, I think, whether this statute was intended to apply when the wife withdraws from the protection of the husband, and lives separate from him without any reasonable excuse [...]. The legislature could not have intended that the court should ever award to the mother the care and education of her minor children when she had wrongfully, and without pretense of excuse, abandoned her family and the protection of her husband, if he was in a situation to take care of them, and no well founded objection existed in the case.[13]

---

12 People ex rel. *Brooks v. Brooks*, 35 Barb. 85 (1861). The court never tries to give any meaning to the suggestion that a statute could have "grave consequences for good."

13 Brooks at 94, quoting The People ex rel. *Nickerson v.* _____, 19 Wend. 16. (N.Y. 1837). Regarding the 1830 statute the *Brooks* court plausibly noted: "This statute does not declare on what grounds the court shall proceed, but confides the whole matter to its discretion, and hence the occasion, cause and circumstances of the separation, and the relative merits and demerits of the parties may be taken into account." Id at 89. Thus the decision in *Nickerson*, while frustrating the wishes of the reformers, left the statute having significant meaning. The same cannot be said of the effect of *Brooks* on the 1860 statute.

While one might well criticize the reasoning of the 1837 decision, it is at least a plausible interpretation of the 1830 law, which had not altered the basic common law provision that made the father the sole head of an intact family and guardian of his children. The 1860 revisions did just that.

Despite the clear wording of the 1860 statute *supra*, the *Brooks* court majority argued that it had failed to "impose upon her corresponding duties and responsibilities, and confer the necessary power to discharge them" and therefore "confers no rights upon the mother, except such as may be enjoyed jointly and upon an equality with the father" (Brooks 1861: 91). This the court claimed despite the statutory language giving the wife "equal power, rights and *duties*" regarding the children (Laws of New York, 1860, Chap. 90, Section 9 [*emphasis added*]). Here, even more shockingly, the court made itself deaf to the spirit of the law and blind to its letter. The opinion elaborated:

> The statute makes her "the *joint* guardian of her children with her husband." So far as this guardianship includes the custody and care of the person, it must be exercised with her husband, and not away from or exclusive of him. It is only in connection with her husband that she takes any right of guardianship, under the [1860] statute. (Brooks 1861: 90)

Courts at that time were entitled to construe a statute in derogation of the common law narrowly, but they were not entitled to ignore it.

Thus, after first denying that the 1860 legislation sought to enlarge the wife's custodial rights, the court ignored and denied the plain text that imposed upon her equal duties of support and care that were the basis for these enlarged rights. It was then able to argue that the father's duty of support and protection gave him, and him alone, "correlative and dependent" rights to be the head of the family that entitled him to the custody and labor of the children. If the law were to take away those rights, the majority decreed, then the duties would also be abrogated "and the child is then left without lawful protectors, and society is without any security for the proper performance of important social duties" (Brooks 1861: 90). According to the majority, the "powers, rights and duties" of the wife are made "equal" not superior to those of the husband, and they "can only be enjoyed and exercised under circumstances in which the husband's equal rights may be secured to him" (Brooks 1861: 92). The statute gave the wife only those rights over the children as she can exercise "when being with her husband and acting in concert with him." Thus, "[t]he law can only be carried into effect while the parents are living together." If the couple separates and husband and wife live independently of each other, "the joint guardianship cannot be exercised, and the husband is remitted to his common law rights" (Brooks 1861: 92).

In a liberation from the formal constraints of legislation similar to what pragmatists currently urge would allow them to act more equitably and serve the common good or substantive justice, the majority opinion in this case amounted to something sinister: if the wife could not prove that she was justified in leaving her husband, she should never be awarded custody of the children. Otherwise the courts could be encouraging wives to decide for themselves when to leave an unsatisfactory marriage, which the courts deemed to be vicious and immoral conduct.

Unlike the 1837 decision, which gave the 1830 law a narrow interpretation but left it with meaning, the *Brooks* court gave the 1860 act a strained interpretation, and justified its refusal to apply the law by essentially denying the act had any meaning. Working as pragmatic social engineers of their era, the majority in *Brooks v. Brooks* applied their forward-looking perspective to reinterpret what the legislature "intended" in order to pretend to be upholding the law, but they make very plain by their use of the term "under pretense" that the legislature must have intended not as it did, but as the court decided it should have.

> It cannot be that by the act of 1860 the legislature intended that a wife, by her own immoral and illegal disregard of her marriage vows and her duty as a wife, could deprive her husband of the companionship and education of his children, under pretense of giving her equal rights and making her joint guardian with him. Her sins, in that case, would work a forfeiture of his rights in her favor. [...] I am of the opinion that while living in a state of voluntary separation from her husband, the wife has no rights under the act of 1860 which could be enforced by habeas corpus, or in any other way. (Brooks 1861: 94–95)

3 Roe v. Wade (1973): standing

Roe v. Wade, the famous 1973 Supreme Court case that made abortion legal in the United States, includes an often neglected but revealing interpretation of the Court's rules regarding which parties have standing to litigate cases in the federal courts. Because the Constitutional provision creating federal courts specifies that they are to decide "cases" and "controversies," federal courts have long refused to give advisory opinions to other branches of government or to make what they call hypothetical decisions. They require that there be a case or controversy before they will issue a decision, and thus require plaintiffs to have an actual interest in a case from inception to adjudication, or what is called "standing," before they will allow the case to go forward.[14] In the early

---

14 US Const. art. III, sec. 2 specifies a variety of cases and controversies over which it extends federal judicial power. See *Lujan v. Defenders of Wildlife*, 504 U.S. 555, 560–561 (1992).

1970s many different parties throughout the United States were challenging the constitutionality of criminal laws forbidding or limiting abortion (Rubin 1982: 29–55). *Roe v. Wade* arose as a consolidation of two similar cases heard together and decided by a three-judge district court convened under a special procedure providing for a direct appeal to the Supreme Court and used when plaintiffs seek to enjoin the enforcement of a state law. One of the cases was brought by a married couple, John and Mary Doe (pseudonyms) who urgently wanted to avoid pregnancy for medical as well as personal reasons. Mary Doe's medical conditions limited the contraceptives they could use and made pregnancy highly inadvisable, though not sufficiently life-threatening to provide them any clear exemption from their state antiabortion laws (*Roe v. Wade* 121). The other case was brought by an unmarried woman, pseudonymously referred to as Jane Roe, who sought to end an unwanted pregnancy.

The Supreme Court first decided that Jane Roe had standing. She had initially brought her lawsuit when "as a pregnant single woman thwarted by the Texas criminal abortion laws, [she clearly] had standing to challenge those statutes" (*Roe v. Wade* 124). Although the usual rule is that an actual controversy must continue to exist at all stages of appellate or certiorari review, and not simply at the date the legal action was initiated, exceptions are made for cases in which a rigid application of that rule would have pernicious results. The Court recognized that the normal 266-day human gestation period was short enough that any pregnancy would end or come to term before the usual appellate process could be completed. Therefore, if Jane Roe's case were to be dismissed as moot at the end of her pregnancy, "litigation seldom will survive much beyond the trial stage, and appellate review will be effectively denied" (*Roe v. Wade* 125). The Court added the following explanation: "Pregnancy often comes more than once to the same woman, and in the general population, if man is to survive, it will always be with us. Pregnancy provides a classic justification for a conclusion of nonmootness. It truly could be 'capable of repetition, yet evading review'" (*Roe v. Wade* 125). If pragmatism can produce definite goods, the Court's relaxation of its rules for Jane Roe is certainly an example of such, but I want to compare and contrast its reasoning in her case with its reasoning in the case with which hers was consolidated – John and Mary Doe, from whom the court withdrew standing.

Before doing so, however, let us examine a fourth party, Dr. James Hallford, who had joined Jane Roe's lawsuit as a plaintiff-intervener, alleging that he was a licensed physician whose medical practice was inhibited by the antiabortion laws: he had been arrested on several occasions but never prosecuted or convicted, and was at that time under indictment for violating the antiabortion law of Texas. The lower courts grasped that being subjected to such treatment provided a genuine case or controversy, but the Supreme Court dismissed him from the case on the basis that he remained fully able to assert all his federally protected rights against the state prosecutions. Ordinarily a defendant in a pending state criminal case cannot affirmatively challenge in federal court the statutes under which the State is prosecuting him. Rather than enjoining a state court criminal proceeding, federal courts typically wait and give the state courts the opportunity to rule on the alleged unconstitutionality of the state statute under the federal constitution; after a state convicts a defendant, the defendant is expected to appeal to the state appellate courts before he can seek federal review of the constitutionality of the state statute. The Supreme Court also rejected Dr. Hallford's efforts to seek standing solely as a "potential future defendant" and ruled that the three-judge district court erred in allowing him standing on the statute's constitutionality, thus depriving the case of the additional strength and support from the legal arguments that his counsel could have provided (*Roe v. Wade* 125–127). There is no doubt that Dr. Hallford had a real interest, suffering "a concrete and particularized injury that is fairly traceable to the challenged [statute]" and that would be "likely to be redressed by a favorable judicial decision."[15] But here, the Court insisted upon imposing its rules strictly – abandoning Dr. Hallford to such suffering as arrests without prosecutions, or prosecutions without conviction, might inflict upon him until such time as he might succeed in being prosecuted and convicted and then appeal in vain his convictions, until he might then be fortunate enough to gain another audience with the Court. Here, where the Court had little to lose by allowing substantive justice to guide its decision, it insisted upon a formalism that kept the legal resources of Dr. Hallford from making their contribution, and providing a broader face to the issue than did the plight of a single unmarried white woman. Instead, the Court held that unless Dr. Hallford could allege harassment or bad faith prosecution, he had no standing to challenge the statute in an affirmative action.[16]

---

15 *Hollingsworth v. Perry*, 570 U.S. ___, 133 S. Ct. 2652, 2661 (2013). See also, *Lujan v. Defenders of Wildlife*, 504 U.S. 555, 560–561 (1992).
16 Harassment and bad faith prosecution are much too narrow exceptions. Dr. Hallford had already been arrested a number of times without reaching federal court. Being arrested is unpleasant and costly, but it does not become "harassment" just because prosecutors decide not to pursue criminal charges. Even if the prosecutors eventually proceed with a criminal case, juries might well acquit him, especially and ironically in the case of a law that is unpopular as well as unconstitutional. Only a particularly strongly motivated litigant is willing to face multiple arrests and prosecution to remove an unconstitutional law from his state statutes.
  Compare the case of Craig v. Boren, 429 U.S. 190 (1976), in which a seller of alcoholic beverages was allowed to challenge a state statute forbidding the sale of alcohol, specifically 3.2% beer, to males under the age of 21, while females were allowed to drink at age 18. The action had been

The Court's reasoning for denying standing to the plaintiffs whose case was consolidated with Roe's is of even greater interest. John and Mary Doe, the married couple, filed a companion complaint challenging the antiabortion laws of Georgia, claiming similar constitutional deprivations and seeking declaratory and injunctive relief. The Does were a childless couple and Mrs. Doe suffered from a "neural-chemical" disorder such that her doctor had "advised her to avoid pregnancy until such time as her condition has materially improved," but a pregnancy would not have presented "a serious risk" to her life that would have exempted her from the anti-abortion law. Following medical advice, she had stopped using birth control pills, and if she became pregnant, she would want an abortion performed by a competent, licensed physician under safe, clinical conditions. The couple's strong desire to avoid pregnancy, Mary's medical inability to use reliable birth control pills, and the prospect of having to choose between "an illegal abortion" and having to "travel to some place where the procedure could be obtained legally and competently" combined to inhibit their sex life. The Does sought to sue "on behalf of themselves and all couples similarly situated" (*Roe v. Wade* 121).

One virtue of the legal system of the United States is its dedication to permitting litigation to proceed irrespective of the size of the material stakes at issue provided some important principle is contested. Yet with respect to the Does, the Court did just the opposite. The Court began its discussion by discounting the importance of the issues the plaintiffs put before it: "In view of our ruling as to Roe's standing in her case, the issue of the Does' standing in their case has little significance. The claims they assert are *essentially* the same as those of Roe, and they attack the same statutes" (*Roe v. Wade* 127 [*emphasis* added]). The Court proceeded to determine that Mary and John Doe were "not *appropriate* plaintiffs" and should have been dismissed on grounds of standing (*Roe v. Wade* 129 [*emphasis* added]).

How, then we might ask, were the Does not "appropriate" plaintiffs and how, then, were their claims "essentially" the same as Roe's? The Does asserted that they confronted "the choice of refraining from normal sexual relations or of endangering Mary Doe's health through a possible pregnancy" (*Roe v. Wade* 128). Under any linguistic theory of pragmatics, and especially under a maxim of cooperation (that does not exist here), the Does are conveying that they want to enjoy an uninhibited and robust sexual life with coitus (not merely its foreplay

---

brought for declaratory and injunctive relief by Craig, a male then between 18 and 21 years of age, and by a licensed vendor of 3.2% beer. During the appeal process, Craig turned 21 and the Court ruled that the "controversy has been rendered moot as to Craig." The standing of the seller of beer was upheld by the Court; she was not required to break the law and suffer prosecution or to appeal the case up through the state appellate courts.

or surrogates) without present and ongoing fears and concerns of having to bring an unwanted pregnancy to term, or else to risk an illegal or burdensome procedure to terminate it, and that they want to enjoy such sexual freedom and fulfilment for its own sake, without procreation as a goal, indeed with procreation as something to be avoided. How, then was such a claim essentially the same as Roe's, an unmarried white woman who sought an abortion for an unplanned pregnancy, but who never had it, whose mother described her as "a die-hard whore,"[17] and who now claims to be strongly opposed to abortion and has ostensibly dedicated herself to overturning the law that bears her pseudonym?[18] And although the Court did not assert that Roe's claims are "essentially" those of Dr. Hallford, who wanted the liberty to pursue his medical practice absent the ongoing threat and frequent burden of being arrested and/or tried and/or convicted under the Texas anti-abortion law, it is worth emphasizing how unlike hers his were. How, then did the Court in pragmatically denying standing hear the communication of the Does?

The Court reported that John and Mary Doe "fear [...] they may face the prospect of becoming parents" (*Roe v. Wade* 128) and would then want an abortion that they could not obtain legally. They asserted as an "immediate and present injury, *only* an *alleged* 'detrimental effect upon [their] marital happiness' because they are forced to 'the choice of refraining from normal sexual relations or of endangering Mary Doe's health through a possible pregnancy.'" (*Roe v. Wade 128* [*emphasis* added]). The Court characterized John and Mary's allegations as a claim that the risk of pregnancy "might have some real or imagined impact upon their marital happiness" (*Roe v. Wade* 128).

The Court ruled that the Does lacked standing because their alleged injury was merely a hypothetical event in a speculative future:

> Their claim is that, sometime in the future, Mrs. Doe might become pregnant because of possible failure of contraceptive measures, and, at that time in the future, she might want an abortion that might then be illegal under the Texas statutes.
>
> This very phrasing [sic, the phrasing of the Court, not the plaintiffs] of the Does' position reveals [sic, one might say "creates"] its speculative character. Their alleged injury rests on possible future contraceptive failure, possible future pregnancy, possible future unpreparedness for parenthood, and possible future impairment of health. Any one or more of these several possibilities may not take place, and all may not combine. But we are not prepared to say that the bare allegation of so indirect an injury is sufficient to present an actual case or controversy. (*Roe v. Wade* 128)

---

17 Joshua Prager, "The accidental activist," *Vanity Fair*, January 18, 2013, http://www.vanityfair.com/news/politics/2013/02/norma-mccorvey-roe-v-wade-abortion, (last viewed 6/5/2016).
18 "Woman behind *Roe v. Wade*: 'I'm dedicating my life to overturning it'" http://www.lifenews.com/2013/01/22/woman-behind-roe-v-wade-im-dedicating-my-life-to-overturning-it/

It is tempting to conceive of the Court as erroneously regarding the Does' concern with their sexual freedom and its effect on marital happiness as conveyed entirely through *conversational* implicature, and in a fit of Gricean non-cooperation testing the principle of cancelation by creating such a qualifier as, *viz.*, "not to imply your Honors, either through the time, expense and energy reflected in our filing this suit instead of merely grousing about the issue to a neighbor over our backyard fence, nor through anything we say in it that any of the concerns adduced in it are of the slightest importance whatsoever to us or anyone else." The court seems then to have applied this cancelation, thus leaving nothing to consider but the insufficient hypothetical harm detailed above.

Much as happened in *Brooks* where the letter of the law was denied in order to void the import of the 1860 statute, in denying standing to the Does the Supreme Court reduced their concern to a nullity. It is difficult to imagine the Court ruling in, say, the case of a defect in an airplane's navigational system, or an automobile's capacity to accelerate, both of which imposed additional burdens to ensure a nonetheless compromised level of safety, that the alleged harm was merely a hypothetical future event. It is difficult to avoid the conclusion that a married couple's loss of a robust and uninhibited sexual life valued for its own sake, and with the intent to avoid procreation, is just the sort of harm that it wished to refuse to recognize, and did. If the Does choose to forego coitus, the risk of pregnancy is eliminated and the problem solved. And if they decide to engage in coitus, then the Court either disregards Mary's experience of sexual relations with John (as when British women were expected to submit to sex merely as part of their marital obligations, or "lie back and think of England"[19]) or it presupposes that fear of pregnancy has no significant effect upon her sexual pleasure. I am not sure which is worse: that the Court assumes that Mary's sexual enjoyment is likely in any event to be insignificant or that it presupposes that she (and John) will forget all about the risk to her health and experience no inhibition during sexual relations.[20] In either case, in so doing the Court managed to leave the stigma of abortion firmly in place when it might have given the case a different and more legitimizing face that broadened understanding of the wealth of motives for having it as a constitutionally protected right.

---

[19] See http://www.phrases.org.uk/meanings/close-your-eyes-and-think-of-england.html (last visited March 8, 2015).
[20] If the Court assumed that despite the law abortions remained readily available, then the Justices overlooked the urban hospitals that typically had whole wards devoted to the care of women suffering from illegal, botched abortions. An unlikely possibility is that the Court accepts that Mary and John will stop engaging in coitus, but concludes that it is too speculative whether engaging in little or no coitus will damage their marital happiness.

4 The Florida Star v. B.J.F.: sexual abuse, privacy rights, and freedom of the press

In the early 1980s Florida enacted a statute forbidding anyone "to print, publish, or broadcast or cause or allow to be printed, published, or broadcast, in any instrument of mass communication the name, address, or other identifying fact or information of the victim of any [specified] sexual offense."[21] In violation of the statute and of its own internal policy, the *Florida Star*, a weekly newspaper, published the full name of a woman who had reported on October 20, 1983 to the Duval County Sheriff's Department that she had been robbed and sexually assaulted by an unknown assailant. The newspaper obtained the information from a report the Sheriff's Department had placed in the pressroom. Although her name appeared in the *Florida Star*'s "Police Reports" section under the "Robberies" rather than the "Sexual Assault" subsection, the short paragraph describing the crime highlighted the sexual assault as well:

> [...] an unknown black man ran up behind the lady [as she crossed through a park to get to her bus stop] and placed a knife to her neck and told her not to yell. The suspect then undressed the lady and had sexual intercourse with her before fleeing the scene with her 60 cents, Timex watch and gold necklace. (*Florida Star v. B.J.F.* 527)

Shortly after her full name appeared in the *Florida Star*, the woman began receiving threatening and harassing phone calls to her home, including one in which the male caller said that he would rape her "again." As a consequence, she sought police protection, changed her phone number and moved her residence, and obtained mental health counseling (*Florida Star v. B.J.F.* 528).

These threatening calls were among the large list of avoidable evils, to be expanded upon later, from which the Florida statute sought to protect victims of sexual assault and to which she was exposed by publication of her name in the *Florida Star*. She brought a civil lawsuit against the Sheriff's Department for negligently making her name available to the newspapers, and against the *Florida Star* for negligently publishing her name in violation of the Florida state statute. The Sherriff's Department paid a relatively small sum to the plaintiff, now referred to as "B.J.F.," to settle her case against the Department before trial, leaving the *Florida Star* as the sole defendant. The trial judge denied the *Florida Star*'s motion to dismiss the civil suit, ruling against the defendant's claim that B.J.F.'s lawsuit violated the newspaper's First Amendment freedom of the press.

---

[21] Florida Stat. § 794.03 (1987) (cited in *Florida Star v. B.J.F.*). The citation is to the 1987 compilation; the law under discussion was enacted earlier.

At trial, the judge found the statute struck a proper balance between First Amendment and privacy rights, and directed the jury that the *Florida Star*'s violation of the state statute barring publication of the name of a rape victim constituted negligence *per se*. The jury found that the defendant's actions were the legal cause of the plaintiff's damages, assessed her damages in the amount of $75,000 and awarded her that sum in compensatory damages (*Florida Star v. B.J.F.* 528). It also awarded her $25,000 in punitive damages because the jury found that the newspaper had acted with "reckless indifference" when it published B.J.F.'s name. The Florida Court of Appeal upheld the trial court verdict and the Florida Supreme Court let the ruling stand (*Florida Star v. B.J.F.* 529).

The *Florida Star* then appealed to the U.S. Supreme Court, which overturned the verdict in a decision by Justice Marshall that focused the issue as one of state censorship in the service of privacy rights versus freedom of the press. After mentioning "the sensitivity and significance of [...] privacy rights" and making an attempt at evenhandedness by stating that both rights are "plainly rooted in the traditions and significant concerns of our society," in what might pass for a shibboleth of judicial pragmatism, Marshall insisted that his decision relied "on limited principles that sweep no more broadly than the appropriate context of the instant case" (*Florida Star v. B.J.F.* 533). This important focus, carried over from similar cases, implies that the particulars of this case and its relation to precedents would be given especial care and attention; the Court thus signaled that it sought full communication of the relevant facts of the instant case. Marshall then articulated the core principle by which the case was to be adjudicated, a principle used by the Court in a prior case (*Smith v. Daily Mail Publishing Co.*) which states: "[I]f a newspaper lawfully obtains truthful information about a matter of public significance then state officials may not constitutionally punish publication of the information, absent a need to further a state interest of the highest order." Marshall offered three considerations in support of this principle that we need not directly engage here.

Whether or not one agrees with Marshall on this tack, as we shall see, the troubling aspect of his opinion is its failure to recognize and engage the strengths of the opposing side even while claiming to do so. In fact, his arguments are riddled with errors and omissions that flow from a failure to appreciate the nature of the harm that B.J.F. suffered, and how she came to suffer it, whereas by contrast the incisive and sometimes lacerating dissent by Justice White is fueled by an empathic understanding of this harm and a sensitive appreciation of the damage done to society by denying the legitimacy of her claim as the majority did. Whereas Marshall seems to be using a cliché while introducing the subject, "At a time in which we are daily reminded of the tragic reality of rape [...]" (*Florida Star v. B.J.F.* 537) and suggests that the tragedy is completed by the rape itself, White begins his dissent with passionate empathy for the victim:

> "Short of homicide, [rape] is the 'ultimate violation of self.'" *Coker v. Georgia*, 433 U.S. 584, 597 (1977) (opinion of WHITE, J.). For B.J.F., however, the violation she suffered at a rapist's knifepoint marked only the beginning of her ordeal. A week later, while her assailant was still at large, an account of this assault – identifying by name B.J.F. as the victim – was published by The Florida Star. As a result, B.J.F. received harassing phone calls, required mental health counseling, was forced to move from her home, and was even threatened with being raped again. (*Florida Star v. B.J.F.* 542–543 [Square brackets in White's quote from Coker])

At almost every point that White challenges Marshall, he is able to do so because of a rich emotional understanding of the victim and her suffering that Marshall, despite sometimes using the words, which often sound hollow coming from him, seemed to lack.

Marshall makes his opinion seem to follow smoothly from a triad of other Court decisions that his adjudicative principle supposedly embodies, but White will have none of this. He reminds Marshall that this principle, used in the *Daily Mail* case, was merely "suggested" by prior cases rather than being "constitutional dogma" and that these cases that suggested it are decidedly unlike the present one (*Florida Star v. B.J.F.* 545). In *Cox Broadcasting Corp. v. Cohn*, the victim's name had been disclosed at a hearing where her assailants pled guilty and so was contained in judicial records already made fully public in accordance with state law, not contrary to it. White notes that *Cox Broadcasting* states explicitly that if there are privacy rights of the victim, the state must undertake to protect them rather than using press censorship as the first line of defense – which is precisely what the Florida statute did (*Florida Star v. B.J.F.* 544).

The *Daily Mail* case on which Marshall so heavily relies is even worse for his purposes because the plaintiff was the *perpetrator*, also a juvenile, who murdered a 15-year-old student in a notorious case and whatever rights he might have enjoyed, "the rights of crime victims to stay shielded from public view must be infinitely more substantial." (*Florida Star v. B.J.F.* 545) Worse, as White emphasizes, the *Daily Mail* explicitly stated that the "holding in this case is narrow [...] *there is no issue here of privacy*" (*Florida Star v. B.J.F.* 545 [emphasis added by White]). So Marshall's decision to use the principle from the *Daily Mail* lay in tatters even before its application to the instant case, and those tatters are further reduced under White's withering examination. Even while claiming to be open to the relevant particulars, Marshall pointedly ignored them.

In emphasizing that the press obtained the information lawfully and thus should not be punished, Marshall relied upon the principle: "The government's issuance of such a release, without qualification, can only convey to recipients that the government considered dissemination lawful, and indeed expected the recipients to disseminate the information further" (*Florida Star v. B.J.F.* 538–539). The Syllabus had misleadingly set the stage to convey to the reader that an innocent mistake had been committed by "A Star *reporter-trainee* sent to the pressroom [who] copied the police report verbatim [...]" (*Florida Star v. B.J.F.* 524 [*emphasis* added]). White scathingly reminds us that the present release was not "without qualification" because not only did this trainee reporter testify that she knew full well that she was breaking the law, but also she copied the report in a room "that contained signs making it clear that the names of rape victims were not matters of public record, and were not to be published" (*Florida Star v. B.J.F.* 546). Thus, the present case was entirely the opposite of a situation where "the government considered dissemination lawful" (*Florida Star v. B.J.F.* 546). Indeed, it was just the opposite because Florida had followed the Court's advice in *Cox Broadcasting* by passing a law designed to protect the privacy rights of rape victims, and despite this, as White notes, "mistakes happen" (*Florida Star v. B.J.F.* 547). White underscores that whatever vital interests may be served by reporting crime, "it is not too much to ask the press, in instances such as this, to respect simple standards of decency and refrain from publishing a victim's name, address, and/or phone number" as doing so serves no useful purpose (*Florida Star v. B.J.F.* 547).

Marshall's second set of concerns revolved around the law having, as White put it, "too strict a liability standard" so that "a newspaper might be found liable under the Florida courts' negligence *per se* theory without regard to a newspaper's scienter or degree of fault." White then noted that this consideration was "wholly inapposite here, where the jury found that appellant acted with 'reckless indifference towards the rights of others [...],'" a far higher standard of proof (*Florida Star v. B.J.F.* 548). As to the issue of liability generally, White observes that what Marshall's objection amounts to is complaining "that the standard of care has been set by the legislature, instead of the courts," (*Florida Star v. B.J.F.* 548) and that Marshall's concern with strict liability in such cases where the victim "voluntarily called public attention to the offense" are answered by the simple fact that such a victim would not be entitled to much, if any, compensation (*Florida Star v. B.J.F.* 549). But even to make such a comparison between B.J.F. and another victim who calls public attention to the offense trivializes the extent that violent rape can cause damage, disorient, provoke the subjective collapse of a civilized world, make a woman feel like "damaged goods," and arouse her fear of the blood-lust of the male hordes who threaten or harass, or who hope for their turn at a defenseless woman.[22] Certainly B.J.F. never "voluntarily called public attention" to herself or to the offense, and no one suggested she had fabricated the assault or otherwise made herself "a reasonable subject of public concern."[23] The fact that some imagined or even real victims of sexual assault might do so has no bearing on the Florida legislature's recognition that the vast majority of victims does not do any such things, and deserve protection.

But Marshall, applying his third and final reason to reject B.J.F.'s claim, found the protection provided to be unconstitutional and undeserved because

---

22 The feared blood-lust of the male horde is nowhere better depicted than by Hubert Selby, Jr. in *Last Exit to Brooklyn*, (Grove Press, Inc., [1957], 1964, pp. 109–114). I use a fictional example because the details of actual gang rapes, even when horrific, are rarely provided so graphically, but see some actual cases below. Selby describes the misadventures of a hooker, Tralala, returning to her Brooklyn haunts and trying to drink herself out of broken heart, who ends up offering on a dare to gang-bang some men who are kiddingly taunting her at a bar. As the circus proceeds to a vacant lot, it ends up attracting some Greek men at a laundromat across the street and then some sailors from a nearby Navy base until a carnival of them has at Tralala "more came 40 maybe 50 and they screwed her and went back on line and had a beer and yelled and laughed and someone yelled that the car stunk of cunt so Tralala and the seat were taken out of the car and laid in the lot and she lay there naked on the seat and their shadows hid her pimples and scabs and she drank slapping her tits with the other hand" while she laughs drunkenly as beer cans are shoved at her mouth and chip her teeth until she finally passes out, but the party pandemonium continues unabated:

> [...] they slapped her a few times and she mumbled and turned her head but they couldn't revive her so they continued to fuck her as she lay unconscious on the seat in the lot and soon they tired of the dead piece and the daisychain brokeup and they went back to Willies the Greeks and the base and the kids who were watching and waiting to take a turn took out their disappointment on Tralala and tore her clothes to small scraps put out a few cigarettes on her nipples pissed on her jerkedoff on her jammed a broomstick up her snatch then bored they left her lying amongst the broken bottles rusty cans and rubble of the lot and Jack and Freddy and Ruthy and Annie stumbled into a cab still laughing and they leaned toward the window as they passed the lot and got a good look at Tralala lying naked covered with blood urine and semen and a small blot forming on the seat between her legs as blood seeped from her crotch [...]

See also "Femicide is an international crisis that urgently needs attention." By Lauren Duca, May 28, 2016 2:47PM EDT http://www.teenvogue.com/story/brazil-gang-rape (last accessed 6/6/2016); "The Stanford Rape Victim's Letter to Her Attacker Should Be Required Reading" by Lauren Duca, June 4, 2016, http://www.teenvogue.com/story/stanford-rape-letter (last accessed 6/6/2016).

23 Marshall's hypotheses would not require the plaintiff herself to have acted improperly as long as one way or another her identity became a matter of public interest. Of course, in our society in almost any case of sexual assault one can find someone willing to raise questions whether the alleged victim fabricated the crime.

of the "facial underinclusiveness" of the statute that "raises serious doubts about whether [the Florida statute] is, in fact, serving [...] the significant interests [the privacy of victims of sexual offenses; the physical safety of such victims, who may be targeted for retaliation if their names become known to their assailants; and the goal of encouraging victims of such crimes to report these offenses without fear of exposure] which appellee invokes in support of affirmance" (*Florida Star v. B.J.F.* 540). Marshall noted that the statute

> prohibits the publication of identifying information only if this information appears in an "instrument of mass communication," [but] does not prohibit the spread by other means of the identities of victims of sexual offenses. An individual who maliciously spreads word of the identity of a rape victim is thus not covered, despite the fact that the communication of such information to persons who live near, or work with, the victim may have consequences as devastating as the exposure of her name to large numbers of strangers.
>
> When a State attempts the extraordinary measure of punishing truthful publication in the name of privacy, it must demonstrate its commitment to advancing this interest by applying its prohibition evenhandedly, to the smalltime disseminator as well as the media giant. Where important First Amendment interests are at stake, the mass scope of disclosure is not an acceptable surrogate for injury. (*Florida Star v. B.J.F.* 540)

While the notion of evenhanded application of the law is appealing when we consider imposing criminal penalties on rich and poor alike, it has little or no traction here, and Marshall's insensitivity is palpable. Notice how he misrepresents matters by complaining that the statute employs the "mass scope of disclosure" as a "surrogate for injury." It does nothing of the sort, and does something far simpler: it recognizes both the difficulty of enforcement and the severe constitutional dangers of placing overly broad restrictions on the truthful speech of individuals. More importantly, it recognizes the difference between the damage and dangers routinely, and usually automatically, caused by the dissemination of the identity of the victims of sexual crimes through an instrument of mass communication and those that might be caused by the potential malicious gossip, who would be less likely to have access to the underlying facts, and whose limited means of dissemination would create less danger. But to see this, as Marshall is unable to, one must empathize with the victim, and be willing to listen to her plight and recognize the law's remedy for it; then it becomes obvious.

Many such victims are struggling with and warding off feelings of shame and degradation and prefer to do so privately, preserving their dignity and revealing the trauma that they went through, and the trauma with which they still struggle, when they are strong enough, by choosing to whom, and when, and how they want it revealed. The fear and concern that they would almost inevitably be forced to face such ordeals simply because they report a violent sexual crime committed against them stops many women from coming forward, a social harm that the Court mentions but insufficiently heeds. As White put the matter plainly, Marshall's reasoning is defective on two scores. In the *Daily Mail* case on which Marshall so strongly relies, a chief defect of the law was that it forbade publication of the victim's name by newspapers, but not radio or television, and so failed to cover evenhandedly all "instrument[s] of mass communication," a defect corrected by the instant Florida statute. Furthermore, and crucially, the Florida statute reads as it does "because presumably the Florida Legislature had determined that neighborhood gossips do not pose the danger and intrusion to rape victims that 'instrument[s] of mass communication' do. Simply put, Florida wanted to prevent the widespread distribution of rape victims' names, and therefore enacted a statute tailored almost as precisely as possible to achieving that end" (*Florida Star v. B.J.F.* 549). The upshot of this is to reveal as thoroughly misguided Marshall's desideratum that an appropriate remedy "must demonstrate its commitment to advancing this interest by applying its prohibition evenhandedly, to the smalltime disseminator as well as the media giant" (*Florida Star v. B.J.F.* 540). Only the latter agency poses the threat, so Marshall's test is simply inapt.[24]

Marshall may have blunted his sensitivity to the plight of the victims, but at least he paid lip service to their difficulties. Scalia's response is far more disturbing. In a concurring opinion, he elaborated and relied on this third ground of the majority decision as "sufficient to decide this case," focusing upon Marshall's concern about "evenhanded[ness]" (*Florida Star v. B.J.F.* 541–542). In other words, rather than meeting his obligation to be open to communication about the particulars of the case, of the wisdom or substantive justice it might embody, Scalia wished to know nothing of the sort. Scalia's opinion ("concurring in part and concurring in the judgment") declined to endorse Marshall's strong support for freedom of the press, and it revealed a peculiarly limited, Victorian understanding of why victims of sexual assault want their name kept out of mass distribution newspapers or other such news outlets and thereby came to impose the same faulty test used by Marshall of what constituted a "vital state interest." Once a woman is publicly identified with sexual assault in any manner, and particularly as a victim of such assault, the chances of her being targeted and harassed in a variety of ways by any number of confused adolescent boys or dangerous predators increases significantly, and any American knowledgeable about the issue of violence against women would recognize the increased danger

---

24 White also points out how misguided Marshall is in faulting Florida's § 794.03 for providing no grounds for tort against the gossip instead of examining "the whole of Florida privacy tort law [that] does recognize a tort of publication of private facts." (*Florida Star v. B.J.F.* 550)

she faced by being identified by name in the newspaper description of the assault against her. But Justice Scalia did not recognize such issues.

Scalia followed and elaborated Marshall's argument that "a law cannot be regarded as protecting an interest 'of the highest order' and thus justifying a restriction upon truthful speech, when it leaves appreciable damage to that supposedly vital interest unprohibited," [cites omitted] and he made much of such cases as "the backyard gossip who tells 50 people that don't have to know" as though the victim's primary concern must be to safeguard her reputation (*Florida Star v. B.J.F.* 540). Most troubling, however, is that the worst damage that Scalia imagines coming from such publication is "her discomfort at its publication" – again seeming to consider this a matter only of her reputation or public image – or in a worst-case-scenario that her uncaptured assailant might now know where she lives and come to harm her. But he very oddly dismisses this possibility as irrelevant because "the instructions here did not require the jury to find that the rapist was at large" (*Florida Star v. B.J.F.* 542). The possibility that B.J.F. is a single mother with a couple of young children to protect from would-be predators roused by the mass media divulging her identity, as she apparently was, never enters his mind, only the possibility that her "discomfort at the dissemination of news of her misfortune [sic] among friends and acquaintances would be at least as great as her discomfort at its publication by the media to people to whom she is only a name" (*Florida Star v. B.J.F.* 542). Having ignored and misunderstood the problem – the actual plight of the victim and her continuing traumas and vulnerability – that the statute addressed and in large part remedied, Scalia felt at liberty to condemn the Florida statute as "a prohibition that society is prepared to impose upon the press but not upon itself." He then concluded: "Such a prohibition does not protect an interest 'of the highest order'" (*Florida Star v. B.J.F.* 542).

Scalia's callousness derives directly from what White termed "insensitivity" to "rival interests in a civilized and humane society." White illustrated this insensitivity by means of the Florida Star's attorney who argued that the newspaper was not to blame for the fear and anguish that B.J.F. suffered from phone calls from a man threatening to rape her again (*Florida Star v. B.J.F.* 553, note 2).

> [I]n reference to the [threatening] phone call, it is sort of blunted by the fact that [B.J.F.] didn't receive the phone call. Her mother did. And if there is any pain and suffering in connection with the phone call, it has to lay in her mother's hands. I mean, my God, she called [B.J.F.] up at the hospital to tell her [of the threat] – you know, I think that is tragic, but I don't think that is something you can blame the Florida Star for.

It is difficult not to be reminded of the young man who murdered his parents, and then pleaded for mercy from the court on the grounds that he was an orphan.

There was an unwholesome odor even back then to Scalia's narrow focus that shut out the substantive issues of the case, and his strong embrace of the purely technical requirements that a statute must meet in order to count as protecting a "vital state interest," irrespective of what the statute actually accomplished, *viz.*, that it "leaves [no] appreciable damage to that supposedly vital interest unprohibited." There is an unhappy implication to this unnatural standard as we search our minds for examples of when both the lips of all mass communications and those of private citizens must be sealed: state secrets and "national security" come to mind, and very little, if not nothing, else. In what began as a seeming contest between freedom of the press and the state's interest in protecting the vital privacy rights of victims of sexual crime, Justice Scalia's insensitivity to the latter steered him towards dogmatically supporting a test that could be satisfied by considerations of national security and little if anything else. Scalia thus ends by upholding the rights of the federal state against those of its citizens under the aegis of protecting the first amendment rights of the media.

5 Concluding thoughts

In seeking to evaluate the potential usefulness of judges applying a pragmatic interpretation of law, we introduced the notion of a "constrained performative" that points instructively to the institutional norms within which the speaker should operate, and suggested that conformity to or deviation from these norms provides or denies the speaker the legitimacy to be endowed with or deserve the authority of his office. The minimalist norms we imposed require a court to pay attention to and appreciate all legitimate concerns by actively pursuing and attending to relevant communications and considerations, and when consistent with its obligations, accommodating substantive justice. Doing so has hopefully brought a clearer picture of the difficulties faced by feminist and CLS scholars, for which pragmatism offers no promise of relief. It has provided an important corrective to the general picture that the reforms we seek are frustrated primarily by the judiciary's obligations to existing law, abstract principle, or formalized modes of reasoning from which the pragmatist offers to rescue us. By focusing upon the various courts' deficiencies in communication, we found that a principal problem is that the judges themselves embody the prejudices we wish to overcome, and that they often impose these prejudices across-the-board not because of supposed obligations to law or abstract principle, but in flagrant defiance of them. Nor is it surprising that a sharper focus on the minimal requirements of active communicative openness should do so, for each of the constraining elements – law or abstract principle, formal reasoning about the relevant facts of the case, and finally substantive justice – provides the court an opportunity to disguise its bias against any one or more that offends it by shifting responsibility for a biased decision onto one or more of the other factors at the expense of active communicative openness. Indeed, this common effort to disguise the bias by shifting responsibility to another factor, or by denying the existence of a factor that the courts wish to ignore, confirms our original claim that communicative openness to each of the above factors is at least implicitly accepted by the courts themselves as a norm for being invested with the authority that they exercise.

In *Brooks*, where the law and abstract principle were just in awarding equal custody rights to the mother after imposing equal obligations upon her, the court – as though claiming to be the better and more objective forward-looking pragmatically oriented social engineers – refused to hear it and engaged in elaborate contortions to pretend that the legislature had not spoken at all, hence that they had obeyed rather than defied it. In *Roe v. Wade*, considered a cynosure of pro-feminist lawmaking, we nonetheless saw anti-feminist – and perhaps also anti-sexual liberation – prejudice rear its ugly head in the Court's refusal to recognize the standing of a married couple (the Does) who put at issue their right to uninhibited coital pleasure for its own sake coupled with a desire to prevent procreation. There the Court seemed to rule that the loss of coitus if the Does chose that option, was no harm at all but rather a solution to the risk of pregnancy that they wished to avoid; and that the worries, fears and burdens assumed in having coitus without the birth control pills that were incompatible with Jane Doe's medical conditions, were also no harm because they did yet make her have an unwanted pregnancy for which she was unable to obtain an abortion. Finally, in *The Florida Star v. B.J.F.*, the Florida state legislature carefully crafted a law to correct the very defects that the Supreme Court had ruled made prior state laws unconstitutional, thus seeking to protect the privacy rights of victims of sexual abuse, and to serve substantive justice. Here, in perhaps the clearest case of a conflict between an abstract principle – freedom of the press – and substantive justice embodied in the state's protection of privacy rights of victims of sexual assault, the Court refused to hear and recognize the actual nature of the harm and its prepotent cause: dissemination of the victim's identity by means of mass media automatically exposed her to increased risk of threat and humiliation. Instead, the Court emphasized that it could imagine other forms of dissemination of the victim's identity that might result in harm to the victim, and that unless all of these were also prohibited, the legislation could not completely accomplish its ends, and was thus unconstitutional. Scalia's limited concurrence displayed classic callousness and indifference to the nature of threats posed to the victim – he refused to hear or recognize them – and thus was able to enshrine as the "correct" adjudicative principle one that in effect reserved the right of press censorship wholly to the federal government, at the cost of the loss of the rights of its citizens.

Such biases are so deeply ingrained in the thinking, feelings, instincts, sentiments and sensibilities of the court that something loosely termed a pragmatic approach to law would be as likely to perpetuate them as not – depending entirely upon the thinking, feeling, instinct, sentiment and sensibility of the pragmatic judge or judges making the decision. What is of special interest, and what I hope this paper has illuminated, is that judicial bias often operates as an inversion of Sartrean bad faith – it is the very opposite of an individual denying her freedom by claiming to be bound by various legal and social pressures (Sartre 1956: 47–70), despite a superficial appearance of similarity. When implementing judicial bias, the courts exercise their freedom to express their deep-seated prejudices, but in disguising the exercise of this freedom they very often reveal the intentions they wish to conceal by violating minimalist communicative norms. Such violations reveal nothing so exotic as Sartrean bad faith, but its garden variety, all-too-common, and all-too-difficult-to-extirpate, weedy cousin.

References

Austin, John L. 1962. *How to do things with words: The William James lectures delivered at Harvard University in 1955*. J. O. Urmson & Marina Sbisà (eds.). Oxford: Clarendon Press.
Basch, Norma. 1982. *In the eyes of the law: Women, marriage, and property in nineteenth-century New York*. Ithaca, NY: Cornell University Press.
Davies, Bethan. 2000. Grice's cooperative principle: Getting the meaning across. In D. Nelson & P. Foulkes (eds.), *Leeds working papers in linguistics* 8. 1–26.
Dworkin, Ronald. 1986. *Law's empire*. Cambridge, MA: Harvard University Press.
Ertelt, Steven. 2013. Woman behind Roe v. Wade: "I'm dedicating my life to overturning it." *LifeNews.com*, 22 January 2013. http://www.lifenews.com/2013/01/22/woman-behind-roe-v-wade-im-dedicating-my-life-to-overturning-it/ (accessed 5 June 2016).
Goffman, Erving. 1959. *The presentation of self in everyday life*. Garden City, NY: Doubleday Anchor Books.
Gertner, Nancy. 2011. *In defense of women: Memoirs of an unrepentant advocate*. Boston, MA: Beacon Press.
Grice, H. P. 1975. Logic and conversation. In P. Cole & J. Morgan (eds.), *Syntax and semantics*, Volume 3, 41–58. New York: Academic Press.
Posner, Richard A. 1989–1990. What has pragmatism to offer law? *Southern California Law Review* 63. 1653–1670.
Prager, Joshua. 2013. The accidental activist. *Vanity Fair*, January 18, 2013. http://www.vanityfair.com/news/politics/2013/02/norma-mccorvey-roe-v-wade-abortion (accessed 5 June 2016).

Ramsey, Carolyn B. 2013. The exit myth: Family law, gender roles, and changing attitudes toward female victims of domestic violence. *University of Michigan Journal and Gender and Law* 20. 1–32.
Rubin, Eva R. 1982. Abortion, politics, and the courts: Roe v. Wade and its aftermath. Westport, CT: Greenwood Press.
Sartre, Jean-Paul. 1956. *Being and nothingness*. New York: Philosophical Library.
Selby, Hubert Jr. 1964 [1957]. *Last exit to Brooklyn*. New York: Grove Press, Inc.

World Wide Web

How to perform a wedding ceremony. http://www.open-ministry.org/wedding-ceremony.php (accessed 17 June 2016).
Close your eyes and think of England. *The phrase finder*. http://www.phrases.org.uk/meanings/close-your-eyes-and-think-of-england.html (accessed 8 March 2015).
Modern ceremonies. http://www.modernceremonies.com/Samples.html (accessed 22 June 2016).

Cases and statutes cited

Bush v. Gore, 531 U.S. 98 (2000).
Craig v. Boren, 429 U.S. 190 (1976).
The Florida Star v. B.J.F., 491 U.S. 524 (1989).
Hollingsworth v. Perry, 570 U.S. ___, 133 S. Ct. 2652 (2013).
Lujan v. Defenders of Wildlife, 504 U.S. 555 (1992).
People ex rel. Brooks v. Brooks, 35 Barb. 85 (1861).
The People ex rel. Nickerson v. _____, 19 Wend. 16 (N.Y. 1837).
Roe v. Wade, 410 U.S. 113, 127 (1973).
Laws of New York, 1860, Chap. 90, Section 9.
2 Revised Statutes 1830, 148, 149, secs. 1, 2 (New York).
Florida Stat. § 794.03 (1987).

Shurli Makmillen and Margery Fee
10 Disguising the dynamism of the law in Canadian courts: Judges using dictionaries

1 Introduction

Aboriginal rights and title cases are taking up an increasing amount of time in Canadian courts, and more recently a good number of the judgments in them are coming out in favor of rights and title. Dictionaries have played a role in quite a few of these cases, as part of close attention to the language of historical documents, statutes, precedents, principles, and tests.[1] It is often said in the language and law literature that literal, or ordinary, readings serve conservative interests (such as those that would limit Indigenous rights), while looser, more figurative, or dynamic interpretations often accompany more liberalized ideologies (Gibbons 1994: 31; Bix 2012: 154). However, we find that in many Canadian judgments close attention to dictionary definitions are linked with judgments that enhance the legal and other statuses of Indigenous people. When it comes to reading early treaties in Canada, courts must apply principles of liberal interpretation as ruled in *R. v. Badger* (1996), which states that "any ambiguities or doubtful expressions must be resolved in favor of the Indians and any limitations restricting the rights of Indians under treaties must be narrowly construed." Similarly in U.S. courts interpretive processes are mostly framed by principles that favor Native Americans, the insured over the insurer, or disadvantaged groups in general (Solan 1993: 65–66). Leniency towards these groups is often the result of the assertion of ambiguity in the interpretation of statutes and regulations. In deciding such cases, judges can use dictionaries to limit themselves to supposedly unambiguous ordinary meanings, and they can also use dictionaries to expand the category of an ordinary meaning to include

---

[1] Our corpus of all Supreme Court of Canada decisions from 1876 to 2010 reveals that, after a steady rise, the number of cases citing dictionaries peaked in the 1990s (8.2 % of all cases for that decade) and dropped considerably in the decade beginning 2000 (2.8 % for this decade). Judgments in eleven of the 69 total number of cases addressing Aboriginal rights in Canada referred to dictionaries (15%).

Shurli Makmillen, Claflin University
Margery Fee, University of British Columbia

DOI 10.1515/9781501504723-010

alternative readings. This broadening (*extensio*) or narrowing (*restrictio*) of meanings relevant to a decision, according to Pierre Bourdieu (1987), gives law a convenient "elasticity," albeit under the guise of "the principled interpretation of unanimously accepted texts" (818). In the pages below, we follow Bourdieu as well as other language theorists and philosophers to illustrate this elasticity in two Canadian Aboriginal rights cases. We chose these cases because of the heightened socio-political contexts in which they were decided, contexts that bring one of the more mundane routines in writing judgments – that of consulting a dictionary for the meaning of a word – into stark relief. Considering the judges' reasonings around word meanings allows us to forward a claim about the nature of legal interpretation itself, one that may have consequences for how linguists work in the courts.

2 Theory

Drawing from a tradition of language research based in rhetoric, relevance theory (Sperber & Wilson 1986) and integrational linguistics (Harris 1981, 2002; Toolan 1996, 2002), we see meanings as invariably context sensitive. Sperber and Wilson, for example, describe meaning in terms of changes to an addressee's cognitive environment, which they call "contextual effects"; meaning is, in other words, the payoff achieved for cognitive effort expended by an addressee on another's utterance. Because "relevance decreases the more effort is required" (137), addressees tend to take whatever cognitive effects – implications about context; the strengthening or contradicting of previously held assumptions – as most manifest in an utterance. Like many pragmatists, Sperber and Wilson take their examples mostly from contrived exchanges between two in-person interlocutors. As well, contexts and contextual effects are contemporaneous, and idealized for the purpose of theorizing a model.[2] Indeed, this idealization inspires Michael J. Toolan (1996: 143) to point out that "no general pragmatic grammar" can possibly account for the myriad indirect speech acts in real contexts of production and

---

[2] The crux of Harris's (2002) and Toolan's (1996) integrational approach is that processes of communication are best seen as an integration of two ends of a spectrum: the assumption of a mythic code at one end and a free-flowing array of contingencies, activities, abilities, and factors of context at the other. This spectrum can be represented by the formalists on the one hand who seek notional definitions within an abstracted yet ultimately (they hope) knowable system, and those on the other hand who, like Wittgenstein, see language in terms only of what it can do in particular contexts, i.e. what games it permits. Communication for the integrationist is a function of merging past linguistic experience with current "communicational requirements" (Roy Harris [2002] 22). Interestingly, while Sperber and Wilson also ostensibly reject the code model, Toolan argues they tacitly rely on it in their theory of inference (196).

reception. Furthermore, we would add that when, through writing, contexts of production are separated from contexts of reception – sometimes (as in law) by very long periods of time – it is not only problems of interpretation that arise, but also problems in theorizing language and law. Thus what we might call a "technical" gap between an utterance and its uptake – whether across time, across genres, or across cultures – has its theoretical counterpart in the gap between the law, as codified and practiced, and justice as an abstract ideal. Lyotard (1988) describes this as a gap between cognitive and transcendental realms, producing what he calls "*le différend*": "the justice which the victim calls upon against the justice of the tribunal cannot be uttered in the genre of juridical or forensic discourse. But this is the genre in which the law is uttered" (30). Bringing Lyotard's concept to an Australian court case, Freadman (2002) identifies *le différend* as generating the "blocking of semiosis" (44); we suggest it can also proliferate potential meanings across these gaps in time, genres, and cultures in legal processes in settler societies like Canada. In other words, this "inarticulable gap" (Makmillen 2007: 100) can, in Sperber and Wilson's terms, give rise to the expansion of an inferential field out of which potential meanings are made relevant.

3 Case study: Canadian Aboriginal rights and title cases

Our paper explores this gap by looking at two Canadian Aboriginal rights and title cases in which dictionaries are consulted. We identify the larger inferences made possible in the sociopolitical context of Canada through judges' recourse to dictionaries. One important inference enabled by this recourse is that there is a widespread belief in a stable linguistic code that underlies the legal code, and that this linguistic code is neutral, natural and self-evident. Also, because of tensions in the wider socio-political landscape concerning Aboriginal rights throughout the settlement of Canada, judges can be assumed to be aware that their readers will tend to infer bias, given that opinions differ about whether or not increasing Aboriginal people's rights to land, self-government and resources is just and justified. We argue that judges use dictionaries as one way to demonstrate the non-partisan nature of the courts, in that *the* dictionary can be seen as an authoritative and neutral text in the context of conflicted and rapidly changing political landscapes. Thus, in situations where public opinion is both strong and opposed, judges struggle to maintain their preferred location, which is a middle ground, firmly embedded in the larger national "public vocabulary" (Hasian, Condit & Lucaites 1996: 327, 335). By presenting two case studies of dictionary use in Aboriginal rights and title cases, we will argue that judges' dictionary use seeks to manage the implications of certain words in their decisions, to negotiate positions between the extremes in public opinion, and to disguise what we call, drawing from Bourdieu, the rhetorical dynamism of the law.

3.1 R. v. White and Bob, 1965

In the mid-1800s in British Columbia, Canada, when the Hudson's Bay Company, acting as proxy for the British Colonial Office, was establishing a foothold on the coast, its chief factor James Douglas engaged with local First Nations to purchase lands on Vancouver Island – resulting in 14 purchases, recorded in 14 deeds. One of these deeds, signed by the Saalequun (now Snuneymuxw First Nation) in the Nanaimo region, became the focus of a 1960s court case involving two Native men from the area, Clifford White and David Bob, who were charged with hunting deer out of season. White and Bob subsequently claimed an Aboriginal right based on the proviso in the deed that the "Indians" will continue to be "at liberty to hunt over the unoccupied lands as formerly." Claiming that the wording created a treaty right protected under Canada's Indian Act, their case focused on proving that the deed was actually a treaty. Amongst a range of other compelling arguments involving the Royal Proclamation of 1763, the Indian Act, the Game Act, and moral claims about "the word of the white man," Justice Norris, in a concurring opinion, still found it worthwhile to bolster his opinion by appealing to the dictionary. To do so, he first took note that the verb *to treat* was used in the correspondence between Douglas and Archibald Barclay, Secretary to the Hudson's Bay Company, and then applied "the golden rule" to the term: "that the grammatical and ordinary sense of the word is to be adhered to unless that would lead to some absurdity or some repugnance or inconsistency with the rest of the statute, in which case the grammatical and ordinary sense of the word may be modified so as to avoid that absurdity, repugnance and inconsistency, but not further." At this point, he tells of consulting the *Shorter Oxford Dictionary* to find no such "absurdity, repugnance or inconsistency," providing supporting evidence that the deed was the treaty it needed to be for the Saalequun to be able to hunt for food on ceded but unoccupied lands.[3] The elasticity of the law in this case extended Norris's purview

---

3 Interestingly, legal hermeneutics' golden rule, exemplified here by Justice Norris, is an echo of what linguists for a long time believed to be the succession of events in the cognitive processing of language, which is that hearers consult the ordinary or literal meaning of a term first, and only move on to figurative meanings if the literal fails to make sense. Elsewhere, Shurli Makmillen has argued that this obsessive and microscopic attention to linguistic detail in the face of genre-boundary-crossing uptakes is a feature of legal contexts rendered unstable by the contact zone (Makmillen 2007).

to texts completely outside the texts in question, as he adopted language from only one side of an exchange of letters between Douglas and Barclay. Specifically, only Barclay used the noun *treaty* in this series of letters; there was no uptake of the term by Douglas, who continued to use the terms "conveyance" and "deed," suggesting his and Barclay's intentions were not aligned (Makmillen 2010: 112–114). (Douglas named the record book itself *Register of Land Purchases from Indians*.)

Adding to the arbitrariness of this consultation of outside sources, and also of interest from a language and law perspective, is the fact that the wording for Douglas's deed was copied from a deed used for similar purposes a few years earlier, half-way around the world, as part of the New Zealand Company's land grab from the Ngai Tahu of the South Island. Transcribed across time (two years) and distance (a copy went to the Colonial Office in London, then it was transcribed into a letter to colonial officials on Vancouver Island), the New Zealand deed functioned as boilerplate, the language changing only as much as necessary to reflect the land in question and the identities and positions of the signatories. But because of the different national contexts, re-readings of these documents differed widely: in New Zealand paralegal contexts, the Kemp Deed figured in questioning the legality and fairness of the sale of large tracts of land in the South Island of New Zealand (Waitangi Tribunal 27, 2.4), whereas in British Columbia the same phrases were cited in relation to Aboriginal rights to carry on traditional hunting practices. In British Columbia, the text became a treaty in subsequent discourses; in New Zealand, it remained a deed. One explanation for these divergences is that the socio-legal need for a treaty in New Zealand had already been met by the 1840 Treaty of Waitangi, whereas until this decision the Tsawout and other First Nations on Vancouver Island had no local framework within which to manage their ongoing relationship with settler society.[4] In order to support the First Nations claim that the deed represented a treaty, Judge Norris first needed to find the term *treaty* in the archival record. He found it in Barclay's letter, which referred to "treating with the natives." Then he needed to consult the *Shorter Oxford Dictionary* to define the verb. This stroke of magic focused interpretation on the intentions of the Crown, which Judge Norris found represented in Barclay's words, rather than focusing on other issues, such as what was understood by the signatories at the time. In other words, in his efforts to support a Saalequun right to hunt, Norris was able to bolster other perhaps less convincing arguments about the cultural and linguistic abyss between signatories, the power imbalances

---

[4] Between its entry into Confederation in 1871 and 1991, British Columbia did not engage in treaty-making.

between Indigenous and non-Indigenous peoples, and their incommensurable legal and epistemological frameworks[5] with recourse to a neutral discourse of linguistic self-evidence: the noun *treaty* was used at the time; the dictionary definition is clear.

But as one enters this particular fray, original wordings seem to matter less and less, as do the intentions of the writers in colonial correspondence, or even the canons of interpretation. Yet judges still resort to them as if in some after-the-fact justification of what they know the courts need to do. Dictionaries, says Chris Hutton, are consulted by judges because they make good "surrogate expert witnesses," which are "blind to the moral rights and wrongs of the case" (86) but which also can "be ignored if unhelpful" (87).

Even if the courts were to adopt a more linguistically attuned understanding of the intended meaning of such a text at the time, the cross-cultural aspects could prove insurmountable. Institutional speech acts such as treaties require the mutual recognition of the institutional or social norms to work, and Sperber and Wilson (1986) express "no doubt that a cross-cultural study of such speech acts [as promising, expressing gratitude, swearing etc.] would confirm their cultural specificity and institutional nature" (fn28, 245). Scholars are only beginning to explore the consequences of such cross-cultural speech acts in courtrooms (e.g. Eades 2008) and in treaty law (e.g. Dawson 2001) from perspectives similar to those we adopt here.

3.2 R. v. Van der Peet, 1996

In 1987, Dorothy Van der Peet, a member of the Stó:lō Nation just upriver from Vancouver, British Columbia, sold ten salmon that had been legally caught under a license allowing Aboriginal people to fish for food. Selling them, however, was illegal under provincial fisheries law, and she was charged. Her lawyers

---

5 He wrote: "The transaction in question here was a transaction between, on the one hand, the strong representative of a proprietary company under the Crown and representing the Crown, who had gained the respect of the Indians by his integrity and the strength of his personality and was thus able to bring about the completion of the agreement, and, on the other hand, uneducated savages. The nature of the transaction itself was consistent with the informality of frontier days in this Province and such as the necessities of the occasion and the customs and illiteracy of the Indians demanded. The transaction in itself was a primitive one – a surrender of land in exchange for blankets to be divided between the Indian signatories according to arrangements between them – with a reservation of aboriginal rights, the document being executed by the Indians by the affixing of their marks. The unusual (by the standards of legal draftsmen) nature and form of the document considered in the light of the circumstances on Vancouver Island in 1854 does not detract from it as being a 'Treaty'."

argued that section 35 of the Constitution Act, 1982, would allow for the trade and sale of fish as an Aboriginal right, over-riding provincial law. What otherwise might be seen as a small infraction went all the way to the Supreme Court because of the constitutional implications of the case. Under the heading "Rights of the Aboriginal Peoples of Canada," section 35 reads as follows:

> 35. (1) The existing aboriginal and treaty rights of the aboriginal peoples of Canada are hereby recognized and affirmed.
> (2) In this Act, "aboriginal peoples of Canada" includes the Indian, Inuit and Métis peoples of Canada. (Canada 1982)

The justices in this case used dictionaries to find definitions for the words *ancestral*, *distinct*, *distinctive*, *integral* and *tradition*. The case is known for laying out what is now called the "integral to distinctive culture" test or the "Van der Peet" test. We focus on how Chief Justice Antonio Lamer can be said to have been managing inference in his use of *Concise Oxford Dictionary* to define the adjectives *distinct* and *distinctive*. Janet Giltrow (2014) has argued that dictionaries are "a rhetorical resource" designed to both "suspend plausible inference" and "enable a less plausible inference." Turning to the dictionary to disambiguate *distinct* and *distinctive* differs from using it to look up words that have obvious ordinary meanings. *Distinct* and *distinctive* are not all that far apart in their meanings, and they have similar meanings in English and French: the Supreme Court works in both languages. Here, we argue that the recourse to the dictionary was driven by a contemporary political debate: at the time the decision was handed down in August 1996, the word *distinct* brought along with it seriously contested political resonances driven by the rise of Québec nationalism.

Since 1763, when New France was ceded to Britain, the French-speaking and mostly Roman Catholic population of Québec has always formed a large percentage of the Canadian total. Any national government has to pay attention to Québec in order to win or maintain power. Its linguistic, legal, and cultural differences have always supported some opposition to the English-speaking majority in the rest of Canada and its economic domination of Québec. In the 1960s, the violent acts of a terrorist group, the *Front de Libération du Québec*, was the most dramatic manifestation of a burgeoning sovereignty movement. In 1976, the *Parti Québécois*, a party whose central political promise was to take Québec out of Canada, gained power for the first time. Obviously, the attention of the entire country was galvanized by these events. Given this context, we argue that Lamer was influenced by the ubiquity of the use of *distinct* in discussions of Québec sovereignty and was trying to block the inference that the distinctiveness of one's culture could allow one to assert sovereignty in ways that trumped Canadian law, not only for Québec but also for the Stó:lō and other Aboriginal peoples. Given that most of British Columbia is not covered by treaties that extinguish Aboriginal rights and land title, the issue was and is a hot one.

The phrase "distinct society" has been ascribed to Jean Lesage, the Premier of Québec from 1960 to 1966, whose election ushered in a surge of Québec nationalism. Whatever its origins, the phrase came to be frequently used in debates about Québec's relation to the rest of Canada. The phrase was politically useful because it could be interpreted in a variety of ways in both languages. *Distinct* could be read as meaning 'separate' in support of an argument that Québec was a sovereign nation and justified in leaving Confederation, or as meaning 'different,' a difference that had been and could continue to be accommodated within the Canadian state. Obviously, inferences can be drawn from the word to support quite different political positions. Ask yourselves just how distinctive a culture has to be to be 'distinct,' that is, following the definition in a range of Oxford dictionaries, "separate, not identical, individual or different in kind or quality." We argue Lamer was attempting to direct inference in ways that countered both Québec's and Aboriginal peoples' aspirations to sovereignty, aspirations that the majority of Canadians saw as unjustified.

4 The context of Québec sovereignty

Both the Aboriginal peoples and Québec had forged new ideas about sovereignty during the debates leading up to the patriation of the Constitution Act in 1982 from Britain to Canada without Québec's assent. This assent was sought in the Meech Lake Accord (stalled at the provincial level in 1990) and the Charlottetown Accord (defeated in a national referendum in 1992). The "distinct society clause" was one of the constitutional amendments proposed in both failed accords. By the time of Van der Peet, Canadians were well aware of the connections between the aspirations to sovereignty of many Québécois and Aboriginal people and also familiar with the phrase "distinct society." However, like so much in Canada, the resonance of the phrase differed between the English-speaking majority in Canada and the francophone population in Québec, not to mention Aboriginal people.[6] What was a plausible inference very much depended on how you understood "distinct society" – or nation, for that matter.

---

[6] The population of Québec is now around 23% of the total Canadian population, while Aboriginal people (broadly defined) comprise less than 4% of it.

(*Nation* has always been used in Québec to mean 'Québec,' as in the name for what would, in every other province, be called the provincial legislature: *l'Assemblée nationale*.)

In October 1995, a Québec referendum came within a hair's-breadth of victory for the sovereignists, with 49.42% voting 'Yes' and 50.56% voting 'No.' The next month, Prime Minister Jean Chrétien tabled a motion in the House of Commons calling for recognition of Québec as a distinct society on the basis of its French-speaking majority, its unique culture, and its civil law tradition. Here, Chrétien was affirming that a distinct Québec could nonetheless remain in Canada. Just as these dramatic events were unfolding, the Supreme Court was hearing the appeal of Dorothy van der Peet.

If you put *distinct/distinctive* into Google, something that was impossible in 1996, you will pull up many sites where these two words are disambiguated: they are what are sometimes called confusibles, that is, words that are often confused with each other. The doyen of English usage, H. W. Fowler (1926) wrote that these words were "often misused" (118). Not surprisingly, perhaps, the *distinct/distinctive* distinction appears as an entry in the *Guide to Canadian English usage* (Fee & McAlpine 1997), written while debates about Québec were rocking the stability of Canada's Confederation. One quotation taken from the *Financial Post* (Toronto), a national business newspaper, focuses on the overlap between the terms in ordinary speech: "When supporters of Meech Lake assert that 'of course Québec is a distinct society, we can all see that,' what they *really mean* is that Québec is a distinctive society, which it certainly is" (*Financial Post* [Toronto] 14 Nov. 1989; emphasis added).

Here, in a national English-language business newspaper, the word "distinct" requires strict segregation from the word "distinctive." Québec can be distinctive, but should not be described as distinct. Ordinary usage is here policed in order to allow for the distinctiveness of Québec society without supporting any notion of "distinctness" as allowing for political separation.

In the majority decision in Van der Peet, Lamer develops what he calls the "integral to a distinctive culture" test. He clearly limits this test by insisting that although the Aboriginal perspective must be taken into account, "that perspective must be framed in terms cognizable to the Canadian legal and constitutional structure." The Canadian legal framework takes priority, although the Canadian state is an interested party in such cases, particularly when they deal with land, a paradox that many Aboriginal legal theorists have noted. He also says

> A practice, custom or tradition, to be recognized as an aboriginal right need not be distinct, meaning 'unique,' to the aboriginal culture in question. The aboriginal claimants must simply demonstrate that the custom or tradition is a defining characteristic of their culture.

Like the *Financial Post* writer, he is making the difference between these two words extremely clear. In fact, in defining *distinct* as 'unique,' he goes beyond the definition in the dictionary he actually used. We have checked several editions of the *Oxford concise dictionary*, the *Oxford English dictionary* and the *Canadian Oxford dictionary*, and not one defines *distinct* as 'unique.'

> **Distinct:** 1 a) not identical, separate, individual b) different in kind or quality, unlike 2) clearly understandable, definite 3) unmistakable
>
> **Distinctive:** distinguishing, characteristic
>
> **Unique:** 1) of which there is only one, unequalled, having no like or parallel; 2) *disputed* unusual or remarkable (*Oxford concise dictionary* 1990. 8th edn.)

Since, in the end, Lamer decides that the appellant had not made the case that trade or sale in fish was integral to her culture, it seems odd that he brings the definition of *distinct* into play at all. *Distinctive* was central to a preceding case, *R. v. Sparrow*, decided in 1990, but the word *distinct* does not appear in Sparrow. Lamer, like the *Financial Post*, does define the words in a way that allows Aboriginal peoples to be distinctive without making any suggestion that they are distinct (defined as 'unique'). Perhaps, the purpose of this excursion into the dictionary was to demonstrate technical competence or thoroughness: a troubling potential confusion had been rendered clear. However, since both dissenting justices pick up on the distinction and also use the meaning 'unique' to define *distinct*, all of the justices appear to have been implicated in managing the inference that might define these obviously distinctive societies as distinct, even so distinct that they could not be, as Lamer put it, "reconciled with the sovereignty of the Crown." Certainly in managing this inference the justices could all be seen as reassuring the majority of Canadians that the Supreme Court remained a neutral judicial space, free of the messy politics around Québec sovereignty.

5 Conclusion

Regardless of whether dictionary definitions restrict or extend meanings in reasoning about Aboriginal rights cases, dictionaries seem to be reliable resources when the courts are on the brink of leaning one way or another, and when "a choice between open alternatives must be made" (Hart 1994, quoted in Bix 2012: 151) – in the "moment of suspense" between two positions that seem equally coherent (Derrida 1992: 20).[7] As mentioned above, dictionaries are, if nothing else, a rhetorical resource. When cases such as those discussed above have broad sociopolitical implications – as they do in Aboriginal rights cases – the inferential field that is being rhetorically negotiated seems to expand to include two strongly opposed popular assumptions: 1. Aboriginal peoples of Canada deserve to have more rights than they currently have; or 2. Aboriginal peoples in Canada have too many special rights already. Canadians are divided on this issue, and legal reasoning, as part of the sociopolitical fabric of Canada, cannot help but reflect this.[8]

So what do dictionaries lend to processes of inference that are, as so many pragmatists propose, *always* part of any communication? And that, in fact, might be the bulk of what is going on in any communication? What happens in this interlude, this break from so-called pure expert legal reasoning, created by resorting to a dictionary, and how might we explain it? We could think of it this way: resorting to a dictionary is a commonplace, lay activity, and an interruption in the expanse of the typically technical legal language of judgments. The cognitive load in processing judgments is typically high, and any cognitive effects that we might describe as inference – even in this realm of expert discourse – might have a high cost. Could diversions into dictionaries temporarily lower the cognitive threshold for other types of inference, tipping the balance into finding more relevance in the broader socio-political field of attitudes and assumptions about Aboriginal rights in Canada? (Giltrow 2014).

Diversions into dictionaries[9] lower the cognitive load in the processing of complex legal texts, yet when combined with specialized juridical language still confirm and re-inscribe the authority of the juridical field itself and the social space of the legal profession. Bourdieu (1987) calls law "a separate cultural field," where "technical competence" in the "competition for the monopoly of the right to determine the law" is asserted and played out (817). Political differences and

---

[7] Derrida continues: "A decision that didn't go through the ordeal of the undecidable would not be a free decision, it would be the programmable application or unfolding of a calculable process" (24). He continues, "The undecidable remains caught, lodged, at least as a ghost – but an essential ghost – in every decision, in every event of a decision. Its ghostliness deconstructs from within any assurance of presence, any certitude or any supposed criteriology that would assure us of the justice of a decision, in truth of the very event of a decision" (24–25). Justice remains as a horizon of possibilities, maintaining its "à venir" (27).

[8] The law is not outside of culture or society but one integral part of it. Hasian, Lucaites & Condit (1996) define law rhetorically, as "neither a rationally constructed discourse nor simply a dominant ideology, but rather an active and protean component of a hegemonically crafted rhetorical culture" (323).

[9] We could also wonder if other types of diversion – literary references, proverbs, "quotable quips" and sayings – might play similar roles.

power relations, he continues, are masked by "disengagement" in the "neutral space" of the court. The use of dictionaries implies that there is authority in some fixed code of language to supplement the authority of the legal code. This pause in the proceedings provides an inferential bridge for readers to access this more foundational principle. And in keeping with the Sperber and Wilson formula that cognitive effort spent on searching for meaning halts once there has been some comparable pay-off, this might be as far as inference goes. Although not perhaps enlightened by definitions of *treaty*, *distinct*, or *distinctive*, readers can be assured by the thought of a reliable linguistic code, and authoritative judges (supported where necessary by their common sense and dictionaries) to authoritatively decode it. Ruth Sullivan (2001) calls these types of inferences "meta-legal messages," a more general one of which ties principles of plain language drafting of statutes to law's general principle of being functionally responsive to the will of the people in a democracy (148; 161–162). Michael J. Toolan (2002) also hints at similar meta-legal messages in the fixed code myth of language promulgated by both law and mainstream linguistics which supposes meanings as ordained in "transcendental sentences" (163). Judges rely, as do many linguists, on a myth about language: that there is a stable and reliable code with which one can encapsulate intended meanings, which in turn, all going well, can be decoded by others. Our analysis of these two Aboriginal rights cases in Canada demonstrates how terms in legal discourse can resonate with certain values and ideologies from those terms' uses in other contexts of production and reception, contexts not easily recoverable in canonical texts of the law.

Aboriginal peoples continue to take their cases to the courts, and their arguments for rights and title are increasingly meeting with success. The response of John Borrows, an Anishinaabe legal scholar, is to see Canada as always already Indigenous, despite the intrusions of colonization, and in need of "recovery" by Aboriginal people. It is time, he says for "Aboriginal control of Canadian affairs" (2002: 140), and, as his subtitle puts it, the "resurgence of Indigenous law." Others take a more radical stance: Dale Turner's 2006 title, *This is not a peace pipe*, might stand for these stances (see also Coulthard 2014).

The bottom line for many Indigenous legal scholars these days will not be found in the interpretation of Western legal texts; they are asking more foundational questions about Canada as a constitutional democracy. Borrows (2010), for example, argues that Canada's justice system is "incomplete" (20) because of a fundamental constitutional void: Indigenous legal traditions have never been formally supplanted in Canada, and yet they are barely recognized in its legal fabric. (The case discussed above, *R. v Van der Peet*, is actually one exception, and Borrows is optimistic that such cases provide a "nascent framework for extending [the] reach" [26] of Indigenous legal traditions). In the face of these larger questions, it might behoove those of us who think about language and the law to ask about the relationship between these larger socio-political shifts and our own investments in a linguistic pragmatics of sentences. Giltrow (2015) would argue that a focus on "form alone" (here the words themselves) is a way the courts are "masking inference" (214). By favoring knowing all the words rather than "the content of the silence" (211) – contextual factors that pragmatics seeks to explicate and codify – law is able to disavow a consideration of motive, which is "more deeply embedded in the unsaid" (218). If pragmatics pays attention to "the contribution of context to meaning" (Bix 2012: 330), then pragmatics scholars could reach a point at which attention to context extends out so far that there is no way of getting back to the terms in question – or at least no real reason to, apart from our own investments in the idea of a linguistic code. Surface references to a stable linguistic code have been beside the point in these two cases; the inferences we have identified were managed in response not to confusions about words' meanings – although there was a lot said about them – but to larger unspoken shifts in the sociopolitical context.

References

Bix, Brian H. 2012. Legal interpretation and the philosophy of language. In Peter Tiersma & Lawrence M. Solan (eds.), *The Oxford handbook of language and the law*, 145–158. Oxford: Oxford University Press.
Borrows, John. 2002. *Recovering Canada: The resurgence of Indian law*. Toronto: University of Toronto Press.
Borrows, John. 2010. *Canada's indigenous constitution*. Toronto: University of Toronto Press.
Bourdieu, Pierre. 1987. The force of law: Toward a sociology of the juridical field. *Hastings law journal* 38. 814–853.
Canada. 1982. Constitution Act.
Concise Oxford dictionary. 1990. 8th edn. Oxford: Oxford University Press.
Coulthard, Glen S. 2014. *Red skin, white masks: Rejecting the colonial politics of recognition*. Minneapolis, MN: University of Minnesota Press.
Dawson, Richard M. 2001. *The Treaty of Waitangi and the control of language*. Wellington: Institute of Policy Studies, Victoria University of Wellington.
Derrida, Jacques. 1992. Force of law. In Drucilla Cornell, Michel Rosenfeld & David Carlson (eds.), *Deconstruction and the possibility of justice*. 3–67 New York: Routledge.
Eades, Diana. 2008. *Courtroom talk and neocolonial control*. New York: De Gruyter Mouton.
Fee, Margery & Janice McAlpine. 1997. *Guide to Canadian English usage*. Toronto: Oxford University Press.
Fowler, H. W. 1926. Distinctive. *A Dictionary of modern English usage*. 118. Oxford: Clarendon.
Freadman, Anne. 2002. Uptake. In R. Coe, L. Lingard & T. Teslenko (eds.), *The rhetoric and ideology of genre: Strategies for stability and change*. 39–56. Cresskill, NJ: Hampton Press.

Gibbons, John. 1994. Introduction: Language constructing law. In John Gibbons (ed.), *Language and the law*. 3–10. New York: Longman.
Giltrow, Janet. 2014. Personal communication.
Giltrow, Janet. 2015. Form alone: The Supreme Court of Canada reading historical treaties. In Natasha Artemeva & Aviva Freedman (eds.), *Genre studies around the globe: Beyond the three traditions*. 207–224. Winnipeg, MB: Inkshed Publications.
Harris, Roy. 1981. *The language myth*. New York: St. Martin's Press.
Harris, Roy. (ed.). 2002. *The language myth in Western culture*. Richmond, VA: Curzon Press.
Hasian, Marouf Arif, Celeste M. Condit & John L. Lucaites. 1996. The rhetorical boundaries of 'the law': A consideration of the rhetorical culture of legal practice and the case of the 'separate but equal' doctrine. *Quarterly Journal of Speech* 82. 323–342.
Hutton, Chris. 2009. *Language, meaning and the law*. Edinburgh: Edinburgh University Press.
Lyotard, Jean-François 1988. *The différend: Phrases in dispute*. Minneapolis, MN: University of Minnesota Press.
Makmillen, Shurli. 2007. Colonial texts in postcolonial contexts: A genre in the contact zone. [Special issue. Genres and social ways of being. Charles Bazerman (ed.).] *Linguistics and the Human Sciences* 3(1). 87–103.
Makmillen, Shurli. 2010. *Land, law, and language: Rhetorics of indigenous rights and title*. Vancouver. University of British Columbia dissertation.
R. v. Badger. 1996. 1 SCR 771. Supreme Court of Canada.
R. v. Van der Peet. 1996. 2 SCR 507. Supreme Court of Canada.
R. v. White and Bob. 1964. 50 D.L.R. (2d) 613 (also reported: 52 W.W.R. 193). British Columbia Court of Appeal. Web. 1 March 2015. http://gsdl.ubcic.bc.ca/collect/firstna1/import/court%20decision/British%20Columbia/rvwhiteboba.PDF.
Solan, Lawrence M. 1993. *The language of judges* (Law and Society). Chicago: University of Chicago Press.
Sperber, Dan & Deirdre Wilson. 1986. *Relevance: Communication and cognition*. Cambridge: Harvard University Press.
Sullivan, Ruth. 2001. Some implications of plain language drafting. *Statute Law Review* 22(3). 145–180.
Toolan, Michael J. 1996. *Total speech: An integrational linguistic approach to language* (Post Contemporary Interventions). Durham, NC: Duke University Press.
Toolan, Michael J. 2002. The language myth and the law. In Roy Harris, *The language myth in Western culture*. 159–182. Richmond, UK: Curzon Press.
Turner Dale. 2006. *This is not a peace pipe: Towards a critical indigenous philosophy*. Toronto: University of Toronto Press.
Waitangi Tribunal. 1991. *The Ngai Tahu land report*. Wai 27. Wellington, NZ: Department of Justice.

III Across borders: New methods for study of inference

Svetlana V. Vlasenko
11 Legal translation pragmatics: Legal meaning as text-external convention – the case of 'chattels'

> *No discrete boundary can be drawn between linguistic and extralinguistic knowledge, any such boundary ought to be drawn on empirical grounds, not imposed a priori.*
> – Ronald W. Langacker, 2013

1 Introduction

This chapter claims that legal meaning is a pragmatically-conditioned category. Legal meaning is a text-external convention whose conceptual content can evolve over time to meet ever-evolving legal relationships in any one jurisdiction. Theoretical approaches behind this claim depart from two major premises: first, that legal meaning is a text-external convention and, second, that this convention is applied by lawyers in line with their intra-trade, or within-the-trade, agreements on the contents of major terminologies and, therefore, can be regarded as default knowledge. This within-the-trade conventionality is believed to make legal discourse challenging for comprehension by outsiders but, more importantly, even by lawyers themselves (for details on the latter assumption see inter alia Mellinkoff 1963: 24–29; Solan 2005; Tiersma 1999: 203–210). It is particularly true when legal texts are conveyed cross-linguistically, which implies that legal translators are participants in transacting legal knowledge cross-culturally, although their knowledge of the law or awareness of lawyers' immediate professional concerns can be distant from or conceptually incongruent with those of the communicating legal profession.

It goes without saying that in law "the text must be construed as a whole" (Scalia and Garner 2012: 167), and "supremacy-of-text principle" (Scalia and Garner 2012: 56) cannot be disregarded. Nevertheless, where certain textual elements are ambiguous for comprehension, text recipients address those elements selectively. There are arguable issues in legal texts comprehension, which could and should be handled based on large corpora of linguistic data, yet even scarce data can be indicative of conceptual collisions between and/or among different types of meaning within one word-form. Some cases of grammaticalized pragmatic meaning are addressed further in the paper.

Svetlana V. Vlasenko, National Research University Higher School of Economics, Moscow

Exploring technical legal terms used in plural evidences that comprehending even basic legal concepts can be halted by their vague meaning caused by ambiguities in their semantics, which are due to extralinguistic factors. This calls for a broad pragmatic analysis on identifying and defining singularities or regularities in specific uses of technical terms of law, as well as elaborating disambiguation tools for legal translation purposes. A set of methods employed include general semantic and pragmatic analyses and a type of referential analysis called 'referential portraying'. The latter draws on a lexicographic sample of twenty-one specialized dictionaries covering a reasonably long time span. It appears justifiable to suggest that pragmatic meaning 'overrules' grammatical meaning in certain instances analyzed in detail below.

The case studies are selected and designed with a view to casting extra light onto the high import of pragmatic factors for enabling an efficient legal discourse including the prerequisites for a faithful legal translation. The cases detailed below are believed to offer convincing proofs for adjusting the paradigms of pragmatics as an academic discipline to widen its applicability to other areas of research, such as legal discourse, intercultural communication and specialized translation studies.

2 Legal language technicalities as legal translation hurdles

For the past half a century, legal language, legal discourse, and legal translation have merited the focused attention of many a scholar working within one scholarly paradigm or employing cross-disciplinary approaches. The list starts from Mellinkoff (1963), followed onwards by Cao (2004), Coulthard and Johnson (2007, 2010); Galdia (2009), Gibbons (1994, 2003); Gotti and Williams (2010); Solan (1993, 2010, 2013), Scalia and Garner (2012); Šarčević (2000, 2010); Solan, Ainsworth, and Shuy (2015); Tiersma (1999, 2012), Tiersma and Solan (2005, 2012), to name but a few. This fact is not accidental since cases of non-ordinary meanings and non-standard usages observed in legal language and legal discourse across countries are multiple, entailing communicative puzzles and notorious communicative failures (for details on high-profile cases in legal translation/ interpreting see, for instance: Bowcott 2012a, 2012b, 2012c; Glowacka 2012; Legge 2012). This assertion holds true for the entire spectrum of legal translation from courtroom and forensic to signing international legal instruments at summitry.

Problems in legal translation stem from various causes of both linguistic and extralinguistic nature intertwined into a 'tight bond' with instances abundant. Suffice it to refer to "suspects needlessly remanded in custody and denied a fair trial because of a severe shortage of qualified court interpreters" (Bowcott

2012c), unacceptably poor performance by court interpreters jeopardizing court proceedings "leading to courtroom chaos" and forcing "court staff to interrupt their core duties to find interpreters at short notice" alongside triggering a "steep rise in the number of abandoned trials" (Bowcott 2012b), which are among other serious problems.

When globalization prompts distant legal cultures using languages from different language families to embark on professional interaction, more often than not this is likely to provoke predictable hurdles in comprehending and/or conveying legal substance cross-linguistically. Approached from the standpoint of semantic complexities associated with legal concepts, legal translation can be regarded as a research or as, at least, highly ideational exercise. Due to the abstract nature of the law and its underlying theories and principles, legal terminologies denote legal concepts, whose taxonomies are arranged in elaborate hierarchies with sophisticated subject-specific linkages, which in their turn draw on sets of attitudes and assumptions agreed upon among the legal profession over time. This is believed to shape a framework of knowledge underpinning law practices and the legal language servicing those practices. The role of such knowledge cannot be overestimated as it qualifies for default knowledge in any one domestic legal system. Essentially, default knowledge draws on conceptual conventions correlating with pragmatic factors, such as legal customs and traditions, which shape legal cultures and legal systems being in place for decades, if not for centuries, in countries or groups of countries. Normally, legal systems are tailored by nation-specific legal traditions with respective legal frameworks enacted and implemented in those countries where they were elaborated.

Given the global macrocontext, lawyers involved in cross-border transactions and communicating legally meaningful substance internationally are inevitably faced with less familiar legal arrangements in their counterparts' jurisdictions. Naturally, this urges lawyers to explore cognitively dissimilar legal paradigms for the availability and consistency of concepts, principles, and/or institutions to be applied on both ends of the transactions made. Despite numerous harmonization and unification efforts observed worldwide regarding legal principles, procedures and practices, finding readily available correspondences in different legal languages might be an exacting assignment, since prominent national dimensions inherent in legal systems are reluctant to change.

2.1 Can a pragmatic meaning overrule a grammatical one?

Legal discourse in general and certain legal texts in particular are recognized as sophisticated forms of communication containing clear instances where grammatical forms with otherwise predictable meanings are *overruled* by pragmatic meanings unshared by or unknown to same-language speakers. Supposedly, pragmatic meaning fixes different semantic properties of legal lexis and technical terminologies recognized as belonging both to general language and the legal profession. Once 'engaged' only by professional legal communities, legal terminologies seem to lose predictability of their meaning associated with corresponding linguistic word-forms. For instance, there are many cases in legal English of using the plural where no meaning of plurality is actually conveyed. These cases are likely to mislead or puzzle those participants in legal discourse who lack a profound legal background or foreign lawyers and/or translators whose native language may have no plural counterpart.

A closer look at cross-linguistic examples of singular/plural uses in legal terminologies appears sufficient to realize that these uses are instances of fixed semantic properties shaped by a professional convention. For Russian legal translators, this might imply a number of transpositions whereby a preferred form would be a collective noun singular, rather than plural as in English, for instance:

(1) **havings** – *imuščestvo, sobstvennost', avuary* [property, ownership, assets/holdings]
(Faekov 2011(I): 321)

Back translations of the semantic constituencies used to define the concept studied deserve detailing as follows in the order they are cited from the bilateral finance dictionary:

(a) *imuščestvo* denotes 'property';
(b) *sobstvennost'* denotes both [any type of] 'property' and 'proprietorship' as legal ownership ('title');
(c) *avuary* yields a variety of surface forms: 'assets, holdings, havings, currency holdings, foreign exchange holdings'; FX holdings, etc.
(Faekov 2011(II): 12)

It is noteworthy that further detailed profiling of *avuary* (see [1c]) provides a more extended row of collocations where the above array of referred objects is expanded by 'funds', hence making the picture of the core semantics of *havings* still vaguer in terms of its legal content. Using *avuary* as a principal name, the denominator, will only complicate the overall comprehension as it is defined through 'holding; holdings; asset; assets' (ABBYY-6 2014). Note an alteration of singular and plural forms in this dictionary entry, which complicates the search of correspondences in the target language. Principally, the singular and the plural do have difference in meaning, which seems to be lost or is rendered insignificant in legal contexts. Example 2 shows one instance of collocations with *avuary* as a head word:

(2) *blokirovannyje avuary* [blocked balances] – 'blocked funds, frozen assets, attached holdings, immobilized funds'.
(Faekov 2011(II): 42)

Consequently, Examples 1 and 2 illustrate a hierarchical composition of the semantical structure of *havings* whose meaning splits into several immediate constituent sememes. In its turn, one of the constituent sememes – *avuary* – further splits into constituents. An obvious hierarchical semantics of these word-forms points to the complex referential space, which is associated with the meaning of *havings*. In terms of legal translation, this situation is revealing of potential complexities associated with a prolonged search of equivalents or correspondences by translators. Even if found, they still may differ from jurisdiction to jurisdiction requiring different processing techniques to be employed by translators.

Examples of nouns used in the plural have been primarily selected based on the frequency criterion across legal texts, such as various types of contracts, as one of the most popular legal genres. The examples selected are largely border cases showing a close interaction of grammar and semantics. This idea is clearly advocated by Langacker who accentuates that "grammar is meaningful" (2013: 27). The case studies are analyzed with a view to exploring the nature of semantic correlation between lexical meaning and grammatical meaning of legal terminologies frequently used in legal sources either in their singular or plural forms with fixed default meanings ascribed by the legal profession. Along with that, selected examples illustrate that linguistically unusual behavior of legal terms in their singular and plural forms is conditioned pragmatically. As described below, for example, a legal term – *damage(s)* – has both the singular and the plural forms, which overlap semantically and hence can be used interchangeably; however, at the same time it can as properly be used in the plural-only form – *pluralia tantum* – with a different meaning.

2.2 Pragmatic conventions objectified: grammatical level

Legal concepts exemplify a platform, where there is an evident interaction between/among different levels of linguistic meaning: lexical meanings and grammatical meanings overlap and fuse into conceptual blends. Sometimes splitting this fusion seems hardly possible, while comprehending it requires an awareness of existing professional, or intra-trade, conventions agreed upon by lawyers.

2.2.1 Legal semantics as a product of conventional meaning: *damages* as *pluralia tantum*

As mentioned, a legal term *damage* enjoying many uses in general and legal languages alike has two semantically different plural forms: the one which is a regular plural form denoting multiplicity and the other, which is semantically distant. Semantical properties of the legal term *damages* in the plural-only form, *pluralia tantum*, are altered, as compared with *damages* as a regular plural form, since there is an obvious semantic shift into a different representational format. A semantic increment corresponds to *damage suffered/incurred to be reimbursed*, rather than *damage multiplied*, i.e. a big loss. Assessing this case might be revealing of several suppositions, which, if proved true on bulky linguistic data, can be instrumental for arriving at some default regularities regarding the nature and/or the structure of legal meaning.

The case of damages, whose meaning in law is *compensation* (Coulthard and Johnson 2007: 48) or *monetary compensation* (Gale 2010(3): 348), instantiates the validity of default legal knowledge as an intra-trade conceptual convention requiring referential competence on the part of any participant in legal discourse. Semantically, the plural of *damage* has little to do with damages used as *pluralia tantum*, inasmuch as the latter's meaning is defined by authoritative dictionaries of law as follows: (1) "a monetary remedy awarded by the court to a successful claimant" (Oliphant 2008: 295) and (2) "money claimed by, or ordered to be paid to, a person as compensation for loss or injury" (Black's Law 2009: 474). Given that *damages* in its plural-only form means *compensation* or *money awarded to be paid in compensation*, there are reasons to analyze this term's semantics in greater detail.

For the purposes of this chapter, it seems noteworthy to consider the translation of *damages* as *pluralia tantum* into Russian. Relevant laws and regulations contain several counterparts for the term *compensation* in legal Russian. The following correspondences for *damages* are customary: (a) *vozmeščenyje uščerba* [damage recovery], (b) *vozmeščenyje ponesennogo uščerba* [indemnification of loss/damage incurred], (c) *stoimost' vozmeščenyja / kompensacyji pričinjennogo vreda / uščerba* [amount to be reimbursed for loss/harm suffered], (d) *vozmeščenyje/ kompensacyja ponesennych ubytkov* [coverage for loss inflicted], etc. In fact, the referential range of *compensation* is manifestly wider in Russian pointing to the term's context-sensitivity and referential variability.

This case is exemplary as it confirms the conventionality of legal meaning. Besides, the case challenges English grammatical patterning used for modeling *pluralia tantum* by adding *-s* suffix usually to the root of countable words. The semantic dimensions of *damages* in its *pluralia tantum* instantiate an objectified pragmatic meaning. It is not the quantity of *damage* which is multiplied as this grammatical form would normally suggest. It is the term's deep structure which is altered fixing a propositional knowledge in place of nominative. Such evident quasi-plurality has legally essential implications: firstly, *pluralia tantum* implies either an awareness or an acknowledgment of actual *loss/harm/injury suffered* and, secondly, an invoked liability to recover such [recognized/appraised or to be recognized/appraised] *loss/harm/injury suffered*. In terms of frame semantics, a deep structure of *damages* is no longer associated with the frame representational format but, rather, with a scenario of an '[obligation] to compensate loss/harm inflicted'.

For purposes of English–Russian legal translation a semantic bundle of properties for *damages* in *pluralia tantum* can be illustrated by applying an analytical technique known as 'referential portraying'.

3 Referential portraying

The theory of reference has remained for decades a meticulously explored area of studies attracting philosophers (Davis 2005), semioticians (Eco 1984, 1999a), linguists (Kibrik 2011), hence adding inter- and multidisciplinary dimensions to its framework, which was classically positioned within the pragmatics realm. Despite this fact, a 'referent' remains a vague concept in the science of linguistics, at least from the translation studies perspective. What is typically called a *referent* is represented in the translator's (or any other recipient's) psychological reality in the form of an image or its clusters, i.e. the imagery, framing associations to eventually entwine them with the overall mental network.

3.1 Chomskyan "referential variables" on the background of "floating reference" and "diffused reference"

The notion of *referential variables* used by Chomsky (1995: 41) correlates with the concept of *referential range* used by Lyons (1981: 220) in the sense that both concepts treat reference with a certain degree of flexibility allowing semantic adjustments. Applying Chomsky's concept of referential variables facilitates a better delineation of cases where legal terminologies are characterized by *diffused reference* or by *floating reference* (for details on the concept see Počepcov 1982: 7). We derived the notion of diffused reference from the notion of *referential diffusion* (for details on the concept see Irischanova 2004: 302). Floating reference seems to be related to discourse reference, at least as follows from Počepcov's explanation, which reads as follows: "Pragmatic semantics of a word is primarily characterized by floating reference. Dictionary-based (language level) reference is grossly transformed in speech. Where a dictionary strictly fixes a word's referent, colloquial speech can change this referent into floating, so that it might be pointing to a totally different range of objects" (Počepcov Jr. 1982: 6 [translation mine. – S. V.]).

In terms of reference theory, both concepts – *referential variables* and *floating reference* – seem to correlate and be instrumental as they improve the tools for describing the stage of knowledge perception and acquisition, hence permitting a more accurate analysis of and leaving room for more reasonable choices on the part of legal communication participants, including translators.

It is noteworthy that a referential portrait drawn here-and-now can be regarded as a mental imagery stock and, when verbalized, as a label. The more specified referential portrait properties are, the more adjustments can be expected over time. This will predictably entail alterations of the portrait. If a translator interiorizes a new concept by chain-linking its semantic properties and collocations, he/she is most likely to have the portrait shaped and fixed in mind as a *referential frame*, or microgestalt (for details on a referential frame as microgestalts see Vlasenko (2014: 106–114)). It is the alteration of the referential portrait that permits regarding a referent as a flexible substance affected by mental flows of associated images and steered by incoming referential specifications. What stands behind all cognitive efforts is the mere striving by the translator towards sharing the same referential frame with the source-text originator. Such striving and respective efforts underlie the translator's referential competence. "Referential competence" suggested by Eco (1999a: 170–171) appears as an instrumental concept for the purposes of our analysis. Referential competence of communicants, as well as translators, might be challenged in terms of their awareness of default knowledge of the legal profession in specific legal settings.

Essentially, *diffused reference* and *floating reference*, once taken together, contribute to the quantity of *referential variables* any complex legal concept can enjoy. These characteristics may explain a legal term's *referential elasticity*. By introducing the notion *referential elasticity* here, we assume it may help establish the correlation between *semantic flexibility* of legal terms and their *referential range*. For instance, both the terms *chattels* and *property* are believed to qualify for being *referentially elastic* within wide referential ranges and many referential variables in either. Given this, both terms *chattels* and *property* appear to fit into the diffused reference category (when unspecified as *chattels*, which is detailed further in the paper on Figure 1) and a floating reference category (when specified as detailed respectively on Figures 2 and 3 further in the paper), while the term *property* appears to be more attributable to the floating reference case as detailed on Figure 3 below.

Referential portraying aims to profile referential knowledge associated with a core meaning of the concept or concepts under study by particularizing and inventorying pieces of incremental information/knowledge affecting this concept's or concepts' semantic transparency and comprehension[1]. Such profiling is based on definitions provided in mono- or bilingual specialized dictionaries and encyclopedias, as well as legislative sources. Yokoyama's graphic conventions (1986) detailed by Zaitseva (1995, 1999: 511) are used for the portraying of semantic constituents enclosed in the referential knowledge to be conveyed by a legal concept under analysis:
- the figure brackets enclose verbalized referential knowledge
 {referential knowledge},
- the square brackets indicate referential specifications
 [extra referential knowledge, details, specifications], and
- the round brackets contain contextual additional information clarifying the context (contextual knowledge)
 (Zaitseva 1995, 1999: 511).

Therefore, a referential portrait of *damages* can be completed as follows:

{compensation; monetary remedy for damaged reputation or property, or injury},

[harmful or unpleasant effects of something, physical harm caused to a person, situation, or type of activity + an awareness or acknowledgment of actual loss/harm suffered, which is to be reimbursed voluntarily or by adjudication],

(an invoked liability to recover such [recognized] loss/harm suffered).

Where contract law is at stake, the round bracketed details ought to be changed as follows:

(the money paid by a person who has breached a contract to the other party as compensation for any financial loss they have suffered)
(Martin, Gibbins 2014: 62).

In this regard, it is essential to indicate that the *pluralia tantum* word-form conveys the legal meaning of *damages* as "payable" (Anglo-American civil law) or "paid" (Anglo-American law of contract). Accordingly, the conceptual conventions behind this form can be particularized as (1) context-sensitive and (2)

---

[1] For comparison purposes see an earlier analysis of the two referential portraits for a legal concept *disclosure* Vlasenko (2014: 106–109).

pragmatically-conditioned, since the context is an extralinguistic factor dictating the meaning to the form and not the other way around. Consequently, it seems justifiable to suggest that conceptual conventions are shaped over time in the form of legal practices in any one jurisdiction by aligning legal knowledge consistently with judicial rulings and the advancement of legal doctrine.

Collocations with *damages* convincingly instantiate that knowledge embedded in this plural-only word-form is propositional by its nature; see the back translations from Russian in square brackets. English–Russian translation versions are synopsized based on the following specialized legal and financial dictionaries: Faekov (2011(II): 188); Fjedorov (2000: 192); Pivovar (2003: 245).

(3) *damages at large* – *polnoje vozmeščenije [otvetčikom] pričinjennogo uščerba [ponesjonnogo iststom]*[2] [full reimbursement (by the defendant) of damage (inflicted on the claimant)]; pragmatically-conditioned meaning makes itself conspicuous by implying participants in the legal event where damage is suffered – the defendant and the claimant, which makes legal relations more transparent.

(4) *inadequacy of damages* – *vozmeščenije [pričinjennogo] uščerba v nedostatočnom ob'jeme*[3] [insufficient indemnification for loss/harm caused]; it is noteworthy that this dictionary translation explicitly points to an inappropriate amount due for payment in reimbursement of loss suffered; the implication here is that the loss suffered is appraised and an appraised amount is assumed to be awarded by the court [to the claimant]; legal relations in this instance are only seemingly more transparent.

3.2 Parallel uses of *pluralia tantum* and regular grammatical word-forms

Another hindrance in using *damages* as *pluralia tantum* lies in the possibility of actual, non-quasi, plural word-form with the regular meaning of plurality without the incremented pragmatic meaning. In this case *damages* means 'injuries', 'destructions' or 'harms', like in *anticipatory damages, proximate damages, direct damages* (ABBYY-6 2014) or *provisional damages* (Martin and Gibbins 2014: 202). Consequently, along with the semantic formula *damage + s > damages = compensation*, a regular grammatical meaning of *damages*, whereby *damage + s = damages (pl.)* applies. Examples 5 and 6 illustrate both formulas:

---

2 See English–Russian section in (ABBYY-5 2011).
3 See English–Russian section in (ABBYY-5 2011).

(5) *damages in negligence*: *damages* can only be claimed for injuries if they are directly caused by and closely connected with a breach of the duty of care. (Martin and Gibbins 2014: 63);

(6) If the type of *damage* is reasonably foreseeable, then the claimant will be compensated for all the *damage* that occurred even if it was much more than anyone could have predicted, as long as it was the same type of *damage*.
(Martin and Gibbins 2014: 262).

A major translation problem with *damages* as *pluralia tantum* is caused by the fact that it is used in parallel with the regular plural form. However, care should be taken in phrasal terminological expressions, such as *agreed and liquidated damages*, as well as in *general damages* (Martin and Gibbins 2014: 108) where the meaning increments a semantic component denoting 'amount(s) to be reimbursed' (recovered or indemnified). Pragmatic 'strings' are again attached as the incremented meaning of 'amount' implies varying degrees of predictability of risks undertaken in contract law where *damages* are treated as part of remedies for breach of contract (see Example (7) below). Along with that, where *damages* are part of remedies for misrepresentation the amount depends on the type of misrepresentation (see Example (8) below).

(7) damages – a sum of money representing the wronged party's actual financial loss, provided that the type of loss was foreseeable by the parties.
(Martin and Gibbins 2014: 214)

(8) fraudulent misrepresentation: rescission and damages. *Damages* will be assessed on the basis of what is needed to put the wronged party in the position he would have been if the fraud had not been committed. They are not assessed on the basis of putting the wronged party in the position he would have been in if the fraud was true.
(Martin and Gibbins 2014: 215)

Consequently, making decisions on objectifying meaning in legal translation is context-sensitive, i.e. pragmatically-conditioned. In view of this, major translation queries would be related to understanding to what extent extralinguistic information behind the term in question needs to be included and to what extent excluded to enable a translator to identify semantic properties and deliver the meaning cross-linguistically. Given many collocations with the term under study – *liquidated damages, unliquidated damages, statutory damages, general damages, specific damages, punitive damages, prospective damages*, etc. (ABBYY-6 2014), legal translation assignment involving these and other collocations would most probably be associated with weighting pros and cons in identifying relevant information on a text-specific or discourse-specific basis.

Therefore, the Gricean maxim of relevance comes to the fore evidencing pragmatic factors in translation deserve further elaboration. These are exactly the pragmatic factors that necessitate an intelligent legal translator equipped with the knowledge of default connotations from within specific fields of law and/or lawyering to make valid decisions on naming things, facts, legal relations and their parties in legal translation to ensure translation fidelity. However, these are exactly the pragmatic factors that might leave immense room for inference and interpretation in legal discourse and, if it is communicated cross-linguistically, in legal translation as well.

3.3 Referential range for legal terms in plural: legal homonymy

A cursory look at legal usage in plural is sufficient to detect a problem, which is intensified by a seemingly uncomplicated linguistic phenomenon of legal homonymy. This can be illustrated by the word *bonds* characterized by massive intralingual homonymy in ordinary English overlapping with homonymy in legal English yielding a sum of meanings varying within a broad referential range from 'ties/unions', 'promises/oaths' to 'debt certificates', and/or 'pledges', thus making the word, if in general English, and a term, if in legal English, extremely context-sensitive and inference-provoking.

Does the plural of *bond* actually convey the meaning of plurality in legal contexts? If *fruit* comprises all kinds of fruit and the plural word-form *fruits* emphasizes the range of those types, there are more cases where the singular and the plural merge either into one singular-only word-form (singularia tantum) like *furniture* and *fish* forming collective nouns, or into one plural-only word-form (pluralia tantum) like *scissors* or *wages*. Meaningful differences do occur intra-linguistically between legal terms in the singular or the plural, for instance, *debt* and *debts*: the former denoting 'payment past-due' or 'indebtedness'[4], while the latter – 'debt securities', 'debt instruments' or 'claims'.

Langacker's viewpoint can be relied on when he asserts that "meaning is not localized but distributed, aspects of it inhering in the speech community, in the pragmatic circumstances of the speech event, and in the surrounding world"

---

4 Subject to different treatment in government finance statistics, accounting, and a specific branch of law (finance law, corporate law, criminal law) depending on the legal system in the country analyzed.

(Langacker 2013: 28). Following this view, it seems reasonable to assert that pragmatic meaning does 'overrule' a grammatical meaning when legal concepts are scrutinized. The case of *damages* is believed to have illustrated this view with further substantiation to follow on the still more exemplary case of *chattels*.

4 Pragmatic conventions objectified: semantic level – the case of *chattels*

Our ongoing studies of the semantic and pragmatic aspects of grammatical plurality affecting transposition of English legal terminology into Russian have prompted us to conduct another case study. Example 9 contains a phrase *damages for chattels*, where *chattels* is used in the plural. Naturally, this grammatical form was explored to learn whether the term *chattels* qualifies for our postulate of legal concepts having conventional meanings with those conventions being sometimes grammaticalized.

(9) The law affords wide protection to proprietary *interests* over *chattels* [emphasis mine throughout this citation]. Again, this can involve using a proprietary remedy to reclaim goods removed from their rightful owner or to claim *damages for chattels* affected by a tortfeasor's intentional or negligent conduct. Intentional interference with *goods* is unusual and therefore receives specialized treatment by some systems.
(Collins Cobuild 2008 cited in: ABBYY-6 2014).

It is noteworthy that the term *chattels* was shortlisted in the book comprising 100 English words with their detailed etymology, connotations, and the 'influence' on the vernacular English (Crystal 2012). Dating back to the 13th century, an Old French borrowing, *chattels* is defined as 'property and possessions', or 'goods' (2012: 52–54). Given this, a referential portrait of *chattels* can be traced back to medieval times, which cannot aid much in avoiding the controversy over the fuzzy semantic boundaries of the concept used currently. However, this gives us one more proof in favor of it being a collective noun.

4.1 Referential ambivalence of *chattels*

The term *chattels* represents a technical term of property law used across many branches of law. It appears to be defined in legal dictionaries by incorporating two legally conflicting constituent concepts: (a) moveable property, moveables, or *personalty*, and (b) real property, immoveables, or *realty*. Reiterating once again and remaining on the pragmatics plane, we assert that the referential portraying technique allows revealing the term as a complex legal construction and being classified as denoting complex referential knowledge. On the other hand, remaining on the semantics plane, *chattels* represents an ideational semantics construct whose semantic field is borderless and, in legal terms, mutually exclusive. Such ambiguity, according to the reference theory, can be seen as a wide-ranging bundle of referential properties. Therefore, the term *chattels* is still another case of *referential elasticity*.

Any effort to find a counterpart Russian term for *chattels* would necessitate referential specification of a corresponding counterpart. For instance, *chattel*(s) is explained in an authoritative business dictionary as 'moveable property; property' (Hoedt 1999: 165). For lack of specification, a legal meaning of *property* is still more opaque across jurisdictions and will not be of much help for legal translation commissioned by legal scholars, practicing lawyers, or participants in summitry.

Should we treat such semantic ambiguity in terms of lexicology, it would be sufficient to regard *chattels* as a hypernym standing for 'property' and comprising two co-hyponyms 'personalty' and 'realty'. However, when the playing ground is legal linguistics, it is essential to acknowledge that the majority of national legal systems distinguish these types of property envisaging different legal treatment to each. For instance, article 130 of the Russian Federation Civil Code (Part 1) as of 30.11.1994 No. 51-FZ (rev. as of 03.12.2012) clearly distinguishes two types of property – moveable and immoveable (RF CC Part 1, art. 130, rev. as of 03.12.2012).

5 Selected lexicographic sampling and research methodology

A research project was conducted based on lexicographic data sampled, collected, and analyzed. A full dictionary sample comprised twenty-one dictionaries. The sample was compiled by attributes based on the quality of dictionary entries, i.e. the level of details in a definition, including clarity and conciseness in defining immediate semantic constituencies, as well as an availability of synonymic rows with semantically transparent comments on usage and examples. The sample comprised not only specialized dictionaries on law, economics, and finance, but also encyclopedic dictionaries on law, economics, and finance, and linguistic dictionaries, the latter ones comprising Skeat's Etymological Dictionary of English (Skeat [1911] 1972), Webster's Encyclopaedic Unabridged Dictionary of the English Language (Webster's Unabridged 1989), Rodale's Synonym Finder (Rodale 1979) and Roget's Thesaurus (Roget's 2012), etc.

A dictionary sample consisted of three groups of lexicographic sources which enabled us to profile the *chattels* concept:

(1) etymological / linguistic mono- and bilingual dictionaries,

(2) encyclopedic mono- and bilingual dictionaries on law, economics, finance, and

(3) specialized mono- and bilingual dictionaries on law, economics, finance.

In total, the following lexicographic sources were sampled for the analysis:

> ABBYY-5 2011; ABBYY-6 2014; Baskakova 2000; Black's Law 2009; Collins Cobuild 2008; Curzon 2002; Faekov 2011(I, II); Flynn 1976; Fjedorov 2001; Gale 2010(2); Gifis 2003; Hoedt 1999; Korolkevitch and Korolkevitch 2002; Martin and Law 2006; Martin and Gibbins 2014; Pivovar 2003; Rodale 1979; Roget's 2012; Skeat 1972; Stewart 2006; Merriam-Webster's Law 2010; Webster's Unabridged 1989.

A dictionary sample equalling twenty-one dictionaries can be detailed as follows:

(1) etymological / linguistic dictionaries:
   a. monolingual: 5 (Collins Cobuild 2008; Rodale 1979; Roget's 2012; Skeat 1972; Webster's Unabridged 1989);
   b. bilingual: 1 (ABBYY-5 2011; ABBYY-6 2014)[5];

(2) encyclopedic mono- and bilingual dictionaries on law, economics, finance:
   a. monolingual: 3 (Black's Law 2009; Gale 2010(2); Merriam-Webster's Law 2010)[6];
   b. bilingual: 3 (Baskakova 2000; Fjedorov 2001; Korolkevitch and Korolkevitch 2002);

---

[5] ABBYY Lingvo dictionaries represent software products comprising corpora of many technical dictionaries, primarily bilingual, in the format of multi-subject and multilingual dictionaries. Their entries contain wide linguistic coverage including etymology and technical data, which range from meaning and collocations of special lexis and terminologies to idioms, synonymy, antonymy, examples from classic and modern literature (fiction and non-fiction, translated passages in source and target languages, etc.). In view of this, it was difficult to ascribe a definite status to these dictionaries, however linguistic data predominate and are available for technical terminology as well. Since ABBYY-6 version differs considerably from ABBYY-5 version in terms of compilation principles and language data arrangement, references are made to them separately; however, for purposes of our analysis both are counted as one lexicographic source in the sample studied.

[6] Both sources – Black's Law 2009 and Merriam-Webster's Law 2010 – contain the word 'dictionary' in their titles, not 'encyclopedia'. However, judging by the volume of linguistic and technical data available in their terminological entries, including etymology, references to statutes and cases, citations from legal doctrinal papers, both sources are believed to have been justifiably attributed not to dictionaries, but to encyclopedia dictionaries.

(3) specialized mono- and bilingual dictionaries on law, economics, finance:
   a. monolingual: 6 (Curzon 2002; Flynn 1976; Gifis 2003; Martin and Law 2006; Martin and Gibbins 2014; Stewart 2006);
   b. bilingual: 3 (Faekov 2011 (I, II); Hoedt 1999; Pivovar 2003).

5.1 Sampling analysis and methodology

Due to the complexities encountered in identifying semantic constituencies of the legal term *chattels* while compiling its consistent referential portrait, a dictionary definition inventorying method was applied in combination with the referential portraying method described above. The former method ensures the search of correlations in definitions and unanimity of the referential range delineated by specialized and encyclopedia dictionaries, both mono- and bilingual. The sample was selected with a view to avoiding repetition in definitions and synonymic rows for the term analyzed.

An exact-match search across the selected lexicographic sample was aimed to reveal the proximity of definitions, thus enabling effective comparisons of overlapping semantic properties for validating conclusions on *chattels* semantics observed over time. Accordingly, the efforts behind sampling were oriented at and driven by the intention to assess semantic properties of the term analyzed with lesser subjectivity to ensure conclusions that are more consistent. Consequently, the lexicographic sample sources cover a noticeably long time span, which allowed tracing conspicuous semantic shifts, since dictionaries were compiled at different periods, from Skeat ([1911] 1972) throughout Faekov (2011) and ABBYY-6 2014.

5.2 Lexicographic and terminological concerns

The use of dictionaries is indispensable for translating. Nevertheless, dictionary meanings are at times overestimated and overly relied upon. Such exaggerated reliance by many, primarily beginning, translators upon dictionary meanings pave the way to imperfections and flaws in decisions and solutions made in legal translation (for details see a translation case described in Vlasenko 2016). Back in 1963, Katz and Fodor were elaborating the structure of a semantic theory with a view to setting forth a "procedure for determining which of the two proposed dictionary entries is the better for a given language" (Katz and Fodor 1963: 192). Their efforts were aimed to determine an optimal form for dictionary entries. Their opinion is formulated convincingly and reads as follows: "A dictionary usually supplies more senses for a lexical item than it bears in an occurrence in a given sentence, for a dictionary entry is a characterization of

EVERY[7] sense that a lexical item can bear in ANY[8] sentence" (Katz and Fodor 1963: 183).

These scholars considered a lexical item with a view to eliminating semantic ambiguity by finding the best ways and means to be proactively applied in dictionary compilation and rules for predicting unambiguous generation of utterances, i.e. elaborating "a system of rules which solves the projection problem" (Katz and Fodor 1963: 172). The linguists underlined novel sentences comprehension, but the speaker's linguistic knowledge was not measured in terms of professional languages, i.e. domain-specific language codes. Thus, legal translation falls out of any such possible projections or solutions as it mediates legal languages and, undoubtedly, presents a novel case: special linguistic codes denoting country-specific legal systems and nation-specific legal traditions stipulated by long-standing legal cultures.

A more recent observation (2005) was made by Solan on the elevated status of dictionaries. This opinion fits our line of thought and the focus of our analysis:

> Without question, the biggest change in the search for word meaning in the past years is the almost obsessive attention courts now pay to dictionaries, including using them as authority for ordinary meaning. Until the late twentieth century, Supreme Court justices only infrequently used the dictionary as a source of ordinary meaning. For example, they used legal dictionaries only twice for this purpose before 1980, but fourteen times since (Solan 2005: 2051).

It should be considered a matter of serious concern for lexicographers and particularly for lexicographers-terminologists that notes to entries are either lacking significant linguistic data or technical substance. It is their first duty to provide information on the pragmatic dimensions of an entry, be it a word from ordinary language or a technical term from special language. Example 10 evidences that in Martin and Law (2006) no such information is provided, moreover, *chattel* as a dictionary entry is not commented on as having an interchangeable form in plural, while in the body of a definition there is *chattels real* with a head word *chattels* in the plural. The same definition is found in Stewart (2006) cited below.

(10) Chattel – any property other than freehold land (cf. real property). Leasehold interests in land are called *chattels real*, because they bear characteristics of both real and personal property. Tangible goods are called *chattel personal*. The *personal chattels* of a deceased person are comprehensively defined by section 25 of the Administration of Estates Act 1925.
(Martin and Law 2006: 86)

---

7 An uppercase replicates the original spelling. – S.V.
8 An uppercase replicates the original spelling. – S.V.

(11) Chattel – in English law, any property other than freehold land. Interests in land that are not freehold may be called *chattels real*. Moveable corporeal articles of property are *chattels personal*. See Goods.
(Stewart 2006: 210)

Example 10 uses *chattel personal*, with a head word in the singular and prepositioned, and immediately after *personal chattels*, where it is in the plural and post-positioned. Example 11 gives an entry word in the singular and collocations in the plural with *chattels* prepositioned. It is noteworthy that the singular and the plural forms are interchangeable across all the lexicographic terminological sources quoted in this paper. For purposes of our analysis, we assume by inference the admissibility of these forms and their complete interchangeability, however, it might have been the role of a legal dictionary to advise on this.

Another issue which affects this legal term's comprehensibility is its semantics as defined by major legal lexicographic sources. For instance, the Black's Law Dictionary, the last resort for English-speaking lawyers globally, unambiguously and clearly defines *chattel* (sg.) as movable property (Black's Law 2009: 268). It contains no comments on its possible and centuries-old use in the plural either as the basic form to be specified or for the collocations, such as *chattel personal*, *chattel real*, although quite recent usage (Example 9) evidences otherwise.

(12) chattel (usu. pl.) (14c.)[9]. Movable or transferable property; personal property; esp., a physical object capable of manual delivery and not subject matter of real property.
chattel personal. A tangible good or an intangible right (such as a patent). – Also termed *personal chattel*.
chattel real. A real-property interest that is less than a freehold or fee, such as leasehold estate. The most important chattel real is an estate for years in land, which is considered a chattel because it lacks the indefiniteness of time essential to real property. – Also termed *real chattel*.
(Black's Law 2009: 268)

Following Black's Law Dictionary, *chattel* qualifies for the status of a hypernym with two co-hyponyms embedded in its semantics, in terms of a classical linguistic approach. According to this logic, a plotted figure can be presented in a simple graphical way.

---

9 The century of *chattel's* entering English differs from the data given by Crystal (2012: 52) and cited earlier in this paper. Crystal's etymological characteristics make *chattel* one century older. For purposes of this paper we adhere to Crystal's data.

Figure 1 below illustrates *chattels'* referential portrait and the term's complex semantics due to its referential ambivalence. Also, simple graphics help accentuate the concept's referential elasticity as a diffused reference case with two types of property enclosed within the concept – *personal property* {chattels personal} labelled as *personalty* and *real property* {chattels real} labelled as *realty*. Further referential analysis, in Chomskyan terms, may justify attributing *personalty* and *realty* to two individual referential ranges under one label *chattels*. In terms of general reference theory, the *chattels* case may as well fall under *split reference* case with low *referential accessibility* to the *referential variables* if no specifications are available.

In linguistic terms, by plotting chattels as the *hypernym* with two *co-hyponyms*, we do not trespass the term's semantic boundaries but merely state the availability of two different types of property verbalized by one technical term of art known to lawyers from time immemorial. In legal terms, we do not trespass this term's semantic boundaries either, merely indicating the ambivalence of its semantics, a predictable collision of regulatory regimes and/or legal treatments implied within this term. In legal translation terms, this case calls for scrutiny necessitating enforced inference over which verbalization option should be preferred among a wide range available in dictionaries cited above.

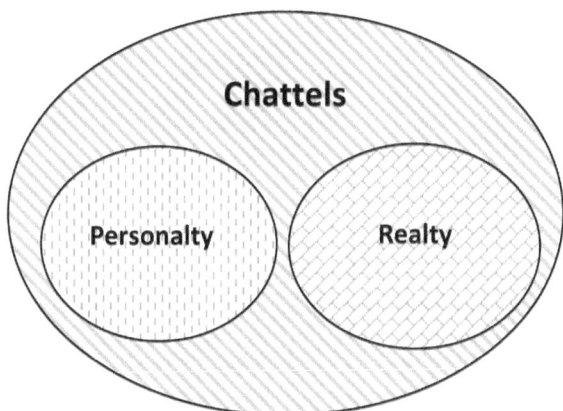

Figure 1: *Chattels'* referential portrait highlighting its referential ambivalence and enclosing two referential ranges labelled {personalty} and {realty}.

For purposes of our analysis aimed to study the plural/singular opposition forms, it is relevant to highlight the labels available for the *chattel(s)'* meaning if the realty-based semantic profile is signified. These are as follows: *chattels real/chattel real, real chattels/real chattel*. The labels available for signifying the personalty-based semantic profile are as follows: *chattels personal/chattel personal, personal chattels/personal chattel* (based on lexicographic sources enlisted above).

6 Referential portrait of *chattels* as personal property

By assuming another view on the meaning of *chattels* as personal, or moveable, property, as its most frequent usage suggests across the majority of sampled dictionaries, the term falls under a floating reference case. Figure 2 plots *chattels* as a floating reference case with the referential bundle of properties in line with the personalty-based profile of its semantics.

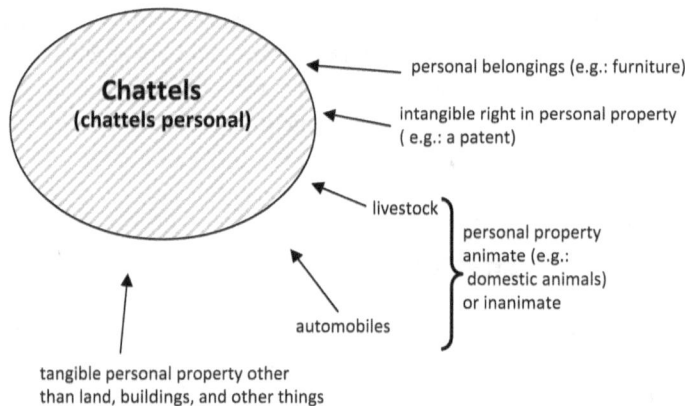

Figure 2: *Chattels* as a floating reference case evidencing its referential elasticity and detailing its referential variables within the range {chattels personal}.

Figure 2 shows *chattels'* referential bundle of properties with specifications detailing its referential range and regular referential variables, which seem sufficient for compiling the *chattels'* referential portrait in the most acknowledged sense known for centuries.

It is noteworthy that the *chattels'* wide referential range plotted on Figure 2 confirms the validity of the Chomskyan concept of referential variables. Indeed, which of the variables might be objectified in specific context of use by a legal translator or any other participant in legal discourse will remain unknown. In view of this, an observation made by Eco in his *Notes on referring as contract* (1999b) seems particularly relevant. The scholar asserts that reference is a prior agreed convention: "[W]e use language for acts of reference; perhaps it has never been stated with sufficient forcefulness that the meaning of a term also includes a series of instructions for identifying the referent of this term" (Eco 1999b: 288). Analyzing and detailing possibilities of what properties are sufficient to identify and, more importantly, to fix the referent, Eco points out that "[t]o give instructions for identifying, in a variety of circumstance, the possible referent of a generic term is not the same as deciding, by pragmatic negotiation, how to fix the referent when referring to individuals" (Eco 1999b: 333).

6.1 Opting for referents: referent sortings, referential conflict

A situation around the *chattels*' referential profile and its immediate constituencies, or variables, can be classified as the *referential choice* problem. It can be described by applying the framework proposed by Kibrik (2011). The linguist addressed arguable issues of categorization of potentially conflicting referents or simultaneous activation of ontologically nonequivalent referents. In so doing, he proposed the notion of a 'referential conflict' and defined it in the following way: "Referential conflicts occur more frequently between referents of comparable inherent properties if they have a different status in the speaker's and addressee's processual cognitive representations. It is this kind of status that serves as the basis for current referent sortings. Current sortings are based on various transient, fluid, contextual properties of referents" (Kibrik 2011: 308). Kibrik's assessment of 'transient' and 'fluid' properties of referents seem to be floating (context-dependent) reference, which is still another evidence of the rightfulness of the approach taken in this paper.

Though Kibrik's examples of referential conflicts largely concern anaphoric uses of pronouns, the notion of a *referential conflict* seems to deserve much greater application, particularly in legal translation, including cases of referentially distant concepts conveying similar messages in source and target languages. Indeed, the *chattels* case is assumed to fall within the referential conflict margins since some dictionaries treat its semantics as denoting *personalty* and *realty* at the same time, implying semantic ambivalence. From the legal perspective, such definition appears unreasonable. It is worth noting that Kibrik points to "contextual properties of referents," thus indicating the inevitable subjectivity by text-producers in attributing referents to individually chosen real/possible world objects, states of affairs or phenomena. If the *chattels*' referential range appears so broad as to comprise two types of properties principally distinguished throughout the world legal systems, then each case of its usage would require the translator's decision-making under uncertainty with heavy focus on the referential range to be signified, while the referent itself would evidently be floating, in Počepcov's terms (Počepcov 1982: 7).

6.2 Further dictionary lookup: mutually exclusive referential labels

American Law Dictionary defines *chattel* as 'any tangible, moveable thing; personal, as opposed to real, property [...]' 'personal property, personalty' are suggested as synonyms (Gifis 2003: 75). This dictionary renders terminological expressions with *chattel* as a head word: *personal chattel* – 'moveable things; personalty which has no connection to real property,' and *real chattel* – 'an interest in real estate less than a freehold or fee; leasehold estates'. The singular is indicated with no mentioning of the possibility of the plural. A referential status of *chattels* ranging from "no connection to real property" to "an interest in real estate" does puzzle, unless the model of 'fruit' or 'furniture' as *singularia tantum* applies.

A clear indication in favor of the plural is given in Skeat's Etymological Dictionary of English ([1911] 1972), where *chattels* is described as plural-only form, i.e. *pluralia tantum*.

(13) **Chattels** (F.–L.) Pl. of M.E. *chatel*, 'property', also 'cattle'. – O.F. *chatel*, O. North F. *catel*, property; see Cattle [Skeat 1972/1911: 86].
Cattle (F.–L.) M.E. *catel*, property; hence, live stock, cattle. – O. North F. *catel*. – Late L. *capitāle*, capital, property; see Capital (2) and Chattels. [...] (Skeat [1911] 1972: 80–81).

Baskakova builds up the following row starting with *chattels* in the plural: *chattels personal, moveables, personal property, things personal, chose transitory* (Baskakova 2000: 108). Given such a long row of labels for the *chattels'* semantics, a customary and proven tool for translator's ad-hoc decision-making has always been checking for synonyms in authoritative thesauri. Therefore, a range of alternative renderings available for the two distinct concepts is remarkable if we rely on Rodale's rows of synonyms (Rodale 1979).

(14) 1. property, estate, estate and effects, holdings, possessions; what one has to one's name, what one can call one's own, *Law* chose; movable, movable article; *Law* acquest; *Law* hereditament.
   2. *Usu.* chattels – belongings, personal belongings, effects, personal effects, personal estate, personal possessions, properties, *Inf.* things, *Sl.* stuff; *Sl.* junk, etc.

All Law: choses, choses in action or possession, choses transitory, personalty; paraphernalia, accoutrements, appurtenances, appointments; appendages, accessories, trappings; goods, goods and chattels, movables, movable articles, furniture.
(Rodale 1979: 160)

It is noteworthy to accentuate that in Baskakova (2000), Rodale (1979), as well as in Black's Law, *chattels* is not accompanied by a rigid pragmatic mark (*Pl.*), but rather by a lesser prescribed plural (*Usu.*).

As follows from Rodale Thesaurus, the concept 'property' appears a hypernym with co-hyponyms to follow across all law fields (see a pragmatic note in this entry – **All Law** [emphasis mine]). Also noteworthy is the marked plurality across quoted usage. Hence conceptualizing *chattels*' referential range by inventorying its immediate semantic constituencies, or variables, is trustworthy when synonyms are cross-checked (Roget's 2012). The synonyms available for *chattels* show neither land, nor landed property:

(15) Belongings, capital, effects, gear, goods, slave, wares.
(Roget's 2012)

Given the inventoried options for the *chattels*' dictionary definitions sampled and studied, synonyms included, its semantics seems more transparent. It signifies moveable property if not accompanied by prepositioned or post-positioned adjective "real." This is a non-pragmatically-conditioned conclusion. Further findings will show that pragmatic conditioning does influence, and even alter, legal meaning of this legal term.

6.3 Quantification markers in the *chattels* semantics

Where quantification operators are involved in defining legal terms, such as 'less than', 'more than' or the like (see Examples 10–12 above based on Black's Law 2009: 268; Gifis 2003: 75; Martin and Law 2006: 86; Stewart 2006: 210), chances are that the precision of potential interpretations might be judgmental with a high degree of subjectivity, which impacts inferencing and interpretation, or even urges enforced inferencing to signify the legal term.

Comparing approaches to defining meaning, Winograd analyzes the structure of dictionaries and word definitions (Winograd 1980). The scholar attempted advocating a new way of looking at words and their representational structures, whereby a systematic reasoning within domain worlds was viewed as part of the overall language comprehension system. The American scholar specifically noted as follows:

The difficulty of formulating appropriate word definitions was apparent even in the simple vocabulary [...] and becomes more serious as the domain expands. [...] The meaning of words like 'big' is always relative to an expected set. The statement 'They were expecting a big crowd' could refer to twenty or twenty thousand, depending on the context. [...] On looking more closely, it became apparent that this problem was not a special issue for comparative adjectives like 'big,' but was a fundamental part of the meaning of most words (Winograd 1980: 216–217).

7 Legal developments as externalities altering lawyers' centuries-old default knowledge

Legal comments regarding insolvency proceedings in the EU member states were published as *Guidance on the concept of establishment in Article 2(h) of the Insolvency Regulation* in the Journal of International Banking Law and Regulation ([2012] J.I.B.L.R, Issue 9. Vol. 27. N–159/160). This *Guidance* targeted the explication of the 'establishment' notion, whose definition contained the word 'goods' with a reference to the two recent cases in the High Court, which provided guidance on the concept of "establishment" in the Council Regulation 1346/2000 art.2(h) for the *Insolvency Regulation Guidance*. "The concept of establishment is defined in art.2(h) of the Insolvency Regulation, as follows: "(h) 'establishment' shall mean any place of operations where the debtor carries out a non-transitory economic activity with human means and goods" ([2012] J.I.B.L.R, Issue 9. Vol. 27. N–159).

Since the insolvency regulations ought to be detailed, the word *goods* was also detailed in an excerpt from *Guidance on the concept of establishment in Article 2(h) of the Insolvency Regulation*, Council Regulation 1346/2000 art.2(h) (*The Insolvency Regulation*) on insolvency proceedings ([2000] OJ L160/1, art.2(h), Pt 7, s.31. Shearman & Sterling LLP ([2012] J.I.B.L.R, Issue 9. Vol. 27. N–159/160), as follows: "The word 'goods' can and should be interpreted more widely than *chattels*. There is an argument that the word is a mistranslation of French and German words and would be better rendered as 'assets.' In those circumstances money and land would also qualify." ([2012] J.I.B.L.R, Issue 9. Vol. 27. N–160).

In the dictionary definitions cited above *land* is excluded from the *chattel(s)* referential bundle of properties and, consequently, from its referential range. The intricacy of the situation with 'chattels' referential portrait is specifically obvious in the Russian law contexts, where *real property* and *personal property* quite predictably fall within utterly different legal treatments and are approached from within different legal frameworks in different law fields, such as civil and criminal law, the latter comprising criminal procedure and penal law. Given this fact, the singular/plural dilemma behind *chattel(s)* loses its momentum and retreats behind a substantive issue associated with the *chattels* core semantic meaning. Hence, the subject-matter issue has been prioritized by the externally imposed developments, i.e. novel regulations of insolvency in the *EU Council's Insolvency Regulation* (2000).

It appears essential to note that the type of proceedings at stake does not matter – insolvency proceedings or divorce proceedings or other. What matters though is the referential portrait of a technical legal term used extensively in handling legal matters for reasoning, construing arguments, and taking legally valid decisions. If *land* qualifies as a rightful constituent, or variable, within the *chattels* referential range, the term appears to qualify for a novel conceptual convention imposed by the development of legal regulation regarding increasing numbers of trans-border insolvency cases and, therefore, meriting the status of new default knowledge introduced within the legal profession as of the *Insolvency Regulation Guidance* release. Under the circumstances, it seems justifiable to share the view expressed by a translation-studies scholar Šarčević (2010) on the Pan-European legal language with regard to the EU private international law framework modeled in DCFR (2009). Šarčević convincingly detailed her approach, which can be extrapolated onto the *chattels* case so that it builds into the Pan-European legal language (English is implied) almost perfectly.

Šarčević does not argue against the striving for greater convergence among the EU member-states admitting that "the intent is not to replace national languages and cultures, but to create a neutral meta-language which would serve as an inspiration to build a new European culture and a common European legal thinking" (2010: 43–44). However, a natural question arises on whether such common legal thinking needs to be based on conceptual default conventions whereby centuries-old usages recorded in dozens of lexicographic sources are challenged by intra-EU usages.

Along with Šarčević, Tiersma (2012), when exploring the practicability of globalizing legal language, persuasively noted as follows:

> Another aspect of globalization is the creation of international alliances or confederations, such as the European Union. Curiously, as the nations of Europe create a common legal superstructure, they have discovered that despite their shared civil law tradition, it can be problematic to translate from one legal language into another. This is an important issue in the EU, which has around two dozen official languages (Tiersma 2012: 25).

Given the statement from the *Insolvency Regulation Guidance* cited above, it seems natural to assume a novel conceptual convention as default meaning imposed on the word *chattels* with a nearly 800-year old usage. Obviously, this is a true pragmatic turn in the word's meaning. Thus far, no specialized dictionary has taken stock of the revised conceptual convention, to say nothing of bilingual dictionaries. Moreover, such conceptual change may have profound implications for legal practices related to property law transactions internationally.

7.1 Overhaul in legal semantics: nearly 800-year usage adjusted

7.1.1 Evolving property rights – evolving concepts

Undoubtedly, the word *chattels* is a remarkable survivor having withstood an enduring history of nearly 800 years of its usage. This word had to put up with and respond to the then-existing property regimes and respective proprietary rights, property allocations and uses, eventualities associated with land property ownership, nationalizations and denationalizations, in a word, following each new form of title under the ever-evolving property systems, as well as judicial practices of conveyancing over an immensely long time span.

Detachment from the original referential variables available over such a vast temporal continuum, changes in the UK historical scenery and environs, revised legal rules and statutory provisions regulating forms of property, proprietary rights, titles and their status throughout those long ages, emerging and dying customs and institutions, political and economic evolutionary developments causing inevitable transformations in forms and types of property and proprietary rights, as well as in related legal regimes towards a new capital-intensive property use, had been providing English speakers across the globe with different referential labels for *chattels*. All those evolving events and factors inevitably altered a *chattels*' semantic contour through expanding referential elasticity of this technical term, its higher referential diffusion contributed to the floating nature of its reference. To this end, the term 'property' as a generic one was plotted with a view to emphasizing the conceptual overhaul and its import on the re-defined *chattels*.

7.2 Referential profile of the generic concept *property*

It is common knowledge that *property* merits elaborated legal treatment in each and every legal system around the world. Property and associated rights, or titles, usually constitute the most profoundly and meticulously regulated legal area in national legal systems. Their treatment is elaborated by lawmakers and rule-makers on a jurisdiction-specific basis. The following steps are made to pool and cross-compare the most essential dictionary definitions available in the sampled dictionaries for the term studied.

Webster's Unabridged Dictionary (1989) provides a systemic definition for the conceptual cluster *property*, which seems worth quoting for purposes of our paper:

(16) **Property** is the general word. [...]

Chattels is a term for pieces of personal property or moveable possessions; it may be applied to livestock, automobiles, etc. [...]

Effects is a term for any form of personal property, including even things of the least value. [...]

Estate refers to property of any kind which has been, or is capable of being, handed down to descendants or otherwise disposed of in a will. It may consist of personal estate (money, valuables, securities, **chattels** [emphasis mine], etc.), or real estate (land and buildings). [...]

Goods refers to household possessions or other moveable property, esp. that comprising the stock in trade of a business. [...]
(Webster's Unabridged 1989: 1153).

A generic term *property* and its immediate constituencies, or referential variables, form a conceptual cluster delineating the respective conceptual domain. A simple graphic representation is plotted below to help visualize the concept's referential elasticity. The referential profile of *property* includes *chattels* under a {personal estate} label according to the bulk of dictionary definitions cited above.

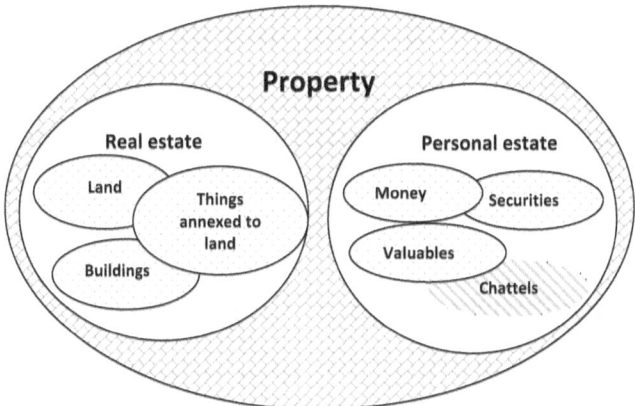

Figure 3: *Property's* referential portrait evidencing its referential ambivalence and elasticity and detailing two major referential ranges {real estate} and {personal estate} with respective referential variables.

Within a classical legal framework, which splits the *property* conceptual domain into two major subdomains – *real estate* and *personal estate* – as shown on Figure 3 above, the following alternative referential labels can be identified for each of these subdomains. These labels are used across law fields for handling property-related matters in lawyering, as well as in legal scholarship.

Labelled *real estate* components
{ chattel(s) real }
{ freehold }
{ immoveables }
{ land }
{ land and buildings }
{ landed property }
{ landholdings }
{ plat } or { plot }
{ real property } or { realty }

Labelled *personal estate* components
{ chattel(s) personal }
{ chose transitory [excludes money][10] }
{ goods }
{ moveables } or { moveable property }
{ personalty }
{ personal property animate } and
{ personal property inanimate }
{ things personal }

Based on: ABBYY-5 2011; ABBYY-6 2014; Baskakova 2000: 108; Black's Law 2009: 268; Collins Cobuild 2008; Curzon 2002: 63; Faekov 2011 (I): 119; Fjedorov 2001: 139; Gale 2010 (2): 342; Gifis 2003: 75; Hoedt 1999: 165; Korolkevitch and Korolkevitch 2002: 70; Martin and Law 2006: 86; Martin and Gibbins 2014: 201; Pivovar 2003: 145; Rodale 1979: 160; Roget 2012; Skeat [1911] 1972: 80–81; Stewart 2006: 72; Webster's Law 2010; Webster's Unabridged 1989: 250, 1153.

A graphic presentation of the *property's* referential profile visualizing its conceptual borders appears to feature what we call the concept's referential elasticity. The efforts did not aim to exhaustively itemize the bundle of referential variables available for the concept *property*, rather to clarify objective challenges likely to be faced by legal translators. There is every reason to agree with Vygotsky who asserted that "[t]he primary word is not a straightforward symbol for a concept but rather an image, a picture, a mental sketch of a concept, a short take about it – indeed, a small work of art." (Vygotsky 1979 [1934]: 75).

7.3 Default knowledge as a set of current conventions

A referential portrait of the generic term *property* is graphed on Figure 3 detailing its referential specifications based on the lexicographic sample selected.

---

[10] This referential label implies referential specification in square brackets.

Those specifications are not exhaustive but allow visualizing the *chattels'* status against the overall portrait of the generic concept. As noted earlier, legal default knowledge can be postulated by employing referential labels, which, in their turn, should be recognized as customary 'stocks' of legal rationale, legal awareness, and eventually legal worldview.

Along with that, referential labels are taken to exemplify mental representations correlating with 'stocked' blocks of legal knowledge. Metaphorically, they can qualify for "off-the-shelf units of legal thought" constituting default knowledge. These units are discrete units of thought, but not necessarily the minimal ones. We name them "referential frames" in terms of frame semantics. Subject knowledge, or expertise, may be taken as of a certain point in time {HERE & NOW} and as such may correlate with certain units of legal and/or linguistic expertise shaped as referential frames. However, any increment in expert knowledge, which is default knowledge based on intra-trade conventions, will automatically allow shaping other mental labels differently from the previous ones, since their time span is different reflecting current default knowledge subject to alteration sooner or later.

As evidenced from the lexicographic sample studied, the plurality of *chattels* appears to have no bearing on its semantics and, evidently, should be perceived as a rudimentary element of its overly long use. This fact needs to be reflected in specialized dictionaries to avoid confusion in comprehending linguistic wordforms by legal translators, who are trained to respect linguistic realizations in any language for special purposes.

8 Research findings

The research was conducted by applying the following methods: (1) general semantic and pragmatic analyzes; (2) a type of referential analysis called referential portraying, and (3) specialized dictionary definitions inventorying method based on the lexicographic sample. The sample comprised lexicographic data from 21 dictionaries and was conducted by attributes with three groups of lexicographic sources studied: (1) etymological / linguistic mono- and bilingual dictionaries, (2) encyclopedic mono- and bilingual dictionaries on law, economics, and finance, and (3) specialized mono- and bilingual dictionaries on law, economics, and finance.

The research findings include an illustrated proof of legal meaning to be pragmatically-conditioned as has been exemplified by the damages and havings cases, and largely by the chattels case. An emphasis was placed on the intra-trade conventionality of legal meaning enclosed in default legal knowledge underlying legal terminologies' core semantics. Such conceptual conventions inherent in nation-specific jurisdictions shape default knowledge of the legal profession.

Some technical legal terms used in *pluralia tantum* were explored and described in detail with a view to showing the level of correlation characteristic of legal translation in its pragmatic aspect. The pragmatic aspect appeared to be strongly dependent on semantic and grammatical means of objectifying sense. This has evidenced that comprehending even basic legal concepts can be halted by their blurred semantics. Along with that, the paper has evidenced that blurred semantic boundaries of technical terms of law are caused by unspecified numbers of variables conventionally comprised within their referential range, hence entailing referential inaccessibility. The core semantics of legal terminologies has been proved to be rooted in extralinguistic factors, thus demanding shared knowledge of referential conventions to be established between/among participants in legal communication. This fact stipulates regarding a dictionary meaning as contingent on text-external factors.

It appears reasonable to suggest that pragmatic meaning does overrule grammatical meaning in certain instances analyzed in this paper. A major finding of the research suggests that even default knowledge of major legal concepts based on conventional usage, which stood the test of time, can be adjusted over time as the case of *chattels* has evidenced. This is believed to be indicative of solid pragmatically-conditioned factors underlying legal meaning in its linguistic realizations. In terms of legal translation fidelity, pragmatic factors, which underlie translation of legal terminologies, appear challenging, hence making cross-linguistic transposition of legal knowledge a non-routine task.

8.1 Dependability of dictionary meanings

Specialized monolingual, bilingual and encyclopedic dictionaries are believed to be the last resort for legal translators' decision-making in terms of impeccability of any dictionary-based solutions. Legal translators, so dependent on the quality of lexicographic sources, run the risk every time if there is no trustworthy dictionary entry or there is contradictory linguistic data for the same entry in different dictionaries. Nonetheless, it is exactly lexicographic sources at large that make any effort behind disambiguation of semantic traps caused by legal terminologies less futile and more rewarding. Certainly, dictionaries and encyclopedias are not panacea but they are crucial for cross-linguistic conveyance of legal and related knowledge.

Given that dictionaries are indispensable tools for translators, no matter legal or otherwise, dependability of dictionary meanings in legal translation has recently been high on the agenda (Aodha 2014; Ramos 2014). In this paper, the lexicographic sample of twenty-one dictionaries was used for two main purposes: (1) to identify any correlation of selected legal terms' grammatical meaning in *pluralia tantum* with their lexical and/or pragmatic meaning, and (2) to profile the semantics of technical terms of law – *chattels* and *property* with a view to highlighting their semantic ambivalence and its pragmatic footing. Lexicographic records of meaning, the quality of linguistic data and validity of dictionary definitions were explored to show their acceptability for general comprehension and their contingency for ensuring conceptual fidelity of legal translation.

The terms *chattels* and *property* manifested themselves both as referentially elastic and referentially ambivalent, which implies a low degree of referential accessibility for either unless the context of use is known and clear to translators. In other words, referential inaccessibility of meanings of legal terminologies is likely to cause situations whereby possible challenges in legal discourse would be predictably faced by participants. As far as referential elasticity is concerned, it can be explained by the terms' broad semantic boundaries aggravated by the need to allocate a referent or referents. In such a case, participants would need to agree on a referent or a range of referents *chattels* would be pointing to for purposes of their legal discourse. Such an agreement signifies that participants in legal discourse need to exercise referent assignment by reaching a referential convention on the term's meaning. As shown in the paper, referential conventions are presumed to underlie intra-trade default knowledge. This default knowledge on intra-trade legal conventions must be accessible to legal translators as a major prerequisite of their trade.

Two types of reference – diffused and floating – which turned to be archetypal for *chattels* and *property*, are believed to be attributable to these concepts' referential elasticity, i.e. their ability to fix a certain set of referential variables within their respective referential ranges by activating certain labels as verbalized options. Once fixed, these variables establish a referential convention used for a certain period of time by participants in legal discourse or by the legal profession at large.

In view of the analysis made, specialized dictionary meanings can be deemed trustworthy for legal translation purposes only conditionally. Therefore, a dictionary meaning of a technical term of law should be regarded as contingent meaning requiring contextualization, i.e. checking contexts. Reasoning over the case of *chattels* gives a clue that any apriori expectations regarding legal meaning should be subject to substantiation and verification across such legal sources as statutory definitions, adjudications, and legal doctrine, along with dictionary lookups. For purposes of legal translation, contingency associated with a dictionary meaning should be regarded as an acknowledged fact.

8.2 Concluding remarks

The paper claimed that pragmatic conditioning of semantic properties of legal terminologies can change over time resulting in major challenges for legal discourse and, particularly, for legal translation. The case studies described have shown that semantic properties of some core terminologies in legal English are pragmatically-conditioned due to being deeply-rooted in extralinguistic, or text-external, conventions underpinning intra-trade default knowledge. This assumption was verified, first, by the analysis of *pluralia tantum* cases covering *damages, debts*, and *havings* in legal contexts, which evidenced grammaticalized pragmatic meaning, and, second, by displaying pragmatic conventions objectified at the semantic level as the case of *chattels* has shown.

The approach used in the chapter targeted primarily the ways of reasoning associated with disambiguation of sophisticated legal knowledge, which is country-specific and rooted in countries' history and culture. More often than not, riddles posed by legal terminologies cannot be easily disambiguated through a dictionary lookup. The paper specifically addressed the issue of non-routine disambiguation of core legal concepts, such as *damages, chattels, property*, encountered in bulky corpora of legal instruments and documentary paperwork available across different branches of law internationally.

The cases described have illustrated that pragmatic conventions can be objectified at least at two linguistic levels – grammatical and semantic. Grammaticalization does not realize its direct function in these cases, inasmuch as surface word-forms convey implied legal meaning comparable with the propositional knowledge. This indicates with a high degree of certainty that the intra-trade default knowledge set by the legal profession attaches pragmatic strings to meaning(s) of legal terminology. Though the disambiguation techniques exemplified in the paper are language-specific involving the Russian–English language pair, nevertheless, they are believed to be applicable to different languages servicing various legal systems.

As seen from the referential analysis undertaken, legal meaning constitutes a pragmatic phenomenon since it appears to be based on text-external conventions agreed upon by the legal profession in a country or countries studied. A legally significant development quoted in the chapter prompted the evolution of the technical term of law in European property law by adding up a new conceptual dimension to the term's core semantics. Such semantic overhaul of *chattels* enjoying a nearly 800-year usage was caused by pragmatic factors. If such a long-standing legal concept can have its semantic properties revised after such extensive use in the Anglo-American property law, there are sufficient reasons to assess this situation as a real pragmatic turn for *chattels*.

This case illustrates the value of pragmatic theory applications to ongoing developments in legal discourse, evolving legal institutions, and consequent implications for legal practices. Moreover, this case is exemplary as it shows the pragmatically-rooted nature of legal semantics. All factors positively or adversely affecting legal semantics by shifting its comprehension cannot be disregarded calling for monitoring of linguistic dimensions across the vast Anglophone world's legal systems, including their evolving institutions.

A referential convention behind a legal term of art is postulated to be a referent or a range of referents known, or shared, by communicants/participants in legal discourse. A referential convention eliminates alternative referents by restricting referential variables (Chomskyan concept) and fixing referents (Eco's concept), thus delimiting the referential range only to those referents which are known to and shared by legal discourse participants. In a word, text-external factors are believed to underlie legal meaning in its linguistic realizations. Legal meaning is a text-external convention whose conceptual content can evolve over time to meet evolving legal relationships in any one jurisdiction, as the case of *chattels* reveals. Along with that, the *chattels* case has substantiated that default knowledge of legal core concepts enjoying sustained legal usage can be adjusted over time. It is exactly due to this that the probability of pragmatic factors affecting some linguistic dimensions of legal knowledge can be expected to grow. Consequently, the value of pragmatic theory for and applications to real-life legal discourse has once again been established.

Disambiguating semantically non-transparent terminologies has always been one of the priorities for specialized translation theories, whose aims encompass the elaboration of appropriate tools. The key technique of referential portraying exemplified here in profiling *chattels* seems instrumental for disambiguating referentially vague and, hence, referentially inaccessible concepts with blurred semantic boundaries. Along with that, the concepts of *diffused reference* and *floating reference* appear fitting for the legal translation pragmatics paradigm allowing the elaboration of a more comprehensive legal translation framework. This framework could benefit from incorporating such concepts as *referential ambivalence, referential convention, referential elasticity* and *referential portrait*, among others, and improve methods of semantic and pragmatic analysis to be employed by specialized translation studies.

Finally, the paper proves that while dictionaries provide general referential profiles of legal lexis and terminologies characterizing a typical or predominant object or classes of objects in real/possible worlds for many uses, actual legal meaning is shaped by default legal knowledge elaborated by the legal profession. This knowledge can be said to comprise a set of fixed attitudes and assumptions underpinning conceptual conventions. Given that practices of implementing statutory provisions and adjudications gradually evolve, professional default knowledge is likely to evolve too. In doing so, further strings are likely to be attached to legal meaning and legal usage in any one country. Consequently, legal terminologies can become more referentially elastic and this referential elasticity will account for the growing number of meanings a legal term can be assigned at a time.

Acknowledgments

It took more time than had been reasonably expected to finalize this chapter. I am indebted to two people who motivated me to accomplish the work.

The chapter would have hardly been possible, if not the inspiring support of my academic mentor, late Professor Alexandra Superanskaya, D.Phil., Institute of Linguistics, Russian Academy of Sciences (Moscow). Fascinated with the semantics of *chattels*, she was sharing her linguistic wisdom and insights with me throughout the entire preparation stage.

Grateful acknowledgments should go to the Latin scholar, Professor Konstantin Krasnukhin, D.Phil., Head of the Indo-European Languages History Section, Institute of Linguistics, Russian Academy of Sciences (Moscow), for valuable comments on Latin sources and historical semantics of *chattels*.

References

Aodha, Máirtín Mac (ed.). 2014. *Legal lexicography. A comparative perspective*. Farnham-Burlington, UK: Ashgate.
Cao, Deborah. 2004. *Translating law*. Clevedon, Buffalo, Toronto: Multilingual Matters.
Chomsky, Noam. 1995. *The minimalist program*. Cambridge, MA, & London: The MIT Press.
Coulthard, Malcolm & Alison Johnson. 2007. *An introduction to forensic linguistics: Language in evidence*. London & New York: Routledge.
Coulthard, Malcolm & Alison Johnson (eds.). 2010. *The Routledge handbook of forensic linguistics*. London & New York: Routledge.
Crystal, David. 2012. *English in 100 words*. London: Profile Books.
Davis, Wayne A. 2005. Nondescriptive meaning and reference: An ideational semantics. Oxford: Oxford University Press.
Eco, Umberto. 1984. *Semiotics and the philosophy of language*. London: Macmillan.
Eco, Umberto. 1999a. *Kant and the platypus. Essays on language and cognition*. Translated from Italian by Alastair McEwen. London: Secker & Warburg.

Eco, Umberto. 1999b. Notes on referring as contract. In Umberto Eco. *Kant and the platypus. Essays on language and cognition.* Translated from Italian by Alastair McEwen, 280–336. London: Secker & Warburg.
Gotti, Maurizio & Christopher Williams (eds.). 2010. *Legal discourse across languages and cultures.* Frankfurt am Main & Berlin: Peter Lang.
Galdia, Marcus. 2009. Legal translation. In Marcus Galdia, *Legal linguistics*, 224–238. Frankfurt am Main & Berlin: Peter Lang.
Gibbons, John. 2003. *Forensic linguistics: An introduction to language in the justice system.* London: John Wiley & Sons.
Gibbons, John (ed.). 1994. *Language and the law.* London & New York: Longman.
Irischanova, Olga K. 2004. *O lingvokreativnoj dejatel'nosti čeloveka: otglagol'nyje imena* [On linguistic creativity of humans: verbal nouns]. Moscow: Izdatel'stvo VTII.
Katz, Jerrold J. & Jerry A. Fodor. 1963. The structure of a semantic theory. *Language* 39(2). 170–210. April–June.
Kibrik, Andrej A. 2011. *Reference in discourse: Cross-linguistic aspects of reference.* Oxford: Oxford University Press.
Langacker, Ronald W. 2013. Conceptual semantics. In R. W. Langacker, *Essentials of cognitive grammar*, 27–54. Oxford: Oxford University Press.
Lyons, John. 1981. *Language, meaning and context.* London: Fontana.
Mellinkoff, David. 1963. *The language of the law.* Boston & Toronto: Little, Brown & Company.
Oliphant, K. 2008. Damages. In Peter Cane & Joanne Conagham (eds.), *The new Oxford companion to law*, 295–296. Oxford: Oxford University Press.
Počepcov, Grigoryj G., Jr. 1982. Jazyk i kommunikacyja: nekotoryje poniatyja [Language and communication: Some concepts]. In Yuri A. Sorokin (ed.), *Text as psychologically real*, 3–7. Moscow: Institute of Linguistics under the USSR Academy of Sciences.
Ramos, Fernando Prieto. 2014. Parameters for problem-solving in legal translation: Implications for legal lexicography and institutional terminology management. In Le Cheng, K. K. Sin and A. Wagner (eds.), *The Ashgate handbook of legal translation*. 121–134. Farnham, UK: Ashgate.
Šarčević, Susan. 2000. *New approach to legal translation.* The Hague, London, & Boston: Kluwer Law International.
Šarčević, Susan. 2010. Creating a Pan-European legal language. In Maurizio Gotti and Christopher Williams (eds.), *Legal discourse across languages and cultures*, 23–50. Frankfurt am Main & Berlin: Peter Lang.
Scalia, Antonin and Bryan A. Garner. 2012. *Reading law. The interpretation of legal texts.* St. Paul, MN: Thomson/West.
Solan, Lawrence M. 1993. *The Language of judges.* Chicago & London: The University of Chicago Press.
Solan, Lawrence M. 2005. The new textualists' new text. *Loyola Los Angeles Law Review* 38. 2027–2062. http://ssrn.com/abstract=719786 (accessed 25 April 2016).
Solan, Lawrence M. 2010. *The Language of statutes: Laws and their interpretation.* Chicago: Chicago University Press.
Solan, Lawrence M. 2013. Judging language plain. *Brooklyn Law School legal studies.* Research paper No. 360. 1–29 (Accepted Papers Series). http://papers.ssrn.com/sol3/papers.cfm?abstract_id=2342350 (accessed 23 November 2015).
Solan, Lawrence M., Janet Ainsworth & Roger W. Shuy (eds.). 2015. *Speaking of language and law. Conversations on the work of Peter Tiersma.* Oxford: Oxford University Press (Oxford Studies in Language and Law).

Tiersma, Peter M. 1999. *Legal language*. Chicago & London: University of Chicago Press.
Tiersma, Peter M. 2012. A history of the language of law. In Peter M. Tiersma & Lawrence M. Solan (eds.), *The Oxford handbook of language and law*, 13–26. Oxford: Oxford University Press.
Tiersma, Peter M. & Lawrence M. Solan (eds.). 2005. *Speaking of crime: The language of criminal justice*. Chicago: University of Chicago Press.
Tiersma, Peter M. & Lawrence M. Solan (eds.). 2012. *Oxford handbook on language and law*. Oxford: Oxford University Press.
Vlasenko, Svetlana V. 2014. Minimal unit of legal translation vs. minimal unit of thought. In Le Cheng, King Kui Sin, and Anne Wagner (eds.), *The Ashgate handbook on legal translation*, 89–120. Farnham, UK: Ashgate.
Vlasenko, Svetlana V. 2016. Where 'fiscal' cannot mean 'financial': A case study at the crossroads of legal and public-service translation taxonomies. *New voices in translation studies* 14. 46–73 [Special Issue]. http://www.iatis.org/images/stories/publications/new-voices/Issue14-2016/articles/VLASENKO_2016.pdf (accessed 10 May 2016).
Vygotsky, Lev S. 1979 [1934]. *Thought and language* [Myšlenyje i jazyk]. Edited and translated by Eugenia Hanfmann and Gertrude Vakar. Cambridge (Mass.): The M.I.T. Press.
Winograd, Terry. 1980. What does it mean to understand language? *Cognitive science* 4. 209–241.
Yokoyama, Olga. 1986. *Discourse and word order*. Amsterdam/Philadelphia: John Benjamins.
Zaitseva, Valentina. 1995. Particles and subtext: Coding referential portraits of the interlocutors. In Yokoyama, O.T. (ed.), *Harvard studies in Slavic linguistics* 3. 213–233. Cambridge, MA: Harvard University Press.
Zaitseva, Valentina. 1999. Šiftery Jakobsona v glagolach recevogo deistvyja [Jakobsonian shifters in speech act verbs]. In Henrik Baran & S.I. Gindin (eds.), *Roman Jakobson: teksty, documenty, issledovanyja* [Roman Jakobson: Texts, documents, studies], 508–518. Moscow: Russian State University for the Humanities (RGGU).

Lexicographic sources

ABBYY-5. 2011. ABBYY LINGVOx5 Electronic Multilingual Dictionary. ABBYY Software Ltd. http://www.lingvo.ru (accessed 23 November 2014).
ABBYY-6. 2014. ABBYY LINGVOx6 Electronic Multilingual Dictionary. ABBYY Software Ltd. http://www.lingvo.ru (accessed 11 February 2015).
Baskakova, M. A. 2009. *Legal glossary: Law and business (Russian–English, English–Russian)*. 8th edn., rev. & amend. Moscow: Finansy i statistika.
Black's Law. 2004. Garner, Brian A. (ed.-in-chief). *Black's law dictionary*. 8th edn. St. Paul: Thomson West.
Collins Cobuild. 2008. *Advanced learner's English dictionary*. New Digital Edition 2008. HarperCollins Publishers. (cited in ABBYY-6 2014. http://www.lingvo.ru (accessed 11.03.2015).
Curzon L. B. 2002. *Dictionary of law*. 6th edn. London: Pearson Education Ltd.
Faekov, Vladimir. 2011. *New finance dictionary*, in 2 vols. 2nd edn. Vol. 1: English–Russian. Vol. 2: Russian–English. Moscow: International Relations Publishing House.
Flynn, William J. 1976. *A handbook of Canadian legal terminology*. Ontario: New Press.

Fjedorov, Boris. 2001. *English–Russian banking and economic dictionary*. Saint-Petersburg: Limbus Press.
Gale. 2010. Batten, Donna (ed.). *Gale encyclopedia of American law* (formerly West's encyclopedia of American law). In 3 vols. 3rd edn.: Gale, Cengage Learning. Vol. 2: Be to Col. http://www.twirpx.com/file/642441/ (accessed 17 December 2015)].
Gifis S. H. 2003. *Law dictionary*. 5th edn. New York: Barron's Legal Guides Inc.
Hoedt, Jorgen (gen. ed.). 1999. *Business dictionary: English–Russian*. 2nd edn., revised. Moscow: Moscow International Publishers; Copenhagen: L&H Publishing Co.
Korolkevitch, Vitaly & Yulia Korolkevitch. 2002. *Modern English–Russian insurance dictionary*. Moscow: Gisbook.
Martin, E. A. & J. Law (eds.). 2006. *Oxford dictionary of law*. 6th edn. Oxford: Oxford University Press.
Martin, Jacqueline & Mary Gibbins. 2014. *A–Z law handbook*. 4th edn. New York: Philip Alan Updates.
Merriam-Webster's Law. 1996. *Merriam-Webster's dictionary of law*. Chicago: Merriam Webster. http://dictionary.findlaw.com/definition/chattel.html#sthash.DwUrrQVu.dpuf (accessed 17 December 2014).
Pivovar, A. G. (ed.). 2003. *Great financial and economic dictionary*. 2nd edn., revised. Moscow: Ekzamen.
Rodale, J. I. 1979. *The synonym finder*. Revised by Lawrence Urdang & Nancy La Roche (eds.). Rodale Press.
Roget's. 2012. *Roget's 21st century thesaurus*. 3rd edn. Paris: Philip Lief Group. http://www.thesaurus.com/browse/chattel?s=t (accessed 09 December 2015).
Skeat, Walter William. 1972 [1911]. *A concise etymological dictionary of the English language*. New and Corrected Impression. Oxford: Clarendon Press.
Stewart, W. J. 2006. *Collins dictionary of law: Law defined and explained*. London: HarperCollins Publishers.
Webster's Unabridged 1989: *Webster's encyclopaedic unabridged dictionary of the English language*. New York: Portland House.

Statutes and regulations cited

DCFR. 2009. Principles, Definitions and Model Rules of European Private Law. Draft Common Frame of Reference (DCFR). Full Edition. Prepared by the Study Group on a European Civil Code and the Research Group on EC Private Law (Acquis Group) / Ed. by C. von Bar and E. Clive. Vol. I–VI. Munich, 2009. 1500 p. Available online at: https://www.law.kuleuven.be/web/mstorme/2009_02_DCFR_OutlineEdition.pdf (accessed: 11 May 2015).
Guidance on the concept of establishment in Article 2(h) of the Insolvency Regulation. Council Regulation 1346/2000 art.2(h) (the Insolvency Regulation) on insolvency proceedings [2000] OJ L160/1, art.2(h), Pt 7, s.31. In: Journal of International Banking Law and Regulation [[2012] J.I.B.L.R, Issue 9. Vol. 27. N–159/160.]. Shearman & Sterling LLP.
RF CC Part 1: Civil Code of the Russian Federation. Part 1. Article 130 as of 30.11.1994 No. 51-FZ (rev. as of 03 December 12.2012). http://base.consultant.ru/cons/cgi/online.cgi?req=doc;base=LAW;div=LAW;n=138738;fld=134;dst=42 (accessed 17 November 2015).

Media sources cited

Bowcott, Owen. 2012a. Courts given green light to hire own interpreters as ALS struggles to cope. *The Guardian*. Thursday, 16 February 2012. http://www.theguardian.com/law/2012/feb/16/courts-hire-interpreters-capita-failing (accessed 15 November 2015).

Bowcott, Owen. 2012b. Court interpreting criticised as 'wholly inadequate' in damning NAO report. *The Guardian*. Wednesday, 12 September 2012. http://www.theguardian.com/law/2012/sep/12/nao-criticises-court-translating-contract (accessed 11 November 2015).

Bowcott, Owen. 2012c. Suspects 'denied fair trial' by shortage of court interpreters. *The Guardian*. Tuesday, 23 October 2012. http://www.theguardian.com/law/2012/oct/23/suspects-remanded-shortage-court-interpreters?INTCMP=SRCH (accessed 22 November 2015).

Glowacka, Magdalena. 2012. Violent clients, traumatised victims, late payment – the life of a court interpreter. *The Guardian*. Thursday, 15 March 2012. http://www.theguardian.com/law/2012/mar/02/ interpreters-courts-protest-privatized-contract (accessed 28 November 2015).

Legge, James. 2012. 'Courtroom chaos': Government accused of endangering justice by using cut-price courtroom interpreters. *Independent*. Tuesday, 23 October 2012. http://www.independent.co.uk/news/uk/home-news/courtroom-chaos-government-accused-of-endangering-justice-by-using-cutprice-courtroom-interpreters-8223381.html (accessed 05 November 2015).

Friedemann Vogel
12 Calculating legal meanings? Drawbacks and opportunities of corpus-assisted legal linguistics to make the law (more) explicit

1 Introduction

In the following contribution I would like to introduce the potentials and the challenges of corpus-assisted legal linguistics. By that I mean computer supported qualitative discourse analysis of legal texts and legal semantics. For this purpose I first give a short introduction to my working area of German legal linguistics and my understanding of jurisprudence as a text based institution (Section 2). Then secondly, I show how corpus linguistics can help us to see legal discourses in a new perspective, and how it gives us methods to analyze speech patterns as indicators of sediments of legal dogmatic (Section 3). Thirdly, I demonstrate the approach of legal corpus pragmatics using the example of the expression *employee* (*Arbeitnehmer*) in a corpus of labor court decisions (Section 4). In my conclusion (Section 5) I try to summarize the drawbacks and opportunities of these methods and present a new research project to develop a German legal reference corpus.

2 Law as institutionalized textual work

The given topic of interest is located in an interdisciplinary working group in the south of Germany, called *Heidelberg Group of legal linguistics* (Heidelberger Gruppe der Rechtslinguistik). This research group was founded in 1984 by the lawyer Professor Friedrich Müller and the linguist Professor Rainer Wimmer. They both had developed an interest in the relationship of legal system, language and speech acts long before they finally met. But they came from different fields, with different theoretical backgrounds and methods. Together with other colleagues they have developed a common theory of legal linguistics over the last thirty years. Today the members of the group come from very different backgrounds, legal scholars and linguists, judges and language practitioners, philosophers and former presidents of parliament. The common understanding of most of these legal linguists might be described in the following principles.

Friedemann Vogel, University of Freiburg

In modern societies, legal work is work within texts and language. When lawyers work with norms they actually work with many different texts. They connect a text with other texts, for example statutes with prior court decisions, texts of the legal scientific community, legal commentaries, texts of external opinions of experts, and, of course, texts describing the controversial "real facts." In other words: The modern constitutional state establishes an intertextual structure (Müller, Christensen, and Sokolowski 1997; Morlok 2004). This is not just another attribute among others. The constitutional state *is* indeed a text structure in itself. Jurisprudence is a "text-based decision science" ("textbasierte Entscheidungswissenschaft," Morlok 2015: 88). This relationship of legal system and text depends on two functions: Language is the most important medium to share and negotiate legal norms as behavioral expectations under a threat of penalty. Furthermore and more important in my opinion, language-based constitutional democracy transforms the brute force of social conflicts into due process and a semantic struggle to find better arguments.

We have to distinguish between at least three levels describing language use: (i) The *surface of language* as sensory stimulus hints, such as expressions like words, phrases, texts, intertextual structures, but also facial expressions and gestures, clothes and architecture forms. In terms of de Saussure but in a broader sense this level can be called "signifiant." On the level of the "signifiant" a sign is constituted if we can associate something with meaning or (ii) cognitive concepts. In the words of Lawrence Barsalou: "By concept I mean the descriptive information that people represent cognitively for a category, including definitional information, prototypical information, functionally important information, and probably other types of information as well. In this regard, my use of concept vaguely resembles intension and sense" (Barsalou 1992: 31).

These concepts or frames (Goffman 1974; Minsky 1975) or, in terms of de Saussure, the "signifié," are dynamic and have been built "bottom up" on a base of sensory perception and socialization. Concepts also preform our perception top down. When the top down process predominates, then we speak of stereotypes or – in a negative form – common prejudice (Nelson 2006). Beside the surface of language (or expressions) and cognitive concepts (or knowledge frames) we must distinguish (iii) the *social practices* constituting the connection between each of them, that is processes of contextualization in the sense of John Gumperz (1982) or Peter Auer (1986). John Gumperz called it a "paradox": "To decide on an interpretation, participants must first make a preliminary interpretation. That is, they listen to speech, form a hypothesis about what routine is being enacted, and then rely on social background knowledge and on co-occurrence expectations to evaluate what is intended and what attitudes are conveyed" (Gumperz 1982: 171).

Gumperz points out that interpretation of an expression depends on our individual experience with its use in the past, our knowledge about situations and the people involved. In that sense we can say, we make expressions or "contextualization cues" (Gumperz 1982: 131) "meaningful" (Hörmann 1980) within a virtual framework or cognitive context model (van Dijk 1999). But we have to consider that contextualization and the production of meaning is not only a question of individual cognition, but of *social* cognition (Schützeichel 2007). Meaning is neither external nor only internal; it is a virtual product of interaction between human beings (Goffman [1967] 2002). In this perspective we have to focus on the procedures of how people learn and constitute meanings in different situations. Or in short: interaction between family members differs from the interaction in institutions like jurisprudence. That's why we talk about legal language as a technical terminology. The main task for students of law is learning an adequate use of this terminology, how to connect and write legal texts with institutionalized methods and how to behave in accepted rituals.

Consequently, as an additional principle, we must distinguish the "text form" of a norm (for example laws, decisions, and commentaries) and the norm as a concept. Norms cannot be inside of a text, ready for use and ready for any subsumption. The law is not a "pot" (Busse 1992: 14). Lawyers must construct a norm actively in a hermeneutic way accepted in the community of lawyers, that is with arguments for their interpretation. They have to contextualize and concretize the expressions of a clause with the help of other texts; they must *ascribe* a norm to a text of law. You can observe these processes especially on the other side of norm text creation. In fact, legal colleagues involved in the legislative process do not try to create one meaning of a law. Instead they try to anticipate the main addressees, their previous knowledge of language and norm structure. They try to anticipate potential different contextualization of the arising text (Vogel 2012a). As a result, we can observe three analytical levels: the world of norms, the world of things (or *Lebenswelt*) and the world of texts. Both the world of norms and the world of things must be constituted by the world of texts. Jurisprudence, in my opinion, is the most important institution of our society to develop methods to bring these three worlds together and in a constitutional (hierarchical) order. In my view, this is also the main question and challenge for legal linguistics: How can we make legal interpretation more transparent? How can we make implicit text connection and legal inferences more explicit, especially in a digitalized world where thousands of texts are available in databases?

These last questions suggest that legal interpretation is not transparent. And often, when legal linguists in Europe talk about discursive construction of legal norms and of normativity within text, some legal scholars disagree. In their view the word "construction" is associated with despotism. But in fact, jurisprudence has developed and used a complex set of institutionalized interpretation methods. For example, Savigny's Canons – grammatical, historical, systematical and theological interpretation – are arguments for expanding and reducing legal meanings; they place an expression in its particular speech context (Kudlich and Christensen 2004: 83). Also theories that aim to structure a hierarchy of legal texts try to bring interpretation under professional control.

However, in that long tradition of methodology of legal text interpretation the important role of introspection often seems to be forgotten. Introspection means that the hermeneutic process depends only on the individual speech experience of the interpreter. In everyday life introspection is important for the ability to judge quickly and effectively. But there are also problems described by cognitive psychology under the topic biases of heuristic in judgment and decision-making (cf. Starck and Deutsch 2002). Especially if we try to make intuitive statements about the frequency of something, for example the use and the meaning of a word in different contexts, we often fail. We can test it, for example, with the following questions:

- How many words can native speakers produce actively and how many words can we understand passively?[1]
- What is the most frequently used word in our or in your language?[2] And which frequency order would you give for the words *candle-light, Gregorian* and *police car*[3]?
- And how many and which meaning versions of the expressions *ship* and *old* do you know?[4]

---

[1] It is very difficult to calculate frequencies of entities in the mental lexicon, we can only estimate them. The biggest problem is to separate so called common language and different institutionalized terminologies. For example, for adults we accept 300-500 thousand words of common language of German. But in everyday life we use only 12-16 thousand words and understand at least 50 thousand words (as a native speaker); cf. Best 2000, 2006.

[2] In German and English the most frequent words are articles (*der/die/das* or *the*).

[3] In German (*Kerzenlicht, Gregorianisch* and *Polizeiwagen*), all these words are in the same frequency-class 17, that is, these words belong to the least frequent expressions in contrast to the most frequent words (articles) in the German Reference Corpus (cf. Korpusbasierte Wortgrundformenliste DeReWo, v-30000g-2007-12-31-0.1, mit Benutzerdokumentation, http://www.ids-mannheim.de/kl/derewo/, © Institut für Deutsche Sprache, Programmbereich Korpuslinguistik, Mannheim, Deutschland, 2007).

[4] The corpus driven online dictionary *Elexico* of the Institut für Deutsche Sprache (Mannheim, Germany) counts five different meanings of the German word *Schiff* (*ship*): ›Wasserfahrzeug‹ (water craft), ›Kircheninnenraum‹ (nave), ›Wasserbehälter‹ (water reservoir), ›Teil des Webstuhls‹ (shuttle of a weaving loom) und ›Zinkplatte‹ (slide of zinc) (http://www.owid.de/artikel/87462, 19.05.2013). For the expression *alt* (old) Elexico counts seven different meanings (http://www.owid.de/artikel/271695, 19.05.2013).

In short: Introspection is a necessary, but not a sufficient resource for certain interpretations. This fact is the starting point of corpus linguistics.

3 Corpus linguistics and legal corpus pragmatics

To control introspection corpus linguists usually use selected text data bases and combine hermeneutic methods with computer assisted analysis methods. By now there are huge text collections (text corpora) for analysing standard languages. Such reference corpora, trying to capture almost all relevant contexts of a language, exist for different languages including German, French, British and American English. For example the British National Corpus (BNC) consists of a 100 Million words, the German Reference Corpus (DeReko) even takes about 8 billion words. However, these corpora are not useful to analyze questions about legal language. And specialized legal text corpora do not exist yet. Currently a Legal Reference Corpus is in preparation (see below), but we will come to that later. What can we do with these corpora?

Corpus linguists develop and use special algorithms and tools realizing one great purpose: They automatically collect those statistically relevant speech patterns which will be overlooked by purely introspective analysis. I will give a brief introduction to the most important algorithms:
- Most systems allow complex search tasks, using special search syntax as *regular expressions*. The results are presented in the form of *concordances* i.e. the "search term" or *keyword in context* (KWIC), as it is realized in the freeware tool *AntConc* (Anthony 2005): Here you can see the search term – for example the expression *arbeitnehm* (employee) in the middle of the window and the particular context right and left. If you sort the results alphabetically you can see recurrent speech patterns distributed in the corpus.
- Furthermore you can create *word lists*, collecting all expressions given in a corpus and count them. Word lists taken separately are hardly meaningful. More interesting is the statistical comparison of two different word lists to get specific *keywords*. For example you can compare the word list of a legal text corpus with the word list of a corpus of newspaper texts. As a result you will get those words which are typical for the one corpus but atypical for the other. For example, see below two keyword lists of German texts (using the toolkit for linguistic discourse and image analysis, LDA-Toolkit, cf. Vogel 2012c), contrasting expressions used from supporters and opponents of nuclear power. As a result we see expressions typically used in arguments as buzzwords or shibboleth.

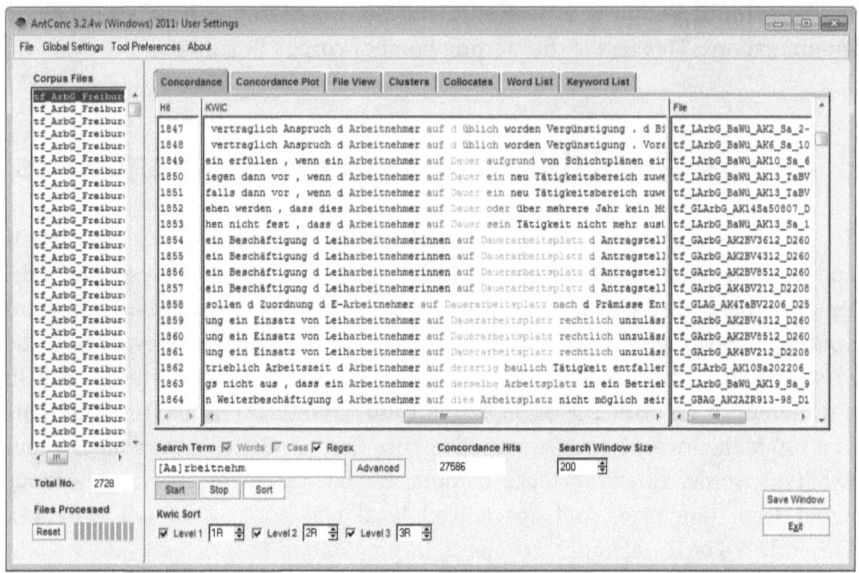

Figure 1: Concordances in the freeware tool AntConc (Anthony: 2005)

- You can also count *multi word units* (MWU) or n-grams to analyze stable phrases. For example, the algorithm separates all texts of a corpus in 5-grams (five-word-units) and creates a list containing the different expression types and their frequency. If you compare different lists, you can analyze *key-multi-word-units*, which are specific for the one and unspecific for the other corpus. See below, for example, a list contrasting three-word-units of left-wing parties and conservative parties in the same corpus of texts discussing pro and contra of nuclear power in Germany.
- In my view the most important algorithm is the analysis of co-occurrences. Co-occurrences are words, which can be found in a defined context of a search expression more often than statistically expected. In simple terms: Co-occurrence algorithms look for the search term in a corpus and count, for example, all the words given on eight places left and right of the search term. The statistical information gives us the degree of cohesiveness between the words. In a pragmatic perspective co-occurrence analysis realizes in a technical and systematical way what Ludwig Wittgenstein had in mind when he said "the meaning of a word is its use in the language" (PI 43). Co-occurrence profiles can be seen as context profiles of an expression. Finally, if you combine multi co-occurrence studies, you can explore the system of language use empirically step by step.

Table 1: Comparing keywords in the LDA-toolkit (Vogel: 2012c)

expression	translation	X²	conservative parties		left-wing parties	
			f	f/10.000	f	f/10.000
FDP	[German liberal party]	168,8	84	146,9	22	12,7
Kernkraftwerk	nuclear power plant	79,5	37	64,7	8	4,6
CDU	[German conservative party]	77,6	34	59,4	6	3,4
ausreichend	sufficient	60,3	28	48,9	6	3,4
Übergangstechnologie	transition technology	52,7	19	33,2	1	0,5
zur	for	52,4	40	69,9	22	12,7
Kernenergie	nuclear energy	51,3	30	52,4	11	6,3
Energiemix	energy mix	43,7	16	27,9	1	0,5
bezahlbar	affordable	37,7	14	24,4	1	0,5
Brückentechnologie	bridging technology	37,7	14	24,4	1	0,5
als	when/as	36,5	44	76,9	38	21,9
BüSo	[small German party]	33,2	11	199,2	0	0
klimafreundlich	climate-friendly	33,2	11	19,2	0	0
Laufzeit	run term	32,5	20	34,9	8	4,6
aber	but	31,2	34	59,4	27	15,6
Neubau	new building	29,8	18	31,4	7	4
können	could	29,2	55	96,2	64	37
lehnen	lean	27,2	13	22,7	3	1,7
Teil	part	25,7	10	17,4	1	0,5
verfügbar	available	24,8	11	19,2	2	1,1
Grüne	[German green party]	48,9	0	0	147	84,9
Linke	[German left-wing party]	35,9	1	1,7	115	66,4
Risiko	risk	29	2	3,4	101	58,3
Atomkraft	nuclear power	25,9	18	31,4	178	102,9
SPD	[German labor party]	23,5	0	0	71	41
ungelöst	unsolved	23,5	0	0	71	41
zudem	furthermore	20,2	0	0	61	35,2
Endlagerfrage	problem of final storage	19,8	0	0	60	34,6
vereinbart	agreed	16,8	0	0	51	29,4
früher	earlier	16,8	0	0	51	29,4
keinesfalls	on no account	16,5	0	0	50	28,9
stoppen	stop	15,8	0	0	48	27,7
deshalb	therefore	15,5	2	3,4	60	34,6
besonders	especially	14,9	1	1,7	52	30
Restlaufzeit	remaining term	14,5	2	3,4	57	32,9
Atommüll	nuclear waste	13,6	2	3,4	54	31,2
Atomausstieg	denuclearization	13,4	1	1,7	47	27,1
unverantwortlich	irresponsible	13,2	0	0	40	23,1
wollen	want	13,2	6	10,4	75	43,3
unsicher	unsafe	12,1	4	6,9	61	35,2

Table 2: Key-multi-word-units

expression	translation	X²	conservative parties		left-wing parties	
			f	f/10.000	f	f/10.000
Ausbau der erneuerbaren	extensions of renewable	19,214	0	0	58	33,536
früher vom Netz	sooner off the net	16,558	0	0	50	28,91
die besonders unsicher	which are very unsafe	15,894	0	0	48	27,754
Atomkraftwerk noch früher	nuclear power plant even sooner	15,563	0	0	47	27,175
und die Endlagerfrage	and the issue of permanent disposal	15,563	0	0	47	27,175
besonders unsichere Atomkraftwerke	very unsafe nuclear power plants	15,563	0	0	47	27,175
das Risiko der	the risk of	14,988	1	1,75	52	30,066
die Endlagerfrage ungelöst	the issue of permanent disposal unsolved	14,899	0	0	45	26,019
Risiko der Atomkraft	risk of nuclear power	14,328	1	1,75	50	28,91
Atomkraft ist unverantwortbar	nuclear power can't be taken responsibility for	8,932	0	0	27	15,611
Atomkraft ist unverantwortlich	nuclear power is irresponsible	6,946	0	0	21	12,142
Endlagerung von Atommüll	permant disposal of atomic waste	2,975	0	0	9	5,204
Frage der Endlagerung	issue of permanent disposal	2,644	0	0	8	4,626
in erneuerbare Energien	in renewable energies	2,314	0	0	7	4,047
unser Kind und	our child and	1,983	0	0	6	3,469

These algorithms or tools allow us to structure big text data and to form corpus-assisted hypothesis about language use. I will use them in a framework of legal corpus pragmatics (Felder, Müller, and Vogel (Ed.) 2012; Vogel 2012b; Vogel (Ed.) 2015) analysing legal speech patterns as a trace or as a trail of sediments of legal semantics. That assumption includes that stable concepts of jurisprudence (dogmatic) are connected with a recurrent use of language. Furthermore, I would argue that in the current environment of an almost exponential growth of legal texts, recurrent speech patterns play an important role for a jurist's take on the state of the art. This indicates that speech patterns in legal contexts symbolize the dogmatic status or/and the degree of institutionalisation of the concept associated with the expression through its "patternedness" ("Musterhaftigkeit"). If these assumptions are correct we should see more patterns in legal texts than

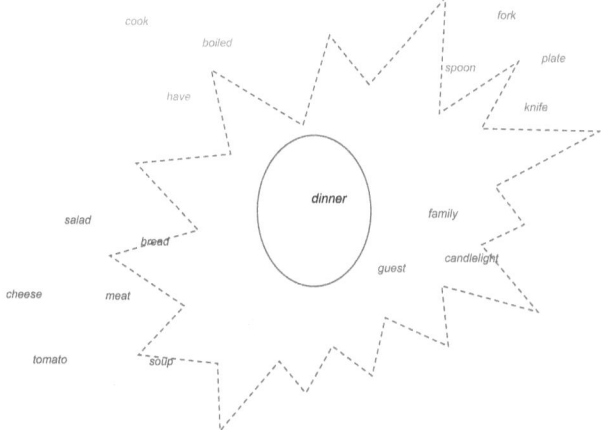

Figure 2: Illustration of different co-occurrence instances exploring the context of the expression *dinner*

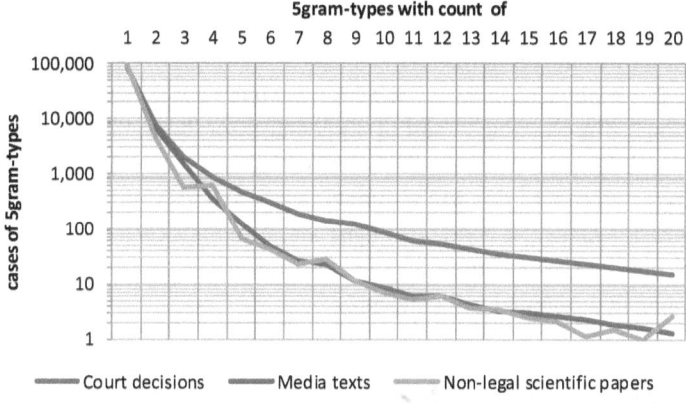

Figure 3: Speech patterns in legal discourses as indicators of legal dogmatic

in media texts or other scientific texts. We can also test this question with corpus linguistic methods.

The chart above illustrates the degree of 'patternedness' contrasting German court decisions, media texts and non-legal scientific texts. The compared corpora are:

- Corpus with 9.085 texts (court decisions) of German Labor Law (about 22,2 million words, 1950–2012; for more details see section 3.)
- Corpus with 474 non-legal scientific texts (papers) of Linguistics, Medical Science and Applied Ethics (about 2,6 million words, 1970–2012)
- Corpus of 17.974 texts in German media (about 10,9 million words, 2000–2012)

For that purpose I divided all texts into five-word-units and counted the hits of different unit types. As expected, using a particular five-word-unit (for example *this is a word unit*) exactly one time is the most frequent case for all three domains. But the case using a particular five-word-unit exactly in ten hits is found ten times more often in legal texts (about 100) than in media or non-legal scientific papers (about 10). That means that judges more often use recurrent multi-word-units in contrast to both of the other domains.

What do these patterns mean? If we look into the corpus and into the texts we can see that most of the speech patterns are references and citations of decisions of higher instances, especially governing arguments of the German Supreme Court (Bundesverfassungsgericht) or other federal courts. We can also see that different types of speech patterns constitute and are associated with different case groups. Of course, the patterns do not decide the case, but they give a macro structure for defining the topic more clearly.

In the following I will illustrate the methodological approach of Legal Corpus Pragmatics using the example of the word *Arbeitnehmer* (employee) in a corpus of labor court decisions[5]. The example is part of a pilot study of Ralph Christensen, Stephan Pötters – both lawyers – and me (2015). We wanted to test corpus linguistic methods in contrast and in addition to traditional legal methods. In this respect the meaning of *Arbeitnehmer* is a good test object, because the expression is not an expression of law (not represented in a statute) but especially of case-law and dogmatics (so called "vague legal concept").

4 The concept of *Arbeitnehmer* (employee) in German labor law

To analyze the concept of *Arbeitnehmer* in labor law we built a corpus of 9.085 decision texts (22,22 Mio. words) of federal, county and European courts,

---

[5] For a first test of legal corpus pragmatics using the example of the expression *human dignity* (Art. 1 Abs. 1 Grundgesetz) see Vogel 2012a.

published between 1954 and 2012. The texts had to be transformed into a simple-text format and annotated with part of speech information. For diachronic analysis the texts were separated in three groups:
(A) 1954 – 1989: 1320 texts / 1, 0 Mio. Words
(B) 1990 – 1999: 5036 texts / 13, 4 Mio. Words
(C) 2000 – 2012: 2728 texts / 7, 9 Mio. Words[6]

To explore the meaning of the expression *Arbeitnehmer* in the sense of Wittgenstein we used corpus linguistic methods to find speech patterns, framing the expression *arbeitnehm* in our corpus. We supposed that the expression *arbeitnehm* at least would be connected with the relevant concept, so called 'minimal assumption'. In the first step we collected several levels of context expressions realizing conceptual attributions of the type >X is Y<:

- Compounds like *Leiharbeitnehmer* (borrowed workforce), *Arbeitnehmerschutz* (protection for employees), *Arbeitnehmerüberlassung* (supply of temporary workers), *Vollzeitarbeitnehmer* (full time employee), *Fremdarbeitnehmer* (foreign employee) etc.: the attribution (Y) is located in the determinans or determinatum;
- Predication phrases like *arbeitnehm* ist Y or *Arbeitnehmer ist nicht/kein* Y (employee is [not] Y);
- Attribution phrases with Adjectives like *junge/alte/gewerbliche/männliche *arbeitnehm* (young/old/commercial/male etc. employee);
- Verb phrases with *arbeitnehm* like *arbeitnehm* müssen/können/dürfen Y (employee must/are allowed to Y);
- Multi-Word-Units with *arbeitnehm*, for example *Arbeitnehmer im Sinne des* Y (employee in the sense of Y);
- Iterations of co-occurrences to the expression *arbeitnehm* (see below).

In the second qualitative step we grouped these context expressions into clusters of meanings or topics, grounded in qualitative micro analysis of the particular expressions in the texts. In the last step we built hypotheses about the most common framing structures associated with the expression *Arbeitnehmer* in contrast to other findings. In the following I give some examples of the different categories:

There are many **compounds** with the expression *arbeitnehm* and they can be distinguished in determinans and determinatum. The determinatum or primary

---

6 Because of inconsistent formats we could only analyze corpora B and C.

word gives a basic frame; the determinative element completes and clears that frame with an attribution. The ten most frequent compounds with *arbeitnehm* as determinatum are the following:

Table 3: Compounds with *arbeitnehm* as determinatum

Nr.	f	Kompositum (Type)	[English translation]
1	851	Leiharbeitnehmer	agency staff
2	371	Wanderarbeitnehmer	migrant laborer
3	125	Teilzeitarbeitnehmer	part-time employee
4	99	Leiharbeitnehmerin	female agency workers
5	66	Vollzeitarbeitnehmer	full-time employee
6	51	Stammarbeitnehmer	permanent employee
7	18	Altersteilzeitarbeitnehmer	partial retirement employee
8	16	Fremdarbeitnehmer	interim/subcontracted employees
9	14	Saisonarbeitnehmer	seasonal laborer
10	14	Gesamtarbeitnehmer [-*vertretung*]	General works council

Compounds like these ones are very concentrated marks of legal case groups and recurrent groups of persons. If we explore particular compounds in a diachronic way we can see that, for example, legal proceedings about temporary agency workers (*Leiharbeitnehmer*) increase.

Figure 4: *Leiharbeitnehmer* in the corpus (screenshot of the concordance plot of AntConc)

Compounds with *arbeitnehm* as a determinative element display how judges try to organize different groups of cases as prototypes. They write about

(1) *Arbeitnehmerähnlichkeit* ('similarity of employee'), *Arbeitnehmereigenschaft* (attributes of employee), *Arbeitnehmerbegriff* (meaning of employee), *Arbeitnehmerstatus* (status of emlployee), [*fiktiver*] *Vergleichsarbeitnehmer* ('comparative employee'), *Arbeitnehmerkategorien* (categories of employee), *arbeitnehmertypisch* (employee-typical)

In this perspective of prototyping a new category called *arbeitnehmerähnliche Person* (referring to § 5 Abs. 1 S. 2 ArbGG) was born. *Arbeitnehmerähnliche Personen* are ›persons, selling their services to someone paying for those services, but these persons have far lower degree of self-determination in regard to time and place of work as prototypical employees‹.

If we search for **predication phrases** like *arbeitnehm is* Y, we get legal efforts to find and to reproduce definitions, created by judges.

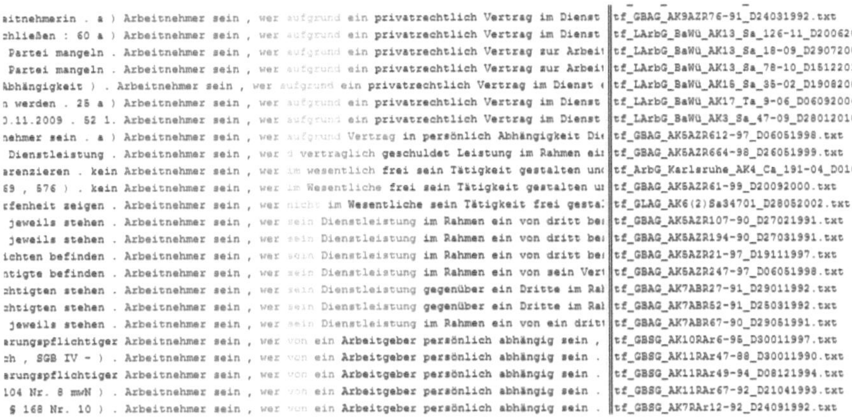

aitnehmerin . a) Arbeitnehmer sein , wer aufgrund ein privatrechtlich Vertrag im Dienst	tf_GBAG_AK9AZR76-91_D24031992.txt
chließen : 60 a) Arbeitnehmer sein , wer aufgrund ein privatrechtlich Vertrag im Dienst	tf_LArbG_BaWü_AK13_Sa_126-11_D20062
Partei mangeln . Arbeitnehmer sein , wer aufgrund ein privatrechtlich Vertrag zur Arbei	tf_LArbG_BaWü_AK13_Sa_18-09_D290720
Partei mangeln . Arbeitnehmer sein , wer aufgrund ein privatrechtlich Vertrag zur Arbei	tf_LArbG_BaWü_AK13_Sa_78-10_D151220
Abhängigkeit) . Arbeitnehmer sein , wer aufgrund ein privatrechtlich Vertrag im Dienst	tf_LArbG_BaWü_AK16_Sa_35-02_D190820
n werden . 25 a) Arbeitnehmer sein , wer aufgrund ein privatrechtlich Vertrag im Dienst	tf_LArbG_BaWü_AK17_Ta_9-06_D0609200
).11.2009 . 52 1. Arbeitnehmer sein , wer aufgrund ein privatrechtlich Vertrag im Dienst	tf_LArbG_BaWü_AK3_Sa_47-09_D2801201
nehmer sein . a) Arbeitnehmer sein , wer aufgrund Vertrag in persönlich Abhängigkeit Di	tf_GBAG_AK5AZR612-97_D06051998.txt
Dienstleistung . Arbeitnehmer sein , wer d vertraglich geschuldet Leistung im Rahmen ei	tf_GBAG_AK5AZR664-98_D26051999.txt
arenzieren . kein Arbeitnehmer sein , wer im wesentlich frei sein Tätigkeit gestalten un	tf_ArbG_Karlsruhe_AK4_Ca_191-04_D01
69 , 576) . kein Arbeitnehmer sein , wer im Wesentliche frei sein Tätigkeit gestalten u	tf_GBAG_AK5AZR61-99_D20092000.txt
rfenheit zeigen . Arbeitnehmer sein , wer nicht im Wesentliche sein Tätigkeit frei gesta	tf_GLAG_AK6(2)Sa34701_D28052002.txt
jeweils stehen . Arbeitnehmer sein , wer sein Dienstleistung im Rahmen ein von dritt be	tf_GBAG_AK5AZR107-90_D27021991.txt
jeweils stehen . Arbeitnehmer sein , wer sein Dienstleistung im Rahmen ein von dritt be	tf_GBAG_AK5AZR194-90_D27031991.txt
ichten befinden . Arbeitnehmer sein , wer sein Dienstleistung im Rahmen ein von dritt be	tf_GBAG_AK5AZR21-97_D19111997.txt
ntigte befinden . Arbeitnehmer sein , wer sein Dienstleistung im Rahmen ein von sein Ver	tf_GBAG_AK5AZR247-97_D06051998.txt
chtigten stehen . Arbeitnehmer sein , wer sein Dienstleistung gegenüber ein Dritte im Ra	tf_GBAG_AK7ABR27-91_D29011992.txt
chtigten stehen . Arbeitnehmer sein , wer sein Dienstleistung gegenüber ein Dritte im Ra	tf_GBAG_AK7ABR52-91_D25031992.txt
jeweils stehen . Arbeitnehmer sein , wer sein Dienstleistung im Rahmen ein von ein drit	tf_GBAG_AK7ABR67-90_D29051991.txt
arungspflichtiger Arbeitnehmer sein , wer von ein Arbeitgeber persönlich abhängig sein ,	tf_GBSG_AK10RAr6-95_D30011997.txt
ch , SGB IV -) . Arbeitnehmer sein , wer von ein Arbeitgeber persönlich abhängig sein .	tf_GBSG_AK11RAr47-88_D30011990.txt
arungspflichtiger Arbeitnehmer sein , wer von ein Arbeitgeber persönlich abhängig sein .	tf_GBSG_AK11RAr49-94_D08121994.txt
104 Nr. 8 mwN) . Arbeitnehmer sein , wer von ein Arbeitgeber persönlich abhängig sein .	tf_GBSG_AK11RAr67-92_D21041993.txt
§ 168 Nr. 10) . Arbeitnehmer sein , wer von ein Arbeitgeber persönlich abhängig sein .	tf_GBSG_AK7RAr12-92_D24091992.txt

Figure 5: Definitions for *arbeitnehm*, created by judges (Screenshot of AntConc)

We see not one definition but competing definitions. One of the most frequent patterns is the following:

(2) ***Arbeitnehmer ist, wer*** *seine Dienstleistung im Rahmen einer von Dritten bestimmten Arbeitsorganisation erbringen muss. Die Eingliederung in die fremde Arbeitsorganisation wird dadurch besonders deutlich, dass ein Arbeitnehmer hinsichtlich Zeit, Dauer und Ort der Ausführung des übernommenen Dienstes einem umfassenden Weisungsrecht des Arbeitgebers unterliegt. Häufig tritt auch eine fachliche Weisungsgebundenheit hinzu.* [Gefolgt von zahlreichen Quellenangaben mit Verweis auf das BAG]

[Translation: ›An employee is someone who has to provide his services in an organisational structure determined by others regarding time, duration and place of services. Often an employee is also bound by professional instructions.‹ [Followed by numerous references to decisions of the same federal labor court.]]

Co-occurrences of the expression *arbeitnehm* refer to broader context relationships. To analyze these relationships we collected all expressions located in a range of 15 words left to 15 words right of our starting expression and filtered these expressions, which are significant in a statistical sense[7]. To cluster the resulting words into different semantic fields we explored the particular (con-)texts in the concordance view and with co-occurrence analysis of secondary or tertiary rank, that is systematic context exploration through co-occurrences of co-occurrences and so on. To get an overview of the data structure we also used visualization methods like network analysis (here: with the help of Gephi[8]):

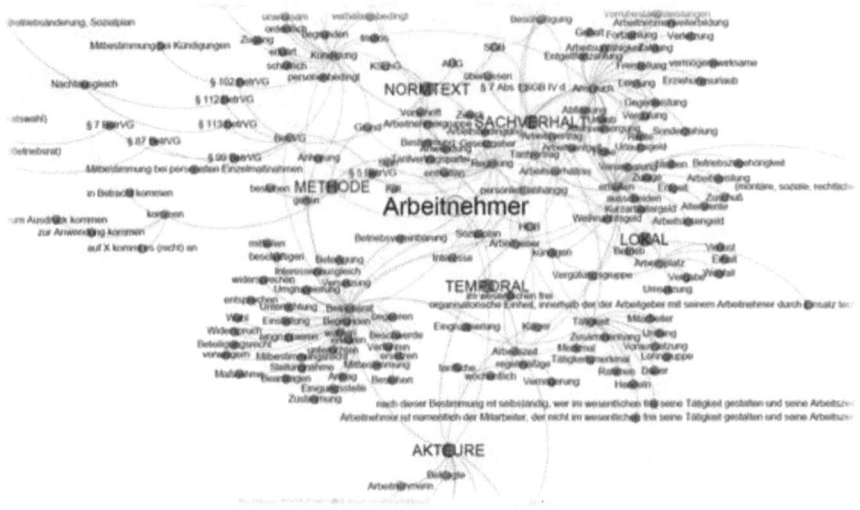

Figure 6: Network analysis: Attribution network of *Arbeitnehmer* (Screenshot of Gephi)

The evaluation of the co-occurrence clusters focuses on important parts of the *Arbeitnehmer*-associated frame, for example:
- Relevant norm texts (laws) and legal domains attributing the *Arbeitnehmer*-Frame: paragraphs of *Betriebsverfassungsgesetz* (BetrVerfG) regarding questions of employee participation and collective protection; German Civil Code (*Bürgerliches Gesetzbuch*, BGB) regarding the relationship between 'service seller' and 'service consumer' and others. Moreover, you can see the methodology judges use, for example a high degree of auto-referentiality (self-citation):

---

7 That means that we used not only a frequency sorted word list but statistical tests in addition (Chi Square) that give information about the specifics of the collected co-occurrences depending on the corpus population and levels of contingency or statistical expectations.
8 http://gephi.org/, The Open Graph Viz Platform (12.07.2013).

BAG ⇒ BAG; BSG ⇒ BSG and so on. Of course, it would be interesting to analyze the full network of citations and the different types of authorities, but that would lead too far.
– Recurrent actors or stakeholders struggling for the *Arbeitnehmer*-Frame: complainer (*Kläger*) and defendant (*Beklagter*), worker's council (*Betriebsrat*) and worker's union (*Gewerkschaft*), employer (*Arbeitgeber*), employee (*Arbeitnehmer*) and the role of female employee (*Arbeitnehmerin*) especially in the last 20 years, framed by European law[9]. We have to point out, that the meaning of employer (*Arbeitgeber*) only is made clear by the negation of employee (*Arbeitnehmer*). A recurrent pattern is: 'employer is who employs an employer' (*Arbeitgeber ist, wer Arbeitnehmer beschäftigt*)[10]. Furthermore, many co-occurrences refer to different case groups, for example distinguishing gender (*männlich/weiblich* [male/female]), age (*jung/alt* [young/old])[11], duration and period of work (*Vollzeit* [fulltime], *Teilzeit* [parttime], *vorübergehend* [temporary], *wöchentlich* [weekly] and so on), healthy (*arbeitsunfähig* [disabled], *krank* [ill], *Prognose* [health prediction]) and others.
– Circumstances and correlating actions framing the *Arbeitnehmer*: The most important point is the expression *Tätigkeit* ('action/employment') because of its role in distinguishing employee (*Arbeitnehmer*) and freelancer (*Selbstständiger*). Regarding to § 84 Abs. 1 Satz 2, Abs. 2 HGB there are two patterns, constituting the employee and freelancer as antonyms:

(3) *Arbeitnehmer ist namentlich der Mitarbeiter, der <u>nicht im Wesentlichen frei seine **Tätigkeit**</u> gestalten und seine Arbeitszeit bestimmen kann.* [Employee is a person who cannot arrange its employment and its working time essentially independently.]

(4) [Als eine Person] *ist selbständig, <u>wer im Wesentlichen frei seine **Tätigkeit**</u> gestalten und seine Arbeitszeit bestimmen kann.* [Freelancer is a person who can arrange its employment and its working time essentially independently.]

– Another symbol for the antonymic relationship is the significant co-occurrence *oder* (or) with its disjunctive meaning: *eine abhängige Beschäftigung <u>oder</u> eine selbständige Tätigkeit* (dependent employment <u>or</u> freelance engagement).

---

9 Art. 8, 11 of 92/85/EWG, *Mutterschutzrichtlinie* and Art. 2 of 76/207/EWG, *Gleichbehandlungsgrundsatz*.
10 The German legal expression *Beschäftigter* (*employer*) (social law) is quasi synonymous with the expression *Arbeitnehmer* (labor law).
11 Cases with young employees increased in the last years because of financial crises and youth unemployment.

These examples should be sufficient to demonstrate the method, using corpus linguistic methods to structure big data of legal texts. Now I will try to summarize the results of the particular pattern analysis to describe our hypotheses bottom up about the **legal *Arbeitnehmer* concept**.

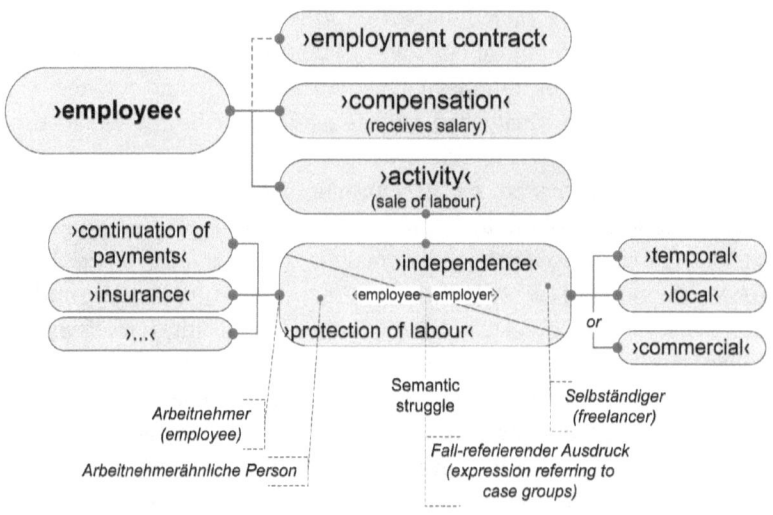

Figure 7: Semantic structure of *employee* in German labor law dogmatic

The semantic structure of ›employee‹ in German labor law dogmatic contains four essential frame slots. The different concretions or fillers (as recurrent expression patterns) of these slots constitute particular groups of persons with different rights and duties. Generally it is a question of ›persons‹ selling their services (first slot) and being paid for it (second slot). This relationship can be, but doesn't have to be formalized as an employment contract (third slot). The fourth slot classifies the circumstances of the offered services within two dimensions, which are the ›degree of independence‹ (regarding temporal, local or commercial aspects[12]) and the ›degree of protection of labor‹ (for example continuation of payments, insurance, dismissals protection and so on). The different expressions and speech patterns negotiated in legal discourses refer to different prototypical combinations of slot fillers. A person called *Arbeitnehmer* (employee) has prototypically no self-determination and therefore full protection of labor. By contrast persons called *selbständig* (freelancers) are totally independent, but have no protection of labor. If we observe the negotiation strategies of the

---

12 Only relevant for the group of *Arbeitnehmerähnliche Personen*, who are independent in regard to time and space of work, but, though, are economically dependent on employers.

struggling stakeholders, we can see that employees usually illustrate their work as bounded by instructions whereas employers emphasize the independence. We can describe labor law as a discourse (in the sense of Michel Foucault 1974a, 1974b: 133), where employers always constitute new types of as-it-were-freelancers ('Als-ob-Selbstständige') and German labor legislation often is late to react (cf. so called *Werkverträge* or *Scheinselbstständigkeit*/ostensible self-employment).

5 Conclusion

This contribution introduced the methodological approach of legal corpus pragmatics, using the example of the concept *employee* in German labor law. Finally I want to discuss possible drawbacks and opportunities of computer assisted studies of legal language and discourse:

On the one hand, corpus linguistics, especially computer based algorithms, cannot calculate legal meanings. Interpretation, that is contextualization of expressions using other sensory input and background knowledge, is and will always be a challenge to human beings. Automata or machines can only connect predefined information; they cannot evaluate this information in a context of struggling interests and the general relativity of ways to describe the world. For this reason, attempts to replace lawyers with computers as "subsumption automats"[13] will always fail. The computer cannot replace the judge; it cannot decide (Kotsoglou 2014).

On the other hand, that does not mean that computer assisted analysis methods are useless. The computer can help us to structure big text data – large amounts of texts – to contrast or control our introspection and – in the words of the lawyer Ralph Christensen (Mannheim) – "lawyer's impressionism." The meaning of a word is its use in the language, but we cannot remember all or at least all of so called 'most important' examples of word use. Even dictionaries often fail (cf. Mouritsen 2010)[14]. Algorithms like co-occurrence analysis are able to support our memory, especially in a digitalized world of growing legal texts and promulgation through media of law. That is to say, legal corpus pragmatics provide a method for 'computer assisted reading' of law.

---

[13] The judge as non-subjective 'automat', cf. from Rave et al. (Ed.) 1971 until Raabe et al. 2012.
[14] Dictionaries are not always a proper source of arguments in a debate about the meaning of a legal clause. Why not? – The first problem is that dictionaries are normally not based upon legal texts, but on different, non-legal speech varieties. Second problem, "the dictionary is not a fortress": As Stephen Mouritsen (2010) pointed out, dictionaries only try to describe the usage in the past, but they do not *prescribe* it. Dictionaries are not 'laws on language use'.

Our pilot studies illustrate that corpus-assisted interpretation methods also work well in legal contexts. In the United States we can already find first court decisions using corpus linguistics[15] and existing text corpora. However, we don't have adequate legal text corpora yet. That's why I have started a project with the duration time from 2014 until 2017, supported by the Heidelberg Academy of Science and Humanities, to develop a legal reference text corpus (*Juristisches Referenzkorpus, JuReko* – www.jureko.de) together with Dr. iur. Hanjo Hamann (Bonn). This corpus will contain thousands of court decisions, texts of legal scholars, commentaries and laws and will be assembled in the next three years (cf. http://www.jureko.de; cf. Vogel/Hamann 2015).

With a legal reference corpus we will be able to describe and to explore legal language and legal discourse in more detail, especially regarding legal vocabulary, citation networks, the most common arguments, rules of establishing authority, the empirical status of standards and indefinite legal concepts and other questions. Furthermore, together with linguists and lawyers of the Federal Ministry of Justice (Germany) we also explore Corpus-assisted methods to optimize legislation. If you create a new text of law you have to anticipate and to connect with future legal language usage. But often it is not clear enough whether you should create a new word or you should better use an existing and established speech pattern associated with the desired concept to prevent misunderstandings.

Last but not least I think we need more interdisciplinary interactions between traditional legal methodology, legal linguistics and corpus linguistics, at the beginning of legal education. Bringing these approaches together would be a contribution to a theory of practice as practice (Bourdieu et al. 2009) with sustainable long-term benefits.

References

Anthony, Laurence. 2005. AntConc: Design and development of a freeware corpus analysis toolkit for the technical writing classroom. *Professional Communication Conference. IPCC 2005. Proceedings.* 729–737.
Auer, Peter. 1986. Kontextualisierung. *Studium Linguistik* 19. 22–47.
Barsalou, Lawrence W. 1992. Frames, concepts, and conceptual fields. In Adrienne Lehrer & Eva F. Kittay (eds.), *Frames, fields, and contrasts: New essays in semantic and lexical organization*, 21–74. Hillsdale, N.J.: L. Erlbaum Associates.

---

[15] Cf. the decision of the Supreme Court of State of Utah, 2011 UT 38, 266 P.3d 702 (available under: http://www.utcourts.gov/opinions/supopin/InReEZ071911.pdf, 04.06.2014). See also: "U.S. Supreme Court uses corpus created by BYU professor Mark Davies" (Deseret News, 13.03.2011; available under http://www.deseretnews.com/article/700118257/US-Supreme-Court-uses-corpus-created-by-BYU-professor-Mark-Davies.html?pg=all).

Best, Karl-Heinz. 2000. Unser Wortschatz. Sprachstatistische Untersuchungen. In Karin M. Eichhoff-Cyrus & Rudolf Hoberg (eds.), *Die deutsche Sprache zur Jahrtausendwende: Sprachkultur oder Sprachverfall?* (Duden 1), 35–52. Mannheim: Dudenverl.

Best, Karl-Heinz. 2006. *Quantitative Linguistik: Eine Annäherung* (Göttinger linguistische Abhandlungen 3), 3rd edn. Göttingen: Peust & Gutschmidt.

Bourdieu, Pierre, Cordula Pialoux & Bernd Schwibs. 2009. *Entwurf einer Theorie der Praxis: Auf der ethnologischen Grundlage der kabylischen Gesellschaft* (Suhrkamp-Taschenbuch Wissenschaft 291), 2nd edn. Frankfurt am Main: Suhrkamp.

Busse, Dietrich. 1992. Textinterpretation: Sprachtheoretische Grundlagen einer explikativen Semantik. Opladen: Westdeutscher Verl.

Felder, Ekkehard, Marcus Müller & Friedemann Vogel (eds.). 2012. *Korpuspragmatik: Thematische Korpora als Basis diskurslinguistischer Analysen*. Berlin [u.a.]: De Gruyter.

Foucault, Michel. 1974. *Die Ordnung der Dinge: Eine Archäologie der Humanwissenschaften* (Suhrkamp-Taschenbuch Wissenschaft), 1st edn. Frankfurt am Main: Suhrkamp.

Foucault, Michel. [1974] 2012. *Die Ordnung des Diskurses*. Frankfurt am Main: Fischer.

Goffman, Erving. 1974. *Frame analysis: An essay on the organization of experience*. Harper & Row.

Goffman, Erving. 2002 [1967]. *Interaktionsrituale: Über Verhalten in direkter Kommunikation*, 6th edn. Frankfurt am Main: Suhrkamp.

Gumperz, John J. 1982. Fact and inference in courtroom testimony. In John J. Gumperz (ed.), *Language and social identity* (Studies in interactional sociolinguistics 2), 163–195. Cambridge: Cambridge University Press.

Hörmann, Hans. 1980. Der Vorgang des Verstehens. In Wolfgang Kühlwein (ed.), *Sprache und Verstehen* (Kongreßberichte der Jahrestagung der Gesellschaft für Angewandte Linguistik GAL e. V), 17–29. Tübingen: Narr.

Kotsoglou, Kyriakos N. 2014. Subsumtionsautomat 2.0: Über die (Un-)Möglichkeit einer Algorithmisierung der Rechtserzeugung. *Juristenzeitung* 69(9). 451–457.

Kudlich, Hans & Ralph Christensen. 2004. Die Kanones der Auslegung als Hilfsmittel für die Entscheidung von Bedeutungskonflikten. *Juristische Arbeitsblätter*. 74–83.

Minsky, Marvin. 1975. A framework for representing knowledge. In Patrick H. Winston & Berthold Horn (eds.), *The psychology of computer vision*, 211–277. New York: McGraw-Hill.

Morlok, Martin. 2004. Der Text hinter dem Text. Intertextualität im Recht. In Alexander Blankenagel, Ingolf Pernice & Markus Kotzur (eds.), *Verfassung im Diskurs der Welt: Liber Amicorum für Peter Häberle zum siebzigsten Geburtstag*, 93–136. Tübingen: Mohr Siebeck.

Morlok, Martin. 2015. Intertextualität und Hypertextualität im Recht. In Friedemann Vogel (ed.), *Zugänge zur Rechtssemantik: Interdisziplinäre Ansätze im Zeitalter der Mediatisierung zwischen Introspektion und Automaten* (linguae & litterae). Berlin, New York: Walter de Gruyter.

Mouritsen, Stephen C. 2010. The dictionary is not a fortress: Definitional fallacies and a corpus-based approach to plain meaning. *Brigham Young University Law Review*. 1915–1980.

Müller, Friedrich, Ralph Christensen & Michael Sokolowski. 1997. *Rechtstext und Textarbeit* (Schriften zur Rechtstheorie). Berlin: Duncker & Humblot.

Nelson, Todd D. 2006. *The psychology of prejudice*, 2nd edn. Boston, MA: Pearson Education.

Raabe, Oliver, Richard Wacker, Daniel Oberle, Christian Baumann & Christian Funk. 2012. *Recht ex machina: Formalisierung des Rechts im Internet der Dienste*. Berlin, Heidelberg: Springer Vieweg.

Rave, Dieter, Hans Brinkmann & Klaus Grimmer (eds.). 1971. *Paraphrasen juristischer Texte*. Darmstadt: Dt. Rechenzentrum.

Schützeichel, Rainer. 2007. Soziale Kognitionen. In Rainer Schützeichel (ed.), *Handbuch Wissenssoziologie und Wissensforschung* (Erfahrung – Wissen – Imagination), 433–449. Konstanz: UVK-Verl.-Ges.

Starck, Fritz & Roland Deutsch. 2002. Urteilsheuristiken. In Dieter Frey & Martin Irle (eds.), *Theorien der Sozialpsychologie: Motivation und Informationsverarbeitung*, 2nd edn. (Psychologie-Lehrtexte 3), 352–385. Bern: Huber.

van Dijk, Teun A. 1999. Context models in discourse processing. In Herre van Oostendorp & Susan R. Goldman (eds.), *The construction of mental representations during reading*, 124–148. Mahwah, NJ: Erlbaum.

Vogel, Friedemann. 2012a. Linguistik rechtlicher Normgenese: Theorie der Rechtsnormdiskursivität am Beispiel der Online-Durchsuchung (Sprache und Wissen 9). Berlin [u.a.]: De Gruyter.

Vogel, Friedemann. 2012b. Das Recht im Text: Rechtssprachlicher Usus in korpuslinguistischer Perspektive. In Ekkehard Felder, Marcus Müller & Friedemann Vogel (eds.), *Korpuspragmatik: Thematische Korpora als Basis diskurslinguistischer Analysen*, 314–353. Berlin [u.a.]: De Gruyter.

Vogel, Friedemann. 2012c. Das LDA-Toolkit: Korpuslinguistisches Analyseinstrument für kontrastive Diskurs- und Imageanalyzen in Forschung und Lehre. *Zeitschrift für Angewandte Linguistik* 57(1). 129–165.

Vogel, Friedemann (ed.). 2015. *Zugänge zur Rechtssemantik: Interdisziplinäre Ansätze im Zeitalter der Mediatisierung zwischen Introspektion und Automaten* (linguae & litterae). Berlin, New York: Walter de Gruyter.

Vogel, Friedemann & Hanjo Hamann. 2015. Vom corpus iuris zu den corpora iurum – Konzeption und Erschließung eines juristischen Referenzkorpus (JuReko). In *Jahrbuch der Heidelberger Akademie der Wissenschaften für 2014*. Heidelberg: Winter.

Ralf Poscher
13 The common error in theories of adjudication: An inferentialist argument for a doctrinal conception

1 Theories of adjudication

Law is about adjudication. Adjudication is not only the center of the law as a social system (Luhmann [1993] 2004: 293, 296), but also what legal practice, legal counseling, trials, procedures and legal scholarship are regularly all about. In modern legislative states legislation is prerequisite for adjudication, but legislation as a process is neither at the center of legal counseling nor at the center of legal scholarship. Theories of adjudication, not legislation, theorize the central element of legal practice.

1.1 Hard cases as the heart of law

Adjudication in turn is all about hard cases, i.e. cases in which fair-minded legal professionals cannot reach intersubjective agreement on what the law demands. Despite their quantitative epiphenomenology with respect to the overall practice of the law, in which uncountable legal relations and transactions run smoothly without ever incurring hermeneutic difficulties, hard cases are central not only to adjudication, but also for the law as a profession and a scholarly discipline. Lower courts may have the function of executing the law in easy cases – the debtor who fails to pay, the thief who has to be brought to justice etc. –, but from the appellate level and upwards, easy cases become scarce. Higher courts predominantly deal with hard cases. It is precisely these cases which are reported in the law reports and reviews and which are of interest to lawyers and legal scholars. It is *Roe v. Wade*[1], *Riggs v. Palmer*[2], *Chevron v. EPA*[3], not everyday, run-of-the-mill easy cases, which lie at the center of the practice of

---
[1] *Roe v. Wade*, 410 U.S. 113 (1973) – Judgment legalizing abortion.
[2] *Riggs v. Palmer*, 115 N.Y. 506 (1889) – Can a murderer be the heir of the murdered person? Used as an example by Dworkin (1977: 23).
[3] *Chevron U.S.A. Inc. v. Natural Resources Defense Council, Inc.*, 467 U.S. 837 (1984) – Court review of the reading of a statute by an administrative agency, so called "Chevron two-step test."

Ralf Poscher, University of Freiburg

DOI 10.1515/9781501504723-013

adjudication and scholarly work in different fields of the law. Carl Schmitt was right when he noted in his (1912: 6) dissertation on adjudication "that the cases of doubt are those which attract academic and practical interest [translation by the author]." Dealing with difficult cases is also what lawyers are trained to do. As H. L. A. Hart (1958: 615) observed: penumbral cases are the "daily diet of the law schools."

With adjudication being the center of law and hard cases the center of adjudication, it is even more disturbing that there is widespread disquiet about adjudication in hard cases in legal theory. To varying degrees, adjudication in hard cases is seen not as a legal, but rather as a non-legal, political, economic, moral or otherwise discretionary practice. Increasingly, the task of adjudication in hard cases is claimed to be the province of rival disciplines such as economics – as in law and economics[4] – or the political sciences – as in the growing industry of law and political studies[5].

This curious state of theoretical self-denial in which legal scholars relegate hard cases to other disciplines delivers the background for the following sketch of a theory of adjudication that attempts to reclaim hard cases for the law. It is subdivided into two major parts. The first part exposes the common assumption that leads theories of adjudication to abandon adjudication as a specifically legal enterprise in hard cases. It demonstrates that this common assumption is entrenched in a variety of different theories of adjudication and portrays them as different reactions to the shared assumption. In the second part a theory of adjudication is presented that refutes the common assumption, demonstrates why it is flawed, and returns the focus to the doctrinal work of courts and lawyers. The central thesis is that adjudication remains a specifically legal enterprise in a doctrinal sense even in hard cases, in which the law is indeterminate. This doctrinal theory of adjudication will be developed as a comprehensive theory of adjudication encompassing a theoretical foundation, a normative defense, and a test of empirical adequacy.

1.2 The common assumption

How did we get there? All major theories of adjudication share a common assumption. According to the common assumption, the indeterminacy of the law entails that a decision made under conditions of legal indeterminacy cannot be a legal decision. The argument for this assumption is simple and straightforward. If legal materials and legal methods do not determine the decision made in a given case, how can this decision still be a legal decision? If legal

---

[4] Early standard volumes include Posner (1972); Landes and Posner (1987); Katz (ed.) (1998).
[5] An excellent overview in Whittington, Kelemen, and Caldeira (eds.) (2010).

criteria are exhausted, a decision must be made with the help of other, non-legal, criteria. Adjudication in cases where the law is indeterminate is no longer considered a legal decision, but as the exercise of some kind of political, moral, economic or otherwise non-legal discretion.

It comes as no surprise that, given such an account of adjudication, other disciplines try to fill the gap. Accordingly, proposals by economists, public choice theorists, political scientists and philosophers abound to offer criteria to guide adjudication in hard cases. This would all be well and good, if hard cases were not central to adjudication. However, theories that give up on hard cases and consign them to other disciplines give up on the heart of the law and give it into hands in which it does not belong. Strange as it may seem, the common assumption, which gives up the 'proprium' of the law, is pervasive in theories of adjudication. Historically and currently there are three basic strategies for coping with the common assumption: the tactics of denial, radicalisation strategies and the mainstream approaches.

1.2.1 The tactics of denial

One strategy is the "tactics of denial." This branch of theories simply denies the existence of the problem by asserting an idea of the law as a seamless web of concepts, precedents, statutes and principles that holds a single right answer for each case.

Continental conceptual jurisprudence in the 19th century[6] and Anglo-American formalism[7] – at least in the stylized accounts given by their critics[8] – are the historic variants. Its modernized forms can be found in Ronald Dworkin's (1977: 81–130) "one right answer thesis" or Michael Moore's (1985) realist conception of the law, which provides a one right answer theory with a naturalist ontological backbone, and in theories of adjudication inspired by Jürgen Habermas' discourse theory – like Klaus Günther's (1993) appropriateness approach –, which deliver idealized and proceduralized versions of the idea (Engländer 2002: 147–151). These theories do not give up on the law. On the contrary, they claim that even in hard cases there is a single right answer. However, it can be shown that they share the common assumption: Adjudication would not be a legal enterprise were the law truly indeterminate, were there truly hard cases

---

6 See e.g. v. Jhering (1857); Puchta (1841, 1842, 1847).
7 For example Langdell (1871), esp. preface, pp. iii–v.
8 For Germany see Ogorek (1986); Haferkamp (2004, 2010). For the American discourse see Sebok (1998: 57–60); Tamanaha (2009).

for which the legal materials or at least the morally enriched legal materials did not hold a pre-existing single right answer to be discovered. The tactics of denial invest heavily in the 'one right answer' thesis to sidestep the problem that the law might really be indeterminate, in which case its proponents, too, would assume that a decision could no longer be a legal one.

The obvious problem for one right answer theories is their high implausibility to anyone familiar with legal practice and hard cases. Is there a single right answer for the tradeoffs between civil liberties and national security in times of terrorist threats? Sure, we can rule out some answers and some false alternatives, for which the encroachment on liberty can even be detrimental to our security. However, that there is only one single right answer in each detail of civil liberty cases brought to the fore seems – pace Hercules – highly implausible. If there is a single right answer to the admissibility of abortion, torture, stem cell research, death penalty and the like, why is disagreement so tenacious even though we share all the factual information that there is to be had and even though every thinkable legal and moral argument has already been made? Disagreements between lawyers and courts abound on most controversial issues of the law and – different from disagreements in the natural sciences – with no scientific evidence even conceivable that could give hope for their resolution.[9] In science there was disagreement over the existence of the Higgs boson, but scientists knew what kind of evidence it took to verify or at least falsify its existence; no such evidence is conceivable in the pro-life vs. pro-choice debate.

Theoretically these difficulties of one right answer theories are mirrored by the underdetermination of their mostly coherentist epistemologies[10] like Dworkin's interpretativism. They might provide a basis to refute radical skepticism and to show – to use one of Dworkin's (1996: 118) examples – that "torturing a baby for fun" is – objectively and really wrong, that the assertions expressing such uncontroversial moral insights have a justified claim to truth. The coherentist strategy, however, only goes so far. In hard cases different and diverging interpretations of the legal materials compete without coherentist epistemological resources to privilege one over the other. The limitations of interpretative theories of adjudication can explain the tenacity of our legal disagreements. The insight to be retained from these approaches, however, is their insistence on the specifically legal nature of legal controversies and decisions even in hard cases. By insisting on the legal quality of our disagreements in hard cases, they capture a feature of our legal practice that every viable theory of adjudication has to account for.

---

9 Cf. Waldron (1992: 176–178).
10 Cp. Stanford (2013).

1.2.2 Radicalizations

The second strategy for addressing the problem of indeterminacy and hard cases is the strategy of radicalisation. Theorists of this approach radicalize the idea that there can be no law in cases of legal indeterminacy by arguing that the law is not only indeterminate in exceptional cases, but is so all or at least most of the time. On the basis of the common assumption, this leads them to advance the thesis that law is not law, but politics, that law is not about justice, but about power, that adjudication is merely politics in disguise.

Historical variants of the radicalization strategy can be found in the Free Law Movement of the early 20th century in German legal thought,[11] the French so-called "Juristes Inquiets" of the same period, Scandinavian[12] and American Legal Realism (Llewellyn 1930), which relied heavily on its German and French predecessors (Herget and Wallace 1987). More recently the Critical Legal Studies Movement aligned itself with this tradition and gave it – at least partly – an even more radical spin (e.g. Kelman 1984), which drew on different analytical or post-modern skeptical views of language and meaning to give their claims philosophical support. The latest addition to this strategy are attempts to align legal theory with the larger trend in philosophy towards naturalism by "naturalizing" the law and especially adjudication (Leiter 2007). Very much in the tradition of legal realism, adjudication is not to be rationally reconstructed, but causally explained by socio-psychological theories.

Unlike the other two strategies, the radicals do not attempt to avoid the calamity caused by legal indeterminacy; they embrace it. They embrace it to expose the ideology of adjudication as a legal, a political enterprise.[13] The radical accounts – criticized even from within the Critical Legal Studies movement[14] – massively distort legal practice. Their obvious problem is that they cannot capture the specificity of our legal practices. The radical indeterminacy thesis is descriptively inadequate, since it is not able to give a meaningful account of the obvious not only institutional but also argumentative differences of our legal practices and politics. Worth preserving, however, is the insight that the application of

---

[11] Ehrlich (1903); excerpts translated in Ehrlich ([1903] 1917); for his foundational work on the sociology of law see Ehrlich (1962), translated by Walter A. Moll, with introduction by Roscoe Pound; Kantorowicz (1906); for an English account of his version of the Free Law Movement as contrasted against Legal Realism see Kantorowicz (1934); Fuchs (1929). See also Muscheler (1984); Moench (1971); Schmidt (1968).
[12] For an excellent comparative overview see Spaak (2009).
[13] For a radical account see e.g. Schlag (1985, 1988).
[14] See e.g. Kennedy (2001) (turning himself against exaggerations within the Critical Legal Studies Movement, often taken by counter-critique as an easy target).

the law is accompanied by a decision in the true sense of the word – as Carl Schmitt ([1934] 1985: 33) had already taken to be pervasive in and characteristic of adjudication. There is something to decide. Adjudication – in hard cases – is not just a cognitive act, but involves volition; it is not about finding a predetermined solution, but about deciding on one by applying the law.

1.2.3 The mainstream

The third strategy is the mainstream strategy, which does not fall for either of the two extremes: it accepts legal indeterminacy on the one hand, but does not throw out the baby with the bath water on the other. For the mainstream, law is indeterminate in some cases, but this does not render the entire practice of adjudication indeterminate. The most common variant of this strategy is the marginalization strategy.[15]

Hard cases are seen as rare cases against the background of myriads of legal transactions in which the law provides a determinate answer. The number of hard cases can be further reduced by canons of interpretation and legal forms of argument. The few genuinely hard cases that remain can be decided on non-legal grounds; they do not threaten the overall determinate practice. The mainstream tries to accommodate the insights of both competing theories by subdividing the law into the overwhelming number of cases for which a right answer can be argued for and the infinitesimally small number of truly hard cases, in which the law is not predetermined and a genuine, non-legal decision must be made.

Other variants of the mainstream approach are essentially similar, but are less timid about hard cases. They see hard cases as an especially suitable aspect of the law through which to introduce interdisciplinary standards into the law.[16] The gap left by the indeterminacy of the law is filled by economics, public choice theory, morality, neuroscience or whatever the fashionable discipline of the day happens to be.

A third variant of the mainstream takes hard cases out of adjudication altogether – at least for some fields of the law such as constitutional or administrative law. These authors attempt to split the law up into easy cases dealt with by the courts and hard cases dealt with by politics on its own terms or by administrative agencies according to their political discretion – sometimes even with institutional consequences (Whittington [1999] 2001).[17] For the US-American

---

15 For a recent explicit account of this often implicit mainstream strategy Leiter (2009).
16 For the German discussion in administrative law e.g. Appel (2008).
17 For German constitutional law cp. Jestaedt (1999: 363–378).

context of constitutional law Keith Whittington (2002) pleads for keeping hard cases out of the Supreme Court and leaving their resolution to the other political branches. In the German and the American discussion in administrative law there is a strong tendency to delegate the decision in cases of legal indeterminacy to the administrative bodies and take them away from the courts.[18]

It can easily be shown that all three mainstream variants rely on the common assumption that the law is inadequate in hard cases. They differ mainly in the effort expended on developing extra-legal standards or institutional solutions for the cases which they no longer consider legal.

The problem with this mainstream approach, however, is that it mistakes quantity for quality. As already stressed in the introduction, adjudication as both professional practice and academic discipline is all about the hard cases the mainstream tries to marginalize. These are the cases that require explanation. The only explanation the marginalization strategy has to offer draws on self-deception or even outright deceit. Lawyers who engage in a legal disagreement in hard cases act either under self-deception or in outright deceit of the public about the true political nature of their argument. In hard cases, in which the law runs out, there is no legal issue to disagree about. Where there is no law, there can be no disagreement about the law and no specifically legal decision. Judges have to exercise their political discretion to decide hard cases. They, however, dress up their political decisions in legal clothes to distract from the political power they exercise (Leiter 2009: 1247). Dworkin (1986: 37–38) had already criticized this explanation as highly implausible. "It is mysterious why the pretense should be necessary or how it could be successful [...] why should the profession fear to correct their error in the interests of a more honest judicial practice? [...] And if the pretense is so easily exposed, why bother with the charade?" The marginalisation strategy dismisses the heart of professional legal practice as a large-scale charade. The psychological or even ideological monstrosity of this claim is not an analytical argument against it – as little as atheism is defeated because people have built cathedrals and fought wars in god's name. However, the monstrosity of the marginalisation strategy has to be made explicit and should let us think twice. If there were an alternative to explain our legal practice in hard cases, the avoidance of monstrous claims should count in its explanatory favor.

---

18 Favoring an expansion of administrative discretion Schmidt-Aßmann ([2003] 2015: paras. 180–187a); for a critique of this tendency Poscher (2011). For the US-American discussion see Sunstein (2006a, 2006b); for two prominent readings of Chevron see Scalia (1989) and Breyer (1986).

1.2.4 The hidden legacy of formalism

All the accounts of adjudication discussed above share a certain perception of the relations between indeterminacy and adjudication. All these approaches assume that indeterminacy represents a threat to adjudication.[19] In a way, all theories of adjudication rest on a formalist foundation. According to formalism – as a construction of its critics, not necessarily as a historical phenomenon[20] –, adjudication aims at the discovery of a pre-determined answer to a legal question by means of legal materials, methods, canons and forms of argument, logic, and the like. If adjudication is understood in this way, indeterminacy is detrimental to law, since there would be no answer to discover. The three branches of theories of adjudication differ only in their presumptions regarding the extent to which the law can fulfill the formalist concept of adjudication, the extent to which the law can live up to what Hart (1977) called the "noble dream." They differ only in their degree of disappointment with the central formalist tenet and in the therapy they choose to handle their disenchantment. The one right answer theories stick to their guns. They are still true believers and keep their formalist faith against all the odds of pervasive and standing legal disagreements. Radical legal critique reacts with frustration and abandons adjudication in the face of radical indeterminacy claims. The mainstream is more moderate and applies different strategies to rein in indeterminacy and place it outside the law and, in some variants of the mainstream approach, even outside judicial institutions. Through all the critique, however, the central claim of formalism remains untouched: if there is to be adjudication it consists in the discovery of predetermined answers; legal indeterminacy and adjudication as specifically legal enterprise are mutually exclusive.

2 A doctrinal theory of adjudication

The theory of adjudication proposed in this essay rejects the common assumption as a widespread error. The common assumption is the common error that plagues the portrayed theories of adjudication. Contrary to the common assumption the doctrinal theory of adjudication to be proposed holds that adjudication remains a specifically legal enterprise even in cases of legal indeterminacy, even in hard cases for which the law holds no predetermined answer. It can be shown

---

[19] Cp. Kutz (1994: 1002–1003), who hints at the theoretical commonalities between the liberal mainstream and CLS-authors regarding the indeterminacy thesis and that they both implicitly rely on a one right answer thesis.
[20] For nuanced historical accounts see the references given in supra note 11.

how the creation of law in the process of adjudication is specifically legal in a doctrinal sense that it has to be defended in a realm of legal argumentation with a specific structure that sets law apart from other disciplines. The creation of law in the process of adjudication does not become mere politics, economics or moral reasoning or legislation. The proposed doctrinal theory of adjudication insists on the autonomy of the law even in cases of legal indeterminacy. As a comprehensive theory of adjudication, the doctrinal approach must be convincing on three different levels:

> first, its conception must be theoretically feasible;
>
> second, it must be normatively defensible;
>
> third, it must be descriptively adequate, if it does not want to formulate a mere ideal without any relation to and – as a consequence – effect on the actual practice of adjudication.

2.1 The theoretical claim

On a theoretical level the doctrinal theory of adjudication must challenge the common assumption. How can adjudication in cases of indeterminacy of the law still be a specifically legal enterprise? Were it true – as the common assumption would have it – that there can be no specifically legal decision in cases of legal indeterminacy, the doctrinal theory of adjudication would never get off the ground. However normatively attractive it might be to have a specifically legal way of deciding hard cases, if the common assumption were correct this would simply not be possible.

The doctrinal theory does not challenge the common assumption by endorsing another one-right-answer thesis. This approach would not only be unconvincing, but would also demonstrably share the common assumption that the doctrinal theory wishes to reject. The whole point of the doctrinal approach is its insistence on the specifically legal character of adjudication in cases for which there is no one right answer. Rather, the central argument rests on the assumption that, even though adjudication has to create law in hard cases, the conditions under which law is created in adjudication distances it from politics, economics and morality in a way that can give it a specifically legal, that is doctrinal, character. The doctrinal specificity of adjudication even in cases of legal indeterminacy follows from the interplay of the exigency to justify legal decisions also in hard cases and the specificities of legal argumentation in a specific sphere of legal meaning.[21]

---

[21] A similar but more sociologically inspired approach can be found in the concept of "legal work" of Duncan Kennedy (1986; 1997, 2001).

2.1.1 Legal decisions and their justification

In the legal context, decisions must be justified. This also holds true for hard cases, for which different lines of legal reasoning are available, justifying different legal decisions. Given the necessity of justifying a decision, even in a hard case, with legal arguments, the decision in a hard case is not only a decision to support of certain outcome, but also in support of a certain line of legal reasoning, a certain doctrinal position. Decisions in hard cases come alongside the baggage of the legal argumentation that supports it. One cannot have one without the other. We cannot endorse a decision, but fail to endorse a legal argument that supports it. The connection of decision and justification requires a commitment not only to the decision but also to the argumentation that supports it. This double commitment has weight not only because it links the decision to a specific line of argument, but also because the arguments the decision is linked to are again linked to other arguments in the sphere of legal argumentation, in which they are interconnected. Chaining a decision to a line of argument immerses it into a context of argumentation that entails far more commitments than the immediate link between the specific decision and its supporting argument. Via the argument that supports it the decision becomes inscribed into a specific sphere of argumentation, bringing with it a potentially unforeseeable number of argumentative commitments.

2.1.2 The legal sphere of argumentation

That decisions require justification and that decisions come with the baggage of their supporting arguments is not unique to legal decisions. This is true also of political and economic decisions as well as of moral choices. However, each of these different areas of discourse has its own sphere of argumentation, in which – as Max Weber describes it – "the 'meaning' of the conduct of the actors [must] be conceptually construed in order to produce an internally consistent conceptual construct of that 'meaning' [...] In other words, we are engaged in what could be called a 'dogmatics' of 'meaning'."[22] The legal sphere of argumentation has a specific content and a specific structure. A legal decision cannot be supported with an argument of party politics and a political decision cannot be supported with an argument from doctrinal history or elegance. Given the legal argumentative baggage that comes along with the decision, the choice to be made in a hard case is a specifically legal one. It is the connection between

---

22 Cf. Weber ([1907] 1977: 112).

the decision and a specific line of argument belonging to a specific sphere of argumentation that makes a decision specific to this sphere even though it is a real decision and not predetermined by – in case of the law – the legal materials. What counts as a specific legal argument or reason and how exactly the sphere of legal argumentation is structured is not only complex, but also in its details specific to a particular legal culture and a particular legal system and most likely even specific to different areas of the law within a particular legal system – the structure and content of the sphere of legal argumentation can vary between tax, tort and constitutional law. Nevertheless, even if the details of the legal sphere of argumentation are specific to each legal culture, there are some general structural elements that can be pointed at to make the claim about the specific structure and character of legal argumentation theoretically more plausible.

2.1.2.1 Time
First, on a very general level there is a specific orientation in time in legal argumentation. Legal arguments have a specific historical, backwards looking orientation. A legal decision has to be justified at least with some reference to the past.[23]

In a case law system the reference has to go to prior cases. The stare decisis rule is a direct emanation of the historical character of legal argumentation.[24] But also in continental legal systems, in which there is no formal rule of precedent, past judicial decisions play an important argumentative role. An argument which can rely on a precedent or at least give a conclusive interpretation of precedents makes a strong case; whereas an argument that does not consider precedents of higher courts or is out of step with them has a difficult stand no matter what are its other merits.

Another obvious aspect of the historical orientation of legal argumentation shows in the importance of legislative acts. It goes without saying that judicial decisions have to take legislative acts into account and are – at least in civil law systems – most often based on legislative acts. Legislative acts though designed to determine the future are from the perspective of the judicial decision acts of the past. The judicial decision has to be argued as one that is either determined or at least consistent with prior legislative decision.

As for the legal methods, historical arguments, and arguments involving the legislative process play an important role. According to the different kinds of

---
[23] Cp. Postema (2010: 52) pointing to the justification of legal decisions with regard to past decisions and actions of a community as the first distinctive feature of legal reasoning.
[24] For the importance of precedent in constitutional adjudication cp. Farber and Sherry (2008: 63–84).

originalism they are even supposed to have a dominant role (Calabresi [ed.] 2007). This does not mean that arguments with the future effects of a decision cannot be found in legal argumentation. They are, however, either linked to a historical perspective or have a kind of last resort, exceptional status averting obviously impractical results.[25] The effects of a certain decision can be introduced into the legal argumentation, not as such, however. To make a legal argument the effects have to be linked to the historic purpose of the precedent or statute or to the historic intention of the legislator. Even though arguments from the effects are directed at the future, they have to be connected to the past.

This historical perspective is very different from the political argumentation in executive or legislative institutions. At least in democracies almost the opposite holds true. The new government and the new parliamentary majority will rather pride themselves on discontinuity. They do not have to justify their politics by appeals to prior decisions of past governments and majorities, but are often elected because they promised to reverse prior decisions and break with them. This is completely different for the courts. New judges can deviate from prior decisions, too. If they do so, they, however, try to show how this shift is consistent with a so far overlooked interpretation of the prior decisions or how the change in the judicature is just unfolding what has been inherent in the precedents all along. Open reversals or overruling of prior decisions are exceptional and rare in judicial opinions. In contrast, political decisions are in the same way directed towards the future as judicial decisions are directed towards the past. It can help in a political context to show that a decision stands in the tradition of prior political decisions, but the standard it is going to be held accountable to is its future effects.

2.1.2.2 Rigidity of legal inferential commitments

Contemporary forms of philosophical pragmatism such as the one prominently developed by Robert Brandom build on the idea that our language and communicative practices in general are to be explained – at least also – by material inferences to which we commit ourselves and to which we are committed by asserting propositions. By stating a single proposition we commit ourselves to a whole series of propositions. To take some humdrum examples from Brandom: "A is to the West of B, so B is to the East of A; This monochromatic patch is green, so it is not red; Thunder now; so lighting earlier. Anyone committed to the premises of such inferences is committed thereby to the conclusions" (Brandom 1994: 168). The commitment entails that we can be legitimately expected and

---

[25] An aspect elaborated by Esser ([1970] 1972: 141), who stresses the "correctness control" (Richtigkeitskontrolle) excluding generally not acceptable practical results as an integral part of the legal argumentative practice.

asked to give reasons, i.e. to justify, the propositions to which we are committed. If we assert that there was thunder, we cannot only be expected to justify that there was thunder, but also why we did not see lightning. Mastering the different inferential relations connected with utterances is what differentiates understanding from just being able to deliver the appropriate sound waves. A parrot – so goes the well-worn example (Brandom 1994: 214) – does not understand an utterance even if he gives the right "answer" when he is asked his name or his favorite food, because he does not master the inferential commitments that come along with the proposition that one's name or favorite food is so and so. Whatever the merits of the wide-ranging aspirations of inferentialist theories of meaning, reference and reason, they make at least plausible that the material inferential structures of our communicative practices are part of the story. If this holds true, it follows that distinct inferential structures that are established for different areas of our communicative practice, can contribute to different spheres of meaning, reason and argumentation.

The law provides for such distinct inferential structures that establish a distinct sphere of legal meaning and argumentation. Unlike in other areas of discourse, in law inferential structures are laid out explicitly by legal rules. Law consists in large parts of explicitly establishing inferential relations, which lead to inferential commitments of those who assert legal propositions. This already happens at the level of individual legal rules. Their conditional structure establishes rigid inferential relation between different propositions. The assertion that some act is qualified as a crime commits due to an explicit legal rule to the inference that a certain punishment has to be adjudicated. In a moral context it might be possible to hold that something qualifies as bad without being committed to some specific reaction. Law, however, is all about establishing rigid inferential relations. It is not the least this rigidity that gives the doctrinal sphere of argumentation a specific character.

This specificity of the doctrinal sphere of argumentation becomes even more prominent by the fact that the rigid inferential relations explicitly established in law carry far beyond individual legal rules. Legal rules are part of an explicit network of rules, which explicitly state a whole network of inferential commitments. If someone is found insane, the law holds a wide range of explicitly and rigidly stated legal consequences ranging from criminal law to civil law to medical law to education law and so forth. This systematic rigidity of explicit inferential commitments in law is escalated further by the systematic rigidity of doctrinal positions and arguments on the different levels of legal argumentation. If a legal concept is defined in one context more often than not it will commit to that definition in other contexts as well. If the protection of free speech is considered to include commercial speech as well,[26] this holds independently of the products or services which are advertised: be it guns or diapers. There might be differences in the reasons justifying the intrusion upon free speech depending on the advertised products. Public safety concern might legitimate an encroachment upon free speech, which could justify limitations on advertisements for guns and not for diapers. The difference in justification of the intrusion would, however, not influence the conceptual stability of the free speech across different factual contexts. In a legal context it would hardly convince to judge advertisements as acts of free speech according to product lines.

Next to their systematic, synchronic side the inferential structure has an important diachronic aspect. In the inferentialist picture speakers have a deontic status defined by the inferential commitments and the respective justificatory obligations they have accumulated over time (Brandom 1994: 157–167). Drawing on David Lewis' metaphor of "Scorekeeping in a Language Game" (Lewis 1983) the accumulation of inferential commitments that amount to a deontic status has been described as a practice of inferential score keeping (Brandom 1994: 180–199). Like the umpires in a baseball game the participants of discursive practices keep score of their own but also of the inferential status of the other participants, which they have acquired by asserting or negating certain propositions.

Again in law also the diachronic inferential structures are specifically rigid because of certain features of our legal practices. Due to the historical orientation of the sphere of legal argumentation the prior assertion of legal propositions establishes strong commitments not only for justification, but also for future decisions and similar cases and legal issues. For an actual legal decision the deontic commitments work in both projections: the past and the future. On the one hand an actual decision will be held accountable to past legal decisions and the inferential commitments that were established; on the other hand making a legal decision will take into account not only the current case, but also how it will affect the deontic status in the future. Legal decisions and their supporting lines of arguments can anticipate the effects of a decision for future cases, in which the decision taken today will create consistency requirements for the future (Gerhardt 2005). Therefore, it comes as no surprise that Brandom illustrates his inferential model by the features of common law adjudication, which produces judge-made law. "But the contents the judges in this sense make is also constrained by what they find, the precedential applications of concepts (both immediate and inferential) whose authority the judges are subject to, at the

---

26 Cp. 113 S. Ct. 1505 (1993); 113 S. Ct. 1792 (1993); 113 S. Ct. 2696 (1993); German Constitutional Court, *Shock Advertisement*, BVerfGE 102, 347 (364).

same time that they inherit it and administer it" (Brandom 2002: 231). In hard constitutional cases a judge might favor politically a decision with advantage for the executive against the legislative branch, because his party is in government and he favors their policy on the issue at stake. However, the judge has to anticipate what kind of inferential commitment his decision and the legal argumentation with which he could support it would create. The consistency requirement of the doctrinal sphere of argumentation forces the adjudicator to generalize the argumentation. In the example he is forced to think about the meaning of the doctrinal argument in favor of the executive in cases where his own party is in the opposition and other issues are at stake. The consistency requirements in the doctrinal sphere of argumentation stand in the way of decisions based on political preferences – even if the constitutional case is a hard one and has no predetermined answer.

A further feature of the law that strengthens the diachronic dimension of the legal scorekeeping lies in the written form and public availability of not only the legal decisions of courts but also of their supporting argumentations. In other areas of our discursive practices the deontic status might be much more ephemeral not the least due to the fact that many assertions will be forgotten or the memory of them becomes imprecise, that they can be contested more easily, etc. In law processes like these are much more unlikely. Legal decisions and the argumentation that supports them are in the law reports to stay. The anticipation of the public record will further lead to a very conscious crafting of opinions and this in a self-reinforcing cycle will lead to more consciously defined legal positions and arguments thus strengthening the inferential structure of the doctrinal sphere of argumentation.

It cannot be stressed enough that the inferential structure of the law does not so much thrive on the decisions taken, but on the arguments that have been laid out to support them. The consistency is not so much a consistency of outcomes but a consistency of argumentation. Judicial decisions on labor law issues do not have to come out consistently, either in favor of workers or in favor of employers. On the contrary, a consistency in political outcome would be suspicious. What has to be consistent is the doctrinal argumentation with which decisions that are not consistent in outcome are supported. The historical perspective of the law leads to a consistency requirement for legal argumentation that is pervasive. If an argumentation is not consistent with prior line of argument it creates at least a problem. This relation of the outcome of decisions and the argumentation that supports it is again different in politics than in law. For politics it is rather the consistency of outcome, which is important. If labor representatives consistently vote for outcomes that favor working class interests, they will not get in electoral trouble just because their argumentation on the different issues is not always consistent. They, however, will not be able to talk themselves out of trouble if they vote for an unfavorable outcome just by pointing out that they have a well-crafted, consistent argument for it.

The rigidity of the inferential structure in the doctrinal sphere of argumentation is reinforced by but not identical with path dependency effects. Path dependency in a most general sense is sometimes stated as the idea "that where we go next depends not only on where we are now, but also upon where we have been. History matters" (Liebowitz and Margolis 2000: 981). As a theoretical concept it borrows from chaos or complexity theory and evolutionary biology which both show that the development of a process is sensitive to the initial conditions and that seemingly minute changes in the initial conditions can have large-scale effects. The concept is prominently employed in economics in which it has a descriptive and a – contested – critical role for describing market inefficiencies caused by lock-in effects due to initial choice which lead to stabilized inefficient outcomes. The QWERTY keyboard was – according to some – deliberately designed to slow down typists and is supposed to be inferior to the Dvorak keyboard, but nevertheless became and remains our standard keyboard due to its early implementation and especially the training costs associated with it (Liebowitz and Margolis 1990). Analytically path dependency links an initial state with a future limitation of alternatives via a *causal* mechanism (Hathaway 2001: 604; Solum 2008: 313). The initial choice of the keyboard type leads to a future situation in which keyboard producers are confronted with a market in which producers, retailers, instructors and consumers have adapted to a specific keyboard design. The causal mechanism consists for a large part in the training and adaption efforts that are needed to master a keyboard, which are prohibitive for changing keyboard types.

In the same way path dependency effects have been described for the law. The role of precedents can be described from a path dependency perspective. Precedents limit later decision alternatives not only via inferential commitments but also via causal mechanisms. The causal mechanisms at work can include the teachability and reliability of the law and the explosion of the workload of courts (Hathaway 2001: 626) if they were to consider every legal issue anew. The effects are reinforced by the anticipations of litigants who will refrain from bringing cases to the fore for which there are strong precedents even if their diverging account of the law might have been an option in the past (Hathaway 2000: 628). Notwithstanding these interconnections, the inferential rational structure of the doctrinal sphere of argumentation has to be kept apart from causal mechanisms that lead to path dependencies.

2.1.2.3 Specific arguments

The sphere of legal argumentation is further determined by a set of arguments which is specific to the law. On the one side there are arguments specific to the doctrinal context of the law, which cannot be used in other areas of discourse. Only in the legal sphere of argumentation do arguments from the doctrinal tradition, precedents, and doctrinal consistency play a role. In a political or moral discussion doctrinal arguments are inappropriate. In a political discussion on the extension of consumer or environmental protection, or on tax benefits an argument from the doctrinal history of the subject would only bewilder friends and foes.

On the other side the legal sphere of argumentation excludes certain arguments from entering a legal debate. This is most obvious for substantial or strategic arguments from party or day-to-day politics. But it also holds for advancing a special professional, regional, political, etc. interest group, which can be a legitimate argument in the political discourse. If a special interest argument cannot be connected to the legislative intent or the purpose of a statute and be transformed into a specifically legal argument, it cannot be introduced into the legal sphere of argumentation.

This does not mean that there is no overlap between legal arguments and arguments of other spheres of discourse. However, arguments of other spheres of discourse have to be translated and integrated into the law in specific ways and not all arguments can be integrated, some are excluded. Whether arguments out of other spheres of discourse can be integrated into the law depends solely on the legal materials and the methodical standards of a specific legal culture. The general debate about the merits and defensibility of the death penalty might be informative to the legal debate. But inside the law the question has to be answered under very different conditions. In Germany the death penalty is an easy case. The German constitution provides an explicit ban.[27] Neither is a moral or empirical argument needed to defend the ban, nor can it be overcome by moral arguments or empirical data in favor of the death penalty.

The specificity of the legal debate, however, holds for hard cases, too. Under the United States Constitution the constitutionality of the death penalty is a hard case. It has to be decided by an interpretation of the 8th Amendment's "Cruel and unusual punishment"-clause. Whether recent empirical data can matter,[28] depends on whether one sides with some kind of originalism or rather with a living constitution type of interpretation – questions and positions irrelevant for any moral or political discourse.

---

[27] Art. 102 of the German Constitution.
[28] Sunstein and Vermeule (2005) (with further references at 706, 710–716).

The different canons of interpretation, the precedents, the legal texts, the different legal forms of argumentation of a particular legal tradition demand a transformation of arguments of other discourses into legal ones. In this respect, law has a King Midas kind of quality: every issue that can be discussed in many other discourses becomes a specifically legal issue if it becomes a matter of law.[29] To integrate arguments from other areas of discourse into the legal sphere of argumentation is a specific task for lawyers, which cannot be taken over by philosophers, economists or political scientists. This explains why even in hard cases, which deal with morally, economically or politically contested issues, judges and lawyers and not moral philosophers, economists or political scientists are called upon to argue and decide.

Historically the legal sphere of argumentation is not necessarily connected to the law. The legal sphere of argumentation is not a conceptual feature of the law, but a cultural accomplishment, which took centuries to develop. The development of the law as a distinct social practice has been a gradual process. This process included the development of a specific set of institutions, but also the development of a specific system of doctrinal legal meaning.[30] The discreteness of legal institutions and a specific sphere of legal argumentation show in the differences between the ancient Greek and Roman law taken as ideal types. The Greek legal system knew courts as legal institutions and certain legal procedures, but legal argumentation was still undifferentiated from general rhetoric also used at other occasions of deliberation.[31] It was only at the dawn of the classical period of the Roman law that specifically legal arguments and a specifically legal sphere of argumentation started to develop.[32] This process of social differentiation led not only to an autonomy of the legal institutions, but also to an autonomy of the legal system of meaning that determines the validity and quality of the argumentative moves in and around the institutions of the law.[33] At least in developed legal systems, such as the ones western civilisations have brought about, the complexity of the institutions and the legal material

---

[29] Cp. for legal concepts Poscher (2009).
[30] For the distinction between law as a doctrinal system of meaning and a system of social action, which receives its identity from its orientation at the doctrinal system of meaning, see Weber (1977: 112, 116–125).
[31] According to Jones (1956: 300–304) with only sparse evidence of specific training in legal rhetoric.
[32] For the Roman Law see Frier (1985: 184–196), describing how a specific legal thinking slowly started to establish itself during the first century B.C. within the Roman legal institutions; see also Fögen (2003: esp. 82–88), linking the autonomous character of the Roman Law especially to its written and secular form.
[33] For a detailed sociological description of the modern law as an autopoietic system see Luhmann (2004).

these institutions have produced, have reached a level at which arguments of other discourses cannot be introduced as such into the law. Even though this autonomy of legal meaning is contingent in the long historical perspective of social differentiation, it is a defining feature of developed legal systems in functionally differentiated societies.

2.1.3 Legal decisions of hard cases

The interplay of decision and justification within a specific sphere of legal argumentation explains why decisions remain specifically legal decisions even in cases in which the law is indeterminate.

First, even if the law is indeterminate the legal sphere of argumentation does not allow for every possible decision, because not every – politically or morally – defensible decision can be supported by a doctrinally valid line of argument. At the beginning of its jurisdiction the German Federal Constitutional Court was faced with the question, if and if so how fundamental rights affect relations between citizens.[34] The legal materials on the question were inconclusive, some historical and textual evidence pointing in this, some in that direction with diverging lines of precedents in different courts in the background. But even though the law was indeterminate on the question, the court could not have decided on just any kind of state action doctrine. It could e.g. not have decided on a binding force of fundamental rights only for employers and landlords, even though such a selective approach could have very well been supported by any left leaning political party. Even though the law was indeterminate this answer would have been excluded because the legal materials would not have allowed a valid line of legal argumentation to support such a selective position.

Second, even the choice between multiple valid lines of legal argumentation in a hard case does not have to be guided by extralegal considerations or criteria. Multiple lines of argument that lead to diverging results might be open in general but not for the court that has to decide on the case because of prior decisions and the consistency requirements of the legal sphere of argumentation. In German constitutional law there are serious arguments not to consider the guarantee of human dignity in the German constitution as a fundamental claim right on its own, but merely as an objective principle of constitutional law guiding the interpretation of the more specific fundamental rights (Enders 1997: 377–425, 501–509) that does not transfer into an absolute, untouchable subjective

---

34 German Constitutional Court, *Lüth*, BVerfGE 7, 198.

right. However, after the Federal Constitutional Court had considered it in its early standing rulings as a fundamental right, it could not retreat from this position when it had to consider a law allowing the shooting down of high-jacked airplanes[35] – even if it would have liked to reject the case on the objective account.

Third, even without such limiting precedents the decision must not be guided by extra-legal criteria. The specific sphere of argumentation gives room for professional standards, commitments and preferences that weigh against an immediate outcome orientation in a specific case. As people have political, economic or moral preferences they also develop professional or in the case of law methodical and doctrinal preferences.[36] These preferences can be found on various levels of abstraction: they can comprise a more formal or substantial understanding of the law; they can be methodical like in the case of originalists of the various brands or they can be more substantial like in the case of a more federalist or more centrist understanding of the US or German constitution. All of these dispositions are specific to the legal sphere of argumentation. None of these dispositions is contrary to the law. All of them are compatible with the legal norms whose application they influence. All of them come to bear if a decision has to be made between competing lines of argument in a hard case that involves the principles, methods and values that are addressed by the doctrinal preferences. But since they differ for different participants they only guarantee the legal – in the sense of doctrinal – character of the decision, not that there is a single right one.

Fourth, even in cases of indeterminacy in which neither the limitations of the doctrinal sphere of argumentation nor prior decisions nor doctrinal preferences distinguish one of the possible options the decision will remain a specifically legal decision, because it will be a decision within the legal sphere of argumentation with its genuine inferential commitments and path dependencies. As seen in the above example of the judge with party politics inclinations in a constitutional case on executive rights, the political inclinations and the doctrinal consequences do not have to map. A decision that conforms to the immediate political inclinations can bear doctrinal consequences that counter these inclinations because of its future effects.

What holds true in a diachronic perspective holds true in a synchronic perspective as well: The legal argument might commit to an argument in different

---

[35] German Constitutional Court, *Aviation Security Act*, BVerfGE 115, 118.
[36] Cp. Kim (2007: 384), contrasting legal preferences to political preferences; Shapiro (2007: 42), on *Tennessee Valley Authority v. Hill*, 437 U.S. 153 (1978), arguing that Justice Burger might have had "a bigger fish to fry" than the snaildarter against the 100-million-dollar project, namely the protection of a more literal standard of legal interpretation.

cases in other areas of the law that do not map in the political sphere. Under the German constitution such diverse areas of the law as national security regulations and reproductive medicine are linked via the constitutional protection of human dignity. After the Federal Constitutional Court construed the guarantee of human dignity as an absolute right in abortion cases,[37] it was forced to stick to its absoluteness in national security issues as well.[38] The doctrinal position on the guarantee of human dignity cuts both ways. Telling in this respect was also a candidacy for the German Federal Constitutional Court supported by the Social Democrats that was effectively opposed by the Christian Democrats, because the candidate suggested that the protection of human dignity might be open for balancing considerations in national security cases (Dreier 2004: para. 133). The Christian Democrats did not oppose him because of these national security considerations, which would be even closer to the agenda of at least some of their politicians, but because of the effects it would have in the area of reproductive medicine and stem cell research (Stolleis 2008). While national security and stem cell research are distinct areas of the political discourse, which allow for non-interdependent political positions, they are linked by the constitutional provision on human dignity and its doctrinal development in the legal sphere.

The special doctrinal structure of the legal sphere of argumentation is distinct from the political or economic sphere of argumentation. It establishes a certain distance between legal arguments and the choice between those arguments and political or economic convictions. This prevents even in hard cases political preferences always being able to be translated one to one into legal ones, in spite of the fact that the decision in hard cases is not legally predetermined. On the other hand it does not exclude that sometimes the choice for a certain legal argument corresponds with a certain political, economic, religious or moral preference, but that this is not necessarily so, showing that even in hard cases specifically legal decisions are possible. Modern legal systems have developed a specific legal sphere of argumentation that allows for specifically legal decisions not only in applying the law in easy cases, but also in developing the law in hard cases.

2.2 The normative claim – justice as impartiality

Why would we do this? Why would we install an institutional system with a system of meaning of its own, besides politics, economics etc. with the risk of

---

[37] German Constitutional Court, *Abortion I*, BVerfGE 39, 1; *Abortion II*, BVerfGE 88, 203.
[38] German Constitutional Court, *Aviation Security Act*, BVerfGE 115, 118.

producing decisions that are politically controversial, economically deficient, etc.? The normative case for this doctrinal approach to adjudication rests on two interconnected arguments: one from justice and one from social differentiation.

The argument from justice relies on the importance of justice as impartiality. Impartiality is constitutive for adjudication not only symbolically, but also in substance. Partial adjudication is an oxymoron. In easy cases, impartiality is established flawlessly by the priority of the norms that govern the case at hand. In easy cases, the legal materials pre-determine the answer to a legal question evoked by a social conflict. Since the law and the right answer to the question raised by the issue were established at a time prior to the case, they cannot be partial with respect to the one or the other of the parties involved in the conflict at hand.[39] In easy cases, the impartiality of adjudication is self-executing if the norms are applied. In easy cases impartiality comes for free. In cases for which the law is indeterminate, the self-executing mechanism that guarantees impartiality in easy cases fails. Impartiality must be guaranteed in a different way.

Impartiality is based on distance. Impartial decisions are decisions in which the decision-maker maintains a distance from the immediate economic, political or moral interest of the concrete parties. By establishing a specifically legal sphere of argumentation with its own doctrinal structures, the law is able to establish such a distance even in cases in which the law is indeterminate and in which impartiality cannot be self-executing like in easy cases. The distance created by the specifically doctrinal approach to open legal questions is the specific form of impartiality that the law has to offer in hard cases. It is not perfect impartiality like in easy cases, but it is the impartiality achievable for hard ones.

Beyond its importance for the procedural justification of a legal decision in the concrete case at hand, the distance created by the legal sphere of argumentation bears on a more general feature of modern societies. The distance the specifically legal sphere of argumentation creates is also a distance to the substantial, non-legal conflicts brought to the fore. People do not have legal disputes. People have disputes about political, economic, moral, personal relation issues and the like. They fight over who gets the children, who has to pay for a damage, whether abortion is to be morally or religiously contested, etc. The substantive conflicts people have are not about the law; they are only transformed

---

[39] Impartiality of adjudication does not exclude a different kind of partiality, the possible partiality of the legislator, who designed the applicable law, with regard to certain group interests. In easy cases judicial impartiality is concerned with the impartial application of the law, not with the impartiality of the law that is to be applied.

by the legal system into legal conflicts. This leaves the underlying substantial issues still open for further discussion. Even if a Supreme Court rules on the constitutional admissibility of abortion, stem cell research, assisted suicide, an environmental or economic regulatory issue, etc., the political, moral, environmental or economic question is still open. The courts only decide on the legal issue within a legal sphere of argumentation. Their doctrinal decisions keep their distance from the substantial, real-world, non-legal issues that lie at the bottom of the legal conflict.

The specificity of the legal sphere of argumentation thus allows the legal system to decide cases authoritatively without deciding on the underlying substantial issues. The legal sphere of argumentation thus combines authoritative decision making with persisting substantive discursive openness. Even if the courts have decided on abortion, they have not decided the moral question; even if the courts have decided on some environmental regulatory policy, they have not decided the issue of global warming and not on some economic theory in the case of economic regulations. The non-legal, substantial discussions are kept open, the public, scientific or academic discussions can continue even though the courts have rendered an authoritative legal decision.

Before the background of theories of social differentiation (Durkheim [1893] 1997; Luhmann 1977) it is a fair guess that modern societies developed a legal system with a specifically legal sphere of argumentation to stay more flexible and retain a greater amount of plasticity[40] despite the need for authoritative decisions of concrete conflicts. The legal sphere of argumentation allows societies to keep the substantive discussions going at multiple levels and thus to stay open for revisions, for new challenges and knowledge. The specific sphere of legal argumentation thus contributes to the flexibility, plasticity, intellectual vitality and viability of modern societies despite their permanent and even increasing need for authoritative decisions.

2.3 The empirical claim – crunching numbers

Besides its analytical and normative aims, the doctrinal theory of adjudication also attempts to explain something about the reality of adjudication. It claims that we are better able to understand what actually happens in adjudication when we see it through the lens of the doctrinal theory. This does not mean that adjudication always follows the model of the doctrinal theory. The doctrinal theory is not undermined by cases in which judges do not take the requirements of doctrinal argumentation seriously – even if there were many such cases. It is

---

40 Cp. the idea of social plasticity (Unger 1987: 139–140).

in part a normative theory and as such always in potential conflict with reality. However, it would be a less interesting theory were it defeated all the time, and did not provide a plausible general account of the practice of adjudication on the ground. A doctrinal theory of adjudication has to confront the empirical data on adjudication, which has been amassed especially on the US-American federal court system. However, all these empirical findings fall within the range of what should be expected on the basis of a doctrinal theory of adjudication.

Political attitudes do influence judicial decision-making. Conservative judges lean towards doctrinal positions that in general tend to promote conservative outcomes and liberal judges lean towards doctrinal positions that tend to promote liberal outcomes (Tamanaha 2009: 139–141). This explains the overall 7% variance (Carp and Rowland 1983: chapter 7) and the higher 44% variance in ideologically contested areas of the law (Cox and Miles 2008: 24). Yet, even in the politically most contested areas of the law the outcomes do not simply map the political preferences of judges in each individual case. Political preferences and doctrinal outcome do not match in numerous cases. The doctrinal theory of adjudication can explain why, in the overwhelming number of all hard cases in ideologically contested areas of the law, courts deliver unanimous decisions. This fact would be difficult to explain if the common assumption were true, that deciding hard cases is a matter of personal politics or morality.[41] The statistical material underlines Dworkin's (1986: 38) well-worn argument, that conceptionalizing hard cases by relying on political discretion cannot explain why judges often decide manifestly against their policy conviction, like Justice Burger in his majority opinion in *TVA v. Hill*, in which he opted for a literal reading of the Species Act of 1973 admitting that it would lead to an $ 100 million dollar waste of public funds without any public benefit worth considering.[42]

A doctrinal theory of adjudication can provide a theoretically feasible, normatively attractive and empirically adequate account of legal decisions and discussions of hard cases which are central to the legal practice in modern legal systems. It builds on a specifically legal sphere of argumentation, which is not conceptually linked to the law and does not necessarily accompany the establishment of legal institutions. The development of a specific legal sphere of argumentation is a cultural development on its own. It is only established through the doctrinal work of courts, lawyers and legal academics, which presupposes and depends on the independence of the legal institutions, but does not follow from their establishment alone. The sphere of legal argumentation is

---

[41] For an illuminating critique of the field see Tamanaha (2009: chapters 7, 8).
[42] On Dworkin's argument Shapiro (2007: 39).

an accomplishment of a legal culture that comes in degrees; it can be gained, but also lost. If, however, it is developed to some substantial degree, it creates a space between the law and other areas of discourse, which allows for specifically legal decisions even in hard cases, in which the law is indeterminate.

References

Appel, Ivo. 2008. Das Verwaltungsrecht zwischen traditionellem dogmatischen Verständnis und dem Anspruch einer Steuerungswissenschaft. *Veröffentlichungen der Vereinigung der Deutschen Staatsrechtslehrer* 67. 226–285.
Brandom, Robert B. 1994. *Making it explicit: Reasoning representing and discursive commitment*. Cambridge, MA: Harvard University Press.
Brandom, Robert B. 2002. Some pragmatist themes in Hegel's idealism. In Robert B. Brandom, *Tales of the mighty dead: Historical essays in the metaphysics of intentionality*, 210–234. Cambridge, MA: Harvard University Press.
Breyer, Stephen. 1986. Judicial review of questions of law and policy. *Administrative Law Review* 38. 363–398.
Calabresi, Steven G. (ed.). 2007. *Originalism: A quarter century of debate*. Washington, D.C.: Regnery Publishing.
Carp, A. Robert & C. K. Rowland. 1983. *Policymaking and politics in the federal district courts*. Knoxville, TN: University of Tennessee Press.
Cox, Adam B. & Thomas J. Miles. 2008. Judging the Voting Rights Act. *Columbia Law Review* 108. 1–54.
Dreier, Horst. 2004. Art. 1 Abs. 1. In Horst Dreier (ed.), *Grundgesetzkommentar* (2nd edn.). Tübingen: Mohr Siebeck.
Durkheim, Emile. 1997. *The division of labor in society*. New York: Free Press.
Dworkin, Ronald. 1977. *Taking rights seriously*. Cambridge, MA: Harvard University Press.
Dworkin, Ronald. 1986. *Law's Empire*. Cambridge, MA: Harvard University Press.
Dworkin, Ronald. 1996. Objectivity and truth: You'd better believe it. *Philosophy and Public Affairs* 25. 87–139.
Ehrlich, Eugen. 1903. *Freie Rechtsfindung und freie Rechtswissenschaft*. Leipzig: C. L. Hirschfeld.
Ehrlich, Eugen. 1917. Judicial freedom of decision: its principles and objects. In Association of the American Law Schools (ed.), *The Science of legal method: Select essays by various authors*, 47–84. Boston: The Boston Book Company.
Ehrlich, Eugen. 1962. *Fundamental principles of the sociology of law*. New York: Russell & Russell.
Enders, Christoph. 1997. *Die Menschenwürde in der Verfassungsordnung: Zur Dogmatik des Art. 1 GG*. Tübingen: Mohr Siebeck.
Engländer, Armin. 2002. *Diskurs als Rechtsquelle? Zur Kritik der Diskurstheorie des Rechts*. Tübingen: Mohr Siebeck.
Esser, Josef. 1972. *Vorverständnis und Methodenwahl in der Rechtsfindung* (2nd edn.). Frankfurt am Main: Athenaeum.
Farber, Daniel A. & Suzanna Sherry. 2008. *Judgement calls: Principle and politics in constitutional law*. Oxford: Oxford University Press.

Fögen, Marie T. 2003. *Römische Rechtsgeschichten: Über Ursprung und Evolution eines sozialen Systems*. Göttingen: Vandenhoeck & Ruprecht.
Frier, Bruce W. 1985. *The rise of the Roman jurists: Studies in Cicero's "Pro Caecina."* Princeton: Princeton University Press.
Fuchs, Ernst. 1929. *Was will die Freirechtsschule?* Rudolstadt: Greifenverlag.
Gerhardt, Michael J. 2005. The limited path dependency of precedent. *University of Pennsylvania Journal of Constitutional Law* 7. 903–1000.
Günther, Klaus. 1993. *The sense of appropriateness: Application discourses in morality and law*. Albany, NY: SUNY Press.
Haferkamp, Hans-Peter. 2004. *Georg Friedrich Puchta und die "Begriffsjurisprudenz."* Frankfurt am Main: Klostermann.
Haferkamp, Hans-Peter. 2010. Die sogenannte Begriffsjurisprudenz im 19. Jahrhundert – „reines" Recht? In Otto Depenheuer (ed.), *Reinheit des Rechts: Kategorisches Prinzip oder regulative Idee?*, 79–99. Wiesbaden: VS Verlag für Sozialwissenschaften.
Hart, Herbert L. A. 1958. Positivism and the separation of law and morals. *Harvard Law Review* 71. 593–629.
Hart, Herbert L. A. 1977. American jurisprudence through English eyes: The nightmare and the noble dream. *Georgia Law Review* 11. 969–989.
Hathaway, Oona A. 2001. Path dependence in the law: The course and pattern of legal change in a common law system. *Iowa Law Review* 86. 601–665.
Herget, James E. & Stephen Wallace. 1987. The German free law movement as the source of American legal realism. *Virginia Law Review* 73. 399–455.
Jestaedt, Matthias. 1999. *Grundrechtsentfaltung im Gesetz: Studien zur Interdependenz von Grundrechtsdogmatik und Rechtsgewinnungstheorie*. Tübingen: Mohr Siebeck.
v. Jhering, Rudolf. 1857. Unsere Aufgabe. *Jahrbücher für die Dogmatik des heutigen römischen und deutschen Privatrechts* 1. 1–52.
Jones, John W. 1956. *The law and legal theory of the Greeks*. Oxford: Clarendon.
Kantorowicz, Hermann. 1906. *Der Kampf um die Rechtswissenschaft*. Heidelberg: Winter.
Kantorowicz, Hermann. 1934. Some rationalism about realism. *Yale Law Journal* 43. 1240–1253.
Katz, Avery W. (ed.). 1998. *Foundations of the economic approach to law*. New York: Foundation Press.
Kelman, M. G. 1984. Trashing. *Stanford Law Review* 36, 293–348.
Kennedy, Duncan. 1986. Freedom and constraint in adjudication: A critical phenomenology. *Journal of Legal Education* 36. 518–562.
Kennedy, Duncan. 1997. *A critique of adjudication: Fin de siècle*. Cambridge: Harvard University Press.
Kennedy, Duncan. 2001. A semiotics of critique. *Cardozo Law Review* 22. 1147–1190.
Kim, Pauline T. 2007. Lower court discretion. *New York University Law Review* 82. 383–442.
Kutz, Christopher L. 1994. Just disagreement: Indeterminacy and rationality in the rule of law. *Yale Law Journal* 103. 997–1030.
Landes, William & Richard A. Posner. 1987. *The economic structure of tort law*. Cambridge, MA: Harvard University Press.
Langdell, Christopher C. 1871. *Selection of cases on the law of contracts*. Boston: Little, Brown.
Leiter, Brian. 2007. *Naturalizing jurisprudence: Essays on American legal realism and naturalism in legal philosophy*. Oxford: Oxford University Press.
Leiter, Brian. 2009. Explaining theoretical disagreement. *University of Chicago Law Review* 76. 1215–1250.

Lewis, Davis. 1983. Scorekeeping in a language game. In David Lewis, *Philosophical Papers*, vol. 1, 233–249. Oxford: Oxford University Press.
Liebowitz, Stan J. & Stephen E. Margolis. 1990. The fable of the two keys. *Journal of Law and Economics* 33. 1–25.
Liebowitz, Stan J. & Stephen E. Margolis. 2000. 'Pathdependency'. In Boudewijn Bouckaert & Gerrit de Geest (eds.), *Encyclopedia of law and economics*. 981–998. Cheltenham, UK: Edward Elgar.
Llewellyn, Karl. 1930. A realistic jurisprudence – The next step. *Columbia Law Review* 30. 431–465.
Luhmann, Niklas. 1977. Differentiation of society. *The Canadian Journal of Sociology* 2. 29–53.
Luhmann, Niklas. 2004. *Law as a social system*. New York: Oxford University Press.
Moench, Dietmar. 1971. *Die methodologischen Bestrebungen der Freirechtsbewegung auf dem Wege zur Methodenlehre der Gegenwart*. Frankfurt am Main: Athenaeum.
Moore, Michael. 1985. A natural law theory of interpretation. *Southern California Law Review* 58. 277–398.
Muscheler, Karlheinz. 1984. *Relativismus und Freirecht: Ein Versuch über Hermann Kantorowicz*. Heidelberg: Mueller.
Ogorek, Regina. 1986. *Richterkönig oder Subsumtionsautomat? Zur Justiztheorie im 19. Jahrhundert*. Frankfurt am Main: Klostermann.
Poscher, Ralf. 2009. The hand of Midas: When concepts turn legal, or deflating the Hart-Dworkin debate. In Jaap C. Hage & Dietmar v. d. Pfordten (eds.), *Concepts in law*, 99–116. Dordrecht: Springer.
Poscher, Ralf. 2011. Geteilte Missverständnisse: Theorien der Rechtsanwendung und des Beurteilungsspielraums der Verwaltung: Zugleich eine Kritik der normativen Ermächtigungslehre. In Ivo Appel, Georg Hermes & Christoph Schönenberger (eds.), *Öffentliches Recht im offenen Staat: Festschrift für Rainer Wahl zum 70. Geburtstag*, 527–551. Berlin: Duncker & Humblot.
Posner, Richard A. 1972. *Economic analysis of law*. Boston: Little, Brown.
Postema, Gerald J. 2010. Law's ethos: Reflections on a public practice of illegality. *Boston University Law Review* 90. 1847–1868.
Puchta, Georg F. 1841, 1842, 1847. *Cursus der Institutionen* (vol. 1, 2 & 3). Leipzig: Breitkopf & Härtel.
Scalia, Antonin. 1989. Judicial deference to administrative interpretations of law. *Duke Law Journal* 1989. 511–521.
Schlag, Pierre. 1985. Rules and standards. *UCLA Law Review* 33. 379–430.
Schlag, Pierre. 1988. Cannibal moves: An essay on the metamorphoses of the legal distinction. *Stanford Law Review* 40. 929–972.
Schmidt, Joachim. 1968. *Das „Prinzipielle" in der Freirechtsbewegung: Studie zum Frei-Recht, seiner Methode und seiner Quelle*. Bonn: Bouvier.
Schmidt-Aßmann, Eberhard. 2015. Art. 19 IV. In Theodor Maunz, Günter Dürig, Roman Herzog, Hans Klein, Udo Di Fabio, Paul Kirchhof, Hans-Jürgen Papier & Ferdinand Kirchhof (eds.), *Grundgesetzkommentar* (76th edn.). München: C. H. Beck.
Schmitt, Carl. 1912. *Gesetz und Urteil*. Berlin: Liebmann.
Schmitt, Carl. 1985. *Political theology: Four chapters on the concept of sovereignty*. Cambridge, MA: The MIT Press.
Sebok, Anthony J. 1998. *Legal positivism in American jurisprudence*. Cambridge: Cambridge University Press.

Shapiro, Scott J. 2007. The "Hart-Dworkin" debate: A short guide for the perplexed. In Arthur Ripstein (ed.), *Ronald Dworkin*, 22–55. Cambridge: Cambridge University Press.

Solum, Lawrence B. 2008. Constitutional possibilities. *Indiana Law Journal* 83. 307–337.

Spaak, Torben. 2009. Naturalism in Scandinavian and American realism: Similarities and differences. In Matthias Dahlberg (ed.), *Uppsala-Minnesota Colloquium: Law, culture and values*, 33–83. Uppsala: Iustus.

Stanford, Kyle. 2013. Underdetermination of scientific theory. In Edward N. Zalta (ed.), *The Stanford Encyclopedia of Philosophy*. http://plato.stanford.edu/entries/scientific-underdetermination/ (accessed 7 July 2016).

Stolleis, Michael. 2008. Konzertierter Rufmord: Die Kampagne gegen Horst Dreier. *Merkur* 62(8). 717–720.

Sunstein, Cass. 2006a. Beyond Marbury: The executive's power to say what the law is. *Yale Law Journal* 115. 2580–2610.

Sunstein, Cass. 2006b. Chevron step zero. *Virginia Law Review* 92. 187–250.

Sunstein, Cass & Adrian Vermeule. 2005. Is capital punishment morally required? The relevance of life-life tradeoffs. *Stanford Law Review* 58. 703–750.

Tamanaha, Brian Z. 2009. Beyond the formalist-realist divide: The role of politics in judging. Princeton: University Press.

Unger, Roberto M. 1987. *Plasticity into power*. Cambridge, MA: Cambridge University Press.

Waldron, Jeremy. 1992. The irrelevance of moral objectivity. In Robert P. George (ed.), *Natural law theory: Contemporary essays*, 158–187. Oxford: Clarendon.

Weber, Max. 1977. *Critique of Stammler*. New York: Free Press.

Whittington, Keith E. 2001. *Constitutional interpretation: Textual meaning, original intent, and judicial review* (revised). Lawrence: University Press of Kansas.

Whittington, Keith E. 2002. Extrajudicial Constitutional Interpretation: Three Objections and Responses. *North Carolina Law Review* 80. 773–851.

Whittington, Keith E., R. Daniel Kelemen & Gregory A. Caldeira (eds.). 2010. *The Oxford handbook of law and politics*. Oxford: Oxford University Press.

Dieter Stein
14 On inferencing in law

1 Linguistics in the law

Given the role of text and meaning in debates about issues of interpretation in law, it seems appropriate to look at these concepts from the point of view of pragmatics, as it deals with the construction of meaning from linguistic and extralinguistic knowledge by the text recipient. While mention of pragmatics in the law has often been restricted to speech act theory, it is the aim of this chapter to extend the application of pragmatic approaches to the analysis of legal communication on a wider scale.

It is surprising that concepts from linguistics have up to now not been taken up systematically by a discipline that deals with a domain that is essentially constituted by language (Stein forthcoming), and works in and through language. The following statement by Toolan (2002: 159–160) aptly sums up the situation:

> [...] recently Christopher Hutton, reviewing contributions to a conference on Law and Linguistics at Washington University, has found not proven the mainstream linguists' claim that linguistics, in its scientificity, had important things to say to lawyers. [Hutton 1998 D.S.] Why so? Essentially, because the legal profession is of the world, and applies on a case by case basis, so that there is far more common ground between the literary critic, entering a plea or making a judgement on a particular unique poem, than with the linguist, hypothetico-deductively elaborating a maximally generalized and abstract system underlying performance in one or all natural languages.

This amounts to a sentiment in the professional law domain that, scandalously, linguistics as it is perceived from the outside through its mainstream orientations, has little to offer to a domain whose materiality is language. It would appear that the type of linguistics Toolan has in mind – basically structure-based, compositionally oriented linguistics – has dominated linguistics to a large extent, defining the picture of the discipline other disciplines have. A more pragmatic approach, advocating less fixity and more the process-oriented, constructive or re-creative aspects of language use, is represented, in its application to the law domain, by the volume "Handbuch Sprache im Recht" (Felder and Vogel forthcoming) containing European contributions only. Significantly, Toolan does not make reference to an intrinsically pragmatic tradition of analyzing the linguistics of law. He frames the difference between the two approaches

Dieter Stein, University of Düsseldorf

in terms of "fixed-code literalist telementation" (Toolan 2002: 164) as against an integrational view of communication, based on Harris' 'language myth' (Harris 1981) view that gives primacy to a live meaning construction process by minds. Another way to frame the differences between two approaches in linguistics is to think of them as meaning minimalism and meaning maximalism. The latter would try to derive meaning primarily through "intensional" information as given by the hypothesized language system, invoking additional language-external information only as a rescue where necessary. Meaning minimalism, a pragmatics-based view (for a consistent application see Bublitz 2001), will include a perspective on the process of how interpreted meaning (pragmatic meanings of real-time utterances) comes to be created by readers and hearers on the basis of system information. These are two basic polar tendencies of how to look at language and communication involving language. They are not identical to, but tend to coincide with, the distinction between more "functional" and more "formal" perspectives. On a deeper philosophical level, a more minimalist-meaning approach congenial to a pragmatic turn implies "the change from interpretation as the identification of pre-existing and immutable meaning to reconstructing the processes that originally created these meaning structures" (Gumbrecht 2012: 183, translated D. S. from the German original "[...] dieser Wechsel *von der Interpretation als der Identifikation von gegebenen Bedeutungsstrukturen zur Rekonstruktion derjenigen Prozesse, durch die die Strukturen der artikulierten Bedeutung überhaupt erst entstehen können*").

The purpose of the present discussion is to see what a meaning-minimalist, processual view can contribute to an elucidation of extracting meanings from legal texts. It first focuses on the issue of what it means, from a pragmatic point of view, to say that "the meaning resides in the text" in normal or in legal discourses, and if it is possible to linguistically explicate a notion of "literal meaning." The chapter then discusses the nature and extent of how meanings are actually construed by way of inferencing in discourse and in law, and how this construction process through types of inferencing works on all hierarchical levels of meaning construction. In addition to legal concepts, the paper argues, legal discourse appears to be characterized by specific rules of meaning-building.

2 Some prolegomena

For a linguist looking at legal language there are basically three options for what to do:
1. The linguist can aim to describe what is characteristic in terms of the meaning management practices (what functions, what forms) in a domain with constituent genres and communities of practice, aiming at identifying what

is specific to this particular domain and how these meaning management practices differ from other domains or from whatever is some "degree zero" type of communication.
2. In a kind of meta-analysis, the linguist can identify and make explicit the specific views, the meta-opinions, the folklore views or the ideology of language present in that community of practice and use these views as explanatory dimensions for specific ways of managing meanings. One of these domain-specific concepts is a notion of literalness that figures prominently in legal argumentation. A linguist's job will then be to explicate the specific version of "literalness" or "plain meaning" that is a central operative concept in legal argumentation. These "operative" concepts in this domain embody a folklore view of language that may be "functional" in the sense that their specific properties are due to perceived needs, and to professional and social conditions in the field.
3. The linguist can take a "didactic" attitude, and, based on Nos 1 and 2, make suggestions for e.g. the formulation or interpreting of texts. Such a stance would to a certain extent treat the legal domain as a case of applied linguistics, and is a priori not likely to make a lot of friends in the legal profession.

The present paper will be mainly concerned with the first-mentioned pursuit, with the second pursuit necessarily involved to some extent. The third pursuit will only be involved to the extent that it is hoped that an insight into the mechanisms of how meanings are created by readers can contribute to an enlightened view of what it can mean to say that, for instance, "the meanings are in the text" or "the law is (in) the text."

As far as "the law" is concerned, there are several types of law, with written statutes in the focus of this paper. Even though there are significant differences between two of the main types of law, Roman (typically continental European law, based on written statutes) and Common Law (typically Anglo-American law, based primarily on precedent), the theoretical issues as discussed in this paper are applicable to both legal cultures. If there are different legal systems in the two areas, these roughly correspond – accidentally or not – to major differences in linguistic thinking. These differences are obvious already from a look at the literature cited in major textbooks and edited collections in the two geographical and intellectual areas. The fact that there is little, if any, mutual referral and citation can also be attributed to linguistic inabilities or to an unwillingness to read languages other than English.

Another initial clarification is necessary. Discussing "language of the law" or "language in the law," involves a generic reference to "the law" as if this were an internally unitary and unstructured domain, delimited only by community of practice. However, the globality of these specifications renders any specification vacuous as the field is internally structured in terms of genres with very different linguistic conventions, knowledge assumptions and practices. A powerful initial differentiation comes from Tiersma (1999: 139-141), who distinguishes between "operative documents" that establish legal rights and obligations, "expository documents" that expound and to a certain extent interpret the law and "persuasive" documents that have a clear rhetorical dimension and try to create, influence and change opinions in a court. Obviously, these three basic types of discourse in the field of law have, beyond shared terminological conventions, very different pragmatic ground rules. They would need to be internally further differentiated by genres. In addition, "persuasive" discourse can be oral, whereas the other types tend to be written. So any discussion of "language in the law" needs to be aware of what genre is referred to.

While legal concepts and legal terminology, the mainstay of most recent, and also corpus-based, work seem to be quite stable across genres, the need to emphasize genre-based internal differentiation seems to be essential for a pragmatic analysis that focuses on the interaction between linguistic surface forms, non-linguistic knowledge types, inference and interpretational conventions and legitimacies, an approach that seems to be much more appropriate to characterize genres than limiting attention to types of surface forms (Giltrow and Stein 2009).

The present study focuses primarily on "operative documents," or statutory texts, but will later extend its focus to "persuasive," oral discourse.

3 The law in the text?

One of the fundamental issues in the law is whether and how much meaning is "in the text." This issue concerns one of the most prominent operative assumptions about language in the professional domain of law. It may also be "functional" to the extent that such an assumption is felt to be necessary – from the practical, operative side – for the law to function. Although the notion of a "literal" meaning has quite a history in linguistics too (e.g. in the shape of the "literal force hypothesis" in speech act theory, Levinson 1983: 263–265 and 274–276) the idea of meaning residing in the text is naturally very attractive in law. In fact, a prominent US judge, James Bradley Thayer, cited in Tiersma (2010: 29), refers to such a state of affairs as a "paradise where all words have a fixed, precisely ascertained meaning; where men may express their purposes, not only with accuracy, but with fullness; and where, if the writer has been careful, a lawyer, having a document referred to him, may sit in his chair, inspect the text, and answer all questions without raising his eyes." Others have referred to this imagined state as a "pious yearning of lawyers and jurists for an objective and stable meaning" (Müller, Christensen and Sokolowski 1997: 26, cited in Vogel forthcoming, 64, by Jäger). The meaning, the sense or message, "Textsinn" is to reside in the text "gleichsam bewegungslos und unabhängig von der Geschichte seiner Auslegungen" (Jäger in Vogel forthcoming, 589) [immutable, transfixed, untouched by any external factor, D. S.].

This view of a meaning "outside the head" (Flanagan 2010: 256) is pervasive in both linguistics and the law. It is misguided and misleading for both. For the law, there are dissenting voices like Easterbrook (1994: 61, "words are not born with meaning"). It has been rejected on independent legal grounds by Flanagan (2010), who argues that there can never be an uninterpreted "literal" meaning. The reason is a very pragmatic one: "Every enactment is the product of finite drafting resources" (Flanagan 2010: 260): it is plainly not possible to imagine all possible scenarios and ex ante formulate exhaustively all possible exceptions. Describing a legal-pragmatist approach, Olsen (this volume) cites the view that "[...] legal controversies arise in specific and often unique contexts [...] and such controversies are better addressed with reference to these contexts than by abstract legal principles." This is why "[...] the literal meaning isn't necessarily its legal meaning," and there may be "[...] scenarios in which literal entailments are *legally* incorrect, not just ethically or prudentially problematic" (Flanagan 2010: 261). Thus there are further criteria which have to be fed into the construction of legal meaning in a concrete case of adjudication. The pragmatic conditions of formulating a statute, the "limited resources" (Flanagan 2010: 263–264), a priori imply the indeterminacy and vagueness of statutes. Especially the concept of indeterminacy as something of a pathological condition seems based on an unrealistic idea that all cases can be covered by language and literalness, and thus all vagaries of interpretation disposed of.

In his discussion of the relationship between norm and text Möllers (2015: 286) points to the identification of norm and text as a strategy of endowing the abstract norm with authority ["Normautorisierung"], with the intended effect of stabilization of a norm, of a kind of an – intrinsically futile – attempt at immunization against norm change (Möllers 2015: 301). Drawing on a distinction between applying the law in a process of adjudication and interpreting the law (Möllers 2015: 302) in a more academic pursuit, he points out that for the practical process of adjudication, of making a concrete decision in a concrete case, apart from further "tactical," social and political criteria, this factually false assumption (norm = text) facilitates the practical conduct of law. The identification of legal norm and legal text can therefore count as another "operative" assumption as the assumption of a "literal" meaning or a "literal" interpretation. It is acceptable as an operative assumption if the best way to describe a norm is to refer to the text in which it is "embedded" (Möllers 2015: 286). In other words, a conceptual confusion is acceptable as a practical procedure. Toolan (2002: 162–166) describes this very effect in law: "For all such reasons, a fixed-code telementational approach remains immensely attractive, so that if it is set aside as ultimately unworkable, it is not without a sense of loss, and a sense of clarity and the promise of perdurable insight being superseded by complexity and only passing illumination" (Toolan 2002: 164).

This misguided, but common and practical, conflation between norm and text shows up as a theoretical problem in discussions of the stability of the legal text vs. the obvious change of norms, so in Möller's (2015: 292) claim that "Der Text bleibt bestehen, auch wenn sich seine Bedeutung ändert." [The text remains unchanged, even if its meaning changes.] The issue is here exactly what it is that remains constant. Underlying this claim seems to be the container idea of a pragmatics-independent stratum of "kernel" propositional meaning as discussed above, with "Bedeutung" (meaning) referring to some higher-order interpreted level of pragmatic meaning construction. It is not clear how any such level of constructed meaning can remain the same if the abstract norm changes. What cannot possibly be meant is the materiality of the text as a structured arrangement of black-and-white contrasts.

Another, related, desideratum is the idea that one form has one meaning, in order to arrive at the meanings without delay or contextual interference, as a "fixed code literalist telementation" (Toolan 2002: 164) view would suggest. In other words, language, and certainly legal language should be, according to these conceptions of meaning, maximally autonomous (Stein 2015), all meanings automatically accessible without interference from any facet of context. Tiersma reports a specific version of this notion of autonomy represented by Justice Antonin Scalia: "He views statutes as heavily textualized and highly autonomous, in the sense that they are not mere evidence of legislative intentions with respect to the law but actually constitute the law" (Tiersma 2010: 162). For Soames (2011: 42) "[...] textualism is typically identified as the doctrine that the content of the legal text (the law it enacts) is the meaning – sometimes "ordinary meaning" – of the text."

The initial citation testifies to a pervasive sense in the legal profession that any departure from this safe haven, the text, is an extraordinary case that needs special justification. It would, then, be good to have a set of rules, ideally codified, by which we or, even better, a machine, could algorithmically determine the outcome of a case at hand. Solan (2012: 88) cites Supreme Court Justice

Benjamin Cardozo, writing in 1921, who expresses this ideal world as a wish for "a code at once so flexible and so minute, as to create for every conceivable situation the just and fitting rule" (Cardozo 1921: 143). If this defines a default situation, interpretation, then, would only be called on as an exceptional life-saving device.

It is perfectly understandable that there is a professionally inherent, operative and functional, desire to have something like a safe handrail in law. A number of papers in this volume emphasize this fact: meaning maximalism is more congenial to the demands of the judiciary to have "surface" evidence, and not have to mind-read if, e.g., a lie was "intended" (Horn, this volume). Slocum (this volume) emphasizes this very point ("the noble dream," the opposite of the open texture, in Hart's words, cf. Poscher, this volume) from a practical point of view. After all, any threat to a stabilized and stabilizing system of norms that holds society together must in principle be undesirable. So, for domain-specific reasons, there appears to be a set of beliefs about how language works that is to some extent also present in everyday folklore views of language, but is present to a much stronger degree in the legal domain.

It seems a surprising fact that several sciences, certainly literary study and linguistics, have had a "pragmatic turn" in their internal development that involved a systematic incorporation of external factors into their theories, especially into the origination of meanings. Law up to now has been singularly unaffected by this movement. One of the reasons may well be the tendency of the pragmatic turn to allow in factors that threaten the assumption of this stability, locked in by the words and their purportedly fixed meanings, an impression actually furthered by, amongst others, the standard language ideology (no variation, no change, one form, one meaning, forever). The domain of law embraces this ideology (Milroy and Milroy 1985) with a vengeance.

The image of a stable system firmly constraining interpretation and really not in need of any additional inferencing work is appropriately referred to as the "container" theory of language and meanings (Bublitz 2001, § 2.4.2), inherent in structuralist, form-based linguistics.[1] One of its core assumptions is that language functions as a "conduit" through which ideas and thoughts are transported as quasi-physical, stable objects from one person to another (Bublitz 2001: 38). This ideology is corroborated by what Peter Tiersma has called "textualization" (Tiersma 2010). It implies the transfer of authority to the written medium, to the text. An effect of this process of literalization is the belief that, as the written

---

[1] Busse (1992:14) refers to this idea, a kernel aspect of legal folklore theory of language, as "Topftheorie," i.e. "pot-theory," i.e. meaning separate and insulated from any producer or recipient waiting to be "used" by such.

text is stable, immutable and forever reliable. So must the message enshrined in it, in its presumed self-sufficiency and, in fact, presumed autonomy, carry all the relevant information to the legal process. In other words, elements of the physical inscription model (permanence and reliability) are inherited by the message carried. To the extent that the law is represented or reflected in a written text, there is really a double inscriptional process. The first step is from a regulatory system of behavior to a system of perceived, abstracted and talked about norms (van Schooten 2007, in Wagner, Werner and Cao) and from there, in a process of "textualization" to a physical form in a written statute. This has significant "performative" and other effects that bear directly on views, current in the legal word, of what "text" and "interpretation" mean. The special status of the text in the legal world derives from the fact that in many cases it is not a report of an act or action, but textualization in the sense of Tiersma (2010) means that the text performatively "[...] constitutes the transaction" (Tiersma 2010: 40).

So there is a tight connexion between the identity of a norm and its concrete linguistic form (Möllers 2015: 280 ["Dieser enge Zusammenhang zwischen der Identität der Norm und ihrer konkreten sprachlichen Verfasstheit [...]"]). The very special status of the text amounts, for most legal cultures, to an attempt to stabilize norms through the preservation of the identity of the text (Möllers 2015: 281: ["Der Versuch, Normen durch die Bewahrung der Identität eines Textes zu stabilisieren [...]"]). One consequence is "the *four corners rule*, in that the meaning of the contract is sought based exclusively on information contained within the four corners of the document. Another name for this principle is the *plain meaning rule*" (Tiersma 2010: 126). Tiersma (2010: 157) also points out that the textualization into written form is also related to the availability of stable copies of legal texts, thereby enhancing the aura of absolute reliability and authority of the text as a safe repository of the expression of the will of the authors.

So it is essentially the process of textualization that is at the bottom of views of, and, in fact, ideologies, of interpretation to the extreme end of seeing the text itself as the law. These views tie in with a-semiotic and a-pragmatic views of meaning outside the comprehending heads. The underlying notion of what "the law" is makes a difference to the notion of interpretation and its place. In a more traditional concept of the law the center of legal activity is the "subsumption," the classification of a criminal event under a legal rubric. Even if this is assumed to be the "primary" locus of the realization of the law, it involves in itself a more basic type of interpretation. As Schuhr (in press, in Vogel) makes clear, even the phrase "clara non sunt interpretanda" needs to be construed in a basic sense of "understood" to be inputted to legal interpretation before it can be used to decide if a case at hand falls within the domain of the "clara." Basically, it is an inference process that relates a case, as it is represented in the judicial narrative, to a norm.

A major issue for the theory of law is, however, how that "norm" exists. A more traditional school claims that it exists "in the language of the law," in some sense of "literalness." Another view holds that it resides primarily as an abstract, social-cognitive system in society (much like the "langue" or "system" sense of language) and that it may be textualized into a written form as depicted above. In a more radically pragmatic orientation as the third type of view, it is claimed that the law has no real a priori existence independent of the history of realization, and that it does not lie dormant in some "text," and that, consequently, it is constituted, or brought into existence, only in the moment of active performance in any act of adjudication in the performance of an act of language (Jäger [in press] in Vogel). The very notion, current in European pragmatically-based legal theory, of "Rechtsarbeit" (=meaning creation activity, Müller 1994; Müller and Christensen 2013) implies that meaning is not pre-existing but is performatively created only in individual processes of meaning construction. This goes hand in hand with a view of law (and, by the way, language itself) as a normative system that has no independent existence in itself, but is really a system of "heuristic hypotheses," and a function of a larger, broader and more primary entity, society.

Obviously, these different views of the ontics of law go with very different views on "Rechtssemantik" (the semantics of the law) and entail very different views of how much meaning is in the text, if any at all, and of what nature, and how meanings are constructed on the basis of the text. So there is a substantive link between the philosophy of law and the role of linguistics in explicating notions of "text" and "inference," as part of a larger dependency of legal concepts on linguistic concepts (Toolan 2002; Stein forthcoming). These issues in the theory of law are relevant here to the extent that they obviously involve different types of inferential processes, not whether or not inference is involved in principle. But the different views of the nature of the legal norm and interpretation do make for very different views as to how much inferencing work – as a presumed source of insecurity and arbitrariness – is assumed in a linguistically-based theory of interpretation: it makes a difference to the nature of the challenge for linguistic theorizing if a case at hand is referred to as a quasi-physical, rock-solid a priori given, or if a new interpretation has to be constructed from a social-cognitively conceived new synthesis based on old decisions. The latter view, built on the re-creation of law in each process, requires much more the application of pragmatic categories of analysis and is much more congenial to a notion of a "pragmatic turn" in the analysis of the linguistic processes in the law than a legal theory based on the stasis and fixity of legal norms enshrined in a text.

From a very pragmatic viewpoint, everybody involved in the practice of law knows that interpretation and inferencing are a blatant reality, and that, obviously, inferencing is a part of the reality of practicing law, including the practice of constitutional law in the United States, – a classic battlefield in the issue of to what extent the "text" constrains interpretation, making inference unavoidable. A first indication is the existence, and the judiciary's awareness of it, of the "canons of interpretation," although these canons are not much loved and considered more of a nuisance. Miller (1990: 1), noting the puzzling persistence of maxims of statutory interpretation, is surprised that these canons still exist and are resorted to, and appear to even be increasing in importance. Miller (1990: 2) points to a side effect of the trend towards textualism, such as evinced in attitudes by Judge Scalia, such that the canons of interpretation are gaining in importance: loss of emphasis on external history of the text's origin leads to more interpretive work on what textual evidence we have as an epiphenomenon of that text origination work, constituting a loss of history of that text.

It should be added that while this discussion of "law in the text" applies in principle to all legal cultures, it is primarily focused on a Roman and a common law situation. It would be interesting to pursue this issue in more depth for legal cultures that view the verbatim text itself as embodying the law in a more radical way, requiring an enhanced degree of "literalness" as part of a unified notion of law and religion represented in the sacred text. On the other end of the spectrum, the precedent-based common law system still requires massive inferencing processes in establishing what counts as precedent (see Condello and Arapinis, this volume) on the basis of written-formulated judgments that still need to be "interpreted" in the non-technical, everyday sense of comprehension.

4 Exactly what is "in the text"?

What does it mean to say that the meaning is "in the text"? We need to have a more precise idea what it means for the "meaning to be in the text," – not just in legal texts, but in any text. In the legal context, any answer to this question is at the base of the issue of a "literal meaning" and notions of the "text only." At one end is the view that the text is something that is immutable and engraved in stone, a view supportive of the "container" view. For the "graven stone" view, obviously quite pervasive in the legal world, to cite Solan (2012: 94), "It is attractive to analyze legal disputes by first determining whether the facts fit within the meanings of the statutory terms, and then rule accordingly." This approach is embodied in the plain language rule of statutory interpretation: "Where [a statute's] language is plain and admits of no more than one meaning the duty of interpretation does not arise, and the rules which are to aid doubtful meanings need no discussion."

The consequence is clear: "De Claris non est disputandum." Interpretation in the traditional sense would not be an issue at all except in cases of "vagueness," or the so-called "hard cases." In any reading of the text, the default procedure is such that the text automatically produces the judgment, and inference processes are only invoked in cases of conflicting legal solutions or in so-called "hard cases." The tenor from most of the legal literature on law is that the default assumption is that notions like "literal meaning," or "what the text says," have a central role in argumentation, in both practical and theoretical reasoning in both law and language.

Any notion of "what the text says," and in fact all of the implicit ideas of a "literal meaning" seem to assume that there is some level of analysis that is stand-alone in terms of language in the sense of the "container" theory. There is, in linguistics and pragmatics, a long-standing discussion of how much meaning is "in the sentence" and how much meaning is extralinguistically fed into an interpretive or constructional process. Notice that the linguistic issue of meaning maximalism vs. meaning minimalism (or linguistics vs. pragmatics) is quite parallel to and in fact forms a linguistic backdrop to the issue in law of how much meaning is "in the text" and how much meaning is a product of the processes of comprehension and interpretation in reaching a judicial decision.

There are really two issues involved here, a linguistic and an applied linguistic/legal or operational one. As a first logical step, linguistic and pragmatic theory can suggest a line or series of steps in an incremental hierarchy of adding meaning from "langue" meanings in the sentence up to conversational implicatures. As a next step, the practice in law of identifying a "literal meaning" or "what is in the text" (on the arguably shaky assumption that there is such a unitary level) can then be explicated in terms of this cline. A next step could then be a reasoned suggestion from the side of linguistics to formulate explicit principles, based on this cline, as to what could operationally be defined as a "literal meaning" in the field of law, based on functional considerations of necessities in this field.

Such a way of proceeding appears to be a promising research paradigm for a linguistically supported judicial practice, even though it presumes substantial communication between disciplines which are at worst suspicious of one another and at best sensitive to interference from one another. Another major issue is the fact that the relative share of linguistic and pragmatically given information has been a classic theoretical battle field, as witnessed by the "border wars" (Horn 2005). A first obvious candidate for a "literal" meaning has been the level at which a "truth value" can be assigned. However, research has shown that even this level needs to have pragmatically, i.e. extralinguistically, determined content in order to be evaluated in terms of truth value. Recanati (2004) has made a distinction between "primary" and "secondary" pragmatic processes that operate on top of and are posterior to the "system," or, in the narrow sense, true "linguistic" meanings. Primary pragmatic processes are of a "saturational" nature insofar as they are necessary to establish a proposition as something that could serve as a "literal" meaning for the linguist. To these saturational processes belong indexicals, cases of reference resolution with null surface forms, but also genitives in which the exact nature of the semantic relationship has to be defined. It is a definitional feature of these primary pragmatic processes that they are "bottom-up" in nature, that they are below the level of consciousness, and are triggered by linguistic expressions. Part of primary saturational processes would presumably also be "semantically implicated" content, such that, for example, "managed to find" implicates that "finding A was expected to involve some difficulty" (Marmor 2011: 89).

Arguably also part of such very early or basic saturational processes, but not as a rule discussed under the heading of "explicatures," are elements of "unrepresented background" (Carston 2002: 253). As Carston points out, the relevance of her examples (Carston 2002: 45 a–c) depends on a number of unarticulated (i.e. not in the text) types of background knowledge:

(1) (45) a: I've had breakfast.
    b: She ran to the edge of the cliff and jumped.
    c: She gave him the key and he opened the door.

"It is important for the interpretation of these sentences that the breakfast (a) took place "today," that the jumping was "off the cliff" (b). "Cognitive effects follow from these. Nothing more follows from the breakfast having been in the normal ingesting way or from the jumping having been subject to gravity, though much may have followed from these *not* being in force. As for the instrumental inference of 'with a key' in (45c) [...] this one comes for free [...] in the door-opening script" (Carston 2002: 254). So we have to assume that there is a prior reservoir of knowledge triggered by genre and Activity Type and types of encyclopedic and professional knowledge triggered by these situations (Carston 2002: 253).

Secondary pragmatic processes, by contrast, are top-down and triggered by broader, hard-to-typify external factors: They typically comprise communicational, discourse and conversational functions, typically the classic conversational implicatures, whereas the primary pragmatic processes seem to cover generalized implicatures. So there seems to be some sort of consensus view in pragmatics that "meaning construction" is based on an assumption of a "strong linguistic underdeterminacy view: encoded linguistic meaning may do little more than provide a skeletal framework which is both augmented (into explicatures) and complemented (with implicatures), by fast, effective mechanisms of pragmatic inference" (Carston 2002: 258). Any notion of "literal" or "in the text" must confront and deal with this strong linguistic underdeterminacy.

Liedtke (2015) has made a three-tier distinction between (1) "what-is-articulated," amounting to a notion of a system sentence and containing all of the polysemous and unresolved ambiguities of whatever kind; (2) "what-is-said," which would contain primary pragmatic inference processes (enrichments); and (3) "what-is- implicated," which is the result of secondary pragmatic processes, including the traditional conversational implicatures. "What-is-said" would arguably be the main site for semantic and pragmatic saturation. In addition to standard situational saturation processes this stage can be conceptualized as the site for specifically legal contextual saturation.

Recanati (2004, §1.8) has specified the concept of saturation by the notion of "availability" of basically a type of knowledge, mutually presumed to be available by the communication partners in a given professional context: "What is said must be intuitively accessible to the conversational participants (unless something goes wrong and they do not count as 'normal interpreters')" Recanati (2004: 10). Liedtke and Schulze (2013, cf. also Liedtke 2015) have suggested a concept of "templates" ("cluster of items of contextual information") that have to be available in order for these primary and secondary pragmatic processes to be possible. Apart from specialized and professional knowledge available at this point, it would be a procedural aspect of this template knowledge to trigger scripts and cognitive inferencing processes in order to arrive at professionally "possible" knowledge states.

So any notion of "literal" meaning is as doubtful as it is difficult to define in more general linguistic terms. If the aim is at all is to define an operational specific legal type of "legal" literal meaning that could hold water, a good candidate might be a level of meaning building after the application of all primary pragmatic processes under the special auspices of specific legal templates. These would naturally be included in any pragmatically satisfying notion of genre and would be different for each type of legal genre.

In particular, it appears not possible to tie a notion of "literal" meaning or what meaning is "in the text" to any traditional notion of proposition. It cannot be anything like the "system sentence," or any abstract construct that would contain all of the meaning potentials of all the morphemes involved. A statute text, although not specific, is still pragmatically specified and thus definite even with respect to an imagined scenario.

Any idea of the text as an ensemble of system meanings – as they are recorded to some extent in dictionaries – is even more unlikely than on the sentence level, unless one wishes to conceive of a text as a kind of hierarchically ordered macro-structural skeleton in the van Dijk-ian sense (van Dijk 1980). The problems with where to draw a line between the relative contributions of system meanings and of pragmatic information are multiplied ad infinitum on the level of the text. While this "internal" type of information is available and triggers and constrains meaning construction, it is – from a linguistic point of view – pointless to try to define some "skeleton" level of analysis, analogous to the proposition, on the level of the text and make it the basis of a text-based notion of literalness.

In a realistic – rather than platonic – view of communication, language occurs in fully specified discourses. The "text" exists only in an interpreted form: legal interpretational work is not an extraction of a preexisting meaning and subsumption of a case, but an always newly happening, inductive amalgamation of previously existing history of interpretive acts with a newly selected "case" (or better: interpretive synthesis that represents a "case") which in itself is already a result of interpretation. This view, leaning more towards pragmatics, that there is no linguistic level of analysis that would qualify for something like the "literal meaning," is represented in a pointed form by Stanley Fish:

> [...] there is no such thing as literal meaning, if by literal meaning one means a meaning that is perspicuous no matter what the context and no matter what is in the speaker's or hearer's mind, a meaning that because it is prior to interpretation can serve as a constraint on interpretation. (Fish 1990: 4)

This view is consistent with a view of the law, sketched above, as a normative system existing only in realizations in individual acts of executing the law, with no independent physical or abstract realization. It is parallel with a view of language as realized only in the individual act of using language, which accords to "the law" a status analogous to the language system as really an abstract hypothesis over histories of use, a view not many linguists will be entirely comfortable with. So both types of norms, language and the law, while realized and changed performatively, have no concrete existence in real time and space except in processes of use and adjudication.

It appears that the competition between intentionalism, originalism and textualism in law is therefore analogous to a parallel discussion in linguistic theory (Bix 2012: 1549):

"New originalism," like older forms of "originalism," focuses on constraining judicial interpretation by reference to a stable and unique "meaning" of the constitutional text, though "new originalism" recognizes that a text's meaning may be only the first step in an interpretive process, by which the meaning may be modified and subordinated in the process of deciding a case [...].

The two issues involved here concern the meaning of the text prior to its identity and free from legally relevant information and the "legal" interpretation proper. Allott and Shaer (this volume) refer to this distinction as "investigative" vs. "creative," where "investigative" refers to the pre-legal information and "creative" to the construction of a legally relevant judiciary conclusion – really the area of classical legal "interpretation," corresponding to the "interpretive process" in the above citation from Bix. This distinction is, however, often more a theoretical than a practically applicable one, as most of the meaning constructions on the pre-legal level are also relevant to the broader issues of the (legal) text.

In both fields there is tug-of-war between meaning maximalism and meaning minimalism: at the interface between semantics and pragmatics there is an ongoing discussion about exactly how much of meaning comes from the intension (with an "s") of an expression, from what is stored in our mental lexicon as a history and abstraction from previous usage history, what is part of "langue" or "the system," and how much is calculated in pragmatic processes of inference. This appears to be analogous to the discussion in law about whether or how much meaning is in the statute and whether and how much is actually constructed in the interpretational process, a point elaborated by Jan Engblom (2012), who, following Christensen and Sokolowski (2002), distinguishes between "weak" and "strong" legal theories, with a "strong" theory of language in law corresponding to a maximalist stance in linguistics that holds that all or most meaning is "contained" in the sentence or text, much in the sense of the "container" theory. By contrast, the "weak" theory of language in law corresponds to the more pragmatic view of ad hoc constructing of meanings, making for an inherent flexibility and enhanced susceptibility to change of any normative system of meanings (Engblom 2012: 177f).

The intention here is not to debunk the "text" or do away with it. After all, "All we have is the text" (Stein 2010), we do have the system meanings, the abstraction from previous uses, as the "linguistic meaning," the technical meanings, all of them "langue" meanings and the identity of the text as an instantiation of a genre, of a type, in a societal domain. The text is the linguistic initiator of communication: the Communicative Principle and the Relevance assumption tell us that we should go on and do certain things, and only legitimate things, with the text. All of the posterior processes are in the nature of constructional inferences.

One aspect of the connected debates in law centers around "intentionalism." If there is no way to think of the text as a stable container, it is equally clear that the structure of the container is as it is because there was an intention by the text creator, and there is only a text because there is an intention. Otherwise the text and a particular individual text would not exist. To discuss the text without a functional reference to its raison d'être is, for the pragmatician, a non-starter. Relevance Theory, studying the relationship between "intended meaning" and "linguistic meaning" (Wilson and Sperber 2012, ix) takes a similar view: "The function of the linguistic meaning of an utterance is not to encode the speaker's meaning, but to provide evidence of her meaning [...] The linguistic meaning is not part of her intended meaning: she uses this expression not to encode her meaning [...]," but to have the hearer construct intended pragmatic meanings. So "the text" is really a symptom, an epiphenomenon, of communication that has taken place in the past.

If it is the case that there is no way to read a text and not fully contextualize it, i.e. synthesize an interpretation with plenty of pragmatic context, real or imagined, how can the meaning be in the text, even exclusively so? The moment you read you interpret, with the linguistically given information only a shred of information, or, more precisely, an instruction to construct a mental entity. Allott and Shaer (this volume) point to exactly this aspect. It is certainly an important step in a pragmatic turn to a view on meanings that meanings are only constructed in use, and that abstractions about previous uses – which is what hypothesized "system meanings" are – are certainly constraints on meaning constructions, but this cannot be the "meaning in the text" of originalists or literalists. It is a further step to be taken in a pragmatic view to de-passivize the statement: it is speakers who, as the agents of communication, have intentions to have later readers construct meanings (and certainly not system-meanings) through the choice of words. So any legally interesting idea of "meaning" must be this original meaning intention, even if it is recognized that there may be uncertainty as to the precise nature and origin of the "intention": "Debates within and about 'originalism' in the United States echo the basic question of legal interpretation [...]: should one focus on speaker meaning or word meaning? If one looks at the intentions of the drafters or ratifiers, which level(s) of intention are relevant? and should one give priority to the choices of the law makers or to the reasonable understanding of those subject to the law?" (Bix 2012: 154).

Apart from the theoretical aspects discussed here, even phrases from statutes like "carry a firearm", that seem at first innocuous with respect to a concrete interpretation, are given an interpretation as a concrete imagined instantiation or a concrete scenario the moment you read it. The reader has at this point already made a decision: does it mean "on the body" or does it mean "in some case below the dash in a car"? There is no way to resort to any "ordinary meaning" here. A computational corpus analysis has turned up great difficulties in defining an "ordinary" or "plain" meaning. Just as the notion of the "meaning in the text" is, if not a legal, but a linguistic fiction, so is "ordinary" meaning.[2]

From the view of a pragmatically oriented semantics, even the folklore assumption of an ordinary, "plain," default and essentially fixed and reliable semantics, as suggested by the fixity and discreteness of written language, is an illusion. Semantic vagueness is not restricted to obvious cases of polysemy, but is in principle inherent in every use of a term, with strict boundaries the exception. Apart from "cases of *semantic vagueness*, where there is no clear cut-off point between whether a predicate is strictly true or what it is not" as in cases of "young" or "child," colors (Carston 2002: 329), or "reasonable doubt," the default situation involves "pragmatically motivated cases of loose use." This also applies to cases discussed by Carston (2002: 328, examples 11a–g), or in the case of "open" (Carston 2002: 364), where many things in this world can be predicated as "open" (mouth, door, milk carton, vowel quality, a discussion and so forth). Based on remembered and abstracted histories of usage, presumed fixed meanings can be more in the nature of "'conceptual encodings' that are not really full-fledged concepts, but rather concept schemas [...] on the basis of which on *every* occasion of their use, an actual concept [...] is inferred" (Carston 2002: 360). In other words, concepts even in individual words used in a text are individually constructed ad hoc.[3]

The problems with whatever is "ordinary" or "plain," which form the basis of interpretational principles like the "strict construction rule" in textualism, have been amply demonstrated, such as in a discussion of the role of inference by Charnock (2007: 39). While "the absence of pre-existing objective meaning" (Charnock 2007: 39) points to the problematic status of discussions around "literal meaning" in the domain of law, it is equally clear that the baby must not been thrown out with the bathwater. After all, the "system" text in a given genre does constrain, and in fact trigger, the constructional process. It is worth quoting Charnock (2007: 39) in more detail:

---

[2] For a critique of this type of "armchair" semantic analysis and the way such a "prelinguistic" "container" theory of language is widespread in legal practice and theory cf. Vogel (2012: 17–26).
[3] The linguistic theoretical underpinning of this view, the inferential ad-hoc-ness of concepts, may be found in the work of Barsalou (1983 and 1987).

If the legal construction of 'what is said' depends to some extent on the domain of discourse, then it seems necessary to accept that the so-called literal meaning, as well as the pragmatic intentional meaning, will vary according to circumstances. To the extent that this is so, it does not appear possible to avoid case-by-case adjudication. However, the rejection of a fixed literal meaning should not be taken as a justification for pragmatic interpretation of speakers' intentional meaning in the sense of Grice. On the contrary, if there is no fixed literal meaning, then there is nothing to which the machinery of pragmatic implicature can be applied in order to yield the desired intentional meaning.

While the view from pragmatic linguistics makes the systematic inclusion of inferencing imperative, the view from legal interpretation (Canale and Tuzet 2007) suggests the same, even if, as is argued in the present paper, the precise forms of typically legal inferencing on all levels need to be worked out, given the recency or novelty of a "pragmatic turn" in the analysis of legal language. Are there processes of inferencing specified by genre rules, typical for oral and/or written legal discourse? Are there genre-specific rules, reflected in the canons of interpretation, for blocking generalized implicatures?

It is one thing to point to the necessity of carrying out a practical legal job of adjudication in a finite time in the machinery of law without on each occasion of adjudication engaging in a time-consuming process of analyzing the inner semantic and pragmatic workings of the machine, but it is another thing to carry out the practical task from a linguistically enlightened and reflected view of what one is doing, that can be called upon if cases of doubt arise, as they keep doing, especially in societally relevant issues.

Comparisons with other domains are always dangerous, but it is tempting to invoke music here. To pretend that there is, and you can extract, and stick by, an uninterpreted level of meaning in a sentence or a text is a bit like saying that it is possible to listen to the score of a piece of music. If you listen to a recorded performance of a given piece twice it will never be the same ultimate listening experience, and the listening experience, what you make of it, is the meaning we are after. You cannot listen to an uninterpreted score. We do not even talk about different performances of the same score, – and different performances of a score are normally taken as a parallel case of text and interpretation. So there is no way to read a text and NOT interpret it, calling into question claims of the "stability" of the text in principle. This view ties in with a view of law as only realized, as finding its mode of existence, in the individual act of adjudication. Just as language really exists and is permanently changed through each act of use, or act of speech, in a vast sea of uses, so the law is changed in each act of adjudication and, like language, law disappears if it is not "read" and applied, as in both cases the individual acts are embedded in individual and ever-changing circumstances. This applies on a more abstract level of "the language" and "the law" just as well as on the level of inferential concept creation in each use of a term as discussed above in this section.

It is not the case that the score, the instigator of the interpretation, does not contain anything constraining interpretation: the language-meanings are abstractions of histories of uses, essentially memories of uses, and there are genre-conventions that indicate legitimacies of inferencing on all levels, from morphemes to the functions of whole texts. "Understanding" or "reading" is always a hic et nunc act, and the question of what the text meant irrevocably implies an archeology of the pragmatics of its creation, including potentialities of the intentions of the creators, no matter how complex this idea may be in the case of law texts. It is a far more linguistically realistic, if less positivistic, idea of what a legal text is.

So inferencing – and interpretation is nothing else but inference – is in reality a very basic and very pervasive process in texts and discourses generally, and it raises one specific issue that the late Peter Tiersma has raised in his writings (2001, 2010: 25–29): the issue of the autonomy of the legal text.

5 Inferencing as the backbone of law

It was argued in the preceding paragraph that a legal text (statute or other types), on top of special legal concepts in special terms, is defined by types of knowledge that, as a case of domain-specific knowledge, is selectively consulted in constructing the meaning of a text. As this knowledge is essentially genre knowledge, it is an essential static component of what a pragmatically-oriented analysis must focus on. In addition to the static availability, focusing and accessing of these knowledge types, dynamic processes of accessing and construing elements and meanings are taking place on all levels. This dynamic aspect of text meaning building will be the focus in this section.

By way of a general definition of inference that can form the basis of a further pragmatic characterization of legal discourse, let us assume as the point of departure of an inferencing process an input information which acts as a prompt, under a communicative presumption (CP), to integrate additional knowledge sources/reservoir (MN) into a new knowledge state, until a point where there is a sense of closure or, in psycholinguistic terminology, "sense constancy" (Hörmann 1976; cf. the discussion in Busse 1991: 141ff), a sense of a reasonable end result of this integrational process. The same basic process of knowledge accrual in linguistic communication is assumed in Relevance Theory: "The claim, then, is that hearers construct and test interpretive hypotheses in order of their accessibility, and once they have found an interpretation which satisfies their expectation of relevance they stop" (Carston 2002: 3).

This end point of the inference process is the "legal meaning" that so centrally figures in discussions of legal interpretation. The "legal meaning" is, then, an end product of inference processes that are compatible with the inference rules that specifically define legal discourse, as Poscher (this volume) elaborates. It may well not be compatible with non-legal, everyday discourse. So "legal meaning" is not something that is embedded in a text, but that is arrived at in each and every individual, contextually new case and circumstance.

This end result is, in a way, a new reality. Following Loflin and Silverberg (1978), each new reality constitution is an act of inference. What is felt to be a "reasonable" closure point is defined by the rules of the game in the professional, legal community of practice. So there are basically two aspects of inference processes, as it seems applicable to the case of interpretation – a static one and a dynamic one:
- the dynamic real-time process of construction and integration
- the static elements of initial state and the types of input or knowledge accessed, and the new end state of the synthesis.

Essential elements on which inferencing operates are the following:
- triggered by logically (not necessarily real-time) anterior structure such as the societal domain, the communicative situation and the genre
- at some point triggered by a "text"
- communicative presumption and relevance
- accessing Mutual Knowledge ("MN"), focused knowledge, constrained by genre and as part of "templates"
- operating as a synthesis-forming process until "closure" is reached, again relative to genre
- submission of intentionality and perlocutionality

For the purpose of the present paper it is convenient to cut off the construction process at a point where a sequence of "words" is available that is a candidate for a "text" that contains propositions, representing some sort of a "baseline" semantic construct. As pointed out above, there is no a priori watertight definition of what a "text" is, and the theoretical construct of a proposition or "what-is-said" itself is already the result of inference processes.

While there seems to be a functional necessity for an operational concept of "literal" meaning in law such as was identified on the level of "what-is-said" in a legal context, it cannot be sweepingly assumed that meanings constructed up to this level are "in the text." It is an issue worth investigating empirically to what extent even "primary," even pre-propositional inferencing processes can become an issue in legal interpretation. So it may not even be undisputed what has been said (in the technical sense of "what-is-said"). It is an empirical question if the following types of examples involved cases in litigation in which the speaker would lie – and be liable to be prosecuted – if the inferred elements of meaning were not true (on the notion of a "lie" cf. Horn, this volume).

(2) John and Mary are married {to each other}
     They had a baby and they got married {in that order}
     (from Horn, this volume, ex. 7)

The bracketed meaning elements are not "in the text," in the sense that they are not represented in words. They are not "said." They can even be felicitously canceled:

(3) John and Mary are married, but not to each other.
     They had a child and got married, but not necessarily in that order

So here is a type of clearly "constructed meanings" that have been termed "implicitures" that are very close to the core proposition, but are in no way "in the text."

The details of the continuing debate in linguistics about which meaning elements belong to pragmatics and have to be construed and which are part of semantics (narrowly conceived as referring to system or language meaning potentials) do not need to concern us here. They are a version of the meaning minimalism vs. maximalism debate. What matters here is the problem of where to draw an operational line for what should or what in legal practice actually in fact is considered part of the "literal" meaning and "in the text," given the relevance of the issue for the textualist and other principles in legal interpretation.

A type arguably further away from core proposition, and not a good candidate for being "in the text" are cases like:

(4) A Is there any evidence against them?
     B Some of their documents are forgeries.
     {Not all of their documents are forgeries.}

Is the inferred meaning, a so-called generalized implicature, available here? Would B be telling a lie if, in fact, all of their documents were forgeries?

(5) I met a woman last night
     {The woman was my wife.}

A standard inference, in fact a generalized implicature, is that this woman is not my wife, otherwise I would say so. But this is not in "the text," and I did not "say" that this woman was also my wife though it presumably would be part of "what-is-said," as a result of implicatures. But would it also invariably count as being in the "text" in legal interpretation? Would the speaker legally lie because s/he did not explicitly say (in the sense of "what is articulated") that there was a formal marital relationship?

To give one last standard example:

(6) John: was the exam easy?
 Mary: some of the students failed
 {A – Not all of the students failed.}
 {B – The exam was not easy.}

A and B are certainly "understood," i.e. inferred, so the meaning is, again, not "in the text." A is a so-called "generalized" implicature, B a "particularized" implicature.

The tentative ordering in the following list represents their "closeness" to whatever is the core meaning of an utterance, ranging from "primary" inferences to "secondary" inferences, not directly triggered by an expression, but by higher-ranking units of the text and by genre knowledge. The following list is ordered in terms of closeness to the proposition (with primary inferences such as explicitures and whatever is asserted and implicated in the sense of Marmor 2011 at the top):

Explicatures
Generalized Implicatures
Particularized Implicatures
Conversational Implicatures

The higher ranking, the more likely the content that is not represented is to be a candidate of litigation. The relevant point here is that all of our meaning construction is so shot through with inference and interpretation that any idea of a self-contained text consisting of words that are put together compositionally into a text that contains all the meanings is untenable, a view expounded in more detail in e.g. Hörmann (1976) and Busse (1991, § 6). A key issue from the point of view not of static knowledge, but of dynamic meaning construction in inferencing, is, for the pragmatician, do these inferences also apply to legal discourse, to put it very generally? Are "generalized" implicatures treated differently, as more usual, common, from "particularized" implicatures, as involving even more shared world interpretation? Do the types of inferences that have been identified in linguistic research constitute some cline of being counted as "in the text" in legal discourse, in some operational sense of text, and are therefore part of some operative notion of "literalness"? And are they treated the same as in non-legal language? In different types of legal language, in different legal genres? In oral legal discourse, like the police interview? In a cross examination? These are challenging research questions, in fact a research program, on issues in pragmatically-oriented research in legal discourse and possibly towards an explicit linguistic basis for legal decisions.

The types of inferencing discussed up to now were relevant to the issue of "what is in the text" and concerned to a large part "covert" inferencing, that non-linguistically trained language users are not normally aware of and that leads to a folklore idea of a "text." Inferencing in law is, naturally, not confined to the types discussed up to now that are at the center of pragmatic theories of inferencing in connection with individual expressions. The mainstay of "legal interpretation" in law concerns a variety of cases that are often the focus of overt debates, including textualist argumentation, with linguists being occasionally consulted, and which are subject of "canons of interpretation." More narrowly "linguistic" or structural cases like syntactic ambiguities (e.g. scope ambiguities) or other cases that are clearly triggered by language-structural optionalities are rarely the subject of "legal interpretation." "Legal interpretation" tends to center more on cases like the following:

- new objects not covered by statute formulations (does "dialing a number" still involve a "dial," or is the telephone book still a "book"?)
- marginal coverage because of changes in the world
- grammatical, structural ambiguities like scope ambiguities, which are often the subject of linguistic canons of interpretation
- ambiguities, including the pragmatic types often overlooked and discussed by Solan (this volume)
- really hard cases like the Boston Charles River Bridge case discussed by Friedman (2002: 49–55), where the economic philosophy is pitched against a literal interpretation (in the sense of propositional content plus primary inferences) of a statute.

In terms of the distinction referred to above by Allott and Shaer (forthcoming) between "investigative" and "creative," it would appear that the latter types discussed fall under the heading of "creative" adjudication: the creative, inferential synthesis accesses a specific type of outside knowledge, gives it preference over a more textualist reading and defines a new legal situation. The meaning construction process results in a new legal meaning, the specific path of inferencing is one of several possible types within the realm of legal dogmatics (in the legal realm as discussed by Poscher).

While the traditional cases of subsumption can tentatively be characterized as processes of deduction, the point to be made here is that all of the traditional cases of "legal interpretation" are of the same basic type of abductive inference, including the special cases of the "reading in" in Canadian law (Allott and Shaer, this volume) or other types of "hard cases": abduction implies the inferential creation of a plausible match between linguistically given information (the text) and various admissible types of legal and non-legal knowledge.

One of the notions that regularly show up in discussions of legal interpretation is "vagueness." There appear to be two versions of this concept, a positive and a negative one. To start with the negative version, vagueness seems to be characterized as a state of affairs that is a departure from a state of normalcy and that calls for additional interpretive work, with the state of normalcy being the "container" situation or lawyer's heaven as adumbrated in § 1, where automatic subsumption disposes of the case at hand. For this view, vagueness is the marked, or something of a pathological case that causes inferential work of the type described here. This is a very far cry from the view espoused here that any act of reference involves, as baseline activity, acts of inference matching memory of previous use with current pragmatic givens.

On the other hand, the term "vagueness" also denotes cases where it functions as a positive and intentional feature of drafting, as it allows formulations that are wide enough to accommodate future developments without the need to keep changing the law (Bhatia et al. 2005).

The two dimensions of inference – the dynamic process and the static aspect of existing knowledge – define variables all along the process, with the constraints on these processes defined by legal genres, or, to be more precise, by the type of legal genre, as it is a gross over-simplification to refer to something like "the legal genre." At best there is a "legal professional domain," with several types of genre, whose mastery is a membership criterion for being a member of that community of practice. It can a priori be assumed that different types of knowledge ("information") are legitimate for different such sub-genres at different stages of the legal process, and that different inductive ("combining") processes are legitimate. For instance, the interpretation rules discussed by Morlok (2012) and the legal canons (Scott 2010; Kudlich und Christensen 2004; Müller und Christensen 2013) are rules for accessing and combining information types in a new synthesis. There is, as a defining element of the community of practice, a clear sense of constraints on which knowledge types may be accessed and which types of inference rules are admissible at what stages of the legal process (Poscher, this volume). In a similar vein, Fiss (1982) refers to "disciplining rules." The differences between methods and schools of interpretation can then be conceptualized as differences between which types of knowledge may be legitimately combined in which ways at which stage of the meaning construction process.

These construction processes work in two directions (cf. Recanati's (2004) primary and secondary inference processes). The logically and temporally primary process is of course a top-down process triggered by the knowledge of the interaction type, Activity Type or genre. It is this knowledge that is "turned on" and interactionally primarily focused as soon as a domain and Activity Type is envisaged: a knowledge of what is legitimately to be expected mutual (technical) knowledge, what are the rules of cooperation, what are possible speech acts or what are possible rules of arguing, questioning and answering in court in a given culture?

While domain-specific language analysis has focused on special language lexis, the parameter of inferencing itself has now been around in discussions of domain-specific language for some time, but hardly in the area of the study of language in the law domain. By way of a first approximation, pragmatically oriented work by Heritage and Drew and by Levinson (Levinson in Drew and Heritage 1992: 76, ex. 10) have identified domain- and genre-specific inferencing processes. The majority of these are top down, such as the pre-assigning of structural-functional slots that interpret and integrate utterances into larger superstructural units. Thus it makes a difference if, in a conversational story, an utterance is classed as part of circumstance or as complicating action. But it seems equally promising to work out how the inferencing processes described in e.g. Levinson (2000), with the highly suggestive title "presumptive meanings," are different for genres in legal discourse.

We owe to Peter Tiersma an initial awareness that there are inferencing rules that are specific to legal discourse. Some of these are cases where generalized inferences that are current in ordinary conversation obviously do not hold in legal discourse. Peter Tiersma (2001, 2006) has given us a list of such rules, where normal inferencing procedures are obviously suspended, such as in the case of "I met a woman last night," when the assumption is that this was not my wife, or that the two NPs refer to different entities in legal language, but not in ordinary language (as in "John kissed John's girlfriend," we assume two different Johns, but in "Buyer promises that Buyer will pay" we infer that it is the same person).

There is, in law, another pointer to an awareness that there have to be such inference rules to get from text to interpretation. They are, as part of legal methodology, embedded in the "canons of interpretation." Scott (2010) has identified some 90 such canons of interpretation, amongst them a larger number of "textual" or linguistic canons in the widest sense (Scott 2010, II A) that vary considerably not only from US state to state, but also differ in part from similar rules in non-legal language, such as in the area of reference resolution. These canons testify to an awareness in the legal professions that there have to be rules of inference, i.e. of meaning construction. Their status, although "methodological law" (Scott 2010: 350), appears to be in-betweenish:

> The common law should be understood to encompass judicial methodology in addition to the traditional substantive common law subjects, such as the law of torts. Black's Law Dictionary does not treat the canons as common law, saying that "most jurisdictions treat the canons as mere customs not having the force of law." Such "custom," however, is law-like. The common law of interpretation develops because methods of legal reasoning attach to results and weakly constrain judges in future cases. Like the development of the common law generally, common law interpretive rules develop by "experience," including "[t]he felt necessities of the time, the prevalent moral and political theories, [and] intuitions of public policy, avowed or unconscious."
>
> As a result, various methods of legal reasoning become widespread because they produce substantive results in which the public has confidence and on which legal actors rely. (Scott 2010: 345)

Scott (2010: 343) also points to the fact that they are "vulnerable to the criticism that they are not authoritative because they are not the work of legislature" – so the fact that they are not inscribed in written statutes makes them only "weakly" constrain meaning extraction.

There are more cases where "inference" seems to be "genre-grammaticalized" such as cases like the following one described by Slocum (this volume) where meaning construction seems to be relative to a particular genre:

(7) "Gin, bourbon, vodka and other beverages are not allowed in this building"

What about "coke"? This is surely an "other beverage." What happens is that a whole class of items is inferred. It can be argued that the case will be resolved by a "noscitur a sociis" principle.

The varying versions of the canon of *expression unius* (Scott 2010: 354f) in different states of the US testify to the linguistically problematic status of some of these canons, and to the impossibility of trying to resolve the issue sentence-internally. Another example for a very different way of handling meaning extraction is the marked difference in handling punctuation. In "ordinary" language, punctuation serves as instruction for the construction of syntactic and pragmatic meanings, but in American statutes that role in meaning construction is dispreferred. The following citation from Scott (2010: 260f) is symptomatic: "[...] punctuation is an inert source of meaning." Statutes tend not to allow punctuation to have meaning-creation status, or only whatever is a "weak source of meaning," or a "last-ditch alternative aid in statutory construction." This is of course a massive departure from normal written language, where punctuation can in fact be meaning-discriminating.

In this way, a linguistic, pragmatic explicitation of canons would go some way towards establishing inference rules that are definitional for legal genres only. So at this point in the present discussion, the pragmatic characterization of legal discourse includes not only specific versions of inference strategies for "filling in," "saturation," types of implicatures on all levels of language, but also rules for accessing paths or inferential strategies and types of knowledge "legitimately" accessed by different schools and methods of interpretation. Arguably, these are all part of the "template" of a given legal genre. With respect to the canons of interpretation, it will be a challenge to reformulate them in technical linguistic terms and identify where they differ from each other and from a hypothesized "degree-zero" language use. For instance, exactly what is the domain of "sociis" in "noscitur a sociis"? Is the notion of frames useful in describing the effect of this rule in law? A pragmatics-based research program will try to identify these differences and formulate them as elements of genre or of templates.

6 On the wrong side of the legal process: language crimes

We have up to now only considered the situation where normative texts have to be "interpreted." The issue of interpreting (in a non-legal, non-technical sense) logically precedes "legal interpretation." The prior task is to establish if an actionable offense was committed that can then, packaged in the genre of a police report, be subjected to the application or not of statutes or parallel cases.

In the case of a punishable, actionable offense involving language ("language crimes") inferencing is involved to the extent that the interpretation of utterances can lead to the conclusion that a language crime has been committed. The question here is very often: Can you be done in for what you have not said, for what is not "in text," for inferences and implicatures? While explicatures as inferences "filling in and adjusting the semantic scaffolding provided by the linguistic expression used" (Carston 2002: 366) are not likely to be a problem, "implicatures are derived wholly pragmatically, though that inferential process may be constrained by encoded procedural meaning" (Carston 2002: 366). The important point here is that they "may constitute the primary point of the utterance, that is, the *main focus of cognitive effects* [my emphasis]" (Carston 2002: 366). In other words, the reason why they are communicated, i.e. why the understander legitimately feels prompted to construct them, is the incriminated language act, although they are not encoded in language. So punishment would really be for something you have not "done," but for what you had someone else do. Punishment would be for an intent, similar to the argument put forward by Horn in his paper on lying in the present volume.

The difficulty for the practical side of the law, for the judge, in most language crimes is that the "enaction" of the incriminated act is not tied to a surface linguistic form in the way the judiciary would like to see. Few people actually say "I herewith threaten to beat you up": but threats take more likely the very indirect formulation like "I know where your daughter lives." As has been convincingly shown in work on the act of lying (Horn, this volume) the criterial element for lying is, in ordinary conversation, the recognized intention to lie, – not even actually offering a false statement. You can lie by mistakenly saying something that is true but by meaning to lie. A recent study of the act of threatening Muschalik (forthcoming) shows that it is not possible to linguistically identify an actionable threat in a watertight way. Put differently, there is no reliable, IFID-like, "grammaticalized" correlation between form and function to which a judge could point and use as "hard evidence" for a crime. There is no formal substance on which she or he can rely.

The problem is there are a couple of statistical tendencies, but nothing approaching anything like a canonical linguistic form associated with an "insult" that a judge can "read off" and pinpoint in a "text" the fact that an utterance is an insult. It is a fact everyone, and certainly the legal practitioner, and in fact a lot of, if not most, linguists, if they are not of a more semiotic bent, will feel uncomfortable with. It explains the search for linguistic indicators of speech acts (illocutionary force indicating devices, "IFIDs") for all kinds of speech acts that are at the center of legal prosecution or other legal processes, such as contracts. The attempt to identify linguistic indicators of pragmatically defined speech acts like insult, defamation, promise, threat is at the core of a substantial body of more linguistically oriented work with the aim of identifying more "hard and fast" linguistic surface cues and, legally speaking, evidence, rather than having to rely on "mens rea."

7 Inference and interpretation beyond the sentence and the text

The pervasiveness of inferencing in the law is also manifested in stages and processes in the legal domain that go much beyond the meaning construction in individual sentences and text chunks that were the focus of the discussion up to this point and operate on the highest level of adjudication. A very basic operating principle of common law is a massive process of inferencing in establishing what counts as a precedent. As Fish (1990: 94) points out, the choice of precedent involves selecting "appropriate" cases that are "arguably similar": "Notice that the similarity is 'arguable', which means it has to be argued for [...]." Similarity judgments are interpretive acts that select – tactically select – relevance criteria (Condello, this volume). Kischel (2015: 246–249) describes in detail the inferential processes of induction and deduction involved in establishing what counts as a precedent in any given individual case in the version of common law practiced in England, where precedent-based law is much more widespread than in the United States, where the culturally, politically and legally most significant processes of interpretation are triggered by the touchstone of a written constitution, such as England does not have. Jeand'heur (1998, 1992) refers to this process as a "Zubereitungsfunktion," i.e. a selective readying and trimming of potential facts into a "story."

A difference between the more local linguistic issues discussed in the previous section and the higher-order selections is the availability and the admissibility of these types of knowledge. In the case of the linguistic forms discussed these choices were as a rule subconscious and not the result of premeditated strategic manipulation. One of the hallmarks of a pragmatic approach to analysing communication in the legal domain is the identification of the admissible static knowledge types to be accessed in inference processes. The acceptability of the end result of an adjudication process is relative to standards of acceptability and consistency in the domain. Poscher (this volume) makes the point that notions of consistency in politics are different from consistency in law, which amounts to saying that inference processes and legitimate constraining knowledge types are domain- and genre-specific. Fish (1990: 98) emphasizes the role of these doctrinal constraints: "[...] interpretation is a structure of constraints, a structure which, because it is always and already in place, renders unavailable the independent or uninterpreted text and renders unavailable the independent and freely interpreting reader." These, then, are rules of the genre game (Fish 1990: 98): "Interpreters are constrained by their tacit awareness of what is possible and not possible to do [...]," such as what implicatures can legitimately be construed.

The differences between schools of interpretation – textualist, new textualist, intentionalist, pragmatic (Scott 2010: 347) – mean for the pragmatician essentially which types of knowledge can legitimately be accessed in meaning construction processes. Poscher (this volume) argues that legal argumentation should strictly be internal, i.e. referring to doctrinally relevant texts, such as statutes, commentaries etc. that already exist, and not look to external, essentially political, intentions to change the world. This is where he sees the borderline between a truly legal, internal, inferencing type on the one side and externally guided, essentially non-legal argumentation on the other. Basically, legal-internal argumentation means consulting different legal documents (statutes, commentaries, previous cases). So it essentially is a process of amalgamating previously existing knowledge types with a selection of new facts in a new synthesis, just as, in principle, every learning process happens.[4] The options are between choosing different such texts and text types, such as expounded by Busse (1998, 2000) and accessing external, social, political, philosophical knowledge. He shows that legal interpretation is "[...] ein Wissen über *zulässige Operationen mit Textelementen* [sic], nicht über deren 'Bedeutungen' im gewöhnlichen Sinn" [a type of knowledge about admissible operations with text elements, and not their meanings in the conventional sense, D.S.] (Busse 2008: 160). What matters here is the emphasis on inferential construction, not on invariant meaning chunks, whatever the status of such entities.

These meaning construction processes would equally apply to top-level strategic argumentation in law. Pointing to a very modern concept of legal decision-making, Ladeur (in Vogel, 32) has argued that while there cannot be any doubt about the continuing fundamental role of so-called static legal concepts, the emerging new practice in "Güterabwägung" (pitting and weighing social concepts against each other with a view to deciding to which one to give preference in a specific case, rather than establishing for-ever principles), rather than deduction, seems to call more for a study of the higher construction rules and the micro-processes, all of them induction processes, of how these processes are forming, and what the nature of this type of induction (or even abduction) is, and what the legitimacies and specifics of the synthesis-forming knowledge-accessibilities are. Current examples include privacy and data protection vs. national security, freedom of speech vs. protection of personal rights and the right to oblivion. Legal decision-making is developing away from the handling of absolutes into a "management of rules" (Ladeur forthcoming: 33), a flexible

---

4 This fact plays a central role in Tomasello's (1999: 122) account of the ontogeny and phylogeny of language. His theory of the primacy of cognitive development in the development of language in both perspectives is also very relevant in the present context of discussion as it emphasizes the logical and functional precedence of social activity engaged in as a repository of informational redundancy. Primacy is not with language and morphemes but with "... an interactive format (form of life, joint attentional scene) that she first understands non-linguistically, so that the adult's language can be grounded in shared experiences whose social significance she already appreciates" (Tomasello 1999: 109). Primacy, ever already in place and a main source of inference and interpretation, is thus for the genre or the template, the modern theoretical inheritors of the "forms of life" and Activity Types.

consideration of what the options are for selecting suitable rules. There is a tendency towards "proceduralization" (Ladeur forthcoming: 34), resulting in a drift from inherent "text sense" to "procedural sense" (Textsinn" vs "Verfahrenssinn"). Rigid rules are subordinated to evolving a new interpretive synthesis. It would probably be good to see that there is some standardization of practices, and not only ad-hoc-ness in this move away from "digging out" law towards making law. So even more importance accrues to the job of the pragmatician to figure out the law-specific constraints on these induction rules and inference procedures. This tendency in law reflects a tendency in which the law is embedded, in society: a move away from social structures that are experienced as stable and axiomatic first principles to more of a fluid, ad hoc, negotiation of terms. In terms of the major schools of interpretation in law, this tendency would seem to be a move away from textualist positions to a more pragmatic theory of interpretation, given priority to external criteria, with canons of interpretation no longer absolutes, but themselves being chosen tactically and subservient to higher-ranking considerations.

To conclude, this chapter has tried to show how core notions of the law are dependent on notions about language. In particular, the chapter has argued for a re-focusing of our analysis of legal discourse towards making more explicit the steps involved in constructing meanings in discourse and what the principles at work are, using the analytical tools of a broadly-conceived discipline of pragmatics. This may or may not have repercussions in the practice of the decision-making business. Ruth Sullivan, a famous student of High Court decisions, has forcefully argued, in the nineties, for making explicit the process of inferencing and the kinds of knowledge that is implicitly or tacitly accessed in guiding inference processes, – basically an early proponent of what a pragmatic turn could achieve.

References

Bhatia, Vijah K., Jan Engberg, Maurizio Gotti & Dorothee Heller (eds.). 2005. *Vagueness in normative texts*. Bern: Peter Lang.

Bix, Brian. 2012. Legal Interpretation and the Philosophy of Language. In Peter M. Tiersma & Lawrence M. Solan (eds.), *The Oxford Handbook of Language and Law*, 145–155. Oxford University Press.

Breheny, Richard, Napoleon Katsos & John Williams. 2005. Are generalised implicatures generated by default? An on-line investigation into the role of context in generating pragmatic inferences. *Cognition* XX, 1–30.

Bublitz, Wolfram. 2001. *Englische Pragmatik. Eine Einführung*. Berlin: Erich Schmidt Verlag.

Busse, Dietrich. 1992. Textinterpretation. Sprachtheoretische Grundlagen einer explikativen Semantik. Opladen: Westdeutscher Verlag.

Busse, Dietrich. 1989. Was ist die Bedeutung eines Gesetzestextes? Sprachwissenschaftliche Argumente im Methodenstreit der juristischen Auslegungslehre – linguistisch gesehen. In Friedrich Müller (ed.), *Untersuchungen zur Rechtslinguistik. Interdisziplinäre Studien zu Praktischer Semantik und Strukturierender Rechtslehre in Grundfragen der juristischen Methodik*. 93–148. Berlin: Duncker & Humblot.

Busse, Dietrich. 2000. Textsorten des Bereichs Rechtswesen und Justiz. In Gerd Antos, Klaus Brinker, Wolfgang Heinemann, Sven F. Sager (eds.), *Text- und Gesprächslinguistik. Ein internationales Handbuch zeitgenössischer Forschung*. 1. Halbband (Handbücher zur Sprach- und Kommunikationswissenschaft, Band 16.1), 658–675. Berlin & New York: de Gruyter.

Busse, Dietrich. 2001. Bedeutungsfeststellung, Interpretation, Arbeit mit Texten? In Ulrike Haß-Zumkehr (ed.), *Juristische Auslegungstätigkeit in linguistischer Sicht*. Sprache und Recht (= Institut für deutsche Sprache, Jahrbuch 2001), 136–162. Berlin & New York: de Gruyter.

Busse, Dietrich. 2008. Interpreting law: Text understanding – Text application – Working with texts. In Frances Olsen, Alexander Lorz & Dieter Stein (eds.), *Law and language. Theory and society*, 239–266.

Canale, Damiano & Giovannia Tuzet. 2007. On legal inferentialism. Toward a pragmatics of semantic content in legal interpretation? *Ratio Juris* 20(1). 32–44.

Carston, Robyn. 2002. *Thoughts and utterances: The pragmatics of explicit communication*. Malden MA: Blackwell.

Easterbrook, Frank. 1994. Text, history, and structure in statutory interpretation. *Harvard Journal of Law and Public Policy* 17. 61–70.

Engberg, Jan. 2012. Word meaning and the problem of a globalized legal order. In Lawrence M. Solan and Peter M. Tiersma (eds.), *The Oxford handbook of language and law*, 175–186. Oxford: Oxford University Press.

Felder, Ekkehard & Friedemann Vogel (eds.) (forthcoming). *Handbuch Sprache im Recht*. Berlin: Walter de Gruyter.

Fish, Stanley. 1990. *Doing what comes naturally: Change, rhetoric, and the practice of theory in literary & legal studies*. Duke University Press.

Flanagan, Brian. 2010. Revisiting the contribution of literal meaning to legal meaning. *Oxford Journal of Legal Studies* 30(2). 255–271.

Friedman, Lawrence M. 2002. *Law in America. A short history*. New York: The Modern Library.

Giltrow, Janet. 2002. Meta-Genre. In Richard Coe, Lorelei Lingard and Tatiana Teslenko (eds.), *The rhetoric and ideology of genre: Strategies for stability and change*, 187–206. Cresskill, NJ: Hampton.

Giltrow, Janet & Dieter Stein (eds.). 2009. *Genres in the internet. Issues in the theory of genre* (Pragmatics & Beyond New Series 188). Amsterdam & Philadelphia: John Benjamins Publishing Company.

Gumbrecht, Hans Ulrich. 2012. *Präsenz*. Berlin: Suhrkamp.

Harris, Roy. 1981. *The language myth*. London: Duckworth.

Horn, Larry. 1984. Towards a new taxonomy for pragmatic inference. In Deborah Schiffrin (ed.), *Form and use in context. Linguistic applications* (GURT '84), 11–42. Washington, DC: Georgetown University Press.

Horn, Larry. 2005. The border wars. In K. von Heusinger and K. Turner (eds.), *Where semantics meets pragmatics*, 21–48. Amsterdam: Elsevier.

Hutton, Christopher. 1998. Law lessons for linguists? Accountability and acts of professional classification. *Language & Communication* 16(3). 205–214.

Kischel, Uwe. 2015. *Rechtsvergleichung*. München: Beck.
Kudlich, Hans & Ralph Christensen. 2004. Die Kanones der Auslegung. In Dieter Maihold und Christian Wolf (eds.), *Juristische Arbeitsblätter*, 74–83. Köln: Volters Kluwer.
Levinson, Stephen C. 2000. *Presumptive meanings. The theory of generalized conversational implicature*. Cambridge, Mass.: The MIT Press.
Liedtke, Frank & Cornelia Schulze (eds.). 2013. *Beyond words. Content, context, and inference.* Berlin/Boston: Walter de Gruyter.
Liedtke, Frank. 2013. Pragmatic templates and free enrichment. In Frank Liedtke & Cornelia Schulze (eds.), *Beyond words. Content, context, and inference*, 183–206. Berlin/Boston: Walter de Gruyter.
Loflin, Marvin D. 1978. Discourse and inference in cognitive anthropology. In Marvin D. Loflin (ed.), *Discourse and inference in cognitive anthropology. Approaches to psychic unity and enculturation*, 3–18. Paris: Walter de Gruyter.
Marmor, Andrei. 2011. Can the law imply more than it says? On some pragmatic aspects of strategic speech. In Andrei Marmor & Scott Soames (eds.), *Language in the law*, 83–104. Oxford: Oxford University Press.
Milroy, Jim & Leslie Milroy. 1985. *Authority in language*. London: Routledge.
Möllers, Christoph. 2015. *Die Möglichkeit der Normen. Über eine Praxis jenseits von Moralität und Kausalität*. Berlin. Suhrkamp.
Morlok, Martin. 2012. Die vier Auslegungsmethoden – Was sonst? In Gottfried Gabriel und Rolf Gröschner (eds.), *Subsumtion. Schlüsselbegriff der juristischen Methodenlehre*, 179–214. Tübingen: Mohr Siebeck.
Müller, Friedrich. 1994. *Strukturierende Rechtslehre*. Berlin: Duncker & Humblot.
Müller, Friedrich & Ralph Christensen. 2013. *Juristische Methodik. Grundlegung für die Arbeitsmethoden der Rechtspraxis*. Auf neuestem Stand bearb. und erw. Aufl. 11. Aufl. Berlin: Duncker & Humblot.
Möllers, Christoph. 2015. *Die Möglichkeit der Normen. Über eine Praxis jenseits von Moralität und Kausalität*. Berlin: Suhrkamp.
Muschalik, Julia. Forthcoming. *Threatening in English: Form and function.*
Olsen, Frances, Alexander Lorz & Dieter Stein (eds.). 2008. *Law and language: Theory and society*. Düsseldorf: Düsseldorf University Press.
Poscher, Ralf. 2012. Ambiguity and vagueness. In Lawrence M. Solan and Peter M. Tiersma (eds.), *The Oxford handbook of language and law*, 128–144. Oxford: Oxford University Press.
Posner, Richard A. 1998. Pragmatic adjudication. In Morris Dickstein (ed.), *The revival of pragmatism. New essays on social thought, law, culture*, 235–253. Duke University Press.
Solan, Lawrence M. 2005. Vagueness and ambiguity in legal interpretation. In Vijay K. Bhatia, Jan Engberg, Maurizio Gotti & Dorothee Heller (eds.), *Vagueness in normative texts*, 73–96. Bern: Peter Lang.
Recanati, Francois. 2004. *Literal meaning*. Cambridge: Cambridge University Press.
Scott, Jacob J. 2010. Codified canons and the common law of interpretation. *The Georgetown Law Journal* 98. 341–431.
Soames, Scott. 2011. What vagueness and inconsistency tell us about interpretation. In Andrei Marmor & Scott Soames (eds.), *Language in the law*, 31–57. Oxford: Oxford University Press.
Stein, Dieter. 2015. "Words, words, words" – but what's in a legal text? In Lawrence M. Solan, Janet Ainsworth & Roger Shuy (eds.), *Speaking of language and law. Conversations on the work of Peter Tiersma*, 51–55. Oxford: Oxford University Press.

Stein, Dieter. Forthcoming. Sprachtheoretische Aspekte rechtstheoretischer Ansätze im Überblick. In Ekkehard Felder & Friedemann Vogel (eds.), *Handbuch Sprache im Recht*. Berlin: De Gruyter Mouton.

Sullivan, Ruth. 1999. "Statutory interpretation in the Supreme Court of Canada." *Ottawa Law Review* 30(2): 175–227.

Tiersma, Peter M. 1999. *Legal language*. Chicago: The University of Chicago Press.

Tiersma, Peter M. 2001. A message in a bottle: Text, autonomy, and statutory interpretation. *Tulane Law Review* 76. 431–483.

Tiersma, Peter M. 2006. Some myths about legal language. *Law, Culture and the Humanities* 2. 9–50.

Tiersma, Peter M. 2010. *Parchment, paper, pixels: Law and the technologies of communication*. Chicago: Chicago University Press.

Tiersma, Peter M. & Larry Solan (eds.). 2012. *The Oxford handbook of language and law*. Oxford: Oxford University Press.

Tomasello, Michael. 1999. *The cultural origins of human cognition*. Cambridge: Harvard University Press.

Toolan, Michael. 2002. The language myth and the law. In Roy Harris (ed.), *The language myth in Western culture*, 159–182. Richmond: Curzon.

Toolan, Michael. N.d. *The language myth and the law*. http://artsweb.bham.ac.uk/MToolan/newsite/languagemyth.htm (downloaded June 2, 2015).

Van Dijk, Teun A. 1980. *Macrostructures. An interdisciplinary study of global structures in discourse, interaction, and cognition*. Hillsdale: Erlbaum.

Van Schooten, Hanneke. 2007. Law as fact, law as fiction: A tripartite model of legal communication. In Anne Wagner, Wouter Werner & Deborah Cao (eds.), *Interpretation, law, and the construction of meaning: Collected papers on legal interpretation in theory, adjudication and political practice*, 3–20. Dordrecht: Springer.

Vogel, Friedemann. 2012. *Linguistik rechtlicher Normgenese. Theorie der Rechtsnormdiskursivität am Beispiel der Online-Durchsuchung* (Sprache und Wissen 9). Berlin & Boston: Walter de Gruyter.

Vogel, Friedemann (ed.). Forthcoming. *Zugänge zur Rechtssemantik. Interdisziplinäre Ansätze im Zeitalter neuer Medien*.

Wagner, Anne, Werner Wouter & Deborah Cao (eds.). 2007. *Interpretation, law, and the construction of meaning: Collected papers on legal interpretation in theory, adjudication and political practice*. Dordrecht: Springer.

Subject index

Aboriginal rights and title 5–8, 14, 233–234, 235, 239, 241–244
abstract principle 205–206, 229–230
abuse (verbal) 12, 188, 191–193, 194–195, 197–203
abuse (sexual) 13, 198, 221–225, 225 fn22, 227–230
abuse (juridical) 189
Activity Type 3–4, 59, 347, 356, 359, 364 fn4
adjudication 8, 11–13, 15–16, 24, 207, 215, 222–223, 231, 257, 279, 282, 307–316, 319–321, 323, 328–331, 328 fn39, 339, 343, 348, 352, 357, 363
alignment 9, 168, 173–179, 184, 237, 258
ambiguity 11, 40–41, 47, 58, 87, 97–99, 99 fn17, 100, 106, 110, 112, 112 fn26, 114, 116, 119, 136, 145–151, 155–158, 160–162, 192–193, 198, 233, 249–250, 262, 265, 278, 347, 357
analogy 11, 113, 167–72, 174–184, 205–206, 348
assertion 25–27, 29–30, 32, 39–40, 45, 48–52, 103, 131 fn18, 137, 180, 195, 233, 310, 318–321, 356
attitudinal model 329–331
arbitration 148, 157–158
Austin, John L. 1–2, 4, 13, 30, 30 fn3, 105, 182, 207–208, 208 fn5
autonomous text 1, 4, 315, 324 fn32, 325, 340, 342, 353

Bach, Kent 41–3, 87, 88 fn3, 147
Bix, Brian 4, 146, 155, 195, 197, 233, 242, 245, 348–350
Bourdieu, Pierre 234, 236, 243, 304
Brandom, Robert 318–321
bullshit 26, 28, 51

canons of interpretation 11, 17, 26, 128–135, 142, 145, 148, 162, 238, 244, 290, 312, 314, 324, 344, 352, 357–362, 365
Carston, Robyn 41, 96, 100, 105, 131, 136–139, 141–142, 346–347, 351, 354, 361

Chinese courtroom discourse 9, 57–59, 62, 75–76, 78–81
Chomsky, Noam 96, 162, 255, 267–268, 281
classification 102, 135, 167–175, 177–179, 191, 203, 262, 269, 281, 290 fn3, 302, 242, 359–360
class gifts 156–157
code, linguistic 1, 4, 12–13, 17, 50, 87, 88 fn3, 94, 94 fn11, 95 fn12, 96–97, 100–102, 102 fn19, 105, 109–110, 114–116, 126, 130, 136, 161–162, 202, 234 fn2, 235, 244–245, 265, 336, 340–341, 347, 350, 360, 361–362
coherence 11, 63, 169, 171, 179, 310
cognitive linguistics 11, 84, 91–93, 114, 135–137, 155, 167–168, 174–176, 178, 182–184, 234–235, 236 fn3, 243–244, 251–252, 256, 269, 288–290, 343, 346–347, 361, 364 fn4
computer-assisted legal linguistics 287, 291, 303–304
consent 101, 146, 158–160, 212
context 1–11, 14, 17–18, 23, 35–36, 41, 43, 50–51, 58, 84–85, 91, 91 fn7, 94 fn11, 99, 103–105, 113, 115–116, 119 fn1, 120, 124–126, 127 fn13, 129–131, 131 fn19, 135–142, 145 fn1, 145–149, 151, 154–155, 157, 161–162, 168–171, 173–174, 179–180, 192, 195, 197–203, 205 fn1, 206–207, 222, 234 fn2, 234–235, 236 fn6, 237, 239, 240, 244–245, 252–254, 257–260, 269, 272, 279–280, 288–292, 294–295, 297, 300, 303–304, 316, 318–320, 323, 339–340, 344, 347–348, 350, 354, 364 fn4
– macrocontext 251
contracts 11, 29, 45, 60, 73, 77, 85, 90, 99 fn17, 145–148, 157–159, 159 fn21, 160, 162, 167, 209, 253, 257–259, 268, 302, 342, 362
conversation 1, 9–11, 17–18, 36, 38, 57–58, 61, 63, 65, 79–80, 84, 113–116, 126, 131–132, 142, 191, 208, 347, 359, 362

conversational maxims 9, 58, 61, 63, 65, 67–69, 77, 109 fn23, 130, 132, 137, 141, 208
cooperation 9, 57–59, 61–70, 72–81
cooperation, continuum 10, 61–62, 80–81
cooperation, degrees of 58–9, 61–64, 67, 72–73, 75–76, 80–81
cooperative principle 9, 11, 13, 57–58, 108 fn23, 130–132, 207, 208 fn4, 210
corpus linguistics 8, 12, 15, 59–60, 187, 199–202, 206, 287–288, 290 fn3, 290 fn4, 291-2, 294–8, 300 fn7, 302–304, 338, 351
corpus pragmatics 288, 291, 294, 296, 296 fn5, 303
critical legal studies 205, 207, 229, 311, 311 fn14, 314 fn19

data-based qualitative research 9, 57–60, 63, 76, 80, 126, 187, 199–202, 250, 254, 262, 263 fn5, 263 fn6, 265, 266 fn9, 277–279, 287, 289, 291, 294, 298, 300, 302–3, 323, 330
Davies, Bethan 9, 58, 61, 63, 80, 208 fn4
definite descriptions 147–148, 156–57, 159, 159 fn21, 161
dictionaries 10, 12–14, 17, 83, 112–113, 112 fn26, 122–23, 127, 138, 187–189, 198–200, 200 fn24, 201–203, 203, 233, 233 fn1, 234–40, 242–245, 254, 256–258, 261–282, 263 fn5, 263, fn6, 264–275, 277–281, 303, 303 fn14, 348, 360
disambiguation 98, 112, 136, 198, 250, 278, 280
dogmatics 229, 287, 294–296, 302, 316, 357
Dworkin, Ronald 15, 111 fn25, 206, 307 fn2, 309–310, 313, 330, 330 fn42

Ehrlich, Eugen 311, 311 fn11
ejusdem generis 128–131, 133–135, 142, 148, 162, 178, 178 fn1
Endicott, Timothy 10, 84, 89–91, 90 fn6
enforced inference 267
enrichment, free 104–106, 108, 115, 136
enrichment, pragmatic 41–43, 87, 101–102, 104–106, 108, 113–115, 125–126, 136, 139, 141, 347

feminism 206–207, 211, 229–230
first-order conceptualizations 14, 196–197, 197 fn20, 199, 202
formalism 15, 161–162, 179–180, 183–184, 205–207, 207 fn3, 211, 214, 217, 229–230, 234 fn2, 309, 314, 336, 362
free-law movement 311
freedom of speech 169, 187–190, 221–222, 227, 229–231, 319–320, 364

gender bias 12–13, 205, 207, 209 fn6
goals 9, 12, 26, 31, 35, 57–8, 63, 74–6, 78–81, 84, 99 fn17, 121 fn6, 132, 175–176, 184, 199, 210
goal relationship 74–76
goal-driven principle 56, 63, 78, 80
Goffman, Erving 15, 33, 210 fn8, 288–289
Grice, Paul 1–3, 9, 11, 13, 18, 23, 29, 30, 32, 35–36, 39, 50 fn11, 51, 57–58, 63, 75, 80, 83, 85–86, 50 fn11, 51, 57–58, 63, 75, 80, 83, 85–87, 87 fn2, 91, 95, 108, 108 fn23, 130–132, 137, 141, 195, 207, 208 fn4, 210, 220, 260, 352

Habermas, Jürgen 309
hard cases 15, 169, 307–316, 323–328, 330–331, 345, 357–358
Hart, H. L. A. 120–122, 122 fn7, 173, 242, 308, 314, 341

indexicals 1–3, 41, 48, 86–87, 96, 96 fn13, 97, 102, 102 fn19, 106, 115–116, 346
induction 179–180, 182–183, 363–365
inference 2–8, 9–10, 12–17, 35–36, 37 fn7, 39–40, 83–88, 88 fn3, 89, 91–99, 99 fn17, 100, 101 fn18, 102–106, 108–116, 119–120, 124–127, 129–130, 135, 137, 139, 141, 147, 155–156, 167–168, 175, 177–181, 184, 191–193, 196, 199, 205 fn1, 234 fn2, 235, 239–240, 242–245, 260, 266–267, 271, 289, 307, 318–322, 326, 335–336, 338, 341, 343–347, 349, 351, 351 fn2, 352–364, 364 fn4, 365
Inferentialism 318–322
integrational linguistics 234
intentionalism 10, 12, 30–32, 34, 40, 83, 85, 89, 95, 109, 111, 120 fn3, 142, 142 fn25,

193, 195–198, 202, 348, 350, 352, 363
interpretation, statutory 5, 93, 99 fn17, 146, 150, 155, 158, 162, 178, 178 fn1, 195, 203, 214, 279, 344–345, 360
implicature 2–5, 7–10, 16–17, 27, 30, 32, 35–37, 37 fn7, 40, 50–51, 51 fn12, 58, 63, 89, 92 fn9, 94–95, 108 fn23, 115–116, 121, 125, 130–137, 140–141, 208, 220, 345, 347, 352, 355–356, 361, 363
implicature, conventional 51 fn12, 108 fn23, 121, 130–131, 131 fn18, 132–133, 135, 140, 220, 345, 347, 356
implicature, conversational 51 fn12, 108 fn23, 121, 130–133, 135, 140, 220, 345, 347, 356
implicature, false 9, 27, 32, 37, 40, 50–51, 51 fn12
implicature, weak 3–5, 8
impartiality 13, 190, 207, 210–211, 327–328
impoliteness 190–193, 200

juristes inquiets 311
jurisprudence 23, 114, 173, 205, 287–290, 294, 309
– conceptual jurisprudence 309

legal hermeneutics 236 fn3, 289–291, 307
legal linguistics 15, 262, 287, 289, 304
legal realism 311, 311 fn11
legal semantics 254, 274, 279, 281, 287, 294, 343
Levinson, Stephen C. 3–4, 33, 59, 133, 135, 137, 190, 191 fn13, 338, 359
Lewis, David 46, 320
lies and lying 8, 23–31, 31 fn4, 31 fn5, 32–34, 37–41, 44–7, 47 fn9, 48–52, 49 fn10, 51 fn12, 341, 355–356, 362
literal truth defense 39, 46
Luhmann, Niklas 307, 324 fn33, 329

Marmor, Andrei 10, 83, 85, 88 fn3, 93–94, 94 fn11, 95–97, 100, 104, 108–109, 115, 131, 131 fn18, 132, 346, 356
maxim of manner 58, 76, 88, 131
maxim of quality 9, 23, 32, 51, 58, 62, 65, 76, 102, 130

maxim of quantity 9, 35–37, 39, 58, 76, 102, 130
maxim of relevance 39, 58, 61–62, 130, 132–133, 138, 195, 208, 260
meaning-textualism 10, 110–113
meaning, communicative 10, 119–120, 120 fn3, 121, 121 fn5, 122–124, 126–131, 133, 140, 142
meaning, encoded 50, 87, 88 fn3, 94, 95 fn12, 96–98, 100, 102, 106, 109, 110, 114–116, 126, 347, 361–362
meaning, legal 10, 14–5, 91, 119, 121–122, 124, 132, 140–141, 249, 254, 257, 262, 271, 277–282, 287, 290, 303, 315, 320, 325, 339, 354, 357
meaning, linguistic 1, 41, 88 fn3, 97–98, 101 fn18, 107 fn22, 108, 119 fn1, 120, 121 fn5, 136, 172, 253, 346–347, 349–350
meaning, literal 4, 9–11, 14, 16–17, 30, 38–39, 46–47, 50, 106, 119, 119 fn1, 120, 120 fn3, 121, 121 fn5, 124, 126–130, 131 fn18, 132–135, 140, 200, 208, 234, 236, 326 fn36, 330, 336, 337–348, 350–352, 354–355, 357
meaning, plain 4, 10, 17, 196, 198, 202–203, 337, 342, 351
meaning, pragmatic 1, 3, 249–252, 255, 258, 261, 278–280, 336, 340, 350, 360
meaning, sentence 124–125
meaning, speaker 1, 3–4, 41, 58, 86–87, 88 fn3, 100 fn17, 109, 197, 350
meaning, utterance 63, 92, 99
mental reservation 40, 41, 45–47, 47 fn9, 49
misleading (vs. lying) 23–24, 30–32, 34–36, 38–41, 44, 46, 50–51, 194, 224, 252, 339

narrowing and broadening 30, 48, 87, 92, 105–107, 107 fn21, 108, 115, 129, 134–135, 189, 214–215, 229, 233–234
naturalism 309, 311
norm, including normal and normative 16, 75–76, 80, 83–4, 110–111, 115, 126, 127 fn13, 132, 161, 167–168, 170–173, 176–177, 179–180, 184, 206–211, 229–31, 238, 255, 288–289, 300, 308, 315, 326–330, 336, 339–344, 346–49, 358–359, 361

Subject index

opacity 11, 145–155, 157–158, 160, 162, 262
originalism 318, 323, 326, 348–50
ostensive 5, 8, 136

performative, constrained 12–13, 205, 208–211, 229
perjury 9, 27–29, 37–40, 50
plain language 4, 11, 150, 244, 345
plain meaning rule 4, 10, 16–17, 196, 198, 202–203, 337, 342, 351
poetic effects 2, 4–5
pragmatic turn 1, 3–4, 16, 162, 205, 273, 280, 336, 341, 343, 350, 352, 365
pragmatism, judicial 12–13, 206–207, 207 fn3, 216, 222
precedent 13, 36–8, 150, 167–172, 205–206, 222, 233, 309, 317, 317 fn24, 318, 320, 322–326, 337, 344, 363
Principle of Communicative Impartiality 13, 210–211
prosecution thresholds 188
prototype and prototype theory 11–12, 26, 167–168, 171–176, 181–183, 298
public order offence 188, 192

Québec 14, 106, 239–243, 240 fn6

reading down 106, 108, 115
Recanati, François 10–11, 41–2, 92 fn9, 96, 105, 124–126, 127 fn13, 128, 130, 346–347, 359
reference 1–3, 11, 126, 136, 140, 171, 187, 255–57, 262, 267–269, 274, 279, 281, 319, 346, 349, 358, 360
referential accessibility 267, 279
referential ambivalence 261, 267, 269, 275, 279, 281
referential conventions 278–279, 281
referential elasticity 257, 262, 267–268, 274–277, 279, 281–282
referential portrait 14, 256–7, 257 fn1, 261, 264, 267, 268, 272–73, 275–276, 281
diffused reference 255–7, 267–269, 281
floating reference 255–7, 268–270, 274, 279, 281

relevance and relevance theory 3–4, 11, 15, 58, 62, 74, 120–121, 135–143, 172–173, 179, 184, 195, 205, 208, 234, 243, 260, 346, 349–350, 353–355, 363
pragmatic relevance 205
Roe v. Wade 13, 215–219, 230, 308

Savigny, Friedrich Carl von 290
Scalia, Justice Antonin 13, 113–114, 129, 153–154, 162, 227–30, 249–250, 313 fn18, 340, 344
Searle, John 30, 45, 95, 95 fn12, 115
sediments 4, 287, 294
semantics 1, 6, 10, 44, 58–59, 83, 87–88, 88 fn3, 94, 94 fn11, 97, 102 fn19, 108–109, 122–124, 125 fn11, 128, 133, 135, 145, 147, 155, 169, 173, 188 fn6, 192, 195, 198, 199–201, 203, 208, 250–259, 261–262, 264–271, 273–274, 277–282, 288, 294, 300, 302, 343, 346–347, 349, 351, 351 fn2, 352, 354–355, 361
similarity 11–12, 167–184, 363
Sperber, Dan and Wilson, Deirdre 1–4, 50, 58, 86, 87 fn2, 88 fn4, 92, 92 fn9, 96, 105, 135–136, 234, 234 fn2, 235, 238, 244, 350
statutes 4–5, 10–12, 27–29, 38, 83–85, 89, 93, 95 fn12, 97–99, 102 fn19, 107, 109–114, 129, 132, 138, 140, 146–157, 161–162, 169, 178, 188 fn6, 196, 198, 202, 205, 207 fn3, 212–213, 213 fn12, 213 fn13, 214, 216–217, 217 fn16, 218–223, 226–229, 233, 236, 244, 263 fn6, 285, 288, 296, 309, 318, 323, 337, 339–340, 342, 345, 347, 349–350, 353, 357, 360–361, 363–364
substantive justice 206–207, 210–211, 215, 217, 227, 229–230
Supreme Court, Canada 6–7, 99 fn17, 233 fn1, 233, 239, 241, 242
Supreme Court, Germany 296
Supreme Court, United Kingdom 109
Supreme Court, United States 13, 127, 138, 140, 161, 174, 212, 215–217, 220, 222, 265, 304 fn15, 313, 329, 340

textualism 4–5, 10–12, 16, 85, 109, 109 fn24, 110–115, 123, 142, 142 fn25, 195–197, 202, 340, 344, 348, 351, 357, 363, 365
textualization 341–343
threat 45, 79, 188–189, 190–191, 202, 216, 219, 221, 223, 225, 227–228, 230–231, 288, 362
– face-threat 190–192
Tiersma, Peter 1, 9, 39, 47, 197, 199 fn23, 249, 250, 273, 338, 340–342, 353, 359
transparency 145, 147, 149–150, 153, 155, 157–159, 159 fn21, 160, 257–258, 262, 271, 281, 289

treaties 6, 13–14, 91, 233, 236–238, 237 fn4, 238 fn5, 239–240, 244

underspecification 96, 100, 138

vagueness 41, 91 fn7, 99 fn17, 119, 122, 128, 162, 250, 252, 281, 296, 339, 345, 351, 358

Weber, Max 316, 324 fn30
wills 11, 85, 93, 146, 156–158, 162
Wittgenstein, Ludwig 1, 12, 182, 234 fn2, 292, 297

www.ingramcontent.com/pod-product-compliance
Lightning Source LLC
Chambersburg PA
CBHW030431300426
44112CB00009B/944